RECIPES,
PARTY PLANS,
and GARNISHES

by Sadie
Le Sueur

Hearthside Press, Inc.

Publishers • New York

(Originally published as Sadie LeSueur's RECIPES
AND PARTY PLANS)

Copyright © 1958, 1970 by Sadie LeSueur

Library of Congress Catalog Card Number: 70-92494

ISBN 0-8208-0224-7

Revised and enlarged in 1970
Tenth printing

Printed in the United States of America

Gratefully dedicated
to
THE BOARD AND MEMBERS OF CENTENNIAL CLUB
Whose encouragement and cooperation
have made this book possible

CONTENTS

CONTENTS

SUPPLEMENT

INDEX

☆ FOREWORD ☆

Some twenty years ago, when I came to the Centennial Club as executive secretary and hostess, I found myself faced with the problem which tries the patience of every club director, that of providing an endless stream of new menus.

Since both club functions and parties given by club members brought together guests who were largely the same, month after month, new and different recipes were necessary in order to maintain the club's long-standing reputation for a distinctive cuisine. In addition, my menus had to be flexible enough to accommodate groups ranging from half a dozen to several hundred in number. My duties included serving refreshments following committee meetings and lectures, planning luncheons and receptions for the large club membership, and arranging parties of all sizes and types for members who wished to entertain at the club.

As ammunition for this battle, I brought my own personal recipe file, together with a number of my mother's treasured family recipes and many good recipes of generous friends who were noted for their ability to entertain and were willing to part with their secrets.

In the succeeding years I have been constantly on the alert to add to this nucleus of tested recipes. As a result I have accumulated a tremendous number of recipes which I believe will be helpful both to the club hostess and to the woman who is entertaining in her own home.

While the majority of my suggestions unquestionably have a Southern flavor, I have included a number of recipes gleaned from other localities as well. Therefore I hope that some of my ideas will add zest to the menus of hostesses in all parts of the country, and thus fulfill the expectations of the club members and personal friends who have suggested that I compile them in book form.

Nothing would please me more than to think that some of my suggestions might bring to other club hostesses the same rewarding experience I have had in receiving comments and notes of appreciation for my efforts.

Since notable speakers are a part of the program of the club I serve, we have entertained countless celebrities, and many of the recipes in this book have received their accolade. The letters they have sent me have been heart-warming, and I have been especially pleased when they have actually requested the recipe for some dish served them. Two in particular come to my mind. The first, from an eminent neurosurgeon, who asked if I would tell him how we made the Goldenrod Eggs served at a breakfast given in his honor. The second letter came from the editor of a national magazine, who wanted the recipe for the sweet potato ring with caramel topping which he had eaten at the club. Both are relatively simple dishes, but each letter provided a moment of triumph for me. It's nice to think that I can please the men, even though I manage a club for women!

 # PREFACE

The picture of one of my large buffet suppers is shown on the cover of this book and the menu and recipes used for it are within. They are all written for relatively small groups since they were originally planned for parties at home. I have found them equally as useful for large crowds, however, since the size of club parties vary and I use these recipes only as a base —once the pattern is set simple arithmetic will make my basic plan for six serve sixty if necessary. All items mentioned in the various menus will be found in the index.

I am grateful for the help and interest shown by friends in my efforts to compile these recipes and for the ones which some of them have contributed to the list.

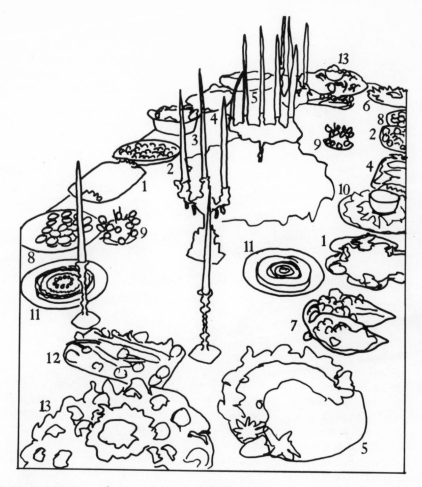

Elaborate buffet supper or smorgasbord (see cover)

A table for a very large crowd, with both sides of the buffet identical to simplify the service. (Dessert table not shown.)

1. Sliced baked Tennessee country ham
2. Deviled eggs
3. Potato salad
4. Sliced baked turkey
5. Fish mold of crab meat salad in lake of cucumber aspic, egg pond lilies
6. Rye bread and butter sandwiches
7. Relish tray
8. Southern beaten biscuits
9. Ripe and stuffed olives stuck in grapefruit with cocktail picks
10. Molded vegetable salad
11. Hors d'oeuvre circle
12. Pickles and radishes
13. Tomato aspic with shrimp

PART I

Party Plans

☆　　BREAKFASTS　　☆

The breakfasts mentioned here are more or less formal affairs which are served around noon in lieu of luncheons. The menus are somewhat different from those served at luncheons, however, since they are made up of recipes which utilize typical breakfast foods.

They can be planned for numerous occasions. A wedding breakfast, for instance, is usually an elaborate party with as many dainty and attractive touches as possible, while a football breakfast caters largely to men guests and therefore is a substantial meal with fewer feminine touches. The latter is quite popular since it can be served at an earlier hour than a luncheon and the rush to get away to the game is thus eliminated. They have also become a popular form of entertainment with people who simply prefer breakfast menus or perhaps have a special reason for wanting a noontime party.

The table decorations for breakfasts vary. The conventional white flowers are usually used for wedding breakfasts while for less formal occasions, either fruit or a combination of fruit and flowers can be used.

At a very large breakfast the guests can be seated in congenial groups instead of at tables and the dining room table can have a center arrangement of the chosen flowers. On the other hand, if a breakfast is given for a small informal group I sometimes seat them at a table on which I use gay colored linen place mats with a fruit design appliqued on both the mats and the matching napkins. At a wedding breakfast the guests can be seated in groups but the bridal party is usually seated at a long beautifully decorated table.

Football breakfasts are sometimes served buffet style, but I have found that most men prefer to be seated so arrange small tables for their use.

A fruit course is usually served first which follows much the same pattern as that served at a luncheon. The main course, however, is entirely different.

I have found that having a variety of molds for the food adds a great deal to any party, but this seems especially true where breakfasts are concerned. Ring molds are nice to use for "Rice or Grits Rings" which are filled with chicken or turkey hash, but the mold that attracts the most attention is one in the shape of a life-sized hen. A rice hen surrounded by turkey hash and a garnish of parsley is always attractive for the main course. When the hen is unmolded on a platter I attach a bright red comb, cut from a pimento, to the top of her head, make eyes of cloves and paint her bill with yellow fruit coloring. Different shaped molds are usually available at large stores that sell kitchen gadgets. A heart-shaped mold is suitable for Valentine or brides' parties and star-shaped molds are used at Christmas time to make party fare out of simple foods.

I usually include eggs in some form in every one of my breakfast menus. A cheese souffle ring filled with creamed ham or sweetbreads, for example, introduces eggs into the menu in a satisfying yet glorified form. Creamed eggs surrounded by clear fried apple rings make a pretty platter, particularly when little broiled breakfast sausages are slipped in the center of each apple ring. You will find numerous recipes in this book for cheese and egg dishes, any one of which would be suitable for a party breakfast.

The type of dessert to be served is a matter of varying opinion but one of my favorites is crisp waffles put together in pairs with a layer of guava jelly spread between them. These are dusted with powdered sugar and served with a square of cream cheese instead of butter. Ice cream molded waffles are usually available and they are delicious served with maple syrup sauce filled with pecans. Large oranges can be scooped out and packed with firmly frozen ice cream which is sealed in with a meringue and baked quickly. (See "Orange Alaska.") Cantaloupes and grapefruit make delicious desserts when treated in this way.

While all of my menus here are planned for parties, many of the recipes will be suitable for family use also, and you will not need to wait for a party to use them.

BREAKFAST THE MORNING BEFORE THE WEDDING

This is served at noon the day of the wedding to take care of the out-of-town guests, the attendants and the families of the bride and groom. It is a rather large affair and is usually given by the ushers and their wives or by some other group of friends. It is often served at a club or at the home of one of the hostesses, and can be either elaborate or simple. Since the guest list may be uncertain it is a good idea to let them serve themselves from a large, attractive buffet table. Small tables can be set up with coffee cups at each place; coffee is poured after the guests are seated. Orange juice, tomato juice, or other drinks are passed among the guests before they go to the buffet table which has an array of attractive dishes on it, each garnished with parsley buds. Several different meats, side dishes and desserts are set out. Hot breads and coffee are passed after the guests have served themselves; perhaps a relative or friend wouldn't mind carrying the bread and coffee around.

SIMPLE BREAKFAST (MORNING BEFORE THE WEDDING)

Orange Juice, Tomato Juice, Other Drinks (Before the Breakfast)
Rings of Cheese Soufflé with Creamed Sweetbreads or Chicken
Fried Tomato Slices   Gingered Fig Compote
Small Buttered Biscuit Filled with Broiled Sausage Patty
Waffles or French Toast   Strawberry Preserves or Guava Jelly
Coffee
(Waffles and French toast are both available at frozen foods departments and can be toasted in the oven in quantity following the directions on the package.)

WEDDING BREAKFAST
Pass Tray of Tomato Juice, Orange Juice and
Green Minted Grapefruit Juice
Pastry Cones of Chicken Hash   Baked Stuffed Apple
Creamed Eggs—Cheese Sauce, Surrounded by Broiled
Tomato Topped with Stuffed Mushroom Cap
Individual Coffee Cakes with Rum Butter Top
Blueberry Muffins   Banana Muffins
Coffee
Pass Wedding Cake—Sliced

LARGE BUFFET BREAKFAST
Turkey Hash   Casserole of Southern Spoon Bread nearby
Thin-Sliced Baked Ham with Crumb Topping
Casserole of Eggs in Cheese Sauce   Clear Apple Rings with Breakfast Sausage
Casserole of Curried Fruit
Blueberry Muffins   Small Hot Biscuits
Coffee
Macedoine of Fruit and/or Molded Sabayon
(If Macedoine of Fruit is used, dispense with the Casserole
of Curried Fruit.)

SMALL WEDDING BREAKFAST
Fruit Bouquets
Individual Rice Rings Filled with Chicken Hash
Baked Stuffed Eggs—Cheese Sauce
Apple Sauce Ring, Tinted Green, Filled with Honey Dew Balls
Orange Marmalade Muffins   Coffee
Sliced Wedding Cake and Molded Ices

EASTER BREAKFAST
Fruits on the Half Shell
Rice Hen with Chicken or Turkey Hash   Parsley Garnish
Tomatoes Stuffed with Mushrooms   Goldenrod Eggs
Ginger Muffins   Coffee
Cake Ring "Nest" Filled with Different Colored Ice Cream Eggs
Wine Sauce

FOOTBALL BREAKFAST
Broiled Grapefruit
Broiled Country Ham   Egg Cutlet—Tomato Sauce
Crusty Peaches
Rolls   Coffee
Pineapple Alaska

BREAKFASTS

Football Breakfast (2)

Orange or Grapefruit Juice
Individual Grits Rings with Turkey Hash
Baked Apple Stuffed with Sausage   Goldenrod Eggs
Rolls   Coffee
Waffle Molded Ice Cream
Maple Nut Sauce

Football Breakfast (3)

Tomato Juice
Broiled Sweetbreads on Canadian Bacon
Clear Apple Rings Around Creamed Eggs
Corn Fritters
Blueberry Muffins   Coffee
Waffles with Guava Jelly and Cheese

BREAKFAST

Cranberry Juice Cocktail   Frosted Red Grapes
Turkey Hash in Grits Ring
Baked Stuffed Tomato   Broiled Pineapple
Creamed Riced Eggs on Toast
Rolls   Coffee
Big Orange Alaska

Breakfast (2)

Ring of Scalloped Biscuit Filled with Chicken Hash
Bell Pepper Filled with Cheese Souffle
Corn Fritters   Baked Peaches
Ginger Muffins   Coffee
Cantaloupe Baked Alaska

Breakfast (3)

Tomato Juice   Rosebud of Olive and Cheese
Toasted Cheese Wheels
Broiled Sweetbreads, Bacon and Grilled Pineapple
Broiled Tomatoes Around Creamed Eggs   Clear Apple Rings
Corn Meal Biscuit   Coffee
Fruit Compote with Cheese at Center
Melba Sauce Glaze
Hot Salted Crackers—Buttered

BREAKFASTS

Breakfast (4)

Cantaloupe Pond Lily
Pastry Cornucopias with Chicken Hash
Clear Apple Rings with Breakfast Sausage
Eggs with Cheese Sauce
Corn Fritters   Coffee   Marmalade Muffins
Waffle Molded Ice Cream
Maple Syrup Sauce with Chopped Pecans

Breakfast (5)

Hot Pineapple Juice
Cheese Souffle Ring with Chicken Livers and Mushrooms in Center
Clear Apple Stuffed with Orange Marmalade
Broiled Tomatoes   Cheese Potato Strings (Canned)
Banana Muffins   Coffee
Grapefruit Baked Alaska

Breakfast (6)

Minted Grapefruit Juice
Brain Cutlets—Mushroom Sauce   Rice Balls with Jelly
Goldenrod Eggs   Broiled Tomatoes
Rolls   Coffee
Baked Peach—Macaroon-Meringue

Breakfast (7)

Orange Juice
Individual Corn Meal Muffin Rings with Turkey Hash
Baked Apple Stuffed with Sausage
Creamed Eggs   Broiled Tomatoes
Rolls   Coffee
Pineapple Baked Alaska

Breakfast (8)

Pineapple Points Served with Powdered Sugar
Big Uncapped Strawberries
Ham and Cheese Rolls on Toast   Baked Eggs Stuffed with Mushrooms
Crusty Bananas   Fried Corn   Rolls   Coffee
Ginger Waffles with Ice Cream Ball

Breakfast (9)

Broiled Grapefruit
Stuffed Lamb Chops   Grilled Pineapple
Broiled Tomatoes Around Shoestring Potatoes (Canned)
Creamed Riced Eggs
Rolls   Coffee
Chocolate Waffles—Whipped Cream

Breakfast (10)

Bunch of Honey Dew "Grapes"
Cheese Souffle Rings with Creamed Sweetbreads Surrounded by
Shad Roe Balls on Lemon Slices
Broiled Tomatoes   Crusty Fried Corn
Rolls   Crepes Suzette   Coffee

BREAKFASTS

Breakfast (11)

Honey Dew Sections with Melon Balls

Baked Apples Stuffed with Sausage   Egg Cutlets

Broiled Tomatoes and Cheese on Toast   Blueberry Muffins

Coffee

French Toast   Strawberry Jam and Whipped Cream

Breakfast (12)

Green Minted Grapefruit Juice

Frosted Green Grapes

Individual Rice Rings with Chicken Hash

Broiled Tomato   Goldenrod Eggs

Rolls   Coffee

Party Waffles with Guava Jelly and Cream Cheese

Breakfast (13)

Grapefruit Half   Center Filled with Maple Syrup

Cheese Souffle Ring Filled with Creamed Sweetbreads and Ham

Baked Tomato Stuffed with Mushrooms

Clear Apple Rings

Blueberry Muffins   Coffee

Pound Cake "Toast" Slices   Molded Ice Cream Eggs with Wine Sauce

HUNT BREAKFAST

Drinks   Orange Juice   Tomato Juice

Baked Ham Cut in Serving Portions

Turkey Hash   Southern Spoon Bread

Eggs and Mushrooms   Clear Apple Rings (Fried)

Coffee   Sweet Rolls

Hot Buttered Sally Lunn

CHRISTMAS MORNING EGGNOG PARTY

Eggnog

Little Biscuits with Smithfield Ham or Home-Baked Ham

Cheese Straws   Cocoanut Balls Topped with Cherries

Fruit Cake Fingers   Coffee

Arrange cocoanut balls on serving tray in the shape of a tree, starting at the top with 1 ball, then 3 balls under that, 5 balls under that and so on. The trunk of the tree can be formed by putting two balls, one on top of the other, at the base of the tree.

☆ COFFEES AND TEAS ☆

Afternoon teas have always been popular because they provide a charming, gracious and, at the same time, an informal means of entertaining. In some localities, however, morning coffees have often been substituted for afternoon teas. These are served from 11:00 to 11:30 A.M. and follow much the same pattern of teas since the food is essentially the same.

The coffee idea evidently originated in the Deep South, possibly because the mornings were more pleasant than the afternoon heat; however, since the morning hours seem more convenient for many of the guests, they are gradually gaining favor farther north.

Both coffees and teas can be as elaborate or simple, as desired, but the serving table should be attractively arranged in either case. Refreshments can be passed to the guests at formal parties or tea can be poured from a silver service placed at one end of the table. In that case, platters of sandwiches and small dainty cakes are put on the table so that the guests can serve themselves. Tea napkins and plates are placed near the tea service for the convenience of the guests. It will be necessary for sandwich platters to be refilled quite often when serving a party of this kind as the table should always look attractive. In warm weather iced tea or coffee can replace the hot beverages.

Sandwiches for teas and coffees are practically the same, although I like to have some kind of toasted sandwich, tiny sweet rolls, or muffins included in the coffee menu. Many canapé ideas can be utilized as sandwiches for a tea or for a coffee, so I have included canapés with my sandwich recipes. A variety of sandwich cutters is a great asset, as sandwiches cut in fancy shapes add a good deal to the occasion. Usually I plan four varieties of sandwiches for a party and have found that a meat, a cheese, a vegetable and a sweet sandwich make a good combination.

Since coffees are served in mid-morning, it is wise to make sandwich fillings ahead of time, and also to plan one or more sandwiches that can be made in advance. Most sandwiches that are to be toasted can be made the day before the party. They should be brushed with melted butter, covered with a damp cloth, and kept in the refrigerator until time to run them in the oven to toast. Rounds of toast for open-faced sandwiches, cheese wheels, orange toast, etc., can be made a day in advance.

Seasonal menus may be prepared for Christmas, Easter and Valentine's Day. Refreshments for brides also lend an added interest to a party.

Sandwiches for a formal party should never be large, but I always plan one or two of moderate size along with the smaller variety. I have found that decorating the tops of sandwiches adds much to their appearance. Olive slices and stars or hearts cut from canned pimento make attractive decorations.

Sets of tiny cutters are sold for canapé decorations. They are first used to remove a piece of bread from the top of the sandwich and then used to cut the decorations from pimentoes. Pimento cutouts then replace the bread that has been removed. Large or small circles can be cut from the tops of tomato and carrot sandwiches to let the bright color of the fillings show through, or an inch circle of bread can be removed from the top of a sandwich and the bread replaced by a clear pickle ring. Pimento decorations can be cut ahead of time and placed on a flat plate. It is then an easy matter to take them up on the point of a toothpick and insert them in the proper space on the sandwich.

The work of making sandwiches is simplified if the bread is cut in the desired shapes and put together in pairs with mayonnaise between them. They are then kept covered until the filling is added. When they have been filled they should be covered with damp cloths and kept in the refrigerator until serving time.

MORNING COFFEE MENUS

MORNING COFFEE
Christmas Season

Individual Oyster Loaves   Tomato Open-faced Canapés
Cheese Dreams—Christmas Tree Shape
Star-Shaped Cinnamon Toast   Coffee
Small Square Individual Cakes, Iced in White and "Tied"
With Red Ribbon Icing to Resemble Christmas Package

Morning Coffee (2) Christmas Season

Christmas Tree Shaped Chicken Salad Sandwich—Pimento Star at Top
Cheese Wheel Christmas Wreath with Pimento "Holly" and Parsley Garnish
Round Tomato Sandwich with Inch Circle Cut from Top
Toast Star with Philadelphia Cheese and Guava Jelly at Center
Cheese Pastry Christmas Trees Filled with Mincemeat
Coffee

Morning Coffee (3)

Toasted Tomato Sandwiches   Cheese Puffs
Cucumber Sandwiches   Stickies
Pastry Cups with Cherry Preserves or Lemon Filling
Topped with Whipped Cream
Coffee

Morning Coffee (4)

Toasted Mushroom Sandwiches   Open-faced Tomato Sandwich
Swiss Cheese and Bell Pepper on Rounds of Rye Bread
Rolled Cinnamon Toast
Coffee   Rum or Bourbon Balls

COFFEES AND TEAS

Morning Coffee (5)

Toast Cups Filled with Crab Supreme   Tomato Sandwich, Crescent Top
Tiny Sausage Turnovers   Orange Marmalade Muffins
Chocolate Cornflake Cookies   Coffee

Morning Coffee (7)

Cheese and Cucumber Sandwich   Ham Squares
Egg and Anchovy Sandwich   Toasted Rolled Asparagus Sandwich
Fudge Cake   Coffee

Morning Coffee (7)

Rounds of Toast with Canapé Marguery   Cheese Sandwich No. 3
Spring Sandwich   Small Banana Muffins
Brown Sugar Fudge Cake   Coffee

Morning Coffee (8)

Cheese and Bacon Toasted Sandwich   Carrot Sandwich
Ripe Olive and Nut Sandwich   Orange Marmalade and Cheese Toast
Cake Squares with Mocha Icing Covered with Grated Almonds

SUMMER COFFEE

Watermelon, Cantaloupe and Honey Dew Melon Balls on Cocktail Picks
Cucumber Almond Sandwich   Toasted Cheese Dreams
Tomato Sandwich   Orange Marmalade Muffins
Iced Coffee   Brown Sugar Kisses

Summer Coffee (2)

Chicken Salad in Cream Puff Shells   Cheese Puffs
Carrot and Black Olive Sandwich   Orange Bread and Butter Sandwiches
Iced Coffee with Vanilla Ice Cream Topping
Hot Spice Cup Cakes

BRIDE'S TEA

Heart-shaped Chicken Salad Sandwich with Tiny
Pimento Heart at Center
Tomato Sandwiches with Large Circle or Heart Removed from Top of Sandwich
Calla Lily Sandwich   Bell-shaped Orange Toast
Petits Fours   Tea

Bride's Tea (2)

Toast Cups Filled with Crab Salad   Heart-shaped Spring Sandwiches
Ribbon Sandwiches with Green Tinted Cheese Filling
Rolled Asparagus Sandwiches
Pale Green Iced "Marshmallow Towers"   Tea

Bride's Tea (3)

Puff Shells of Chicken Salad   Cucumber Sandwiches
Cheese Lily of the Valley Sandwiches
"Valentine" Sandwiches
Angel Food Rum Balls   Tea

CHRISTMAS TEA
Round Turkey Sandwich—Cranberry Jelly Garnish
Philadelphia Cheese and Olive Sandwich Christmas Tree Shaped
Pimento Star Garnish at Top
Open-face Tomato Sandwich (See Tomato Canapé)
Cheese Wafers—Cut in Christmas Bell and Star Shapes
Small Snowball Cocoanut Cakes with Holly Spray Iced on Top
Tea

VALENTINE TEA
Valentine Sandwich, Heartshaped Open-face
Heart-shaped Tongue and Olive Sandwich with Pimento Heart Garnish
at Center
Round Cucumber Sandwich on Whole Wheat Bread
with Stuffed Olive Center
Heart-shaped Orange Toast
Heart-shaped Teacakes   Tea

HALLOWEEN TEA
Boston Brown Bread Halloween Sandwiches with Jack-o'-Lantern Faces
Round Carrot Sandwiches on Whole Wheat Bread with Inch
Circle Cut from the Top—Garnish Tray with Cheese Pumpkins
Ham Squares
Tomato Sandwiches
Chocolate and Orange Cakes   Tea

ST. PATRICK'S TEA
Shamrock-shaped Chicken Salad Sandwiches   Water Cress Sandwiches
Green-tinted Cheese Ribbon Sandwiches
Cucumber Sandwich—Inch Circle Cut from Top and Parsley Spray Inserted
Cocoanut Ball Cakes—Tops Decorated with Shamrock
Cut from Green Mint Cherries

GEORGE WASHINGTON TEA
Hatchet-shaped Parmesan Cheese Toast (See Cheese Wheels)
Tomato Sandwiches
Rolled Chicken Salad "Logs" with Tiny Favor Hatchets Across Each One
Cucumber and Almond Sandwich
Tricorne of Toast Filled with Cherry Preserves
Tea

SUMMER TEA
Chicken Salad Sandwich   Tomato Sandwich
Date Bread Sandwich   Cucumber Sandwich
Iced Tea with Pineapple Sherbet Topping
Hot Cup Cakes

AFTERNOON TEA
Shrimp Ovals   Spring Sandwiches
Philadelphia Cheese and Stuffed Olive Sandwiches
Brown Bread and Crystallized Ginger Sandwiches
Small Spice Muffin Cakes   Tea

21

Afternoon Tea (2)
Chicken Mushroom Open-faced Sandwiches
Cheese and Olive Flower Sandwiches
Avocado Sandwiches   Cinnamon Toast Sticks
Date Bars   Tea

Afternoon Tea (3)
Hot Rolls Stuffed with Chicken Salad   Cucumber and Cheese Sandwiches
Celery Sandwiches   Nut Bread and Butter Sandwiches
Date Nut Kisses   Tea

Afternoon Tea (4)
Rolled Chicken Salad Sandwiches   Russian Cheese Sandwiches
Tomato Sandwiches   Egg and Almond Sandwiches
Caramel Thins   Tea

Afternoon Tea (5)
Ham and Olive Sandwiches   Cucumber and Almond Sandwiches
Rolled Asparagus Sandwiches   Brown Bread Wedges
Angel Food Rum Balls   Tea

LUNCHEONS—
PLATE LUNCHEONS

Luncheons range from simple salad plates through lap tray and bridge luncheons to very elaborate formal luncheons of several courses. This chapter will deal mainly with the elaborate type, although I have also added some menus for the lap tray and salad plate luncheons. The hostess without help will probably be more interested in the buffet luncheons which I will feature in another chapter.

Most of these menus have been used for parties at the Centennial Club and I think it would probably be interesting to show what we have done during the past months since all of the menus would also be quite suitable for a party at home.

For formal luncheons we use beautiful, carefully chosen linens, china and silver and the first course always harmonizes, as far as possible, with the color scheme of the flowers used as decoration. In the spring when we use yellow daffodils for decoration, the first course for a luncheon might be a salad made of a grapefruit half in a lettuce nest, topped with a natural-looking daffodil made of varieties of yellow cheese. The cheese daffodil is flanked with green leaves cut from sections of avocado pear. A summer luncheon table might be decorated with yellow day lilies, calling for a first course of yellow cantaloupe cut to resemble a pond lily. When pink flowers are used, I often feature watermelon balls for a first course. Sometimes I arrange the melon balls like a French bouquet, with a lace paper frill and single mint leaves around the outer edge of the fruit cup. Or I might use half of an avocado pear filled with frozen tomato mayonnaise, which is a lovely pink color.

In very warm weather I plan elaborate cold luncheons. One of my favorite salad platters features a salmon mousse molded in the shape of a large fish with a slice of stuffed olive for his eye. The fish mold is curled in a pool of green cucumber aspic with a garnish of pond lilies made from hard-boiled eggs. Flat leaves cut from green peppers are placed under each lily.

In the fall harvest luncheons feature food that harmonizes with decorations of fruit, sprays of wheat and other symbols of plenty. Christmas, Valentine, Easter and May Day parties, too, are planned to make the food fit the seasonal decorations.

One of the most effective Christmas luncheons we ever served featured food that tied in with the holiday decorations. For it I used a first course which gave the effect of a miniature holly wreath at each place. Pineapple with the hull left on was cut in thick slices and the fruit

23

was removed, leaving a circle which resembled a wreath. This was filled with a colorful serving of a fruit cup and topped with a bright red cherry. At the top of each wreath I placed a spray of real holly berries, tied with a fluffy red bow. This fruit plate was put on the table before the guests came into the dining room.

Of course Valentine luncheons are easy to plan, with the heart motif predominating.

At a recent Easter luncheon at the club, we used Easter-bonnet cake "hats" as part of the dessert course. The little "hats" were all iced in different pastel shades and decorated with flowers, such as roses, lilies of the valley, orchids and daisies made of icing. Each cake was large enough to serve eight or ten guests, so we used one of the hats for each luncheon table. The hats were decorated differently, so that each table had a distinctive dessert.

For a May Day luncheon dessert I once used a May basket made of cake, iced and decorated, with a ribbon-tied handle. The basket was filled with individual ices, each molded in flower shape.

Although these are elaborate luncheon ideas, I also have recipes for many parties which are much simpler but just as good; in fact, the informal lap tray luncheon that we serve is one of our most popular parties.

The club's tin lap trays have red, black, green, yellow, blue and peach-colored borders, and on them we use bright-colored tray covers made of hand-hemmed linen. Napkins used with them are exactly the same size as the tray covers and are folded four times into a long narrow shape. These napkins, in colors which contrast with those of the tray covers, lend a gay note to the informal luncheon. On a black-bordered tray, for example, I might use a coral cover and a turquoise napkin; a yellow tray might have a teal blue cover and an orange napkin; while a red tray would perhaps get a dark green cover and a chartreuse napkin. Since all napkins and covers are the same size, numerous color combinations are possible by using them interchangeably. The covers are made to fit the inside of the trays so that the colored border of the tray is in direct contrast with the cover.

Guests at the lap tray luncheons sit around in groups and the maids at the club are instructed to take as many different colors as possible to each group.

The food at such parties is usually served in two courses. For the first course, we send in, on the tray, a plate with a service of meat (such as curried chicken in individual rings, a salad (perhaps a molded vegetable salad), and a hot roll. One side dish is passed and coffee is poured by the maids into the cups which have been sent in on the tray. Loaf sugar is sent in on the saucers to facilitate service. Rolls are passed again and the plates and cups are then replaced by the dessert.

An interesting luncheon plate that I like for these lap tray parties is a salad plate containing three varieties of salad. Stuffed eggs and olives are placed between the lettuce cups of salad. This, with iced tea, hot cheese dreams, and a simple dessert, makes a very satisfying luncheon in warm weather. A young newspaper woman, writing about the salad plate, once called it my "toothsome threesome." A wise combination for such a plate would be a chicken or crab meat salad, a vegetable salad and a molded fruit salad. Since the latter is sweet, dessert can be dispensed with, if you are planning a one-plate party.

LUNCHEONS

At our club we entertain many literary clubs, garden clubs and art groups who have morning meetings, followed by a light luncheon. Our salad plate, with sandwiches, a drink and cookies passed, is quite popular for these gatherings.

Since many of these groups come once or twice a month, I plan a large number of menus and nothing pleases me more than to have a member of one of the clubs remark, "You never seem to serve the same thing twice."

The following menus have been used for various types of parties at the club.

BRIDE'S LUNCHEON
"Fruit Bouquets" of Melon Balls
Stuffed Squab—Orange Sauce
Clipped Corn   Stuffed Eggplant
Hot Rolls   Peach Pickle
Party Ice Tea   Orange Slices
Mint Bubble Garnish
Individual Ices, Bride and Bridesmaid Designs
Little Cakes Iced in Flowers

Bride's Luncheon (2)
Bunches of Honey Dew Grapes on Galax Leaves
Pastry Cones Filled with Crab or Shrimp Newburg
Garnish of Green Bell Pepper Slice Filled with Pickle Relish
Cauliflower Bouquet with Carrot Roses   Fresh Garden Peas
Rolls
Pale Green Meringue Hearts Filled with Ice Cream
Coffee

THANKSGIVING LUNCHEON
Grapefruit Juice Cocktail (Minted)
Frosted Grapes on Galax Leaf
Sliced Turkey on Rounds of Turkey Dressing
Mushroom Gravy
Rice Ball on Ring of Cranberry Sauce
Casserole of Hot Fruit Compote No. 1
Green Asparagus   Rolls
Individual Mince Pies   Hard Sauce
Coffee

CHRISTMAS LUNCHEON

Tomato Juice Cocktail   Bell-shaped Cheese Wafers
Olive, Radish "Christmas Tree Garnish"
Sliced Spice Round or Baked Ham   Clear Pickle Rings
Bright Red Bell Pepper Stuffed with Creole Cauliflower
Star-shaped Beaten Biscuit
Two-toned Christmas Salad
Round Slice of Plum Pudding—Molded Bell of Eggnog Ice Cream on Top
Fluffy Bow Red Ribbonzene on Top of Bell

HALLOWEEN LUNCHEON

Golden Salad
Halloween Puff Pastry Shell Filled with Creamed Ham or Sweetbreads
Stuffed Yellow Squash   Green Gage Plum and Apricot Compote
Pass Cabbage Spook Head Filled with Olives,
Celery and Radishes (See Garnishes)
Rolls   Coffee
Sunshine Cake Rings with Uncooked Orange Icing and Garnish of Pumpkins
Made of Icing, Filled with Yellow Lemon Ice Cream
Coffee

SUMMER LUNCHEON

Jellied Bouillon   Assorted Crackers
Sliced Turkey and Fresh Fruits
Hot Blueberry Muffins   Iced Tea
Broken Orange Chiffon Cake with Serving of Pineapple
or Lime Sherbet Garnished with Orange Sections

Sliced turkey breast in center of plate surrounded by Della Robbia wreath of fruits on lettuce hearts. Fruits used are watermelon, cantaloupe and honey dew balls, fresh peach halves filled with red raspberries or blueberries, peeled fresh plums, fresh apricots, sections of fresh pears, tiny bunches of green grapes and black cherries. Celery seed or poppy seed dressing should be passed several times.

Summer Luncheon (2)

Sandwich plate, consisting of Holland rusk, buttered with anchovy paste, on shredded lettuce, covered in turn with sliced baked ham, sliced chicken breast, thick slice of tomato and two halves of deviled eggs. Cover all completely with Russian dressing. Serve with ripe and stuffed olives and iced tea.

Chilled platter with lime sherbet heaped in center of dessert tray. Around this put fresh apricots, plums and large black cherries. Tuck in ivy leaves under fruit. Allow one of each kind of fruit for each person to be served.

Summer Luncheon (3)

In center of each plate put a ring of cantaloupe or honey dew melon. Surround this with lettuce leaves, on which are placed small groups of fresh fruit: fresh peach halves filled with raspberries, green grapes, melon balls, blue plums stuffed with cheese balls rolled in nuts, sliced bananas, orange sections, etc. Just before serving fill the center of the melon ring with raspberry or lime sherbet and garnish with mint spray. Serve with "Wine Dressing" and pass buttered "Nut Bread Sandwiches."

CHRYSANTHEMUM LUNCHEON

Orange Chrysanthemum Filled with Molded Fruit Salad
Crackers
Rice Rings with Curried Chicken   Stuffed Yellow Squash
Baked Peach Half Stuffed with Bananas   Cocoanut Topping
Rolls
Individual Iced Chrysanthemum Cakes Around Apricot Ice Cream
Coffee

ROSE LUNCHEON

Lime Cocktail   Olive and Cheese Rosebuds (See "Garnish")
Crackers
Tomato-Cheese Rose Salad   Baked Country Ham
Eggs and Mushroom, Swiss Cheese Sauce, Casserole
Pickle Rings   Beaten Biscuit
Individual Pink Rose Ices in Cake Basket—Iced in Pale Green
Coffee

CAMELLIA LUNCHEON

Salad of Grapefruit Half with Pink Cheese Camellia on Top Avocado Leaves
French Dressing   Assorted Crackers
Deviled Chicken
Broiled Tomato Slices Topped with Individual Molds of Corn Pudding
Broccoli   Beaten Biscuit   Red Crab Apple Pickle
Tennessee Baked Country Ham
Strawberry Sherbet on Platter Surrounded by Macaroon-dipped Ice Cream Circles
Fresh Strawberry Garnish
Coffee

This "Camellia Luncheon" was served at a luncheon given in honor of Vicomtess Antionette de Bellargue and, as we wanted it to be typically Southern, we decorated the tables lavishly with lovely shaded pink camelias. The menu, as you can see, was typical of the South.

DAFFODIL LUNCHEON

Grapefruit Half, Daffodil of Cheese on Top   French Dressing
Crackers
Fish Pudding Ring with Potato Balls   Lemon Cups with Tartar Sauce
Cucumber-Radish Garnish   Cauliflower-Carrot-Rose Bouquet
Stuffed Yellow Squash   Little Corn Meal Muffins
Orange Pudding Ring   Whipped Cream
Coffee

PINK LUNCHEON

Avocado Filled with Frozen Mayonnaise
Crackers
Baked Ham Slice   Creole Crumb Topping
Baked Stuffed Tomato
Casserole of Baked Fruit Compote
Pickle in Pepper Ring (See "Garnish")
Large Ring of Devil Food Cake
Pink Peppermint Stick Candy Ice Cream
Coffee

This luncheon was planned in honor of Vera Michaels Dean, who spoke at our club.

YELLOW LUNCHEON

Cantaloupe Pond Lilies
Cheese Souffle Ring Filled with Creamed Sweetbreads, Bordered with
Parsley and "Carrot Flower Garnish"
Green Asparagus with Riced Egg
Yellow Squash, Fried Whole   Rolls
Golden Charlotte Russe   Coffee

PURPLE LUNCHEON

Purple Grape Juice Cocktail   Frosted Pink Grapes
Pastry Cornucopias Filled with Lobster Newberg
Individual Molds of Bing Cherries and Grapefruit Salad   Rolls
Stuffed Egg Plant   Green Peas
Purple Cabbages Stuck with Radish Roses and Carrot Flowers, Center
Filled with Celery Curls and Olives (See "Garnishess")
Black Rasperry Ice Cream on Platter Surrounded by Individual Chrysanthemum
Cakes, Iced in Shades of Lavender and Pink
Coffee

☆

This menu was served at a luncheon given at our club for Region Six of the Associated Junior Leagues of America a year or so ago. The guests were seated in groups around the club and the dining room table was used only as a decoration.

The Victorian note of the club furnishings inspired the unusual arrangement and the color scheme blended with the club decor. The large round table was draped in a soft shade of Burgundy velvet which fell from the top of the table to the floor and which extended around the edge of the table, where it was caught down in plaits. A flat plaque of green magnolia leaves came almost to the edge of the table and in the center a two-foot high tripod of wrought iron was hung with specimen bunches of pink Tokay grapes which formed a tree. Small chrysanthemums, shading from pink to lavender, outlined the branches. At the base of the tree, extending almost to the edge of the magnolia leaves, was banked an arrangement of purple egg plant, green artichokes, limes and avocados. The young artist who arranged it was a Junior League member and also a member of the club.

Our menu, as you see, was planned to tie in with the purple and green color scheme.

MONTHLY CLUB LUNCHEONS

Our monthly club luncheons are usually attended by 150 to 175 guests seated at tables holding from six to ten. The decorations are planned by the Home Department of the club and many attractive and unusual ideas are carried out by their untiring efforts.

The first course is usually on the table when the guests come in the dining room, and it is always planned to tie in with the table decorations.

The meat is usually put on the plate for the main course, with some sort of garnish, and often one vegetable, such as a stuffed pepper, tomato or squash, is also on the plate. If the salad is served with the main course, it is on the plate with the meat and the vegetable platters are passed. This is an easy way to serve large groups.

The following suggestions show how we plan the different monthly menus:

JANUARY LUNCHEON

Frosty Salad Rings Filled with Grapefruit and Russian Dressing
Crackers
Noodle Ring Filled with Tuna Fish Creole
Stuffed Patty Pan Squash Around Green Peas—Parsley Garnish
Green Asparagus, Lemon Butter and Toasted Almonds on Top
Rolls   Pickles
Green Mint Ice Cream   Cocoanut Balls
Coffee

Decorations for the luncheon were little snow men and snowballs made of styrofoam.

FEBRUARY CLUB LUNCHEON
(George Washington)

Tomato Juice Cocktail	Hatchet-Shaped Cheese Toast
Olives	Celery Curls
Baked Ham Slices	Creole Crumb Topping

Bing Cherry and Grapefruit Salad

Baked Stuffed Tomato	Beaten Biscuit

Chocolate Marshmallow Roll iced in chocolate to resemble a log. Platter decorated with sprays of artificial cherries. Pasteboard hatchet across the roll.

(Pasteboard hatches about 10 inches long are available at stores specializing in favors.)

Logs 4 inches in diameter and about 14 inches long had three holes bored down the length; these held red candles which were decorated around the base with artificial bunches of cherries. These were used for our table decorations.

MARCH CLUB LUNCHEON
(Saint Patrick)

Green Pineapple and Cucumber Aspic Salad
Individual Rings of Fish Pudding Centered with Tartar Sauce
and Parsley Bud Garnish
Potatoes in Cream Sauce   Riced Eggs
Green Bell Peppers Filled with Creole Cauliflower
Slice of Lemon on Plate with Pickle Relish on Top of It
Green Asparagus
Little Hot Corn Meal Muffins
Green Meringue Rings Filled with Vanilla Ice Cream
Green Marshmallow-Mint Sauce
Coffee

Decorations for this luncheon were jonquils put into green pasteboard Irish top hats. Little green shamrocks for place cards. Hats can be ordered from a firm who deal in favors.

APRIL CLUB LUNCHEON
(Easter Season)

Pineapple Quarters with Fruit Garnish
Half Deviled Chicken   Orange Slice with Jelly Garnish
New Green Peas   Hot Fig Compote
Rolls
Ice Cream   Pass Easter Bonnet Cakes
Coffee

Decorations for this luncheon were little round bandboxes covered with orchid-covered wallpaper. The tops were off to one side and pale pink tissue paper was fluffed inside the boxes.

In each box was a little toque made of flowers with a pink tulle veil on it. The hats were fashioned of an iris surrounded by rosebuds and weigela. These were made by the club members who decorated the club luncheon tables under the direction of the chairman of the home department.

MAY CLUB LUNCHEON

Grapefruit May Baskets Filled with Fruit
Molded Chicken Salad with Tomato Aspic Top
Stuffed Green Patty Pan Squash
Casserole of Lima Beans and Mushrooms
Crab Apple Pickle   Hot Rolls
Iced Tea
May Basket Cakes Filled with Molded Flower Ices

(Ice cakes in pastel shades and fill with Easter lilies, roses, yellow Calla lilies of ice cream.)

May baskets filled with roses and "baby breath" were on each table.

JUNE CLUB LUNCHEON

Cantaloupe Pond Lilies
Toast Boats Filled with Sweetbreads, Chicken and Mushrooms
Broccoli with Lemon Butter Sauce
Broiled Tomato Slices with Individual Corn Pudding on Top of Tomato
Peach Pickle   Hot Rolls
Iced Tea
Apricot Ice Cream   Broken Sunshine Cake

(Yellow garden lilies in different shades were used for this luncheon.)

JULY CLUB LUNCHEON

Watermelon Balls on Green Ice
Tomatoes Stuffed with Chicken Salad
Corn Pudding   Lima Beans
Ice Tea   Hot Rolls
Platter of Green Mint or Lime Ice with fresh fruits at either end. (See "Summer Delight.")

Shaded pink specimen zinnias were used for this luncheon.

LUNCHEONS—PLATE LUNCHEONS

AUGUST CLUB LUNCHEON

Cantaloupe Rings Filled with Fruit
Molded Lamb Ring Filled with Potato Salad—Surrounded by Tomato,
Cucumber and Stuffed Pickle Slices Placed One on Top
of the Other (See "Pickle Garnish")
Stuffed Eggs   Hot Banana Muffins
Frozen Party Iced Tea with Ginger Ale
Frozen Macaroon Pineapple Dessert
(White spider lilies on these tables)

SEPTEMBER CLUB LUNCHEON

Half Grapefruit, Crystallized Ginger Center
Broiled Sweetbreads on Ham—Mushroom Sauce
Squash and Egg Casserole   Broiled Tomatoes Around Green Peas
Iced Tea   Blueberry Muffins
Sunshine Dessert

Yellow and orange colored large fluffy marigolds for table decoration.

OCTOBER CLUB LUNCHEON

Cream of Corn Soup
Crackers
Baked Ham   Tomato-Cheese-Artichoke Salad on Plate
Stuffed Egg Plant
Crusty Peaches   Rolls
Charlotte Russe Ring—Wine Jelly Top
Coffee

Fall flowers used on these tables.

NOVEMBER CLUB LUNCHEON

Egg Appetizer on Tomato Slice   Crackers
Turkey Ball on Pat of Dressing
Mushroom Gravy
Clear Apple with Orange Marmalade Glaze
Green Asparagus   Little Fried Yellow Squash
Rolls   Pickle
Molded Ices in Fruit Shapes
Broken Sunshine Cake
Coffee

Combine bunches of grapes, apples, pears, peaches, bananas of ice cream
on platters surrounded by galax leaves.
(Small gilded pumpkins filled with yellow chrysanthemums were flanked with
bunches of red grapes. The grapes were highlighted with gold paint.)

DECEMBER CLUB LUNCHEON
(Christmas)
Pineapple Ring Christmas Wreaths Filled with Fruit   Holly Garnish

Sliced Turkey on Pat of Dressing
Mushroom Gravy   Cranberries
Star-shaped Mold of Rice with Star of Pimento on Top
Baked Stuffed Tomatoes
Red Crab Apple Pickle   Hot Rolls
Christmas Dessert

Little styrofoam sleds filled with packages tied to resemble Christmas gifts and drawn by "Rudolph the Red-nosed Reindeer" were placed down the center of the tables. (Holly decorations were also used.) The packages were from 1 to 3 inches long and were really small blocks of wood tied in gay wrappings.

SALAD PLATE LUNCH
Bing Cherry and Grapefruit Salad
Chicken Salad in Hot Rolls   Open-faced Tomato Sandwiches
Cheese and Water Cress Sandwich
Tea or Coffee   Canadian Cookies

Salad Plate Lunch (2)
Sweetbread and Cucumber Salad in Tomatoes
Individual Oyster Loaves   Cheese Sandwich
Asparagus Sandwich
Chocolate Cup Cakes   Tea or Coffee

Salad Plate Lunch (3)
Perfection Salad
Tongue and Olive Sandwich   Cheese Sandwich
Egg and Anchovy Sandwich
Brown Sugar Muffin Cakes   Tea or Coffee

Salad Plate Lunch (4)
Molded Jewel Salad
Chicken Salad Sandwich   Tomato Sandwich
Olive Nut Sandwich
Angel Food Rum Balls   Tea or Coffee

Salad Plate Lunch (5)
Tomato Stuffed with Eggs and Caviar
Ham Squares   Carrot Sandwiches
Cucumber and Olive Sandwiches
"Monkeys"   Tea or Coffee

Salad Plate Lunch (6)
Jellied Tongue Ring Filled with Chopped Vegetable Salad
Egg Sandwich   Water Cress Sandwich
Swiss Cheese and Bell Pepper Sandwich on Rye Bread
Peanut Butter Cookies   Tea or Coffee

Salad Plate Lunch (7)
Tomato Aspic with Celery   Crab Mayonnaise
Hot Cheese Dreams
Roll Stuffed with Tongue   Asparagus Sandwich
Tea or Coffee   Spice Muffin Cakes

Salad Plate Lunch (8)
Molded Grapefruit and Pineapple Salad
Chicken Salad Sandwich   Tomato Sandwich
Cheese Dreams
Tea or Coffee   "Rocks"

Salad Plate Lunch (9)
Tomato-Cheese Layer Salad
Tongue and Olive Sandwich
Egg and Anchovy Sandwich
Bacon Twists
Tea or Coffee   Hot Cup Cakes

Salad Plate Lunch (10)
Molded Ginger Ale Salad with Fruit
Tomato Sandwich   Snappy Cheese Sandwich
Tuna Fish Sandwich
Tea or Coffee   Cocoanut Corn Flake Cookies

Salad Plate Lunch (11)
Crab Salad Molded   Cucumber Aspic Top
Spring Sandwich
Cheese and Bacon Open-faced Sandwich
Asparagus Sandwich
Tea or Coffee   Fruited Cookies

Salad Plate Lunch (12)
Molded Pear and Cheese Salad
Toasted Mushroom Sandwich   Spring Sandwich
Ripe Olive and Nut Sandwich   Tea or Coffee
Brown Sugar Fudge Cake Squares

Salad Plate Lunch (13)
Grapefruit-Asparagus Salad   Red Dressing
Cucumber Sandwich   Cheese Dreams
Hot Sardine Biscuit
Tea or Coffee   Bittersweet Chocolate Cookies

Salad Plate Lunch (14)
Individual Frosty-Salad Rings Filled with Shrimp
Russian Dressing
Cucumber and Tongue Sandwich   Egg and Almond Sandwich
Carrot Sandwiches on Whole Wheat Bread
Tea or Coffee   Chocolate Corn Flake Cookies

Salad Plate Lunch (15)
Chicken-Vegetable Molded Salad
Roquefort Cheese Sandwich on Rye Bread
Tomato Sandwich
Carrot Sandwich on Whole Wheat Bread
Tea or Coffee   Date Bars

Salad Plate Lunch (16)
Molded Apricot Salad   Chicken Salad Sandwich
Philadelphia Cheese and Olive Sandwich
Tea or Coffee   Fudge Cakes

Salad Plate Lunch (17)
Tomato Stuffed with Eggs and Caviar
Ham Squares   Cheese Dreams
Cucumber and Almond Sandwiches
Tea or Coffee   Chocolate Macaroons

Salad Plate Lunch (18)
Frozen Fruit Salad
Rolled Cheese Dreams   Spring Sandwiches
Olive and Nut Sandwich
Tea or Coffee   Torte Cakes

PATIO PICNIC LUNCH

Each guest is given his picnic basket or box with napkin tucked inside. A table with coffee urn and iced soft drinks is also placed nearby for his convenience. Each basket is packed with the following items and each item is put in an individual plastic sandwich bag.

(1) Fried chicken (usually a piece of breast or thigh)
(2) Stuffed deviled egg, cut in half
(3) Swiss cheese and rye bread sandwich cut in half (serve ½)
(4) Ripe olive and nut sandwich cut in half (serve ½)
(5) Cheese biscuit or beaten biscuit buttered with slivered baked ham in them (optional)
(6) 2 olives and 2 small gherkin pickles
(7) 2 Rocky Road Fudgies

An idea conceived by a talented young woman in our community is to "cater" the picnic. She supplies attractive small round wicker baskets without handles, and red-and-white checked napkins. She has quite a business, not only packing these baskets for picnics, but for other informal or formal gatherings. They are a boon to the hostess who is without help as they are dainty and attractive as well as good. All the hostess needs to do is to prepare drinks for her guests, whether sewing club, garden club or bridge club members!

☆ LAP TRAY LUNCHEONS ☆

Avocado Half Filled with Crab Meat   Russian Salad Dressing
Molded Perfection Salad
Molded Grapefruit-Pineapple Salad
Ripe Olives   Hot Rolls   Stuffed Olives
Iced Tea or Coffee

Arrange the three salads in separate lettuce cups in clover-leaf shape. Put olives between each serving of salad.

LAP TRAY LUNCHEON
Individual Mold of Chicken-Vegetable Salad
Slice of Tomato, Philadelphia Cheese on Top with Garnish
of Artichoke Heart
Molded Bing Cherry and Grapefruit Salad
Olives   Marmalade Muffins   Stuffed Eggs
Iced Tea or Coffee
Individual Chocolate or Lemon Tarts

Lap Tray Luncheon (2)
Individual Mold of Chicken Salad with Tomato Aspic Top
Green Asparagus Salad with Stuffed Egg Garnish
Hawaiian Salad—Cream Cheese Topping
Banana Muffins   Ripe Olives
Iced Tea or Coffee
Individual Iced Cake Rings Filled with Strawberry Ice Cream

Lap Tray Luncheon (3)
Tomato Stuffed with Vegetable Cottage Cheese
Small Mold of Salmon Mousse
Mold of Fruit Salad
Ripe Olives   Hot Rolls   Green Olives
Iced Tea or Coffee
(No dessert necessary unless desired)

Lap Tray Luncheon (4)
Grapefruit Salad in Avocado Pear (on Plate)
Pass Platters of Chicken Valenciana
Toasted French Bread
Tea or Coffee
Individual Chess Pies

35

Lap Tray Luncheon (5)
Individual Cucumber Aspic Rings Filled with Crab Salad (on Plate)
Baked Stuffed Tomato (on Plate)
Pass Casseroles Creamed Asparagus and Almonds
Hot Corn Meal Biscuits
Iced Tea or Coffee
English Trifle in Individual Compotes
Whipped Cream Topping

Lap Tray Luncheon (6)
Individual Rice Rings Filled with Curried Chicken (on Plate)
Large Red Bell Peppers Stuffed with Creole Cauliflower (Pass)
Individual Mold of Apricot-Cheese Salad (on Plate)
Hot Rolls   Pickle   Tea or Coffee
Meringue Rings Filled with Vanilla Ice Cream   Fresh Red Raspberries

Lap Tray Luncheon (7)
Baked Ham—Creole Dressing (on Plate)
Mold of Tomato Aspic with Celery and Olives (on Plate)
Pass Casseroles of Baked Stuff Eggs and Mushrooms
with Cheese Sauce
Blueberry Muffins   Peach Pickle
Tea or Coffee
Broken Sunshine Cake with Vanilla Ice Cream and Strawberries

LAP TRAY LUNCHEON FOR BRIDE'S SUMMER SHOWER
Chilled Vichyssoise Sprinkled with Chives
Cantaloupe Rings Filled with a Variety of Fresh Fruits (on Plate)
Finger-length Apricot Bread and Butter Sandwiches (on Plate)
Tiny Hot Buttered Cheese Biscuits Filled with Slivers of Baked Ham (on Plate)
Cucumber Sandwiches (on Plate)
Iced Tea with Scoop of Lime Sherbet in Each Glass (Garnish with Mint Sprig)
(No dessert necessary)

LAP TRAY LUNCHEON FOR BRIDE'S WINTER SHOWER
Mugs of Hot Cream of Corn Soup (Served in Living Room)
Fruit and Ginger Ale Salad in Lettuce Cups with Mayonnaise (on Plate)
Curried Eggs Sprinkled with Canned Chinese Noodles (on Plate)
Small Hot Buttered Rolls   Coffee
Rum Balls

Buffet parties have become a favorite means of entertaining since they have solved many problems for the hostess who is without help. These parties usually consist of one very satisfying dish, a vegetable (optional), and a dessert and are planned so that they can be prepared ahead of time.

The buffet table is attractively arranged with plates, silver and napkins placed at one end of the table. A central arrangement of flowers is usually planned for the buffet luncheon, but an arrangement of candelabra and single candlesticks is often more effective for the buffet supper.

Platters of food are placed at intervals along the table with service forks and spoons by each platter so that guests find it easy to serve themselves. The food should be bountiful so that second servings are available.

Sometimes individual trays are provided for each guest, and again small tables are placed around for their use. Coffee cups are placed on these tables and the hostess pours coffee while the guests are serving their plates. The coffee can be poured from one end of the buffet table, however, if preferred. Dessert is either passed by the hostess or brought to the buffet table so that guests can serve themselves.

When an elaborate buffet luncheon or supper is planned, it is wise for the hostess not to attempt it without help.

MENUS

SUMMER BUFFET LUNCHEON
Platter of Cold Sliced Turkey or Chicken Breast
Ring of (Fruit Ball) Jewel Salad
Philadelphia Cheese Thinned with French Dressing   Potato Chips
Nut Bread Sandwiches   Cucumber Sandwiches
Iced Tea   Lime Sherbet   Small Muffin Cakes

BUFFET LUNCHEON
Chicken Breasts with Mushroom Sauce   Rice and Carrot Ring
Philadelphia Cheese Ring Salad Filled with Grapefruit Sections
and Balls Cut from Avocado with Melon Scoop
Crab Apple Pickle   Rolls   Coffee
Frozen Lemon Icebox Dessert

Buffet Luncheon (2)
Stuffed Eggs with Newberg Sauce in Shells
Tomato Aspic with Shrimp in Ring Mold
Beaten Biscuit   Coffee
Orange Chiffon Cake—Center Filled with Whipped Cream
Surround Cake with Spoons of Wine Jelly

Buffet Luncheon (3)
Chicken or Turkey Divan
Molded Grapefruit and Pineapple Salad
Watermelon Pickle   Coffee   Rolls
Orange Chiffon Dessert

Buffet Luncheon (4)
Casserole of Scalloped Shrimp
Salad of Avocado Pear Halves Filled with Orange or Grapefruit
Sections—French Dressing
Green Lima Beans in Cream   Rolls
Coffee
Cocoanut Bavarian with Butterscotch Sauce

Buffet Luncheon (5)
Ring of "Chicken-Vegetable" Salad Surrounded by Slices of
Tomato and Cucumber and Lettuce Hearts
Stuffed Deviled Eggs
Pickle   Potato Chips
Rye Bread and Butter Sandwiches   Iced Tea
Pineapple Sherbet   Muffin Cakes

Buffet Luncheon (6)
Salmon Mousse in Fish Mold Shape
Potato Salad   Pickle
Cucumber and Whole Wheat Sandwiches   Iced Tea
Raspberry Sherbet   Broken Chiffon Cake

Buffet Luncheon (7)
Individual Molds of Chicken Salad with Tomato Aspic Top
Casserole of Cauliflower and Mushrooms
Peach Pickles   Rolls   Coffee
Orange Pudding

Buffet Luncheon (8)
Ring of Tomato Aspic with Bowl of Crab Meat Mayonnaise in Center
Casserole of Stuffed Eggs with Swiss Cheese Sauce
Beaten Biscuit   Pickle
Coffee
Raspberry Chiffon Cake Dessert

Buffet Luncheon (9)
Chicken a la King
Individual Molded Apricot Cheese Salad in Lettuce Cups
Green Asparagus Sprinkled with Riced Eggs
Coffee   Rolls
Rum Charlotte Ring with Whipped Cream

BUFFET LUNCHEONS AND SUPPERS

Buffet Luncheon (10)

Crab Supreme in Shells Around Outer Edge of Large Platter
Canned Potato-Cheese Strings in Center of the Tray
Molded Pineapple and Cucumber Salad
Hot Corn Meal Biscuit Brushed with Melted Butter
Golden Charlotte Russe

Buffet Luncheon (11)

Platter of "Eggs and Mushrooms" Surrounded by Border of
Fried Chinese Noodles (Canned)
Molded Vegetable Salad
Casserole of "Fruit Compote"
Rolls   Tea or Coffee
Pineapple Icebox Pudding

Buffet Luncheon (12)

Chicken Tetrazinni
Perfection Salad—Apricot Green Gage Plum Compote
Rolls   Coffee
Lemon Tarts

Buffet Luncheon (13)

Chicken Valenciana
Molded Grapefruit Salad   Green Asparagus
Toasted French Bread   Pickles
Chess Pies   Coffee

Buffet Luncheon (14)

Creamed Ham, Sweetbreads and Black Olives
Tomato Aspic with Celery   Squash and Egg Casserole
Beaten Biscuit   Relish Tray
Rum Charlotte Ring   Coffee

Buffet Luncheon (15)

Tomato Aspic with Crab Mayonnaise
Curried Eggs   Peas and Pimento
Celery Hearts and Carrot Sticks
Rolls   Coffee
Lemon Tarts

Buffet Luncheon (16)

Chicken and Shrimp Casserole
Grapefruit and Pineapple Molded Salad
Cauliflower and Mushroom Casserole
Corn Meal Biscuit   Coffee
Fudge Pie with Peppermint Ice Cream

39

BUFFET LUNCHEONS AND SUPPERS

ELABORATE BUFFET SUPPER OR SMORGASBORD
Platters of Cold Sliced Baked Country Ham and Turkey Breast
Individual Molds of Tomato Aspic with Shrimp
Molded Vegetable Aspic
Crab Salad Molded in Shape of Fish, Surrounded by Green
Cucumber Aspic and Egg Pond Lilies
Potato Salad   Deviled Eggs
Huge Ripe and Stuffed Olives   Celery Hearts and Carrot Curls
Radish Roses and Pickles   Hors d'Oeuvre Circles
Rye Bread and Butter Sandwiches   Beaten Biscuit
Cheese Platter of Varieties of Cheese   Coffee
Lime Ice in Watermelon Halves Scooped Out and Cut in Points Around Edge
Garnish of Melon Balls and Fresh Fruits

CHRISTMAS BUFFET SUPPER
Sliced Turkey   Sliced Baked Ham or Spice Round
Pickles, Celery Hearts, Carrot Curls and Radishes
Cinnamon Apples or Cranberry Sauce
Casserole of Lima Beans and Mushrooms or Creole Eggs
Rolls   Coffee
Fruitcake Slices Around a Variety of Cheeses
Christmas Candy or Nuts

Buffet Supper (2)
Chicken Indian Curry with Condiments
Celery Hearts   Carrot Strings   Radishes
French Bread   Coffee
Orange Ice   Cookies

Buffet Supper (3)
Deviled Oysters
Baked Sliced Ham   Cranberry-Pineapple Salad
Asparagus and Cheese Casserole
Rolls   Coffee
Macaroon Pudding

Buffet Supper (4)
Creole Chicken
Bing Cherry and Grapefruit Salad   Rolls
Asparagus and Egg Casserole
Chocolate Icebox Pudding
Coffee

Buffet Supper (5)
Italian Spaghetti
Grapefruit Salad with Cucumber Dressing
French Bread   Coffee
Date Crumble

Buffet Supper (6)
Baked Sliced Ham   Boston Baked Beans
Chopped Vegetable Salad
Toasted and Buttered Boston Brown Bread Slices
Rolls   Coffee
Trifle

Buffet Supper (7)
Brunswick Stew
Slaw No. 1   Hot Biscuit
Rolls
Individual Chess Pies   Coffee

Buffet Supper (8)
Creamed Crab and Rice
Tomato Aspic with Avocado Mayonnaise
Apple Compote   Green Lima Beans
Beaten Biscuit   Coffee
Golden Charlotte Russe

Buffet Supper (9)
Chicken with Sausage Balls   Fluffy Rice
Tomato Aspic with Celery
Casserole of Fruit Compote   Rolls
Coffee

Buffet Supper (10)
Chicken Chop Suey over (Canned) Chinese Noodles
Molded Vegetable Salad
Rolls   Celery   Olives
Chocolate Tarts
Coffee

ENGAGEMENT ANNOUNCEMENT OPEN HOUSE BUFFET
Fish-shaped Shrimp Dip with Sliced Olive for Eye
Beef Squares in Chafing Dish with Burgundy Sauce
Tiny Hot Rolls   Stuffed Eggs with Caviar Topping
Cheese Dip   Clam Dip
Melba Toast or Assorted Crackers
Olives Baked in Cheese Pastry (Served Warm)   Deviled Pecans
Little Cheese Biscuits Filled with Slivers of Baked Ham
Champagne   Coffee

SIMPLE ENGAGEMENT PARTY BUFFET
Mock Champagne Punch with Fruit-Filled Ice Ring in Punch Bowl
Tiny Puff Shells Filled with Chicken Salad
Cheese Straws   Salted Nuts
Petits Fours

☆ BRIDGE PARTIES ☆

Bridge parties can be divided into several groups. The simplest of these is the dessert bridge which is served at two or three o'clock in the afternoon followed by cards. The dessert is a rather rich or elaborate one and is accompanied by coffee and perhaps salted nuts. Since it is simple to serve, it appeals especially to the hostess who is without a maid. Another type of afternoon bridge is followed by a salad plate or by sandwiches and cookies, while still another variety is preceded by a simple luncheon. This usually consists of a salad, one hot dish, coffee and a simple dessert.

If the hostess prefers, a morning bridge party can be followed either by a salad plate or a luncheon. If the party is at night a dessert is the logical choice to serve.

BRIDGE PARTY MENUS

DESSERT BRIDGE
Large Egg Kisses Filled with Vanilla Ice Cream
Strawberry Sauce
Coffee   Salted Pecans

Dessert Bridge (2)
Fudge Pie   Peppermint Candy Ice Cream
Coffee   Salted Almonds

Dessert Bridge (3)
Broken Orange Chiffon Cake   Vanilla Ice Cream
Cherry Jubilee Sauce
Coffee   Salted Mixed Nuts

Dessert Bridge (4)
Vanilla Ice Cream   Eggnog Sauce
Fruitcake   Coffee
Salted Nuts

Dessert Bridge (5)
Almond Macaroon Icebox Pudding
Salted Pecans   Coffee

Dessert Bridge (6)
Large Cream Puff Shells Filled with
Ice Cream—Chocolate Sauce
Coffee   Salted Pecans

42

Dessert Bridge (7)

                    Rum Charlotte   Whipped Cream
                         Coffee   Salted Nuts

Dessert Bridge (8)

     Pecan Crisp Cups   Vanilla Ice Cream with Butterscotch Sauce
                         Coffee   Salted Nuts

Dessert Bridge (9)

     Chocolate Cake Ring   Peppermint Candy Ice Cream
                    Salted Almonds   Coffee

Dessert Bridge (10)

               Fruit Icebox Pudding   Coffee
                         Salted Nuts

Dessert Bridge (11)

                    Mocha Cake   Whipped Cream
                         Coffee   Salted Nuts

Dessert Bridge (12)

               Strawberry Torte   Coffee
                         Salted Nuts

AFTERNOON BRIDGE REFRESHMENTS

Menu No. 1

               Cheese and Pineapple Aspic Salad
          Tomato Sandwiches   Cucumber Sandwiches
          Brown Sugar Fudge Squares   Coffee

Menu No. 2

               Fruit Salad in Aspic
          Orange Bread and Butter Sandwiches
               Chicken Salad Sandwiches
          Tea   Angel Food Rum Balls

Menu No. 3

               Cherry-Orange Salad, Frozen
          Nut Bread and Butter Sandwiches
               Cheese and Olive Sandwiches
                    Tea   Chews

Menu No. 4

               Frozen Fruit Salad No. 1
          Spring Sandwiches   Cheese Wheels
                    Tea   Ham Squares
                    Brown Sugar Kisses

Menu No. 5

               Ginger Ale Salad
          Ripe Olive Sandwiches   Cheese Dreams
                    Tea   Chocolate Thins

Menu No. 6

Pineapple and Cucumber Salad
Tomato Sandwiches   Toasted Mushroom Sandwiches
Tea   Date Kisses

Menu No. 7

Pear and Cheese Salad, Frozen
Date and Nut Bread and Butter Sandwiches
Chicken Salad Sandwiches
Tea   Fruited Cookies

BRIDGE LUNCHEON

Apricot Cheese Molded Salad
Stuffed Eggs Newberg Sauce in Shells
Rolls   Coffee or Tea
Chocolate Tarts

Bridge Luncheon (2)

Frosty Salad Rings Filled with Shrimp
Russian Dressing   Cheese Fondue
Rolls   Coffee
Date Crumble

Bridge Luncheon (3)

Chicken Vegetable Salad   Creole Eggs
Cheese Biscuit   Coffee
Fudge Cake

Bridge Luncheon (4)

Tomato Aspic   Crab Mayonnaise
Baked Stuffed Eggs—Cheese Sauce
Rolls   Coffee
Cherry Tarts

Bridge Luncheon (5)

Frozen Cream Cheese and Jelly Salad with Grapefruit Sections
Asparagus and Egg Casserole No. 1
Blueberry Muffins   Coffee
Corn Flake Cookies

Bridge Luncheon (6)

Chicken Salad Molded with Tomato Aspic Top
Corn Pudding   Rolls   Coffee
Chocolate-Orange Cup Cakes

Bridge Luncheon (7)

Molded Vegetable Salad
Creamed Asparagus with Almonds
Banana Muffins   Coffee
Spice Meringue Cake

44

☆ COCKTAIL PARTIES ☆

Informal cocktail parties, where the guests serve themselves, have become increasingly popular as they require relatively little preparation although they are quite bountiful. If the party is a formal one, however, canapés and relishes can be passed by the waiters who serve the cocktails. Occasionally a guest will not care for alcoholic cocktails and it is wise to include a few tomato juice cocktails to take care of that emergency. As each host prefers his own variety of cocktails, I am only giving suggestions for canapés and the other items suitable for cocktail parties in the following menus.

COCKTAIL PARTY SUGGESTIONS

INFORMAL COCKTAIL PARTY
Cold Sliced Turkey   Sliced Country Ham
Sliced Sandwich Bread (Crusts Removed)   Sliced Rye Bread
Bowls of Whipped Butter   Prepared Mustard   Small Hot Biscuit
Relish Trays of Olives and Celery Hearts
Bowls of a Variety of Cheese Spreads
Crackers and Potato Chips
Jumbo Shrimp on Cocktail Picks
Russian Dressing
Stuffed Deviled Eggs   Sliced "Cheese Nut Roll"
Cocktails

LARGE FORMAL COCKTAIL PARTY
Hot Cheese and Bacon Canapés
Chicken Salad in Tiny Cream Puff Shells   Beaten Biscuit with Baked Ham
Shrimp Ovals   Water Cress Canapés
Cucumber or Tomato Open-faced Sandwiches
Relish Tray with Stuffed Eggs, Olives, Celery, etc.
Cocktails

All arranged on attractively decorated platters and passed continuously among the guests.

COCKTAIL PARTY
Hot Ham and Cheese Pinwheels   Cheese and Pepper Canapé
Chicken Canapé   Tomato Canapé
Bacon Twists   Stuffed Celery and Olives
Cocktails

COCKTAIL PARTIES

Cocktail Party (2)
>   Hot Ham Squares   Crab Meat in Toast Boats
>   Cheese and Anchovy Canapés   Water Cress Canapé
>   Stuffed Deviled Eggs   Carrot Sticks
>   Cocktails

Cocktail Party (3)
>   Hot Sardine Turnovers   Cheese and Pepper Canapé
>   Cheese Puffs   Cucumber Canapé
>   Relish Tray of Olives, Stuffed Beets and Celery
>   Cocktails

Cocktail Party (4)
>   Fish Roe Canapé   Tomato Canapé
>   Chicken Salad in Toast Cups   Cheese Dreams
>   Olives   Chipped Beef and Cheese Rolls
>   Celery Hearts
>   Cocktails

Cocktail Party (5)
>   Cheese and Bacon Open-faced Sandwiches
>   Individual Oyster Loaves   Toasted Rolled Asparagus
>   Crab Meat Canapé   Relish Tray with Olives and Radishes
>   Cocktails

Cocktail Party (6)
>   Anchovy and Cheese Canapé   Water Cress Canapé
>   Cheese and Poppy Seed Open-faced Sandwiches   Beaten Biscuit and Ham
>   Relish Tray with Celery and Carrot Sticks
>   Bacon Twists
>   Cocktails

46

☆ DINNERS ☆

The very elaborate, formal dinners, consisting of six or seven courses, are almost a thing of the past, and a simplified menu seems to fit the needs of the present-day hostess. For that reason I have planned a series of menus which will be flexible, so that a salad course can be introduced after the meat course in some of them, or perhaps a soup or fish course added to others. This will be optional with the hostess, as they are complete just as they are for most occasions.

The American custom of serving a salad as a first course is a clever way of combining the appetizer and salad course, and cocktails served with canapés in the living room can also take the place of one of the dinner courses. A separate fish course is rarely served now, but again the fish can be introduced into the menu in the form of an appetizer or soup. If the dinner is informal, the salad course can be put on the table and served with the meat course. These suggestions tend to simplify the dinner and they are often necessary when the maid service is limited.

Although I think the hostess of today will prefer menus I have suggested, I am also including one of the formal ones, with several more courses, simply as a means of showing how it should be served.

FORMAL DINNER MENU

Rose Apple Appetizer   Anchovy Circles   Olives
Clear Tomato Soup   Crackers
Shrimp Sea Shells   Tiny Corn Meal Muffins
Chicken Breasts with Wine Sauce   Rice Rings with Pimento Peas
Peach Pickle   Green Asparagus   Rolls
Head Lettuce   Roquefort Dressing
Lime Sherbet with Fruits (Summer Delight)
Coffee

CHRISTMAS DINNER

Grapefruit Halves with Crystallized Ginger
Maraschino Cherry Garnish
Baked Turkey   Cranberry Relish   Celery Hearts
Sweet Potato Ring Filled with Apple Balls
Cauliflower with Tomato Curry Sauce
Green Beans with Toasted Almonds
Rolls
Plum Pudding—Eggnog Sauce
Coffee

47

DINNERS

THANKSGIVING DINNER
Oyster Cocktail
Hot Tomato Bouillon Celery Olives Crackers
Baked Duck or Goose Clear Apple Filled with Orange Marmalade
Wild Rice Ring Filled with Green Peas and Pimento
Spinach Souffle or Broccoli with Hollandaise Sauce
Individual Mince Pies with Cheese Pumpkin Garnish
Coffee

DINNER
Avocado Appetizer
Shrimp Bisque
Deviled Chicken Peach Pickle
Lima Beans with Sour Cream
Clipped Corn Rolls
Cocoanut Bavarian Cream
Coffee

Dinner (2)
Crab Salad in Avocado Pear
Russian Dressing Crackers
Chicken Ring Surrounded by Crusty Peaches
Creole Cauliflower in Bell Peppers
Baby Lima Beans Rolls
Charlotte Russe
Coffee

Dinner (3)
Individual Tomato Aspic Rings with Stuffed Egg in Center
Chicken Breasts in White Wine
Rice and Carrot Ring Filled with Peas
Green Asparagus
Cherry-Sherry Ring
Broken Orange Chiffon Cake Coffee

Dinner (4)
Frosty Salad Rings with Grapefruit and Avocado
Fish Creamed with Shrimp Sauce
Baked Stuffed Tomatoes Potato Balls
Corn Meal Muffins
Peach or Strawberry Meringue
Coffee

Dinner (5)
Frozen Consommé with Shrimp
Creamed Chicken in Noodle Ring
Broccoli with Lemon Butter Sauce Fig and Ginger Compote
Salad Can Be Added Here (Optional)
Rolls
Macaroon Pudding Coffee
48

DINNERS

Dinner (6)

Grapefruit and Black Grape Salad
Cream of Mushroom Soup (Optional)
Stuffed Squab   Crab Apple Pickle
Corn Timbales on Broiled Tomatoes
Stuffed Squash
Rolls
Macaroon Meringue Ring with Vanilla Ice Cream
Coffee

Dinner (7)

Tomato and Egg Appetizer (Optional)
Sliced Baked Country Ham   Clear Pickle Rings
Casserole of Deviled Oysters
Snap Beans with Toasted Almonds   Rolls
Peppers Stuffed with Cheese and Tomato Catsup
Rum Charlotte Ring
Coffee

Dinner (8)

Grapefruit Half with Ginger (Optional)
Cream of Celery Soup
Carrot Sticks   Radishes
Fish Cutlets   Tartar Sauce
Cauliflower with Tomato Curry Sauce
Green Peas—French Style
Corn Meal Muffins   Slaw No. 1
Strawberry Torte
Coffee

Dinner (9)

Tomato Juice   Bacon Twists
Chicken Cutlet—Mushroom Sauce
Hot Fruit Compote   Asparagus and Almonds
Salad May Be Added Here (Optional)
Chocolate Icebox Pudding
Coffee

Dinner (10)

Soup (Optional)
Canapé Marguery
Creole Chicken   Rice Balls
Green Asparagus with Toasted Almonds
Sweet Potatoes and Pears
Trifle
Coffee

Dinner (11)

Shrimp Cocktail   Crackers
Lamb Chops Stuffed with Mushrooms   Pear Garnish
Asparagus with Almonds   Baked Stuff Tomato
Salad Can Be Added Here (Optional)
Rolls   Pickles
Almond Macaroon Icebox Pudding
Coffee

49

Dinner (12)

Cream of Corn Soup   Crackers
Sweetbreads Broiled   Tomato Sauce
Lima Beans Creamed   Stuffed Squash
Baked Bananas   Rolls
Salad (Optional)
Apricot Ice Cream   Orange Chiffon Cake
Coffee

Dinner (13)

Tomato Juice Cocktail   Bacon Crisps
Stuffed Celery   Blue Cheese Canapé
Turkey Balls   Cranberry Relish
Asparagus in Bell Peppers   Sweet Potato Ring
Salad (Optional)
Mocha Cake
Coffee

Dinner (14)

Oyster Soup   Crackers
Celery   Radishes   Olives
Sweetbread Cutlets
Lima Beans and Mushrooms   Broiled Tomatoes
Apricot and Green Gage Plum Compote
Salad (Optional)
Pecan Crisp Rings   Ice Cream
Butterscotch Sauce
Coffee

Dinner (15)

Avocado Appetizer
Crab Bisque (Optional)   Crackers
Barbecued Chicken
Snap Beans with Mushroom Sauce   Baked Stuffed Tomato
Hot Fig and Ginger Compote
Rolls
Strawberry Torte
Coffee

Dinner (16)

Individual Cheese Rings with Grapefruit Sections
Shrimp Creole in Rice Ring
Green Peas with Pimento   Rolls   Stuffed Squash
Frozen Lemon Icebox Dessert
Coffee

SWEET SIXTEEN AND OTHER TEEN PARTIES

Our parties for teen-age girls are usually divided into three categories. The formal teas planned by grandmother; the morning coffees or chocolates which mother suggests; and the "pop" parties, cook-outs, or poolside refreshments which are planned by the girls themselves and which are really the most popular of all parties for that set.

For sweet sixteen parties that include boys, the food should be plain fare, totally different from the dainty sandwiches and cakes served at the teas or chocolates.

A "pop" party, when served indoors, is not quite as informal as a poolside one—but the drinks are different. At times our huge silver punch bowl was filled with crushed ice and the coke bottles were buried in the ice. They had been previously refrigerated so were thoroughly chilled. A tray of soda straws was near the punch bowl. When a punch bowl is not available the soft drinks can be served in glasses over ice cubes.

MORNING POP PARTY, Served Indoors
Cheese Dreams (Round or Rolled)   Egg and Almond Finger Sandwiches
Tomato Sandwiches with Crescent-Shaped Tops   Sausage Roll-Ups Served Hot
Soft Drinks
Butterscotch Fudge Cake

SWEET SIXTEEN COFFEE OR CHOCOLATE
Ripe Olive and Nut Sandwiches   Spring (Vegetable) Sandwiches
Cheese and Bacon Open-faced Sandwiches   Orange Toast
Fudge Cake
Chocolate or Coffee, Hot or Iced

SWEET SIXTEEN TEA
Chicken Salad in Puff Shells   Cucumber Sandwiches
Philadelphia Cheese and Olive Sandwiches   Cinnamon Toast Sticks
Tiny Meringue Shells Filled with Angel Pie Filling
Punch Bowl with Party Punch in which Floats a Fruit-Filled Ice Ring

MORNING SUNDAE PARTY
Sundae Dessert Parties are popular and quite easy to prepare as each guest assembles his own sundae. Several varieties of ice cream such as vanilla, chocolate, peppermint, coffee and maple-nut are emptied into one large punch bowl or put in separate smaller bowls. Surrounding the ice cream are small bowls with varieties of sundae sauces, chopped nuts, whipped cream, chocolate sprinkles and sections of bananas which have been rolled in lemon juice to prevent discoloration. Page numbers for recipes for Chocolate Sauce, Butterscotch Sauce, Maple-Nut Sauce, Minted Marshmallow Sauce or Simple Tutti-Frutti can be found in the Index.

SWEET SIXTEEN AND OTHER TEEN PARTIES

TEEN-AGE POOLSIDE LUNCH

Potato Salad with Tomato Wedges   Hot Wiener and Cheese Rolls
Doughnuts
Have a milk bar with individual cartons of sweet milk and chocolate milk. Or have a tray of thoroughly chilled soft drinks with soda straws nearby.

Poolside Lunch (2)

Po'Boy Sandwiches   Soft Drinks
Peanut Butter Cookies

Poolside Lunch (3)

Have your bakery bake a 6-foot loaf of French or Italian bread. Slice it through once horizontally, butter inside and fill with assorted cold cuts: slices of turkey, baked ham, corned or roast beef, bologna, and cheese. You will need about 12 pounds of filler to serve 36. Each guest is served about two inches of sandwich, which is sliced vertically at the table.

Punch   Soft Drinks
Decorated Birthday Cake

TEEN-AGE POOLSIDE SUPPER

Cocktail Party Drumsticks with Tomato Dip
Impromptu Pizzas   Chopped Vegetable Salad
Garlic Bread Sticks   Parmesan Cheese Potato Chips
Cocktail Cheese Dip
Rocky Road Fudgies   Soft Drinks

POOLSIDE LATE SUPPER

Cheese Fondue   Hot Biscuits with Sausage or Ham
Relish Tray of Celery, Carrot Sticks and Radish Roses
Tray of Watermelon, Honey Dew and Cantaloupe Balls with
Cocktail Picks Nearby
Soft Drinks

COOK-OUT

Tray of Hamburger Buns   Bowl of Tomato, Onion and Bell Pepper Slices
Platter of Hamburgers to Barbecue (or Cook Them Inside and Serve Outdoors)
Casserole of Baked Beans
Soft Drinks   Small Chess Pies

TEEN-AGE CHRISTMAS PARTY

Christmas Wassail (Mulled Cider)
Hot Pizza Toast Rounds
Tomato Sandwiches
Rocky Road Fudgies

Teen-age Christmas Party (2)

Christmas Punch
Biscuits with Tiny Hamburgers
Cheese Dreams
Date Bars

LATE SUPPERS AND
☆ AFTER-THEATRE SNACKS ☆

LATE SUPPERS

(1)

Crab Meat Luncheon Salad
Thousand Island Dressing and/or Roquefort Cheese Dressing #2
Garlic Bread Sticks   Corn Meal Biscuits
Butterscotch Fudge Cake   Coffee or Iced Tea

(2)

Casserole of Sweetbreads and Olives   Molded Beet Salad
Hot Rolls
Chocolate Tarts   Coffee or Iced Tea

(3)

New Orleans Seafood Gumbo   Fluffy Rice
Asparagus and Artichoke Salad with Anchovy Dressing
Coffee   Date Balls

(4)

D'Anjou Pear Salad with Cheese Mayonnaise
Tongue and Olive Sandwiches
Hot Pecan Muffins
Iced Tea or Coffee   Caramel Bars

(5)

Shrimp Jambolaya
Grapefruit Salad with Caper Dressing
Iced Tea or Coffee   Rocky Road Fudgies

(6)

Cocktail Party Chicken Drumsticks
Sauce for Dunking—Kept Warm over Hot Plate
Garlic Bread Sticks   Toasted Crackers or Corn Chips
Onion Soup Mix with Sour Cream Dip   Clam Dip

(7)

Meat Balls in Sauce in Chafing Dish   Cheese Dip
Tiny Hot Sesame Rolls   Potato Chips Toasted with Parmesan Cheese
Cereal Tidbits

AFTER-THEATRE SNACKS

(1)

Welsh Rarebit   or   Cheese Fondue

(2)

Hot Oyster Soup   Celery Hearts   Oyster Crackers

(3)

Creamed Oysters in Chafing Dish   Sesame Rolls

(4)

Chicken Terrapin in Chafing Dish   Toast Circles

(5)

Philadelphia Cheese Squares, Guava Jelly and Round Butter
Crackers—Serve with Butter Spreaders

(6)

Warm Buttered Bishop Bread Served with Hot Chocolate
Topped with Marshmallow or Whipped Cream

PART II

Recipes

AMOUNTS OF FOOD NEEDED FOR LARGE GROUPS

☆ ☆

1 turkey, dressed, 20 pounds, and 4 bunches of celery make salad for 40.

4 turkeys, 20 pounds, baked and sliced, with dressing, serve 150.

7 turkeys made into turkey á la king serve 300.

3 turkeys, 20 pounds, made into turkey hash fill 75 individual rice or grit rings.

1 turkey, 20 pounds, makes 55 turkey balls or cutlets.

6 hens, 5 pounds each, make chicken salad for 50.

2 hens, 5 pounds each, and two bunches of celery make chicken salad to fill 125 tiny puff shells or 100 sandwiches.

30 pounds thinly sliced cooked spice round serve 180.

5 baked hams, 15 pounds each, serve 150.

5 pounds sweetbreads, creamed, will fill 20 pastry shells.

36 pounds of boned red snapper will make fish pudding rings or fish cutlets to serve 200.

1½ pounds cooked and peeled shrimp made into "Shrimp Creole" will fill a very large "Cheese Soufflé Ring" (3 times recipe) and will serve 10 to 12.

2½-pound box frozen asparagus serves 10.

5 pounds frozen peas serve 30.

3 pounds coffee for 100 large cups or 175 small cups of coffee.

1 cake of yeast makes 30 rolls.

☆ APPETIZERS ☆

AVOCADO APPETIZER

1 avocado
1 firm tomato
¼ head of lettuce, shredded

4 strips breakfast bacon cooked until crisp
Russian dressing

Cut avocado and tomato into small cubes; marinate in French dressing. When ready to serve, combine with lettuce and bacon, which has been crumbled in bits; add Russian dressing. Serve on small curled lettuce hearts, in cocktail glass, as first course. Serves 6.

AVOCADO AND SHRIMP COCKTAIL

½ pound cooked shrimp   1 avocado

Cut avocado into cubes; sprinkle with lemon juice; clean shrimp; combine with the same cocktail sauce that is given for "artichoke and egg appetizer." Serves 6.

ARTICHOKE APPETIZER OR SALAD

1 can baby artichokes
1 diced pimento
1 small diced cucumber
2 tablespoons lemon juice

1 tablespoon gelatin
¼ cup cold water
1 cup boiling water
¼ cup sugar

Make cucumber aspic of gelatin, lemon juice, water, sugar and cucumber; tint green with a few drops of green coloring; add other ingredients; mold in very small molds. Serves 8.

ARTICHOKE AND EGG APPETIZER

1 No. 2 can artichoke hearts—diced
6 hard boiled eggs—chopped

1 cup finely diced celery
2 slices crisp breakfast bacon, crumbled

Mix with Russian dressing made of

½ cup of mayonnaise
1 tablespoon Worcestershire sauce
1 tablespoon chili sauce

1 tablespoon catsup (tomato)
1 tablespoon horse-radish. Serves 6.

BACON ROLL-UPS

Cut slices of bacon in four pieces; wrap around olives, cocktail sausages, oysters, or pecan halves put together with Roquefort cheese spread; dip in Burgundy wine and broil; serve hot, speared on cocktail picks.

STUFFED BEETS

Scoop out centers of tiny rose-bud beets; fill with highly seasoned, riced, hard-boiled eggs; bound together with a bit of cooked dressing or with seasoned and sweetened vinegar. Put cocktail picks in sides of the beets and serve on relish tray.

CHIPPED BEEF ROLLS

1 part Roquefort cheese spread   2 parts cream cheese spread

Smooth together with a little wine; spread a layer of cheese on each slice of chipped beef. Roll up. Chill. Cut in bite-size pieces and spear with colored cocktail picks.

CHIPPED BEEF AND CHEESE ROLLS

Season cream cheese with onion juice, minced parsley, Worcestershire sauce, and horse-radish; shape into narrow cylinders, size of little finger; roll in thin slices of chipped beef; trim the ends evenly; chill and use to garnish salads or on hors d'oeuvre tray.

CODFISH BALLS

1 cup salt codfish	1 egg, well beaten
4 potatoes, cut in small blocks	1 large pinch cayenne pepper
1 tablespoon butter	

Soak codfish an hour in cold water, shred, remove bones; cook in boiling water with potatoes. When almost done, drain off water and cover vessel, letting it stay over very low heat until they are dry; mash fine; add seasoning and well beaten egg; shape into small balls. Roll in flour and put several at a time in frying basket. Cook in deep fat several minutes, until brown. Drain on unglazed paper; serve hot on cocktail picks. 20 small balls. Serve with a bowl of tartar sauce to which a few capers have been added.

CEREAL CRUNCHIES

1 pound margarine	1 box Rice Chex cereal, 12-ounce size
1 tablespoon Worcestershire sauce	1 box Cheerio cereal
2 teaspoons salt	1 jar pretzel bits
1 teaspoon garlic powder	½ pound each of almonds and pecans

Blanch almonds; cut in half lengthwise and toast in oven to a light brown. Melt margarine; add seasonings; combine with cereals, pecans and toasted almond. Put in a large, flat pan and toast slowly for two hours at 250°. Thin pretzel sticks can be substituted for the pretzel bits if desired. These can be served at cocktail parties or with tomato juice. They keep well in air-tight containers.

CUCUMBER PICKLE AND CHEESE APPETIZER

Select large, sour, firm pickles; scoop out centers with an apple corer; if pickle is very large cut in halves, crosswise, before scooping out centers. Stuff holes in pickles with snappy yellow cheese spread; chill; cut in half-inch thick slices.

CHEESE PUFFS

1½ cups grated American cheese	2 egg yolks
2 egg whites	1 teaspoon Worcestershire sauce

Grate cheese; add beaten yolks and Worcestershire sauce; beat egg whites very stiff; combine with cheese. Toast rounds of bread on one side; spread untoasted side with cheese mixture. Put in hot oven until puffed and brown. Serve at once.

STUFFED CUCUMBER SECTIONS

Cut unpeeled cucumbers in two-inch thick sections. Scoop out to make little containers. Remove narrow sections of the cucumber peel leaving an alternating strip of peel as you go around the container. Chop scooped out cucumber; add a little grated onion, a package of Philadelphia cream cheese, a tablespoon of French dressing and a little Worcestershire sauce and chili powder. Season to taste. Put mixture in cucumber containers; mound high and top with parsley bud.

STUFFED CELERY SECTIONS

Mix equal amounts of Philadelphia cream and Roquefort cheese, or use Roquefort spread cheese. Pull ribs off of celery stalk until you reach the center; then put it together again with thick layer of cheese between each layer of ribs; tie firmly and chill. Slice in 1-inch sections. The same cheese mixture may be used to stuff small pieces of celery hearts.

STUFFED CELERY HEARTS

Use a combination of Roquefort and cream cheese (or cream cheese seasoned with Worcestershire sauce, onion juice and horse-radish) with an equal amount of finely-mashed shrimp added, stuff celery; sprinkle with paprika.

CHEESE ROLL

½ pound yellow cheese	1 small onion
½ pound Philadelphia cream cheese	1½ cups chopped pecans
¼ pound Roquefort cheese	

Grind onion, yellow cheese and Roquefort cheese together, knead with Philadelphia cheese; add ½ cup pecans, form into 2 narrow cylinders; roll in the rest of the finely chopped pecans. It will take a cup of pecans for this. Chill for 24 hours; when ready to serve, slice into round slices; place around the edge of a platter containing crackers. 20 slices.

CHEESE BALLS OR SPREAD

Combine 3 packages Philadelphia cheese, 4 teaspoons horse-radish, drained, 2 teaspoons highly seasoned mayonnaise; ⅛ teaspoon salt, 1 teaspoon Worcestershire sauce and 1 teaspoon onion juice. Chill; form into balls; roll in minced parsley or paprika. Can be used as a spread if desired. 20 balls.

Another version of cheese balls is made from creamed Old English cheese made into balls and rolled in chopped pecans.

HAM AND EGG APPETIZER BALLS

½ pound baked ham, ground	5 hard boiled eggs
1 teaspoon minced onion	Mayonnaise to bind

Mash egg yolks, add onion, season with salt, paprika, and a little Worcestershire sauce; add mayonnaise to bind together; mix with ham and riced egg whites. Form into balls an inch in diameter; roll in minced parsley; chill; serve on cocktail picks.

HORS D'OEUVRE CIRCLES

Cut thin center slices from flat round loaf of rye bread about 8 inches in diameter, trim off crusts so that you have a perfectly round circle of bread to work with. Spread the round with butter mixed with a small amount of anchovy paste, putting it on rather thickly so that the decorations will stick to the surface. In the exact center of the round put a small circle of caviar; around it put a row of rolled anchovies which form a wall to hold the caviar in place. Next to the anchovies put a half inch circular band of riced egg whites; outside the eggs put a band of smoked salmon, cut or ground; then put a band of riced egg yolks; followed with a band of finely-minced parsley. A band of little cocktail shrimp is then put on; followed by a piping of highly seasoned cream cheese that is fluted on with a pastry tube; this is followed by a circle of red caviar. Tiny sardines come next, laid around and around, overlapping a bit. Another row of cheese (this time a yellow cheese) can be fluted around the outer edge of the circle. Take care that each row is put on in an evenly spaced circle. These directions can be varied to make each circle different; make each one as colorful as possible. Put on flat platter, cut in small pie-shaped wedges by pressing knife down carefully instead of using a sawing motion to cut it. See front cover. Each circle should serve 10 to 12.

EGG APPETIZER

8 hard-boiled eggs, grated
4 crackers grated or rolled into
  fine crumbs

4 ribs of celery, chopped fine
½ teaspoon dry mustard
1 tablespoon Worcestershire sauce

Bind ingredients together with highly seasoned mayonnaise to which 1 tablespoon lemon juice has been added; season with salt and pepper; pack into small molds; chill until firm. Spread slices of Holland rusk with anchovy paste; cover with slice of tomato; turn out molds of eggs on tomatoes; top with small amount of caviar. Serve on lettuce hearts as an appetizer salad.

STUFFED EGGS

Hard boil eggs; plunge into cold water; shell at once; cool; cut in half, lengthwise; remove yolks and press them through a sieve; season highly with salt, red pepper, a little dry mustard and a bit of anchovy paste or caviar. Moisten with French dressing to bind together; stuff back into the whites. Decorate tops with parsley bud, stuffed olive, or anchovy fillet.

STUFFED MUSHROOMS

Fill large mushrooms with Smithfield deviled ham. Broil. Serve on cocktail picks while hot.

STUFFED MUSHROOM CAPS

Cut stems from fresh mushrooms; sauté in butter; chop stems fine; sauté them with either chicken livers or smoked sausage. Mash well and season with salt and pepper. Stuff in mushroom caps and place cocktail pick in each.

OLIVE-CHEESE APPETIZER

Ice large stuffed olives with a highly seasoned cream cheese mixture; roll in ground nuts.

PECAN-CHEESE APPETIZERS

Spread a thick layer of Roquefort spread cheese between two large halves of pecans. Press together and chill until time to serve.

ROSE APPLE APPETIZER

2 cups finely minced celery
6 hard-boiled eggs, riced

6 chopped anchovies
Mayonnaise to mix

Combine ingredients; fill rose apple (pimento) and put on appetizer plate, on lettuce hearts. Serves 8.

SALMON STRIPS

Spread finger-length toast strips with mayonnaise; dip edges in minced parsley; cover with thinly-sliced smoked salmon. Garnish top with slice of stuffed olive or cocktail onions.

TOMATO APPETIZER OR SALAD

Butter Holland rusk with anchovy paste; top with a slice of tomato; on top of tomato put a "stuffed egg"; flank this with two small sardines; serve on shredded lettuce; cover with Russian dressing.

TOMATO-EGG APPETIZER

Use a large firm slice of tomato for each serving. Sprinkle with salt and scrape a suspicion of onion juice on it. Rice hard-boiled eggs separately; put a border of the riced whites around the outer edge of each slice; just inside that put a band of riced yellows. Arrange a spoonful of stiff mayonnaise in the center; top with a bit of caviar; serve on lettuce hearts.

CANAPÉ MARGUERY APPETIZER

1 5-ounce can white tuna fish
2 hard-boiled eggs—cnopped
1 pimento cut in small pieces

1 medium sized tomato—chopped
½ bell pepper chopped
1 cup Russian dressing

Pour boiling water over tuna fish; drain and shred; add other ingredients. Just before serving, put 1 tablespoon butter in skillet; heat the mixture well; put on large rounds of toast; sprinkle with Parmesan cheese; run under the broiler. They must be served hot. Serves 6. When used as a canapé spread on small toast rounds.

COCKTAILS

CRAB-MEAT COCKTAIL

1 cup mayonnaise
½ cup tomato catsup
1 teaspoon anchovy paste
1 teaspoon Worcestershire sauce
1 teaspoon horse-radish

1 tablespoon lemon juice
1 can crab meat—6-ounce size
½ cup chopped celery
Salt and cayenne pepper to taste

Combine seasonings with mayonnaise. Flake crab meat, add celery and mayonnaise. Line cocktail glasses with small pieces of lettuce hearts and add cocktail. Serves 4 to 6.

OYSTER OR SHRIMP COCKTAIL

Allow six or eight oysters for each person. Serve in cocktail glasses covered generously with "Cocktail Sauce." Use the same recipe for shrimp cocktail.

COCKTAIL DIPS

ANCHOVY CHEESE DIP

8 ounces Philadelphia cream cheese
1½ teaspoons anchovy paste
1 tablespoon Worcestershire sauce

1 teaspoon onion juice
¼ cup cream
Salt and cayenne pepper

Mash cheese; thin to dipping consistency with cream; add seasoning; using more or less anchovy paste as desired. Serve with potato chips or crisp crackers.

AVOCADO CHEESE DIP

3-ounce package Philadelphia cheese
1 large ripe avocado
1 teaspoon onion juice

1 tablespoon mayonnaise
1 tablespoon French dressing
Salt and cayenne pepper

Press avocado through a sieve; mash cheese; mix French dressing and onion juice with avocado pulp, add mayonnaise to cheese; combine. Serve with potato chips.

CHIVE CHEESE DIPS

1 wedge chive cheese
1 teaspoon onion juice
2 teaspoons Worcestershire sauce

1 tablespoon French dressing
Cream as needed
Salt and cayenne pepper

Smooth cheese with French dressing; combine with seasoning; add cream to make dipping consistency; correct seasoning if necessary. Grated salted almonds can be added, if desired.

CLAM DIP

2 packages (3 ounces) Philadelphia cream
  cheese
1 small can minced clams
1 teaspoon Worcestershire sauce

1 teaspoon onion juice
⅛ teaspoon cayenne pepper
Salt if needed

Mash cheese; drain clams, add clam juice to cheese until it reaches dipping consistency; season; add minced clams. Serve with potato chips.

ROQUEFORT CHEESE DIP

2 packages (3 ounces) Philadelphia cream
  cheese
2 packages Roquefort cheese, large size

Sherry wine
Cream

Mash cheese thoroughly with a silver fork; season with cayenne pepper and salt. Thin to dipping consistency with wine and cream. Serve with potato chips.

ROQUEFORT CHEESE TOMATO DIP

Use the preceding recipe, substituting tomato paste for the wine and cream. If necessary, add a little cream to make dipping consistency. Serve with potato chips or crisp crackers.

GUACAMOLE DIP

2 ripe avocados
1 teaspoon onion juice
1 ripe tomato diced and drained

1 teaspoon lemon juice
French dressing as needed
Salt and cayenne pepper

Sieve avocado; add seasoning and finely chopped tomato. Thin to dipping consistency with French dressing. Serve with crisp crackers.

SHRIMP DUNK

1½ pounds green shrimp (Large size)
  1 bay leaf
  2 teaspoons salt
  1 pod red pepper

2 ribs celery, cut in pieces
1 teaspoon pickling spice
Juice ½ lemon
4 cups boiling water

Combine ingredients; boil ten or twelve minutes; peel shrimp and remove black line. Impale shrimp on cocktail picks and stick close together on a large grapefruit. Serve with a bowl of "Russian Dressing." Dunk shrimp in dressing.

VEGETABLE DUNKING BOWL

Cut raw carrots, cucumbers and sections of celery hearts in long slender strips; soak in ice water until crisp; drain and dry between cloths. Arrange on a platter; decorate with raw cauliflower flowerettes and radish roses. In the center of the platter put a bowl of "Sour Cream Dressing" which has had several tablespoons of chopped water cress added to it.

BEVERAGES

PERCOLATOR COFFEE

Use 1 heaping tablespoon of percolator or all purpose grind coffee to each measuring cup of water. When coffee begins to percolate reduce heat and let percolate for 5 or 10 minutes, or until has reached the desired strength.

COFFEE FOR LARGE PARTY

It is advisable to use a hotel size coffee urn when making coffee in large quantities. When this is not available, coffee can be made in kettles, each holding 2 gallons of boiling water. Allow 1 pound of coffee to each kettle of water. Tie coffee loosely in muslin bags, put in boiling water; reduce heat; cover and let stand 10 minutes. Uncover and dip bags up and down to extract coffee flavor. Remove coffee bags, when the desired strength, and cover until ready to serve. Each pound of coffee will make 40 cups.

ICED COFFEE

Make coffee double strength; pour immediately over glasses of crushed ice. Pass sugar and cream, or sweeten before serving and top with slightly sweetened whipped cream or with a scoop of vanilla ice cream.

FROSTED COFFEE

Make 3 pints of iced coffee; break 1 quart of vanilla ice cream in pieces; combine with coffee and blend in cocktail shaker or with a wire whisk. Serve in tall glasses. Serves 10.

TEA

Allow about 1 teaspoon of tea for each person to be served. Have water boiling hot and pour over tea. Remove from heat and let it stand 3 to 5 minutes. Strain. Never boil tea.

TEA FOR LARGE PARTY

Tie cup of tea leaves loosely in a cheese cloth bag. Have several kettles of boiling water in readiness on the stove. When ready to serve the tea, dip out a pitcher-full of boiling water and immerse the tea bag in the pitcher. Dip the bag up and down until the tea is the desired strength. Usually 1 or 2 dippings is sufficient. Do not leave the bag in the pitcher. Take out and put on a plate until the next pitcher is needed. The tea bag can be used repeatedly for the party.

ICE TEA

Make a tea infusion, allowing ½ cup of tea to 6 cups of boiling water. Remove from fire at once and strain. Add cold water until tea is desired strength. It should take 6 cups of cold water to make tea for 12, or more glasses. Use half recipe for 6 glasses.

PARTY ICE TEA

4 tablespoons tea	1 quart boiling water
4 cups sugar	12 lemons (juice of)
1 bunch fresh mint	6 oranges (juice of)

Pour boiling water over tea, sugar and mint and let stand a short time. Strain, add fruit juices and enough water to make a gallon. Serve over cracked ice. This is also nice frozen and served in tea glasses covered with ginger ale. Garnish with orange slice and sprig of mint. Serves 15.

RUSSIAN TEA

Tie 1 stick cinnamon and ¼ teaspoon whole cloves in bag and bring to a boil in 6 cups water. Let simmer 10 minutes before adding 4 teaspoons of tea. Strain tea, add juice of one lemon and 2 oranges and sweeten to taste. Serves 8.

HOT CHOCOLATE

2 quarts sweet milk	2 cups sugar
8 squares (½ pound) bitter chocolate	

Grate chocolate; add to sugar; melt over hot water; add to hot milk. Cook in double boiler until thoroughly blended. Serve with whipped cream or marshmallow on top of the chocolate. Serves 10.

FROSTED CHOCOLATE

Make chocolate; chill. To 3 pints of chocolate use 1½ pints of vanilla ice cream. Break ice cream in pieces; put in shaker; add chocolate; shake until blended. If shaker is not available, let ice cream become somewhat soft; blend into chocolate with wire whisk. Serves 10.

SPANISH CHOCOLATE

1 package Nestle's semi-sweet chocolate morsels	2 egg yolks
	3 pints milk
1 cup hot coffee	2 teaspoons vanilla

Scald milk in double boiler. Melt chocolate, over hot water, with coffee; add milk. Just before serving, beat egg yolks; add to chocolate slowly; beat well with wire whisk. Sweeten to taste. Flavor with vanilla. Serve topped with whipped cream. Serves 8.

FROSTED MINT COCOA

6 tablespoons cocoa	5 cups milk
8 tablespoons sugar	6 drops essence mint or to taste
1 cup boiling water	1½ pints vanilla ice cream

Cook cocoa, sugar and water 5 or 10 minutes. Scald milk in double boiler; add cocoa and mint flavoring; stir until blended. Chill. Break ice cream in pieces; add to cocoa and shake in cocktail shaker or beat with wire whisk. Serves 10.

PARTY COCOA FOR CHILDREN

Follow directions for cocoa, in above recipe, omitting mint and ice cream. Serve hot, flavored with 1 teaspoon of vanilla. Beat with rotary beater just before serving and top with marshmallow.

COCKTAILS

CRANBERRY JUICE (1)

1 quart red ripe cranberries	½ cup lemon juice
1 quart boiling water	½ cup orange juice
1 cup sugar	½ cup pineapple juice

Cook cranberries in boiling water until perfectly soft. Strain and add sugar. When cold add fruit juices and serve over cracked ice. Serves 8.

CRANBERRY JUICE COCKTAIL (2)

1 bottle cranberry juice cocktail—16 ounces	1 can pineapple juice—12 ounces
	1 can grapefruit juice—18 ounces

Combine ingredients and pour over ice. Serves 12.

GRAPE JUICE COCKTAIL

1 quart grape juice	1 pint ginger ale

Combine and serve over cracked ice. If preferred the plain grape juice can be served in the same way. Serves 12 to 15. Use half of recipe for 6 to 7 servings.

LIME COCKTAIL

2 cups white grape juice	1½ cups lime juice
1 cup pineapple juice	1 quart ginger ale

Combine fruit juices and store in refrigerator. Just before serving add ginger ale and garnish with mint. Color green with fruit coloring. Serves 15.

MINTED, GRAPEFRUIT JUICE COCKTAIL

1 46-ounce can unsweetened grapefruit juice	1 No. 2 can of pineapple juice
	3 drops essence of mint

Combine and serve cold. Color green with fruit coloring. Serves 15.

HOT SPICED PINEAPPLE JUICE

1 14-ounce can pineapple juice	1 stick cinnamon
1 lemon—juice of	Sugar if necessary

Heat pineapple, lemon juice and cinnamon. Let simmer slowly for 15 minutes. Serve hot. Serves 4.

TOMATO JUICE COCKTAIL

1 16-ounce can tomato juice
1 lemon—juice of
Salt to taste

1 tablespoon (or more) sugar
1 tablespoon Worcestershire sauce

Combine. Each pint of liquid will fill five average cocktail glasses.

PUNCH

GINGER ALE PUNCH

3 dozen lemons
2 dozen oranges
4 quarts ginger ale
6 cups sugar (more or less)

2 tablespoons tea
2 quarts boiling water
2 gallons lime sherbet

Pour water over tea, add sugar and steep for few minutes. Strain and add fruit juice when cold. Just before serving add ginger ale and lime sherbert. Do not use as much sugar as specified unless the lemons are very juicy. It will be best to use only part of it at first and the rest if necessary. Serves 50.

GRAPE JUICE PUNCH

1 dozen lemons
6 oranges
1 quart water
1 large (40 ounces) can pineapple juice

3 quarts grape juice
3 quarts ginger ale
Sugar to taste

Combine juices and water. Add ginger ale when ready to serve. Makes 50 cups.

Grape Juice Punch (2)

For an inexpensive punch use equal parts of grape juice, water and ginger ale. Sugar if necessary.

PARTY PUNCH

3 gallons tea
1 gallon orange juice
4 (46 ounces) cans pineapple juice

5 dozen lemons
6 quarts ginger ale
Sugar

Pour hot water over large bunch of mint or add a little essence of mint to the punch. Sweeten tea to taste. When cool, remove mint and add fruit juice. Slice 1 dozen small oranges and cut each slice in half to use as decoration for the punch bowl.

Slice 4 small bottles of green cherries in half and pin each piece to an orange slice with a small section of fresh mint, using a piece of toothpick to hold it in place. Float these in the punch bowl. Add ginger ale just before serving. This will make about 8 gallons and will serve over 200 cups of punch. Put large piece of ice in punch bowl with bunch of grapes on top of ice.

FROSTED COFFEE PUNCH

6 cups double-strength coffee
6 tablespoons sugar
1 cup Jamaica rum or to taste

5 pints vanilla ice cream
2 cups whipped cream

Sweeten coffee; whip cream; break ice cream in small pieces; combine ingredients; add rum to taste. Serves 15 to 20.

MINT COOLER

6 lemons—juice of
2 oranges—juice of
2 cups sugar

2 cups water
1 handful fresh mint, crushed

Boil sugar and water together for 5 minutes. Pour the hot syrup over the fruit juice and mint. Add the grated rind of 2 lemons and 1 orange. Cool, remove mint and store in covered jar. Put in refrigerator. When ready to serve, fill glasses with crushed ice and strain 3 tablespoons of the mixture over the ice. Fill glasses with ginger ale.

MULLED CIDER

8 cloves
 Sugar to taste

4 cups sweet cider
2 sticks cinnamon

Boil 10 minutes, strain and serve hot. Serves 4 to 5.

EGGNOG

8 eggs, separated
1 quart whipping cream

8 tablespoons sugar
1 glass whiskey (more or less)

Beat yolks separately. Add sugar to yolks and beat well; add whiskey. Whip the cream and add to the yolk mixture. Add beaten whites last. More sugar and whiskey can be added to taste. Serves 8 or 10.

RED RASPBERRY SHRUB

Crush 2 gallons red raspberries with potato masher; add enough vinegar to cover. Let stand for 24 hours. Put in cheese cloth bag and squeeze all the juice possible from it. Measure the juice; add 1 cup of sugar to each cup of juice; cook to a nice syrup. Seal in small bottles. When ready to serve, put 2 inches of syrup in each glass; fill with crushed ice and pour in enough cold water to completely fill the glass. Add a sprig of mint to the top of the glass.

SPARKLING LIME COOLER

6 limes
3 oranges
2 lemons

Handful fresh mint
1 pint sparkling water
Sugar to taste

Pour fruit juices over crushed mint; strain after an hour and add sparkling water. Sweeten to taste. Serve over crushed ice. Serves 6.

BISCUITS

BAKING POWDER BISCUITS

2 cups flour
3 tablespoons shortening
¾ teaspoon salt

4 teaspoons baking powder
⅔ to 1 cup sweet milk

Mix dry ingredients; cut in shortening; make a well in the center of the flour; pour in milk, mix lightly with a spoon, letting the dough be as soft as can be handled. Put out on board and knead about 1 minute, roll the dough out to ½ inch thickness. Cut with a small cutter; put ½ inch apart on ungreased cookie sheet. Bake about 10 minutes at 450°

BEATEN BISCUIT

6 cups flour
¾ cup lard
1½ teaspoons salt

2 teaspoons sugar
1 cup milk

Dissolve sugar and salt in milk; cut lard into the flour and mix to stiff dough with milk. Beat or put through biscuit brake until white and smooth. Roll dough to ½ inch thickness, cut out, stick with tines of silver fork and bake about 45 minutes at 375 to 400°.

CHEESE BISCUIT

½ pound butter, creamed
½ pound cheese (sharp American)
2 whole eggs, beaten together

1 teaspoon salt
1 pinch cayenne pepper
flour

Grate cheese; add butter, then beaten eggs, salt and pepper. Mix lightly with enough flour to make a soft dough. Roll thin; cut and bake carefully 425°.

Cheese Biscuit (2)

1 pound sharp American cheese
½ pound butter

1 tablespoon Worcestershire sauce
2 cups flour

Grate cheese; cream butter and combine. Add Worcestershire sauce and gradually work in the flour. Roll thin; cut with a small cutter and bake at 425°.

Cheese Biscuit (3)

2 cups flour
3 tablespoons shortening
1 cup sharp grated cheese
¼ teaspoon soda

¾ to 1 cup milk
1 teaspoon baking powder
1 teaspoon salt

Sift dry ingredients; cut in shortening and cheese; add milk to make a soft dough. Roll ¼ inch thick, cut out bake at 450°.

CORN MEAL BISCUIT

1½ cups sifted flour
½ cup corn meal
3 teaspoons baking powder

1 teaspoon salt
4 tablespoons shortening
⅔ to ¾ cups milk

Sift dry ingredients; cut in shortening; add milk and mix lightly, turn out on floured board and knead a very few minutes. Roll out ¼ inch thick; cut out and bake 450° for 12 or 15 minutes. Should be thin and crunchy. Nice with salads.

SCALLOPED BISCUIT RING

Make recipe for soda biscuits and cut biscuits with a scalloped cutter. Cut a circle the size of the ring desired, from waxed paper and put on a cookie sheet. Arrange the biscuits around this circle, putting them close together. Brush the tops with melted butter and cover them with another row of biscuits. This will make a wall high enough to accommodate the hash that is to be served in the ring. Bake at 425°. Slip the biscuit ring off onto a platter and fill with chicken or turkey hash. Enough biscuits should be used to make a rather large ring. If they break apart, just push them together again.

SODA BISCUITS

2 cups flour
¾ teaspoon salt
2 teaspoons baking powder

½ teaspoon soda
3 heaping tablespoons lard
1 cup buttermilk

Sift dry ingredients, mix by directions for "Baking Powder Biscuits," and bake at 425 to 450°.

WHOLE WHEAT BISCUITS

2 cups whole wheat flour
⅔ teaspoon salt
1 teaspoon sugar
1 cup buttermilk

2 teaspoons baking powder
½ teaspoon soda
2 heaping tablespoons shortening

Sift flour, sugar, salt, and baking powder together; add soda to buttermilk. Combine as directed in "Baking Powder Biscuits."

MUFFINS

BANANA MUFFINS

2 cups flour
1 teaspoon soda
1 teaspoon baking powder
¼ cup buttermilk

1 stick margarine
1 cup sugar
2 beaten eggs
3 very ripe bananas

Sift dry ingredients together. Cream butter and sugar, add beaten eggs. Sieve bananas and add to the mixture. Stir in buttermilk. Bake in greased muffin tins at 400° for about 20 minutes.

BLUEBERRY MUFFINS

2 cups flour	1 beaten egg
4 teaspoons baking powder	⅔ cup milk
¼ cup butter—melted	½ teaspoon salt
¼ cup sugar	1 cup floured blueberries

Sift dry ingredients together; add sugar to beaten egg and alternate other ingredients, adding melted butter last. Stir in floured blueberries. Put in hot greased muffin rings and bake at 400°

CORN MEAL MUFFINS

2 cups buttermilk	1 teaspoon soda
1 egg	1 teaspoon salt
2 cups corn meal	1 tablespoon melted lard

Beat egg and milk together and combine with dry ingredients. Bake in hot greased muffin tins in a quick oven about 425°.

CORN MEAL MUFFIN RINGS

Make recipe for Corn Meal Muffins and cook in well-greased individual ring molds, until firm but not dry. These are nice to serve turkey hash in. If preferred, one large ring can be baked and filled with the hash. Bake at 425°.

DATE MUFFINS

1 cup flour	1 egg beaten with
1 cup bran	1 cup milk
2 teaspoons baking powder	2 tablespoons melted butter
½ teaspoon salt	1 cup finely chopped dates

Combine in order given. Bake in hot greased muffin rings at 400°.

FLOUR MUFFINS

2 cups flour	1 egg
3 teaspoons baking powder	1 cup sweet milk
1 teaspoon salt	2 tablespoons Wesson oil
2 tablespoons sugar	

Sift dry ingredients; beat eggs and milk together; combine; add Wesson oil. Bake at 400° in preheated, greased muffin tins.

GINGER MUFFINS

2½ cups flour	1 cup shortening
2 teaspoons soda	1 cup molasses
1 teaspoon salt	1 cup boiling water
1 teaspoon powdered ginger	2 well-beaten eggs
1 teaspoon powdered cinnamon	

Sift dry ingredients. Cream shortening; add boiling water and molasses; combine with dry ingredients, alternating with beaten eggs. Bake at 375° in preheated greased muffin tins.

GRAHAM FRUIT MUFFINS

1 cup graham flour
¾ cup white flour
½ teaspoon salt
1 heaping tablespoon sugar
2 teaspoons baking powder
⅓ stick butter

1 well-beaten egg
1 cup milk
¾ cup chopped dates dredged in white
   flour
½ cup chopped pecans

Cream butter and sugar; add beaten eggs; sift dry ingredients; add alternately with milk; add dates and pecans. Bake in preheated, greased muffin tins at 425°.

ORANGE MARMALADE MUFFINS

¼ cup butter
¼ cup sugar
2 well-beaten eggs
2 cups flour

3 teaspoons baking powder
⅔ cup milk
½ teaspoon salt

Sift dry ingredients. Cream butter, sugar and eggs; add flour, alternating with milk. Drop in greased, small muffin tins, filling them half full, then put in teaspoon of marmalade filling and add more batter to fill rings 2/3 full. Bake at 375° for twenty minutes.

MARMALADE FILLING FOR MUFFINS: 3 tablespoons orange marmalade, 4 tablespoons brown sugar, 4 tablespoons flour, 1 tablespoon melted butter and 1 tablespoon cream. Combine ingredients.

MUSH-MUFFINS

1 quart sweet milk
1 cup corn meal

1 teaspoon salt
2 eggs, beaten separately

Let milk come to a boil in top of a double boiler. Sprinkle in the meal, to which the salt has been added, stirring constantly until smooth and thick. Cook about half an hour and cool. Add beaten yolks to the cooled mush; fold in the beaten whites. Bake in very hot, well-greased muffin rings at 425° for about 25 minutes. This can also be baked in a cake tin and cut in wedges. Put chicken hash over the wedges.

PECAN MUFFINS

2 cups flour
3 level teaspoons baking powder
⅓ cup butter, melted
¾ cup chopped pecans

¾ cup milk
2 well-beaten eggs
2 tablespoons sugar

Beat eggs; add melted butter and milk. Sift dry ingredients and combine; add pecans. Bake in preheated, greased muffin tins 20 to 25 minutes.

WHOLE WHEAT MUFFINS

1 cup whole wheat flour
1 cup white flour
1 cup milk
1 egg

3 teaspoons baking powder
½ teaspoon salt
4 tablespoons melted butter
2 tablespoons sugar

Sift dry ingredients; beat egg and milk together; add melted butter; combine with dry ingredients. Bake at 400° in previously heated, greased muffin tins.

ROLLS

ROLLS

1 cake yeast	1 cup mashed Irish potatoes
½ cup lukewarm water	1 cup scalded milk
⅔ cup shortening	1 teaspoon salt
2 well-beaten eggs	Flour to make stiff dough
½ cup sugar	

Dissolve yeast in warm water. Add shortening, sugar, salt and mashed potatoes to scalded milk. When cool add yeast. Mix well with eggs; add flour. Turn out on floured board and mix to dough. Put dough in greased bowl; brush with melted butter; cover and put in refrigerator. About 2½ hours before needed take out and make into rolls; let rise 2 hours; bake at 425° for twenty minutes.

CINNAMON ROLLS

2 yeast cakes	½ teaspoon salt
1 cup milk, scalded and cooled to luke-	7 cups flour
warm	6 tablespoons butter or margarine
1 cup warm water	2 eggs, beaten together
1 tablespoon sugar	

Dissolve yeast and sugar in lukewarm water and milk combined; add half of the flour; beat until smooth. Cream butter and sugar; add eggs and combine with the above mixture. Make a soft dough by adding the rest of the flour sifted with the salt. Let rise until doubled in bulk in a covered, greased bowl. Take half of the dough and roll into a thin rectangle; spread with melted butter; sprinkle with sugar and cinnamon which have been sifted together; cover with chopped raisins and pecans. Roll up lengthwise; cut in 1 inch slices. Spread a biscuit pan thickly with butter and brown sugar; sprinkle cut pecans over the sugar. Put the rolls, cut side down, over this, let rise about 1 hour. Bake at 415°. Turn rolls out carefully; let cool until caramel syrup hardens. Watch while cooking to see that sugar does not burn. The other half of the dough can be made into rolls or put in the refrigerator for future use.

ICE BOX ROLLS

2 cakes yeast	2 kitchen spoons shortening
¼ cup lukewarm water	½ cup sugar
1 beaten egg	1 teaspoon salt
4 cups flour, sifted	1 cup boiling water

Dissolve salt, sugar and shortening in boiling water. Cool and add beaten egg. Mash yeast and mix with lukewarm water till smooth. Add this to the cooled egg mixture, then add sifted flour. Put in bowl and cover. Let rise one hour. Work down and put in refrigerator. When ready to make into rolls, take out on floured board. Cut rolls, brush with melted butter and fold over in pocketbook shape. Let rise two hours in warm place. Bake at 425°. Use dough as needed, keeping remaining dough in refrigerator.

73

PARKER HOUSE ROLLS

2 cups flour
2 teaspoons baking powder
½ teaspoon salt

1 egg
1 cup milk
2 tablespoons butter

Mix dry ingredients; cut in shortening. Beat egg; add to milk, and combine. Roll thin; cut in rounds; brush with butter and fold over. Brush tops with melted butter; bake at 450°.

RUM-BUTTER COFFEE CAKES

4 cups flour
½ teaspoon salt
½ cup butter
½ cup sugar
2 eggs

1 cake yeast
1 cup lukewarm milk
1 cup mixed candied cherries and citron
  chopped fine

Crumble yeast; add to luke warm milk; cream butter, sugar and eggs; add flour and yeast mixture alternately. Knead until smooth. Cover and put in warm place to rise until double in bulk. When risen, roll out in thin oblong; brush with melted butter; sprinkle with additional sugar and chopped fruits. Roll up like jelly roll; cut in ½ inch thick slices. Grease muffin tins heavily; put a spoonful of "rum-butter mixture" in each. Put slices of dough over this; let rise to double in bulk; bake ½ hour at 350°. Take care not to burn sugar.

RUM-BUTTER MIXTURE: 1 cup brown sugar, ½ cup melted butter, ¼ teaspoon powdered nutmeg and cinnamon and a pinch of powdered cloves. Flavor with rum.

BATTER BREADS

CORNMEAL BATTER CAKES

1 cup corn meal
2 tablespoons flour
1 teaspoon salt

1 teaspoon soda
1 pint milk (sour)
2 eggs, beaten separately

Sift dry ingredients. Add beaten yolks to milk and combine with dry ingredients. Beat whites stiff and pour the batter into the whites with a folding motion. Pour on greased baker by tablespoonfuls, dropping batter from the tip of the spoon. This makes a perfectly round cake. When bubbles appear turn the cakes and brown on the other side.

CORNMEAL-CHEESE SPOON BREAD

½ cup cornmeal
2 cups milk
2 eggs

4 tablespoons grated cheese
1 teaspoon baking powder
1 teaspoon salt

Cook meal and milk in double boiler 10 minutes. Add cheese. Stir until melted. When cool add beaten eggs, baking powder and salt. Bake in greased casserole about half an hour or until set.

CREPES SUZETTE

2 cups flour
2 cups milk

¾ cup powdered sugar
5 eggs beaten separately

Beat yolks of eggs, add sugar; alternate rest of ingredients. Flavor with 1 teaspoon each of orange and lemon juice; add teaspoon grated lemon rind. Make thin pancakes; spread with jelly and roll up. Keep rolls warm over hot water. When ready to serve dip each roll quickly into the following orange sauce:

ORANGE SAUCE

1 teaspoon grated orange rind
6 tablespoons butter

1 cup powdered sugar
1 cup orange juice

Cook together and keep over hot water. If preferred add liquor instead of orange juice (a small glass each of brandy and cointreau). Touch a match to the mixture and let burn; spoon over the crepes. Sprinkle powdered sugar over the rolls.

GEORGIA BREAD

2 cups sifted meal
1 pint milk
1 heaping teaspoon baking powder

1 tablespoon butter
½ teaspoon salt
1 cup cooked grits

Sift dry ingredients, add milk, melted butter and grits and bake in greased casserole at 375°.

GRITS BREAD

2 cups freshly cooked hominy grits
1¾ cups milk

1 tablespoon butter
2 eggs beaten separately

Combine and bake in greased casserole for half an hour or until done at 375 to 400°.

HUSH PUPPIES

2 cups corn meal
2 tablespoons flour
2 eggs
2 teaspoons salt (scant)

2 teaspoons baking powder
Milk as needed
Grated onion (optional)

Break eggs in pint measure and add milk until three fourths full. When ready to fry add this to dry mixture and beat until smooth. Drop by small teaspoonful in deep hot fat. Drain on brown paper when done. The original Hush Puppies had grated onion, to taste, in them.

MUSH SPOON-BREAD

4 eggs beaten separately
¾ cup corn meal
2 cups sweet milk

½ teaspoon salt
2 tablespoons melted butter

Cook meal and milk in double boiler; stir constantly until smooth and thick; add salt, butter and beaten yolks. When cool, fold in whites and bake in casserole about half an hour.

PANCAKES

2 cups flour
1 teaspoon baking powder
2 cups milk
1 teaspoon sugar

2 tablespoons melted shortening
3 eggs beaten together
¼ teaspoon salt

Sift dry ingredients; beat eggs and add milk; combine with flour. Bake by pouring tablespoonful on hot greased griddle.

RICE GRIDDLE CAKES

1 cup flour
4 teaspoons baking powder
1 tablespoon sugar
1 teaspoon salt

1 egg
1¾ cups milk
1 cup cooked rice

Sift dry ingredients; beat egg and add milk, combine with flour and rice, bake by pouring tablespoonful on hot griddle.

WAFFLES

WAFFLES

2 eggs beaten separately
1 stick butter, melted
1 tablespoon lard, melted
¾ cup sweet milk
¾ cup water

1 teaspoon salt
1 teaspoon sugar
4 teaspoons baking powder
2 cups flour

Sift dry ingredients; add combined egg yolks, milk and water; beat until smooth. Fold in stiffly beaten whites. Bake in hot waffle irons.

Waffles (2)

2 cups flour
2 teaspoons baking powder
½ teaspoon salt
½ teaspoon soda

1¾ cups buttermilk
1 egg, beaten
4 tablespoons melted shortening

Sift dry ingredients together. Add beaten eggs to milk; combine with dry ingredients. Add melted shortening last. (Makes 7 waffles.)

PARTY WAFFLES

2 cups flour
2 teaspoons salt
4 teaspoons baking powder
1 teaspoon corn meal
1 cup milk (sweet)

1 cup cream
1 stick butter (melted)
8 tablespoons melted lard
5 eggs beaten separately

Sift dry ingredients, beat yolks; add flour and milk alternately; add melted shortening; fold in beaten whites. Serve with guava jelly spread between two waffle sections. Dust with powdered sugar and place a small square of Philadelphia cream cheese to the side of each serving. Do not serve butter. This waffle is used for dessert at breakfasts or simple luncheons.

CHOCOLATE WAFFLES

1½ cups flour
2 teaspoons baking powder
½ teaspoon salt
3 eggs beaten together
1 cup sugar

½ cup butter
3 squares bitter chocolate
1 teaspoon vanilla
½ cup milk

Sift dry ingredients; melt butter and chocolate over hot water. Beat eggs, add sugar; combine with chocolate mixture. Add vanilla, milk and flour. Bake. Serve with whipped cream or ice cream.

GINGER WAFFLES

2 cups flour
½ teaspoon salt
1½ teaspoons powdered ginger
1 teaspoon baking powder
1 cup molasses

½ stick butter
1 teaspoon soda
½ cup buttermilk
2 eggs

Sift first four ingredients together. Heat butter and molasses; remove from heat; add combined soda and butter milk; add beaten eggs and flour mixture. Bake in waffle irons, being careful not to get them too hot. Serve with whipped cream.

ORANGE WAFFLES

1¾ cups flour
¼ teaspoon salt
2 teaspoons baking powder
2 eggs
½ cup sugar

½ cup milk
4 tablespoons orange juice
1 tablespoon lemon juice
2 teaspoons grated orange rind
4 tablespoons melted butter

Sift dry ingredients. Combine beaten eggs, sugar and liquids; add to dry ingredients with orange rind; add melted butter last. Serve with whipped cream and orange sections between two waffles. Top with sifted powdered sugar. A delicious dessert for a breakfast.

RICE WAFFLES

1¾ cups flour
2 teaspoons baking powder
1 teaspoon salt
¾ cup cold cooked rice

2 eggs
2 tablespoons sugar
1½ cups milk
4 tablespoons melted shortening

Sift dry ingredients. Beat eggs, shortening and milk together; combine with rice and dry ingredients. Bake in hot waffle iron.

CORN MEAL WAFFLES

1½ cups flour
½ cup corn meal
4 teaspoons baking powder
½ teaspoon salt

2 teaspoons sugar
2 eggs
1 pint milk
½ cup melted butter

Sift dry ingredients. Combine beaten yolks and milk. Combine liquid and dry materials; add melted butter last and beat until smooth. Bake on hot irons.

QUICK BREADS

BANANA BREAD

½ cup butter
1 cup sugar
3 large or 4 small bananas thoroughly mashed
2 eggs, well beaten

2⅓ cups flour
1 teaspoon soda
½ teaspoon salt
¼ teaspoon vanilla

Cream butter and sugar; add mashed bananas and eggs. Sift dry ingredients and combine. Flavor. Bake in greased pan 350 to 375° for 45 minutes.

BOSTON BROWN BREAD

2 cups graham flour
1 teaspoon salt
1 cup white flour
2 teaspoons baking powder
1 teaspoon soda
½ cup dark molasses

2 tablespoons melted butter
1 cup buttermilk
¾ cup sweet milk
½ cup chopped seeded raisins
½ cup chopped pecans
½ cup sugar

Dredge raisins and nuts in part of the flour. Sift dry ingredients; combine all ingredients. Grease 1 pound baking powder cans; fill half full, put on tops; set in vessel half full of boiling water; cover tightly; steam slowly 3 to 4 hours. Turn out of cans; dry in slow oven 15 minutes.

Boston Brown Bread (2)

1 cup molasses
4 cups graham flour
1 cup sugar
1 cup meal
2 cups buttermilk
2 teaspoons soda
1 teaspoon salt
1 cup raisins cut fine

1 teaspoon baking powder
1 teaspoon cinnamon
1 teaspoon cloves
1 teaspoon nutmeg
1 teaspoon ginger
3 tablespoons melted butter
1 cup blackberry jam
1 cup chopped nuts

Dredge fruit in part of flour. Sift dry ingredients. Combine all ingredients. Grease one pound baking powder cans, including tops, thoroughly, fill half full of mixture; put on tops; set in vessel of boiling water, let water come a little over half way up the cans. Boil 3½ hours, adding more water as needed. Dry in oven 15 minutes after removing bread from cans.

DATE BREAD

2¾ cups flour
2 level teaspoons baking powder
2 level teaspoons soda
1 teaspoon salt
1½ cups sugar
1 teaspoon vanilla

2 tablespoons melted butter
1½ cups boiling water
1 cup chopped pecans or black walnuts
2 cups dates—chopped
2 eggs

Pour boiling water over dates; add soda. Mix butter, sugar, and well-beaten eggs; add flour alternately with water from the dates; add dates, nuts, salt and vanilla. Pour into well-greased loaf pans and bake in moderate oven (350 to 375°) one hour.

FRUITED BROWN BREAD

½ cup sorghum
1 teaspoon soda
2 cups buttermilk
3 cups whole wheat flour after sifted

1 level teaspoon salt
1½ cups crystallized fruits: cherries, citron, pineapple, etc., dredged in flour
1 cup chopped pecans

Add soda to milk and combine with other ingredients. Bake in greased pan in slow oven.

NUT BREAD

3 cups graham flour
1½ cups pastry flour
1 cup brown sugar
2½ cups buttermilk

¾ teaspoon salt
2 teaspoons baking powder
½ teaspoon soda
1½ cups chopped pecans

Sift dry ingredients and combine with other ingredients. Put in greased bread pans; heat oven, while mixing, to 350°. Cook for about ¾ hour.

Nut Bread (2)

1 cup sugar
1 egg
4 cups flour
4 teaspoons baking powder

1 teaspoon salt
1 cup sweet milk
1 cup chopped pecans

Sift dry ingredients, mix sugar with beaten egg; add milk and flour; add nuts. Put in greased pan and bake 1 hour at about 350°.

ORANGE BREAD

3 cups flour
4 tablespoons sugar
3 teaspoons baking powder
½ teaspoon salt
1 egg

½ cup orange marmalade
1 cup milk
1 tablespoon grated orange rind
1 cup chopped pecans

Beat egg; add milk. Sift dry ingredients and combine with egg and milk mixture; add marmalade, nuts and orange rind. Bake in well-greased bread pan at 350°.

(MISCELLANEOUS)

CHEESE STRAWS

1 pound grated sharp cheese, 1 stick of butter, 2 cups flour sifted with large pinch of red pepper. Cream butter; add grated cheese. Knead together by hand adding flour gradually. Roll up and put in cookie press. Grind out in 3 inch pieces and cut off dough. Bake at 425°. These can also be cut in strips with pastry wheel.

FRENCH TOAST

1 egg
½ cup milk

Pinch of salt
4 slices bread

Beat egg; add milk and salt; trim crusts from bread, dip in egg mixture on both sides and cook on griddle that has been greased with butter. Turn toast to brown. Serve with a tart jelly for breakfast.

SALLY LUNN

3 eggs
3 cups sifted flour
3 teaspoons baking powder

1 scant cup sweet milk
2 tablespoons butter
8 tablespoons sugar

Cream butter and sugar; add beaten eggs; sift flour and baking powder, combine, alternating with milk. Bake in greased round cake tins. Cut in wedges.

STICKIES

3 cups sifted flour
4 teaspoons baking powder
1½ teaspoons salt

½ cup shortening
1 cup milk

Make dough and roll ¼ inch thick. Cover with a brushing of melted butter and sprinkle with 4 teaspoons brown sugar and 2 teaspoons powdered cinnamon. Over this put ½ cup each of chopped nuts and raisins. Roll up, as for a jelly roll and cut in 1 inch slices. Put in pan over a syrup made of ¼ cup of butter, ¼ cup of brown sugar and ¾ cups Blue Label Karo syrup which have been cooked together about 1 minute. Bake at 375° half an hour or more. Turn out of pan and take up with a spatula. As soon as the air strikes the Stickies they can be easily handled.

ROSETTES

1½ cups sifted flour
2 teaspoons sugar
¼ teaspoon salt

1 cup milk
2 eggs

Sift dry ingredients together. Beat eggs slightly; combine with milk. Pour mixture into dry ingredients and beat until smooth. Heat deep fat to 365°; dip rosette iron into fat for half minute; drain a moment and then dip into batter until it is just even with top of iron. Put directly into hot fat and fry until brown. This should take about 1 or 2 minutes. Take from fat and loosen carefully from iron. Drain on absorbent paper. Sift a mixture of confectioners' sugar and powdered cinnamon over rosettes. Allow to 2 tablespoons of powdered cinnamon to 1 cup of sugar. Nice for morning coffees.

GARLIC-CHEESE ROSETTES

Make rosettes by recipe, omitting sugar, and adding ½ teaspoon each of garlic and celery salt to batter. Fry as directed and sprinkle with parmesan cheese. These can be run in the oven and toasted long enough to melt cheese slightly if desired.

ROLLED WAFERS

½ pound confectioners' sugar
½ stick butter
3 beaten eggs

1 lemon (juice of)
Flour as needed

Cream butter and sugar; add beaten eggs and lemon juice; stir in sifted flour to make a stiff batter; beat until perfectly smooth. Heat wafer irons on both sides, being careful not to get them too hot. Brush with melted butter between each baking. Put about 2 tablespoons of batter in iron. When one side is baked turn to the other side. Bake a light brown; take off carefully, roll up while hot over a spoon handle.

TOAST BOATS

You will need two large slices of bread for each toast boat. Trim crust off and brush with melted butter, then fit them into large muffin rings overlapping edge of each slice at the center of the muffin ring and letting the opposite points of each slice extend out on either side of the muffin tin. These are overlapped at least half the distance from point to point and are fitted around in the ring to form a cup with two pointed ends extending to form a boat shaped container. Nice to use for creamed chicken, fish, etc.

TOASTED FRENCH BREAD

Cut a long loaf of French bread in half-inch slices, cutting almost through, but leaving the bottom crust uncut. Put a thin slice of butter between each slice; brush the top with melted butter, and toast in oven until butter has melted and loaf is hot through. Send the loaf to table to be served whole. This is especially good served with Italian spaghetti. If desired the butter can be creamed and a small amount of garlic powder added before buttering bread.

WHIRLIGIGS

2 cups flour
2 tablespoons baking powder
½ teaspoon salt

1 tablespoon sugar
2 tablespoons lard
½ cup milk

Mix first 4 ingredients. Cut in lard and add milk to make a medium soft dough. Roll to ¼ inch thickness and cover with the following mixture: ½ cup brown sugar, ¼ cup butter, creamed together with ½ teaspoon cinnamon. Sprinkle a few raisins and chopped nuts over the surface. Roll up and cut in ½ inch sections. Place in greased pan, cut side down, and bake 15 to 20 minutes.

TOAST WHEELBARROWS

Body—3¼x2¼x2 inches—cut 1
Handles—1¾x½x½ inches—cut 2
Legs—1¾x½x½ inches—cut 2

Wheel bars—1¾x½x½ inches—cut 2
Wheel—⅜ inch thick; 1½ inches in diameter—cut 1

Use day old, unsliced bread. Cut pieces according to measurements. Snip out the inside of the box shaped body to form a container, using scissors to remove the bread. Leave a half inch wall. Dry out all parts of wheelbarrow in oven, but do not toast at this time. Fasten legs to back end of body with toothpicks, letting one end of toothpick go through the leg and the other end go through the body using the entire toothpick for this. Fasten handles on in horizontal position at the upper edge of the body in the same manner. Stick toothpicks at the top edge of the body in a slanting position; fasten wheel bars to these toothpick extensions; put wheel between bars; press bars against wheel and fasten in place with a short piece of toothpick. The wheelbarrow is now ready to be brushed with melted butter and toasted in oven to a light brown. Fine textured bread is best to work with when making wheelbarrows. These can be filled with creamed chicken and mushrooms and are very attractive.

BUTTER CAKES

APPLE SAUCE CAKE

1 cup sugar
⅓ cup margarine
1 cup unsweetened apple sauce
2 eggs well beaten
1 cup chopped raisins
1 cup chopped pecans
2 tablespoons drained orange marmalade

1¾ cups flour
½ teaspoon salt
⅔ teaspoon soda
1 teaspoon vanilla
¾ teaspoon powdered cloves
1½ teaspoons powdered cinnamon
½ cup crystallized pineapple

Chop fruits and nuts. Sift dry ingredients together; add 1/3 of flour mixture to fruit and nuts. Cream butter, add sugar and eggs; beat until fluffy; add remaining flour, alternating with apple sauce; add fruit and nuts. Bake in greased layer cake pan at 350°. Ice with "caramel icing."

BANANA CAKE

1 cup margarine
2 cups sugar
4 eggs beaten separately
4 large ripe bananas

⅓ cup buttermilk
1½ teaspoons soda
3 cups flour
1 cup chopped pecans

Sieve ripe bananas. Cream margarine; add sugar; beat together until smooth; add beaten yolks. Mix buttermilk with sieved bananas. Sift dry ingredients together; add to mixture alternating with bananas; fold in beaten whites. Bake in greased layer pans at 350°. Ice with "caramel icing."

CARAMEL CAKE

1 cup margarine
2 cups sugar
6 egg yolks
1 teaspoon vanilla

3 cups flour
3 teaspoons baking powder
1 cup milk

Sift dry ingredients. Cream margarine and sugar; add beaten yolks; add dry ingredients alternately with milk; flavor. Bake in greased and floured layer cake pans at 375°. Ice with "caramel icing No. 2."

COCOANUT CAKE

Follow recipe for white cake; bake in 2 layers. Make "white icing"; spread thickly on each layer; put a thick coating of fresh grated cocoanut on bottom layer; cover with the other layer, putting the iced side down on the cocoanut; ice all over with remaining icing; sprinkle with cocoanut, covering the entire surface. At Christmas time, outline the top edge of the cake with a narrow border of chopped crystallized fruit or ice little holly sprays on the corners. If thicker icing is desired, make once and a half the recipe for "white icing."

COCOANUT-SPICE CAKE

1 cup butter
2 cups sugar
6 egg yolks
1 cup buttermilk
½ pound seeded raisins
1 cup sliced citron, cut fine
1½ cups chopped pecans

3 cups flour
2 teaspoons baking powder
1 teaspoon soda
1 teaspoon cinnamon
1 teaspoon allspice
½ teaspoon cloves

Sift dry ingredients. Cream butter and sugar; add beaten yolks; add flour and milk alternately; add fruit that has been dredged in part of the sifted flour; add nuts. Bake in greased cake pans at 350°. Put together and ice with cocoanut filling.

COCOANUT FILLING: 2 cups sugar, juice and rind of orange and lemon, 1 cup water, 4 tablespoons flour, 1 package cocoanut: slice and grind orange and lemon, including peel; add to sugar, water and flour; cook until thick; add cocoanut last; cool; frost cake.

BITTERSWEET CHOCOLATE CAKE

Follow recipe for white cake or for devil's-food cake. Ice with "white icing." Let stand several hours. Melt 3 squares of chocolate in double boiler with 1 tablespoon of butter; cool slightly; pour slowly over the iced cake, letting it drip down sides of cake.

CUP CAKES

1 cup butter
2 cups sugar
3 cups flour
4 eggs

1 cup milk
2 teaspoon baking powder
1 teaspoon vanilla

Cream butter and sugar; add beaten yolks. Sift dry ingredients; add alternately with milk and flavoring; add beaten whites last. Bake in small greased tins.

BROWN SUGAR CUP CAKES

4 eggs
2 cups brown sugar
1 cup chopped pecans

1 teaspoon baking powder
2 teaspoon vanilla
1 cup flour

Beat eggs separately; add sugar to yolks; flavor. Sift dry ingredients; add to mixture, alternately, with beaten whites; add pecans. Bake in small greased muffin tins.

CHOCOLATE CUP CAKES

3 cups sifted flour
3 teaspoons baking powder
1 teaspoon salt
2 cups sugar
⅔ cup butter

1 cup milk
4 well-beaten eggs
4 squares chocolate melted over hot water
1 cup chopped pecans

Sift dry ingredients. Cream butter and sugar; add eggs: alternate milk and flour; add nuts, chocolate and vanilla. Cook in greased muffin pans at 400°.

CHOCOLATE-ORANGE CUP CAKES

Make once recipe for "Cup Cakes"; cook in very small tins; cover with chocolate icing. When nearly dry, put teaspoon of orange icing, stiff enough to stand up in a peak on top of cakes.

CHOCOLATE ICING FOR CHOCOLATE-ORANGE CUP CAKE

1 pound confectioners' sugar
4 tablespoons melted butter
1 teaspoon vanilla

6 tablespoons cocoa
Cream, to make spreading consistency—about 6 or 8 tablespoons

ORANGE ICING FOR CHOCOLATE-ORANGE CUP CAKE

½ pound confectioners' sugar
2 tablespoons melted butter
2 tablespoons grated orange rind

Enough orange juice to make into a stiff fondant that will stand up in peaks

FRENCH POUND CAKES

5 eggs
1 pound sugar
1 pound flour
½ pound butter
½ teaspoon soda

1 cup cream or milk
1 teaspoon cream of tartar
1 teaspoon vanilla
1 tablespoon whiskey

Sift dry ingredients. Cream butter and sugar; add eggs, one at a time, beating after each addition; add dry ingredients alternately with milk; flavor. Bake in greased muffin rings.

SPICE CUP CAKES

1 cup butter
1 cup sugar
1 cup milk
2 well-beaten eggs
2 cups flour

2 teaspoons cinnamon
2 teaspoons baking powder
1 cup chopped raisins
1 cup chopped pecans
1 teaspoon vanilla

Cream butter and sugar; add well-beaten eggs. Sift dry ingredients; add alternately with milk; flavor with vanilla; add pecans and raisins. Bake in hot, greased muffin rings. If desired these can be flavored with whiskey or sherry wine, omitting equal amount of milk.

CHILLED FRUIT CAKE (Uncooked)

½ pound graham cracker crumbs
1 cup dates—chopped
½ cup raisins—chopped
2 tablespoons orange peel—ground
½ cup citron, sliced thin
¼ teaspoon nutmeg
¼ teaspoon allspice

2 tablespoons crystallized cherries
1 cup marshmallows cut fine
1 cup thick cream
¼ cup currants
1 teaspoon cinnamon
¼ teaspoon cloves
1 cup nut meats, chopped

Mix above ingredients, as for any other fruit cake. Place mixture in shallow pan; put in ice box to chill 3 or 4 hours. When ready to serve, turn out and slice in bars.

DEVIL'S FOOD CAKE

2 cups sugar
½ cup butter
2 eggs beaten together
3½ squares bitter chocolate dissolved in
⅔ cup boiling water and cooled

1 level teaspoon soda
⅔ cup buttermilk
2 cups (packed) sifted cake flour
¼ teaspoon salt
1 teaspoon vanilla

Put chocolate and boiling water in double boiler, over hot water, dissolve; cool. Sift dry ingredients. Cream butter and sugar; add beaten eggs; add flour and buttermilk alternately; add chocolate; flavor with vanilla. Bake in 2 layer cake pans, with greased paper in bottom of pans; bake at 325°. If desired this can be made into cake rings. Grease and flour ring molds before adding batter. Ice with plain white icing or mint flavored icing, tinted pink.

Devil's Food Cake (2)

1 cup butter
¾ cup white sugar
2 cups brown sugar
3 egg yolks
3 whole eggs
2 cups sifted cake flour

1 teaspoon baking powder
1 teaspoon soda
1 cup buttermilk
2 cups cocoanut, grated
4 squares unsweetened chocolate, melted over hot water

Sift dry ingredients. Cream butter and sugar; add egg yolks; beat well; add part of dry ingredients. Add unbeaten eggs, one at a time; beat well after each addition; add rest of flour, alternately with milk. Add cocoanut and chocolate; bake in 3 layer cake pans in moderate oven at 350°, until done. Frost with "white icing" using the 3 eggs whites left over from the cake and 3 added whites to make once and a half the recipe.

JAM CAKE

1 cup butter
1 cup sugar
4 eggs beaten separately
3½ cups flour
1 teaspoon baking powder
1 teaspoon soda

1 teaspoon nutmeg
1 teaspoon cinnamon
1 teaspoon allspice
½ teaspoon cloves
1 cup blackberry jam
1 cup buttermilk

Sift dry ingredients. Cream butter and sugar; add beaten yolks and jam; alternate dry ingredients with milk; add beaten whites last. Bake in layers, in greased tins, at 350°; ice with "white icing."

BLACK FRUIT CAKE

15 eggs
1¼ pounds butter
1½ pounds flour
1½ pounds sugar
4 pounds raisins
1 pound currants
1 pound crystallized cherries
1½ pounds citron
1½ pounds figs

1 pound pecans
1 pound blanched almonds
½ pound crystallized pineapple
1½ water glasses whiskey
1 tablespoon powdered ginger
1 tablespoon powdered cinnamon
1 teaspoon powdered nutmeg
1 teaspoon powdered cloves

Wash currants; spread out in pan; dry in oven; roll between palms of hand to loosen skins; remove stems. Pick over raisins, but do not wash them; cut fine. Slice citron thin; cut in slivers. Cut crystallized fruit and figs in small pieces. Slice pecans and almonds thin. Soak all fruits in whiskey overnight, except citron. The next day sift dry ingredients together; dust citron with a small amount of flour; mix rest of flour with soaked fruit, kneading it well with your hands. Cream butter and sugar; add beaten yolks; fold in beaten whites; combine this with fruit mixture; mix thoroughly. Put double layers of heavy brown paper in bottom of stem cake pans; then cut a long piece to line the sides of the pan; cut about 4 inches wider than the sides of the pan, so that part of the wide paper can overlap part of the bottom of pan; slash at intervals; so that it can be fitted over the bottom. Let top part of paper extend above top of pan about 2 inches. Grease well, both bottom and sides of paper. Fill pans 2/3 full. Place oven rack 4 inches from bottom of range, with pan of hot water under rack; put cake pans on rack; over the top of each cake put several folds of newspaper; letting it rest on the paper that extends above top of each pan. Space pans so the air can circulate around them. Bake at low heat 250° for several hours, depending on size of pans used. Test with straw to be sure they are done. Remove newspaper from tops after cake has cooked 2 hours to brown tops. When cakes are done, remove from oven; cool in pans; then remove from pans and wrap in cloths soaked in whiskey. Leave paper on cakes until ready to use. This makes about 20 pounds of cake. My mother's famous recipe.

WHITE FRUIT CAKE

1 cup butter	1 cup blanched almonds
1 cup sugar	1 cup light citron
2 cups flour	1 cup crystallized pineapple
8 eggs	1 cup crystallized cherries
1 teaspoon baking powder	1 cup white raisins
1 teaspoon vanilla	½ pound fresh cocoanut

Slice almonds. Cut fruits fine and dredge with part of the flour. Sift flour and baking powder. Cream butter and sugar; add beaten yolks and flavoring. Add flour, alternately with beaten whites. Fold in grated cocoanut, nuts and fruits. Bake in greased tube pan lined with heavy greased paper, at 250° for 3 hours or until done, when tested with straw. Chill in refrigerator before slicing.

LIGHT FRUIT CAKE

6 eggs	½ pound white raisins
1 cup butter	1 cup crystallized cherries
1½ cups sugar	½ cup light citron
2 cups flour	½ cup blanched almonds, sliced
Juice and grated rind ½ orange	½ cup sliced pecans
1 teaspoon almond extract	½ cup crystallized pineapple
1 teaspoon baking powder	

Slice nuts. Cut fruits fine and dredge with part of the flour. Cream butter and sugar; add eggs, one at a time, beating well after each addition. Add flavoring, orange juice and grated rind. Sift flour and baking powder; work into mixture. Add fruits and nuts. Bake in tins, that have been greased and lined with heavy greased paper, for 2 hours at 300°. Put a pan of water in oven while cake is baking.

PECAN CAKE

1 cup butter or margarine
2 cups sugar
2 cups flour
1 teaspoon cream of tartar
½ teaspoon soda

5 egg whites beaten stiff
1½ cups sliced pecans
½ cup wine (sherry)
1 teaspoon ground nutmeg

Cream butter and sugar. Sift dry ingredients. Add beaten whites to butter and sugar, alternating with dry ingredients. Add wine and pecans. Bake by fruit cake directions.

SPICE CAKE

1 cup butter
2 cups sugar
4 well-beaten eggs
2½ cups flour
3 teaspoons baking powder

1 teaspoon cinnamon
1 teaspoon allspice
1 teaspoon nutmeg
1 cup milk

Sift dry ingredients. Cream butter and sugar; add beaten eggs; alternate flour and milk. Bake in greased layer cake tins in moderate over at 350°; ice with caramel or with sea foam icing.

SPICE MERINGUE CAKE

2½ cups flour
1 teaspoon baking powder
1 teaspoon soda
1 teaspoon powdered cinnamon
1 teaspoon powdered cloves
½ teaspoon salt
2 teaspoons vanilla

4 cups brown sugar
1 cup margarine
1 cup buttermilk
4 whole eggs
2 more egg whites
1 cup chopped pecans
½ teaspoon cream of tartar

Sift first 6 ingredients together. Beat 2 whole eggs and yolks of 2 more together. Reserve 4 egg whites for meringue. Cream margarine: add 2 cups brown sugar; reserving other 2 cups for meringue. Combine butter, sugar and beaten eggs; add other sifted ingredients and milk alternately; flavor. Spread mixture in greased and floured pan 9x12x2. Before cake is baked, spread meringue made of 4 egg whites and 2 cups brown sugar over batter. Sprinkle with pecans. Bake at 325°. Cut in squares when done. Serve hot. This is delicious.

WHITE CAKE

1 cup butter
2 cups sugar
8 eggs, whites only
3½ cups flour

3 teaspoons baking powder
1 cup milk
1 teaspoon vanilla

Sift dry ingredients together. Cream butter and sugar; alternate milk and flour; add vanilla; fold in beaten whites last. Bake in 2 layers at 350°.

CAKES WITHOUT SHORTENING

ANGEL FOOD CAKE

12 egg whites
1 cup cake flour
1½ cups sugar

1 teaspoon cream of tartar
1 teaspoon vanilla
1 pinch salt

Add salt to eggs; beat until foamy; add cream of tartar; beat until stiff, but not dry. Add sugar, that has been sifted twice, very slowly. Sift flour five times; fold in, with over and over strokes. Do not beat when adding flour. Put in ungreased angel food pan; cut through batter several times with a knife, to release air bubbles. Put in cold oven set at 250°; raise 25° every 15 minutes until it reaches 325°. Will bake in about an hour. Invert pan; remove cake when cool.

CHOCOLATE ANGEL FOOD CAKE

12 egg whites
1 cup cake flour
½ cup cocoa
1 teaspoon cream of tartar

2 cups sugar
2 tablespoons water
1 pinch salt
1 teaspoon vanilla

Sift flour and cocoa together 5 times. Beat egg whites until foamy; add cream of tartar; beat until stiff but not dry; add sugar slowly; fold flour into mixture; then add water and vanilla. Bake in ungreased angel food pan 1 hour at 325°. When done, invert pan until cool.

SUNSHINE CAKE

9 egg whites
4 egg yolks
½ teaspoon cream of tartar

1 teaspoon vanilla
1¼ cups sugar—sifted twice
1 cup cake flour sifted 4 times

Add cream of tartar to whites of eggs; beat until stiff, but not dry; fold in beaten yolks; add sugar and vanilla; fold in flour last. Bake in angel food pan in 325° oven until firm to touch and a delicate brown.

ORANGE SUNSHINE CAKE

6 eggs
2 tablespoons orange juice
3 tablespoons cold water

1 cup flour
1 cup sugar
1 teaspoon cream of tartar

Beat yolks with liquids until double in bulk; sift sugar and flour together 4 times; add to yolks. Beat whites with cream of tartar until stiff; fold into yolk mixture. Flavor with 1 tablespoon grated orange rind. Bake in angel food pan, at 300° for one hour.

ORANGE CHIFFON CAKE

The new chiffon cakes are delicious and easy to make. My favorite is the orange chiffon as it can be used for many dessert bases, as well as for a cake.

2¼ cups sifted cake flour	5 unbeaten egg yolks
1½ cups sugar	¾ cup water
3 teaspoons baking powder	Grated rind 2 oranges
1 teaspoon salt	8 egg whites
½ cup salad oil	½ teaspoon cream of tartar

Sift dry ingredients into a mixing bowl; make a well at center; add salad oil, egg yolks, water and orange rind; beat until smooth. In another bowl, beat egg whites with cream of tartar until very stiff; pour yolk mixture over beaten whites; folding it in. Pour into ungreased angel food pan; bake 55 minutes at 325°; increase heat to 350° and cook until top springs back when lightly touched. Remove and invert pan, putting the tube over the neck of a funnel. Do not let the cake touch any surface until cool. Loosen the cake from the sides of the pan when cool; invert on cake rack.

SPICE CHIFFON CAKE

2¼ cups sifted cake flour	½ cup salad oil
1½ cups sugar	6 eggs, separated
3 teaspoons baking powder	½ teaspoon cream of tartar
1 teaspoon salt	1 tablespoon grated orange rind
1 teaspoon powdered cinnamon	¾ cup cold water
½ teaspoon cloves	1 tablespoon orange juice
½ teaspoon nutmeg	

Sift first 7 ingredients together into a mixing bowl; make a well at center and follow directions for "orange chiffon cake." Ice with "seafoam icing."

CHOCOLATE CHIFFON CAKE

2¼ cups sifted cake flour	½ cup salad oil
½ cup cocoa	6 eggs, separated
2 cups sugar	½ teaspoon cream of tartar
3 teaspoons baking powder	¾ cup cold water
1 teaspoon salt	1 teaspoon vanilla

Sift first 5 ingredients together in a mixing bowl; make a well at center, follow directions for orange chiffon cake. Ice with chocolate icing No. 2.

TROPICAL CHIFFON CAKE

Make "orange chiffon cake"; split in 3 layers; put together with thick layers of "orange filling." Ice cake with white icing and sprinkle thickly with fresh grated cocoanut.

COOKIES AND SMALL CAKES

ANGEL FOOD RUM BALLS

Cut a loaf of Angel Food Cake into squares about 1½ inches across; trim off corners, so that cake will look slightly round. Cream ½ pound butter; add 1 pound confectioners sugar gradually; beat well. Flavor with rum, whiskey, or almond extract; add one or two tablespoons double cream. Completely cover the cake rounds with butter and sugar mixture; roll in ground, parched almonds. Best to serve soon after making.

BITTERSWEET CHOCOLATE COOKIES

½ cup butter
2 cups sifted cake flour
½ teaspoon soda
¼ teaspoon salt
⅔ cup brown sugar pressed down in the cup

1 well-beaten egg
3 squares Baker's chocolate
½ cup buttermilk
1 teaspoon vanilla
1 cup broken pecans

Sift dry ingredients. Cream butter and sugar; add beaten egg; alternate flour and milk; add melted chocolate, vanilla and pecans. Put teaspoonful on greased cookie sheet and bake at 350°.

BRANDY-SNAP ROLLS

½ cup New Orleans molasses
1 stick butter
1 cup flour

⅔ cup sugar
1 tablespoon pulverized ginger
1 tablespoon brandy (optional)

Heat molasses and butter together; blend thoroughly; add other ingredients. Invert cookie sheet; grease well; drop batter by teaspoonful, about 3 inches apart; bake in 350° oven until bubbles appear. Remove from oven; cool two minutes; loosen with spatula; roll over a wooden spoon handle. If they harden too quickly to roll, you can reheat slightly.

BROWN SUGAR CORNFLAKE COOKIES

3 egg whites
¼ teaspoon cream of tartar
1½ cups sifted yellow sugar

½ teaspoon vanilla
3 cups corn flakes

Beat egg whites with cream of tartar until very stiff; add sugar and vanilla; fold in corn flakes. Put on greased cookie sheet by spoonfuls. Bake at 250° until firm to touch.

BROWN SUGAR FUDGE SQUARES

1 pound brown sugar
4 beaten eggs
1½ cups flour

1 teaspoon baking powder
1 teaspoon vanilla
1 cup broken pecans

Beat eggs and sugar together; cook over hot water for 15 minutes; cool. Sift flour and baking powder; add to sugar mixture; add pecans and vanilla. Put in greased, floured pan; bake 30 minutes at 350 to 375°. Cut in squares.

BROWN SUGAR KISSES

3 egg whites
¼ teaspoon cream of tartar
1½ cups yellow sugar

3 heaping tablespoons flour
2 cups broken pecans
1 teaspoon vanilla

Beat egg whites with cream of tartar until very stiff. Sift sugar; add to whites; add vanilla; fold in flour and pecans. Bake on greased cookie sheet at 250° until firm to touch—about 30 minutes. Do not make kisses too large. Put about an inch and a half apart.

CARAMEL THINS

¼ pound butter or substitute
1 cup, well packed, brown sugar
2 cups flour
½ teaspoon salt

1 egg yolk
1 egg white (unbeaten)
¾ cup chopped pecans
1½ teaspoons vanilla

Cream butter and sugar; add egg yolk and vanilla; sift in flour and salt; mix thoroughly. Invert cookie sheet; grease with butter; spread dough over surface; smooth to edges of sheet with rolling pin. It should be very thin. Brush over dough with unbeaten egg white, using a pastry brush; cover surface with chopped pecans. Bake at 350° until brown and crisp. Cut in squares while hot.

FOR CHOCOLATE THINS add 2 ounces of melted chocolate when creaming butter and egg yolk.

FOR CINNAMON THINS sift 2 teaspoons ground cinnamon with flour.

CANADIAN COOKIES

½ cup brown sugar
1 cup flour
¼ cup butter
2 eggs, beaten together
1 cup brown sugar

2 tablespoons flour
1 can Baker's moist cocoanut
½ teaspoon salt
½ teaspoon baking powder
1 teaspoon vanilla

Blend first three ingredients; press on the bottom of a small biscuit pan (6x10 inches); bake in slow oven 15 minutes until slightly dry. Combine other ingredients; spread over first mixture; bake until golden brown, about 15 minutes; cool in pan. Spread with icing made of 1 cup confectioners sugar, 1 tablespoon melted butter, 1 tablespoon orange juice and 1 teaspoon lemon juice.

CHEWS

2 cups sugar
4 well-beaten eggs
2 cups crystallized fruit
2 cups shredded cocoanut

1½ cups flour
½ teaspoon salt
1½ teaspoons baking powder

Sift dry ingredients. Beat eggs; add sugar, fruit and cocoanut; combine with dry ingredients. Spread as thin as possible on cookie sheet—cook at 350° for 20 to 25 minutes. Cut in bars. Sprinkle with powdered sugar.

CHOCOLATE-COCOANUT DROPS

2 egg whites
1/4 teaspoon cream of tartar
1 cup sugar
1/2 cup cracker crumbs
1/2 cup dry cocoanut

1 pinch salt
1/2 cup chopped pecans
2 tablespoons cocoa
1 tablespoon vanilla

Beat eggs, cream of tartar and salt until very stiff; add other ingredients. This should be stiff enough to mold with hands like chocolate drops. Bake on greased cookie sheet, one and a half inches apart.

CHOCOLATE MACAROONS

2 egg whites
1 cup sugar
1/2 teaspoon cream of tartar
1 1/2 cups shredded cocoanut

1 1/2 squares Baker's unsweetened chocolate
1/2 teaspoon vanilla

Add cream of tartar to egg whites; beat until very stiff; add sugar slowly. Melt chocolate over hot water; add chocolate and cocoanut to egg mixture; drop on greased cookie sheet with teaspoon. Bake at 275°.

CORN-FLAKE COOKIES

2 egg whites
1 cup sugar
1 cup broken pecans

1/2 teaspoon vanilla
4 cups corn flakes

Beat the whites slightly, until well mixed, but not stiff and white; add other ingredients; put spoonfuls on greased cookie sheet and bake until firm. This does not make a white cookie, as the egg is used only to bind the corn flakes and nuts.

COCOANUT CORN-FLAKE COOKIES

4 egg whites—beaten stiff
1/8 teaspoon cream of tartar
1 cup shredded cocoanut

4 cups corn flakes
1 1/4 cups sugar
1 teaspoon vanilla

Add cream of tartar to eggs; beat until very stiff; add sugar slowly; fold in cocoanut and corn flakes; add vanilla. Put out by spoonfuls on greased cookie sheet; bake slowly until firm to touch.

CHOCOLATE-CORN-FLAKE COOKIES

1 pound sweet chocolate (shaved)
3 squares (ounces) unsweetened chocolate
1 cup broken pecans

1/8 teaspoon salt
1 teaspoon vanilla
1 medium-sized box corn flakes

Melt chocolate over hot (not boiling) water; add vanilla. Put corn flakes and nuts in a large bowl; pour chocolate over them. With a tablespoon, mound cookies on waxed paper. Put in ice box until nearly ready to serve.

CRESCENTS

½ pound butter
5 heaping tablespoons powdered sugar
2 cups flour

1 cup pecans cut fine
1½ teaspoon vanilla

Cream butter and sugar together; add other ingredients. Break off small amount; roll between palms into finger length pieces; curve each end around in crescent shapes. Bake on top of inverted cake tin, in slow oven until light brown. Roll in powdered sugar when cool.

CRULLERS

3 pounds flour
1¾ pounds sugar
½ pound butter
1 salt spoon liquid aqua ammonia
½ teaspoon baking powder

6 eggs
1 cup sweet milk
1 teaspoon powdered cinnamon
½ teaspoon powdered nutmeg
1 teaspoon vanilla

Cream butter and sugar; add beaten eggs. Sift dry ingredients; add alternately with milk, etc. Roll thin, cut out 3x4 inch rectangles with pastry wheel. Then cut 4 slits about 3 inches long through the rectangle leaving small space at top and bottom of rectangle. Pick up every other strip; give cruller a quick twist; put in hot grease in frying basket; fry until golden brown. Drain on brown paper; sprinkle with sifted confectioners sugar with powdered cinnamon added. This recipe has been used by my family for five generations.

DATE BARS

1 cup flour
1 teaspoon baking powder
1 cup sugar
3 eggs

1 teaspoon vanilla
1 cup chopped pecans
1 package of dates cut fine

Sift baking powder and flour together. Beat eggs; add sugar, flour, vanilla, dates and nuts. Bake 20 minutes at 375° in greased and floured pan; cut in finger lengths; roll in powdered sugar.

DATE KISSES

2 egg whites
¼ teaspoon cream of tartar
1 cup powdered sugar

1 cup walnut meats
1 cup chopped dates
½ teaspoon vanilla

Beat egg whites with cream of tartar until very stiff; add sugar gradually; then add dates, nuts and vanilla. Bake in slow oven at 250° until firm to touch. Kisses should not be too large.

DATE CHEWS

1 cup chopped dates
1 cup chopped nuts
1 cup sugar
1 teaspoon vanilla

2 beaten eggs
¾ cup flour
1 teaspoon baking powder

Beat eggs; add sugar. Sift dry ingredients; combine. Add dates, nuts and flavoring. Spread thin in greased pan. Cook at 325° for 20 minutes.

When done, cut in squares; roll between palms. Dust with confectioners sugar.

DATE CRISPIES

2 cups crispy rice flakes	½ cup sugar
½ cup finely chopped dates	1 teaspoon vanilla
2 egg whites	

Beat egg whites until quite stiff; add sugar slowly; fold in rice flakes and dates; add vanilla; drop on greased cookie sheet; cook in very slow oven at 250°.

DATE-NUT ICE BOX COOKIES

1 cup brown sugar	½ teaspoon salt
1½ cups butter	1 teaspoon cinnamon
1 cup white sugar	1 cup chopped dates
3 well-beaten eggs	1 cup chopped nuts
4½ cups flour	1 teaspoon vanilla
1 teaspoon soda	

Sift dry ingredients. Chop dates and nuts fine. Cream butter and sugar; add well-beaten eggs; make into cookie dough with flour, etc. Form into a roll; wrap in cloth; chill overnight. When ready to cook, slice very thin with a sharp knife; cook in moderate oven.

FRUITED COOKIES

1 cup butter	4 tablespoons milk
2 cups light brown sugar	2 cups crystallized fruitcake fruits
2 eggs beaten together	3 cups flour
2 teaspoons vanilla	1 teaspoon soda
1 teaspoon pulverized cinnamon	

Sift dry ingredients. Cream butter and sugar; add beaten eggs. Alternate dry ingredients with milk; add fruit and flavoring. Bake; cut in bars; roll in powdered sugar when ready to serve.

FUDGE CAKE

2 cups sugar	2 cups flour
½ cup butter	2 teaspoons baking powder
2 eggs	2 cups chopped nuts
4 squares chocolate	1 teaspoon vanilla
1 cup milk	

Sift dry ingredients. Melt butter; add sugar and eggs that are unbeaten; add melted chocolate; add milk and flour alternately; flavor with vanilla; add nuts and spread out in large greased pan. Batter should be about ½ inch deep. Bake in 350° oven—cut in squares and dust with confectioners sugar.

Fudge Cake (2)

1 cup butter	1 pinch of salt
2½ cups sugar	1 teaspoon vanilla
4 eggs	4 squares or ounces bitter chocolate
1 cup flour	1 cup pecans or black walnuts

ICING: 1 pound of confectioners sugar, 3 tablespoons cocoa, 4 tablespoons melted butter. 1 teaspoon vanilla, coffee to mix to spreading consistency. CAKE: Beat eggs; cream butter and sugar; combine; add vanilla, flour, salt and nuts. Put in greased and floured biscuit pan; bake 45 minutes in moderate oven. Put a pan containing a little water under cake for a third of the time. Ice if desired.

GINGER ICE-BOX COOKIES

1 cup sugar
½ pound butter
1 teaspoon soda
1 cup molasses
1 egg

4 cups flour
1½ teaspoons powdered ginger
1½ teaspoons powdered cinnamon
½ teaspoon powdered cloves

Cream butter and sugar; add beaten eggs and molasses, to which the soda has been added. Sift spices with flour; combine with other ingredients. Form into roll, wrap in waxed paper; store overnight in refrigerator. When ready to use, slice very thin; bake on cookie sheet.

ICE-BOX COOKIES

½ pound butter
½ pound brown sugar
3 cups sifted flour
Sift baking powder with flour
2 teaspoons baking powder

¼ pound blanched almonds, shaved very thin
1 egg, beaten
1 teaspoon vanilla

Cream butter and sugar; add beaten egg; combine with flour and nuts, add vanilla; knead dough; form into roll; wrap in waxed paper; put in icebox overnight. When ready to use, slice very thin and bake.

MARSHMALLOW TOWERS

Ice tiny cup cakes in delicate pink, yellow or green; top with marshmallows that have been cut in half.

MONKEYS

1 cup sour cream
2 sticks butter

2 tablespoons sugar
3 cups flour

Cream butter and sugar; add flour and cream alternately; chill for several hours. Roll thin; cut in 3 or 3½ inch squares. Fill with fruit mixture; roll as you would a jelly roll; twist each end around to form horseshoe shape; brush tops with melted butter. Bake at about 400° until brown—about 15 minutes. Sprinkle with powdered sugar.

FRUIT FILLING FOR MONKEYS

1½ cups dates
1½ cups pecans
½ cup sugar

Juice 1 lemon and 1 orange
1 tablespoon flour

Chop dates and pecans fine. Cook until thick.

PEANUT BUTTER COOKIES

1 cup white sugar
1 cup brown sugar
1 cup shortening
1 cup peanut butter
2 beaten eggs

3 cups flour
1 teaspoon salt
1 teaspoon soda
1 teaspoon vanilla

Sift dry ingredients. Mix shortening, sugar and eggs; add peanut butter, flour and vanilla; chill dough. Drop by teaspoonfuls on greased cookie sheet; flatten with tines of a silver fork; press in two directions to give a criss-cross effect. Bake at 375°.

PUFFED RICE COOKIES

1 box puffed rice—medium size
1 cup white sugar
½ cup white Karo syrup
1 pinch soda

1 tablespoon butter
1 teaspoon vanilla
1 cup broken pecans
¾ cup milk

Boil sugar, Karo syrup, milk and soda slowly, to 240°; add butter and vanilla; pour over puffed rice and nuts. Grease finger tips; form into balls; put on waxed paper until needed.

PETITS FOURS

3 egg whites
1 pinch salt
1½ cups sugar
1 cup milk

3 teaspoons baking powder
3 cups cake flour
½ teaspoon almond extract
1 stick butter

Sift dry ingredients. Cream butter and sugar. Beat egg whites stiff. Add milk and flour, alternately, to butter and sugar mixture; flavor; fold in whites last. Bake in greased pan (about 9x15 inches). When cool, cut into oblongs, triangles, diamonds, etc. Ice with tinted, butter cream icing. Decorate with tiny flowers or silver dragees.

ROCKS

4 eggs
½ cup butter
1 cup brown sugar
⅔ cup milk
1 teaspoon soda dissolved in tablespoon hot water
3 cups flour

1 package dates
1 cup seeded raisins
1 cup chopped nuts
1 teaspoon powdered cinnamon
½ teaspoon each, cloves, allspice, and ginger

Chop raisins, dates and nuts; rub a little flour into them. Cream butter and sugar; add eggs, one at a time, beating well; alternate flour and milk; add soda, fruits and nuts. Drop on greased pans; bake 10 to 12 minutes at 375°.

RUM OR BOURBON BALLS

1 12-ounce box vanilla wafers
1 cup pecans
3 tablespoons cocoa

3 tablespoons white Karo syrup
⅓ cup rum or whiskey
1 cup confectioners' sugar

Grind wafers and pecans. Combine ingredients. Make into small balls; roll in powdered sugar: Let dry several hours, then roll again in powdered sugar. Any stale cake crumbs can be utilized for this, allowing 4 to 4½ cups of crumbs to recipe. For variety substitute orange juice for rum and add grated rind of two oranges.

SNOW BALL CAKES

Cut angel food cake into 1½ inch squares; ice thickly on all sides with "white icing"; roll in fresh grated cocoanut. At Christmas time, ice tiny sprays of holly on top of these cakes or make holly berries of small cinnamon drops and leaves of sliced citron.

SAND TARTS

1 cup sugar	3 cups flour
1 cup butter	2 eggs, beaten
1 teaspoon vanilla	Cinnamon and sugar

Cream butter and sugar; add beaten eggs and vanilla, work in flour. Roll out very thin; cut in rounds; brush with slightly beaten egg white; sprinkle with a mixture of granulated sugar and cinnamon. Press half of a toasted almond into each cookie. Bake in a moderate oven at 350°.

SCOTCH SHORT BREAD

4 cups flour	1 cup sliced almonds
1½ cups butter	1 tablespoon grated orange rind
¾ cup sugar	¼ teaspoon salt

Cream butter; add sugar, flour, salt, almonds and grated orange rind. Knead together. Roll out; cut in diamond shape; bake 20 minutes at 350°.

SWEDISH PECAN WAFERS

1 box Swedish milk wafers	Pecan halves
Melted butter	Brown sugar

Brush wafers with melted butter; sprinkle brown sugar thickly over butter; lay pecan halves over sugar. Dribble more melted butter over entire surface; put under slow flame and toast until sugar melts.

SWEDISH ALMOND KISSES

2 cups almonds	2 cups sugar
6 egg whites	1 tablespoon grated lemon rind
½ teaspoon cream of tartar	1 teaspoon powdered cinnamon

Wash almonds, leaving skins on; dry thoroughly in warm oven; put through meat grinder. Beat eggs until frothy; add cream of tartar and beat very stiff. Mix sugar and cinnamon, add gradually to beaten whites. Fold in almonds and lemon rind. Put out by teaspoonfuls on greased cookie sheet. Bake 20 minutes at 325°.

TEA CAKES (FILLED)

4 cups flour	1 teaspoon soda
1 cup butter	2 teaspoons cream of tartar
1 cup sugar	2 eggs
2 teaspoons sweet milk	1 teaspoon vanilla

Sift dry ingredients together. Cream butter and sugar; add flour and milk alternately. Roll as thin as possible; cut out; put on cookie sheet and bake until brown. These are delicious, plain, but are also good as filled tea cakes. Put 2 rounds together with filling between; press edges together with tines of fork; bake.

FILLING: 2 cups sugar, 2 cups dates. chopped, 2 tablespoons flour, 1 cup water, juice of lemon and orange. Boil until thick and add 1 cup chopped nuts.

TORTE BARS

2 cups sugar	3 cups flour
1 cup margarine	½ teaspoon salt
4 eggs beaten together	2 teaspoons baking powder
1½ teaspoons vanilla	2 cups sifted yellow sugar
1 cup chopped pecans	2 egg whites

Sift flour, salt and baking powder together. Cream butter and sugar; add beaten eggs, flour, vanilla and pecans. Spread thin in large 17 inch square pan or 2 smaller greased pans. Make meringue of stiffly beaten egg whites and yellow sugar; flavor with 1 teaspoon of vanilla; spread over uncooked batter. Bake about a half hour at 375°. Cut in bars.

WALNUT KISSES

3 egg whites	1½ cups sugar
½ teaspoon cream of tartar	2 cups broken black walnuts
1 teaspoon vanilla	

Beat egg whites stiff with cream of tartar; add sugar slowly; flavor with vanilla; fold in walnuts. Bake on greased cookie sheet at 350° for ten minutes. Pecans can be substituted for walnuts.

ICINGS

BUTTER-CREAM ICING

1 stick butter	2 tablespoons cream
5 cups confectioners' sugar	2 egg whites unbeaten
Flavor with vanilla or almond	

Cream butter; add sugar, alternately, with the unbeaten whites and cream. Beat well; flavor. Keep icing covered to prevent crusting. Thin with cream if icing gets too stiff while using. Can be tinted in pastel shades when used for petits fours.

CARAMEL ICING

4 cups sugar	½ cup butter
1 cup milk	

Caramelize 1 cup of the sugar in an iron skillet; boil the rest with milk; add caramel mixture and butter; cook to soft ball stage; beat until creamy. If it gets too thick to spread, add a little cream to icing.

Caramel Icing (2)

1 cup buttermilk
2 cups sugar
½ teaspoon soda

½ cup butter
½ cup brown sugar
1 tablespoon vanilla

Combine ingredients. Cook to soft ball stage at 238°. Beat until creamy when cool. If this should get too stiff, thin with a little cream.

CHOCOLATE ICING

3 cups sugar
1 cup milk or cream
1 tablespoon butter

2 tablespoons Karo syrup
4 squares bitter chocolate shaved fine

Combine ingredients; heat slowly; cook to soft-ball stage; beat to spreading consistency.

Chocolate Icing (2)

3 cups sugar
1 cup milk
3 egg yolks

2 tablespoons butter
4 squares bitter chocolate

Beat eggs; add sugar, milk, and butter; cook over hot water until very thick. Melt chocolate over hot water; add to mixture; cool and beat creamy.

CREAM CHEESE ICING

2 cakes Philadelphia cheese (3 ounces)
⅛ teaspoon salt
1 teaspoon grated lemon rind

2 tablespoons rum
2 cups confectioners' sugar
2 tablespoons cream

Cream ingredients together; add more sugar if necessary.

COCOANUT ICING

Make "white icing"; spread on cake; cover thickly with fresh grated cocoanut.

LADY BALTIMORE FILLING

Make "white icing" (4 eggs) add ½ cup chopped raisins, ½ cup chopped English walnuts and ½ cup chopped crystallized cherries to half of the icing. Use as a filling for white cake. Ice cake with remainder of white icing.

LEMON FILLING

2 eggs beaten together
1 cup sugar
3 tablespoons flour

½ cup water
½ cup lemon juice
3 tablespoons melted butter

Add flour to sugar. Beat eggs. Combine ingredients. Cook over hot water in double boiler until very thick.

100

MOCHA ICING

1 box confectioners' sugar	2 tablespoons melted butter
6 tablespoons double-strength coffee	

Sift sugar; add coffee and melted butter; beat until creamy; add more sugar if it seems too thin to spread. Ice cake and sprinkle with ground nuts.

Mocha Icing (2)

½ pound butter	1 tablespoon cocoa
1 box confectioners' sugar	1 teaspoon vanilla
4 teaspoons powdered coffee	1 cup ground salted almonds

Cream butter and sugar; add powered coffee, cocoa and flavoring. If necessary a little cream can be added to make this spreading consistency. This is especially good used on Sunshine or Orange Chiffon cake, cover the surface of icing with ground toasted almonds.

ORANGE FILLING

Follow recipe for lemon filling, substituting 1 cup orange juice for water, and lemon juice. Add 3 tablespoons grated orange rind.

UNCOOKED ORANGE ICING

Sift 1 box confectioners' sugar; add grated rind of 1 large, bright yellow orange, 2 tablespoons melted butter, about 6 tablespoons orange juice. Add more sugar if necessary. Any fruit juice can be used.

PEPPERMINT ICING

Make "white icing"; tint a delicate pink; flavor with several drops of essence of peppermint instead of vanilla. This is especially good on devil's food cake.

SEAFOAM ICING

2 cups yellow sugar	½ teaspoon cream of tartar
2 tablespoons white Karo syrup	½ cup milk or cream
4 egg whites	

Cook sugar, Karo and cream to soft ball stage at 238°. Beat whites with cream of tartar until very stiff; add sugar syrup slowly; beat until it peaks. Ice cake; sprinkle with ground pecans.

UNCOOKED ICING

1 box confectioners' sugar, sifted	2 tablespoons melted butter
6 tablespoons cream or fruit juice	Vanilla or almond flavoring

Combine sugar and cream or fruit juice; add melted butter; tint any desired shade. If too thin to spread, sift more sugar into the icing. Strawberry or red raspberry juice makes a delicious flavored, pink icing.

UNCOOKED CHOCOLATE ICING

1 pound sifted confectioners' sugar	Strong coffee or cream to mix to spread-
4 tablespoons melted butter	ing consistency
¾ cup cocoa	

More sugar can be added if necessary.

101

WHITE ICING

4 egg whites	2 cups sugar
1 pinch salt	½ cup water
½ teaspoon cream of tartar	1 teaspoon vanilla

Add salt to whites; beat until foamy; add cream of tartar; beat stiff, but not dry. Cook sugar and water in covered vessel for few minutes; put in a candy thermometer and cook to 242°. Pour slowly over whites, beat ing constantly. An electric beater is a great help. When using this icing for decorating, add 1 tablespoon sifted confectioners' sugar for each egg white after icing is done.

DECORATED CAKES

When planning an elaborately decorated cake, you should make twice the recipe of white icing. If the cake is to be iced in a color, remove part of the icing and tint it the desired shade with a small amount of color paste. If the paste is not available, use liquid coloring. Spread the icing smoothly over the surface of the cake with a spatula, dipping it in hot water occasionally. Use the remainder of the icing for the decoration. Add about six tablespoons of sifted confectioners' sugar to it so that the flowers will stand upright. Tubes for decorating can be made of very heavy typewriter or bond paper rolled into a cornucopia and pinned securely about two inches from the tip end. Stems are made with a tube that has had the small end clipped off to make a tiny opening. Most flowers are made with a tube from which an inverted V has been cut. Chrysanthemums and daisies, however, are made by cutting an M from the tip end of the tube. Leaves and fluted decorations are made with the V shaped tube and it is also used for the foundations of gardenias and jonquils. To make these, hold the tube flat. Roses, gardenia centers and violets are made by holding the tube in a vertical position. When the icing is put in the tube be sure to fill it only two-thirds full. Then bend the upper end of the tube over until it is completely sealed. Press the tube from the top when making decorations. If the tube should split when in use, cut about one inch from the lower end of the tube and put the tube into another cornucopia. Clip the end of the new tube in the correct shape and continue with the decorating. If shaded flowers are desired, brush a deep shade of icing around the inside of the tube, using only a small amount. Then put a very pale shade or even some plain white icing in the tube. This will give the shaded effect. The cup of a jonquil is molded from icing that has been made into a stiff fondant by adding confectioners' sugar until it can be handled.

Decorated cake rings filled with ice cream make beautiful desserts. When these are made from angel food cakes, a small amount of the cake should be removed from the center before the ring is iced, so that there will be sufficient room for the ice cream. For individual cake rings, the cake can be cut in slices and trimmed into rounds. These are iced and then decorated around the outer edge. The ice cream is put on top of the rounds without removing any of the center of the cake rounds. Large cake baskets can be made in the same manner, and a handle made of wire or of flattened soda straws fastened together and covered with icing, can be put in place on the cake. These cake baskets are usually filled with molded roses, lilies, etc., made of ice cream.

When a club luncheon features Easter decorations or has a fashion show in connection with the luncheon, we often make little Easter bonnets of cake. For a cake to serve ten or twelve people, use a round ten-inch layer of cake for the brim of the hat and a seven-inch layer for the crown. These should be iced in uncooked icing tinted to the desired shade. Flowers and ribbons can be iced on to resemble hat trimmings—a pale green foundation with a crown covered entirely with violets will look exactly like a hat made of flowers.

Fan-shaped cakes can be made by cutting a pattern of an unfurled fan from heavy paper. Lay the pattern on a sheet cake and cut around it to get the fan effect. The top part and the sticks of the fan can be outlined with a narrow band of fluted icing and the fan decorated in flower designs. These are appropriate for summer luncheons. If the odd shape of the fan leaves unusual shaped sections of cake which are not large enough for another fan, these can be placed together to make another fan; when they are covered with icing the piecing does not show.

Small individual cakes can be cut from a sheet of cake, into hearts, rounds or diamonds to be iced and decorated. Little French bouquets, single rose cakes and little cake ladies are attractive as individual cakes. The latter are made of inverted muffin cakes with tiny china doll ladies inserted in the top of the cake. The cake forms a bouffant skirt which can be iced in little ruffles caught together at intervals with tiny pastel flowers. With a little practice, it is surprising how quickly you can learn to do this decorating.

☆ CANAPES ☆

ANCHOVY AND CHEESE CANAPÉS

Mix cream cheese with a little cream; add anchovy paste to taste; spread on Ritz crackers; put parsley bud in center.

ANCHOVY CIRCLES

Make "Philadelphia Cheese Pastry"; roll thin; cut in small circles. Spread with anchovy paste; cover with another circle of pastry; press edges together with tines of a fork. Bake in hot oven for 8 to 10 minutes. Watch carefully. Serve hot.

BACON TWISTS

Twist strips of breakfast bacon around and around long slender snow flake crackers which have been separated into sections. Tuck ends of bacon underneath crackers. Put on a wire rack. Toast in oven 350° until bacon is crisp.

BLEU CHEESE CANAPÉS

½ pound bleu cheese   1 tablespoon brandy
½ cup ripe chopped olives

Cream cheese and brandy until smooth; spread on rounds of toast; sprinkle with chopped olives; heat about 5 to 10 minutes.

CAVIAR CANAPÉS

Spread toast strips with caviar, mixed with a little softened butter to form a paste; sprinkle with lemon juice; garnish with riced egg whites and riced yolks.

CHEESE AND BACON CANAPÉS

Mix cream cheese with chili sauce to right consistency; spread on toast circles. Put minced, crisp bacon on top.

Cheese and Bacon Canapés (2)

Toast finger lengths of bread; spread with a mixture of Roquefort and Philadelphia cheese, moisten with a little cream or mayonnaise; sprinkle crisp, crumbled breakfast bacon on top.

CHEESE AND CAVIAR CANAPÉS

Spread rounds of toast with highly seasoned cream cheese; put minced parsley around the outer edge; decorate the center with red or black caviar.

CHEESE AND HAM PIN WHEELS

Roll out pastry; spread with deviled ham; cover with sharp grated cheese that has been mixed with a little dry mustard and paprika—roll up like a jelly roll; chill for several hours; cut in ¾ inch slices; put in pan with cut side down; bake in quick oven.

CHEESE AND PEPPER CANAPÉS

Cream Philadelphia cheese with mayonnaise; add finely chopped green peppers, chives, and salted almonds. Spread on crackers.

CHEESE ROLL UPS

Spread thin slices of bread with butter mixed with prepared mustard; sprinkle with grated sharp cheese; roll tightly and put a half strip of breakfast bacon around them; skewer end of bacon with a toothpick. Toast in the oven on a rack until the bacon is crisp.

CHEESE CRAB CANAPÉS

1 can (6 ounces) crab meat	½ cup sharp grated cheese
1 cup medium cream sauce	

Add cheese to cream sauce; combine with minced crab; chill several hours or until stiffened. Put on small rounds of toast; sprinkle with grated cheese; toast under flame until heated.

CHICKEN CANAPÉS

Grind chicken; moisten with mayonnaise; season highly; add a little lemon juice and some toasted ground almonds; spread on Melba toast.

CRAB CANAPÉS

1 can crab meat—best grade	1 tablespoon mayonnaise
½ cup sharp cheese	1 teaspoon lemon juice
2 teaspoons horse-radish	

Add horse-radish and lemon juice to mayonnaise; season highly; mince crab meat; grate cheese; combine; if necessary add a little cream to make it spreading consistency. Put on rounds of toast; sprinkle with cheese; heat; serve at once.

CRAB IN TOAST BOATS

Put a can of minced crab in a cup of cream sauce, highly seasoned with red pepper, Worcestershire sauce and a little dry mustard. Fill little toast shells with hot crab mixture; sprinkle with grated Italian cheese; put under broiler to brown.

CUCUMBER CANAPÉS

Peel cucumber; score lengthwise with tines of silver fork; slice very thin; marinate ten minutes in French dressing; drain; butter small rounds of toast with highly seasoned mayonnaise; put slice of cucumber on it; top cucumber with a Jumbo Shrimp that has also been marinated in French dressing and drained. Garnish with a parsley bud.

FISH ROE CANAPÉS

Mash a can of shad roe; season with lemon juice, red pepper and a bit of scraped onion. Bind with a little mayonnaise or cream; spread on toast. Decorate with slices of stuffed olives.

PATÉ DE FOIE GRAS CANAPÉS

Spread toasted strips of bread with *pâté de foie gras;* put tiny pickled onions around edges of canapés.

LIVER CANAPÉS

Cook chicken livers; mash fine; season with salt, pepper, onion juice and small amount of lemon juice. Add mayonnaise to make a paste. Spread on rounds of buttered toast; decorate tops with slices of hard-boiled egg and parsley bud.

PEANUT BUTTER AND BACON CANAPÉS

Spread Ritz crackers with peanut butter; cover top with crumbled, crisp breakfast bacon.

SARDINE CANAPÉS

Mash sardines with a very small amount of mayonnaise; add a bit of grated onion and lemon juice to taste; spread on Melba toast. Garnish with riced egg.

SARDINE AND BACON CANAPÉS

Allow a strip of bacon for each sardine; spread raw bacon lightly with prepared mustard; sprinkle sardines with lemon juice; wrap a slice of bacon around and around sardine; broil on rack until bacon is crisp; serve on buttered toast fingers.

SARDINE AND EGG CANAPÉS

Spread round pices of toast with sardine paste; cover with slice of hard-boiled egg; pipe border of cream cheese around edges; season cheese with onion juice, salt and red pepper; add enough cream to make it proper consistency to use in pastry tube.

SARDINE PASTRIES

Cut circles of pastry; put a spoonful of sardine paste on each; fold pastry over to form a small turnover; press edges together with tines of a fork; bake. Serve very hot.

SARDINE AND PIMENTO CANAPÉS

Butter narrow strips of toast with mayonnaise; put small sardine, and a long narrow strip of pimento, side by side, down length of toast.

TONGUE AND OLIVE BASKETS

Slice salty, "party" rye bread very thin; spread with a mixture mayonnaise and prepared mustard; bend two sides of circle toward each other to form a basket; fill with a mixture of ground tongue, olives and pecans, moistened with a cooked dressing. Hold top of basket together with colored cocktail picks, put in criss cross. A mixture of grated ham and cheese can be used if preferred.

COCKTAIL SAUSAGE ROLL-UPS

Drain cocktail sausage; place each sausage on small square of pastry (diagonally), pinch two corners of the pastry together on top of the sausage, leaving the sausage extending out over the other two corners of pastry; bake, serve hot.

TINY SAUSAGE TURNOVERS

Roll rich pastry thin; cut into small circles; place a small amount cooked, smoked sausage on each circle; fold over in turnover shape; press edges together with tines of fork; bake. These are nice for morning coffees or canapés.

TOMATO CANAPÉ

Toast two inch circles of bread; butter with mayonnaise; cover with a layer of sardine paste and a small slice of tomato; cover with combined riced egg whites and yolks; top with slice of stuffed olive.

Tomato Canapé (2)

Toast rounds of bread the size of a small slice of tomato; butter with mayonnaise. Slice tomatoes, remove seeds; cover toast with tomato slice; fill seed spaces with the following; in one section put riced whites of hard-boiled eggs; in another riced yellows; a parsley bud in another; and a bit of caviar in another.

Tomato Canapé (3)

Toast rounds of bread on both sides; spread with mayonnaise. Make highly-seasoned tomato aspic; congeal in thin layers; cut rounds of aspic to fit toast rounds. Cover toast with aspic circles; decorate center of aspic with large pinch of riced, hard-boiled eggs; put parsley bud at the side of eggs. Canned tomato aspic can be used for this if desired.

WATER CRESS CANAPÉS

Toast circles of bread on one side; spread untoasted side with mayonnaise; place thin slice of cucumber, that has been marinated in French dressing, on toast; put finely chopped water cress around edges of cucumber.

107

CANDY

CHOCOLATE FUDGE

3 cups sugar
1 cup milk
1 tablespoon white Karo syrup
3 squares bitter chocolate

3 tablespoons butter
1 cup black walnuts
1 small package marshmallows (optional)
1 teaspoon vanilla

Dissolve chocolate over hot water, add to sugar, milk and Karo syrup. Cook slowly for 10 minutes; bring to a boil and cook to soft ball stage, 236°, stir often; remove from heat; add butter, vanilla and nuts. If desired, marshmallows may be quartered and put on the bottom of a well-greased pan. Beat fudge when it has cooled slightly, until very thick; pour over marshmallows. Cut in squares.

COCOANUT CANDY

4 cups sugar
1 cup milk
½ stick of butter

½ pound fresh cocoanut
1 teaspoon vanilla

Cook sugar and milk to soft ball stage; add butter and vanilla; beat until very thick; add cocoanut; pour in buttered pan. Cut in squares when nearly cold.

STUFFED DATES

Pit dates; stuff with marshmallows and salted peanuts or pecans. Roll in powdered sugar.

DATE-NUT ROLL

1 package dates
1 cup pecans
8 large graham crackers

16 marshmallows
1 tablespoon cream

Cut dates and marshmallows fine; chop pecans; roll crackers to a powder; combine all ingredients; form into narrow roll; wrap in waxed paper; chill well; slice.

DIVINITY FUDGE

2 cups white sugar
½ cup white Karo syrup
½ cup water

2 egg whites
1 cup pecans, chopped
1 teaspoon vanilla

Cook syrup of sugar, Karo and water until it forms a long thread; pour 1/3 of this over well-beaten whites; cook rest of syrup until it bubbles; add to egg mixture; add flavoring and nuts. Put out on platter by small spoonsful.

CANDY

DIXIE MINTS

2 cups sugar
1 cup boiling water
½ stick butter

1 teaspoon vinegar
6 drops oil of peppermint

Combine sugar, water and vinegar; boil without stirring, to hard crack stage; add butter; take from fire; add peppermint; pour into lightly greased flat platter. When cool enough to handle, pull like taffy candy; cut off little sections with scissors; store in tins until creamy.

FRUIT CAKE CANDY

1 cup crystallized fruitcake mix
1 cup dates
1 cup pecans
½ cup dried figs

½ cup dried apricots
1 cup seeded raisins
4 tablespoons orange juice

Grind all fruits in food chopper; mix well; add orange juice, to hold mixture together. Oil a square cake pan; pat fruit into it firmly; chill in refrigerator several hours or until firm. Cut in squares; roll in powdered sugar: If preferred, this can be cut in smaller squares and dipped in melted dipping chocolate.

CANDIED GRAPEFRUIT PEEL

Cut grapefruit hulls in thin slices; measure by cupfuls before boiling; cover with water; boil 20 minutes after it strikes a boil; drain and repeat until it has been boiled 3 times. Place in sauce pan, after draining again, with ¾ cup sugar for every cup of peel originally measured. Put over very slow fire until sugar melts; do not use any water this time; let cook slowly until practically all syrup cooks away. Remove from fire; roll in granulated sugar.

MARSHMALLOW NUT CANDY

Soak marshmallows in warm wine until soft. Roll in finely ground pecans and cool.

MAPLE SQUARES

1 cup maple syrup
2 cups sugar
1 cup cream

2 tablespoons corn syrup
1 cup broken nut meats

Combine ingredients; cook to soft ball stage 236°. Remove from heat, add nuts; beat until creamy. Pour in buttered dish; cut in squares.

STUFFED FIGS

1 pound pulled figs
¾ pound chopped pecans

1 pound marshmallows, chopped
Sherry wine or whiskey

Let figs and marshmallows stand several hours with sherry to cover; drain; stuff figs with pecans and marshmallows; roll in powdered sugar.

109

MARSHMALLOW NUT BALLS

½ cup sugar
2 tablespoons hot water
2 cups sugar
1 cup milk

1 cup white Karo syrup
1 teaspoon vanilla
2 tablespoons butter

Put the ½ cup of sugar in iron skillet to caramelize; add 2 tablespoons hot water. Boil the 2 cups of sugar, milk and Karo syrup to soft ball stage; do not stir, add caramel syrup, butter and vanilla; beat until creamy. Dip marshmallows into this with two forks; then dip into broken pecans; if the mixture hardens, put over hot water to melt.

SUGARED PECANS

2½ cups yellow sugar
1 cup milk
1 pound pecan meats

1 orange rind, grated
2 tablespoons orange juice

Cook sugar and milk to soft ball stage; add orange rind and juice; beat until sugar gets cloudy; add nuts; when it sugars, break apart.

PRALINES

1 box yellow sugar
1 cup white sugar
¾ cup Karo syrup
1 cup cream

¼ pound butter
1 teaspoon vanilla
1½ cups chopped pecans

Combine first four items; cook very slowly until it reaches soft ball stage; remove from fire; add butter, vanilla and nuts; beat until creamy; drop on waxed paper by teaspoonfuls.

TRUFFLES

¾ pound sweet chocolate
1 15-ounce can condensed milk
½ teaspoon vanilla

¼ teaspoon salt
¼ pound chocolate sprinkles

Cook milk and chocolate in double boiler until smooth; add salt and vanilla; cool; form into small balls with buttered finger tips. Roll in chocolate sprinkles.

☆ DESSERTS AND ICES ☆

DESSERTS

ALMOND-SHEET DESSERT

1 pound confectioners' sugar
2 sticks butter
1 teaspoon almond extract

¼ pound salted almonds, coarsely ground
1 small box graham crackers, rolled into
fine crumbs

Cream butter and sugar; add extract, half of cracker crumbs, and ground almonds; mix well; chill. Pat or roll out on back of cookie sheet, in a very thin layer; refrigerate until ready to use. Cut a 2½ inch square for each serving; put on dessert plate, top with a serving of vanilla ice cream; sprinkle remaining graham cracker crumbs over all.

BOILED CUSTARD

1 quart sweet milk
¾ cup sugar
Pinch of salt

6 egg yolks
2 teaspoons cornstarch
2 teaspoons vanilla

Heat milk in double boiler; beat yolks until thick; add sugar, salt and cornstarch; pour a small amount of hot milk over eggs; stir until well mixed; combine with rest of milk; cook until thick, flavor with vanilla. Sherry wine can be substituted for vanilla. Serves 6.

CARAMEL CUSTARD

3 cups milk
½ cup sugar
6 eggs

1 teaspoon vanilla
1 cup sugar to caramelize

Put 1 cup of sugar in heavy iron skillet; let caramelize; pour directly into a ring mold; beat eggs together; add sugar and scalded milk. Pour this mixture over the caramel; set in pan of hot water; bake in slow oven until set. Test with silver knife blade; it will come out clean when done; chill; turn out on platter. The caramel will drip over the sides when it is turned out. Fill center of ring with whipped cream and sprinkle with macaroon crumbs. Serves 6.

CHOCOLATE CAKE RING MINT ICING WITH PEPPERMINT ICE CREAM

1 cup sugar
¼ cup butter or margarine
1 egg, beaten without separating
2 squares chocolate melted with
⅓ cup boiling water

½ teaspoon soda
1 pinch of salt
⅓ cup buttermilk
1 cup cake flour (packed in cup)
½ teaspoon vanilla

Sift dry ingredients; cream butter and sugar; add beaten egg. Put grated chocolate and hot water in double boiler; melt; cool; add to egg mixture. Add flour and milk, alternately; add flavoring. Pour in 9 inch ring mold, that has been greased and dusted with flour. Bake at 325°. Ice with "white icing," tinted pink and flavored with several drops of essence of peppermint; swirl icing around on top and cover sides; fill with peppermint-candy ice cream. Serves 8.

CHOCOLATE-CREAM ROLL

5 eggs, beaten separately
3 tablespoons cocoa
1 tablespoon flour

¾ cup confectioners' sugar
1 teaspoon vanilla

Combine cocoa, flour and sugar; add well-beaten yolks; fold in stiffly beaten whites; flavor with vanilla. Spread half inch layer of batter on cookie sheet 10x15 (one end open), that has been greased and dusted with flour. Bake at 350° for twenty minutes; turn out on damp cloth; remove crisp edges; cover with another damp cloth for 10 minutes; Spread with 2 cups of cream, whipped, flavored with essence of mint, and sweetend to taste. Roll up carefully. Serve with chocolate sauce. Serves 8.

HOT CHOCOLATE PUDDING

1 quart milk
5 eggs
½ cup sugar

5 squares chocolate
3 heaping tablespoons flour or cornstarch
1 teaspoon vanilla

Make custard of egg yolks, sugar, chocolate, milk and flour; cook until very thick in double boiler; put in baking dish; cover with meringue made of 5 whites, beaten stiff with ½ teaspoon of cream of tartar and 10 tablespoons sugar; bake until meringue is firm. Serve with whipped cream when cold. Serves 6 to 8.

CREAM PUFF SHELLS

½ cup butter
1 cup boiling water
½ teaspoon salt

1 cup flour
4 eggs

Dissolve butter in boiling water; add salt and flour; cook until mixture leaves sides of sauce pan, stirring constantly. Remove from heat; add eggs, one at a time, beating well between each addition. When perfectly smooth put out on greased baking sheet; according to the size desired, with a pastry tube or spoon. For small puff shells a half teaspoonful only is necessary. Bake at 350° for half an hour; raise heat slightly, until they are done, cook about 10 minutes longer. When small puffs are to be used as containers for chicken salad or cheese canapés, the tops can be cut off with a sharp knife, leaving a crisp little shell to fill.

When larger puffs are used for dessert, they are split on one side and filled with ice cream or custard filling. A good filling can be made as follows: 4 egg yolks, 1 pint milk, ½ cup sugar, 1 teaspoon vanilla, 1 tablespoon cornstarch. Cook in double boiler until very thick. These can also be filled with ice cream and served with chocolate sauce.

DATE CRUMBLE

6 eggs
1 cup sugar
1 cup chopped dates

1 cup chopped pecans
1 cup grated bread crumbs
1 teaspoon vanilla

Beat egg yolks with sugar until light; add crumbs, dates, vanilla and pecans; fold in beaten whites; pour into greased pan, dusted with flour. Bake in moderate oven 350°, let cool in pan; when cold, crumble cake into 1 pint of whipped cream. Serve in glasses topped with additional whipped cream. Serves 6 or 8.

DATE-PRUNE SOUFFLÉ

1 package dates
½ pound prunes, cooked and chopped
1 cup pecans, chopped

6 egg whites
½ cup sugar
Pinch of salt

Beat whites very stiff; add sugar slowly; fold in other ingredients. Bake in moderate oven; serve with whipped cream. Serves 8.

DATE PUDDING

1 pound dates, chopped fine
1 pound pecans, chopped
½ cup flour
1 teaspoon baking powder

¼ cup sugar
1 teaspoon salt
2 whole eggs, beaten light
1 teaspoon vanilla

Beat eggs; add sugar and dry ingredients, sifted together; add flavoring; stir in dates and nuts. Bake in pan lined with greased paper, in moderate oven, for 45 minutes. Serve cold, cut in squares, topped with whipped cream. Serves 8.

DATE ROLL

1 box dates
1 small bag marshmallows (4 or 5 ounces)
½ cup pecans, cut fine

2 cups whipping cream
8 large graham crackers
2 tablespoons sherry

Cut marshmallows in small pieces. Roll half of crackers. Whip 1 cup of the cream. Mix these with pecans, dates, wine and marshmallows. Roll the other 4 crackers and spread on a piece of waxed paper. Cover with the date mixture and roll up like a jelly roll. Chill for several hours; slice; top with the rest of the whipped cream. Serves 6 to 8.

FLOAT

1 quart whipping cream
5 egg whites
5 tablespoons sugar
Sherry wine

5 tablespoons tart jelly, preferably, wild plum
Fruit coloring

Sweeten cream to taste; flavor strongly with sherry wine; whip until it begins to thicken slightly. Put egg whites, with 5 tablespoons sugar and 5 tablespoons jelly in electric beater; beat at high speed, pushing the eggs to the center of the bowl as you beat. Tint a pretty light pink, beat until stiff enough to stand in peaks. Fill individual glass compotes with the partly whipped cream, and top with pink egg mixture. This is an old family recipe and we think it is delicious. This should be served soon after it is made. Serves 8.

FUDGE PIE WITH MINT ICE CREAM

2 squares bitter chocolate	2 eggs
1 cup sugar	1 teaspoon vanilla
½ cup butter	½ cup chopped pecans
4 tablespoons flour	Pinch of salt

Melt chocolate and butter over hot water; remove from heat; add sugar, slightly beaten eggs, flour, salt, vanilla and pecans. Put in greased pyrex pie pan. Bake in moderate oven a half hour; cool. Serve, cut in wedges, with a spoon of peppermint candy ice cream on each piece. This can be baked in an oblong pyrex dish and cut in squares, if preferred. It is very rich and servings should not be too large. Serves 6. The pie does not have a crust.

FABULOUS DESSERT

Line a silver bowl with macaroons that have been thoroughly soaked in rum; press them against sides and bottom of the bowl. When ready to serve the dessert, put mocha ice cream over the macaroons until the bowl is filled. Cover top with whipped cream and sprinkle ground macaroon crumbs over the surface—one pound of macaroons, two quarts of ice cream, and a half pint of whipping cream will fill a large bowl and is sufficient to serve ten or twelve people. This makes an attractive dessert to pass at a party. Reserve ten macaroons from the pound to be toasted and ground into crumbs to decorate the top of the bowl.

ICE-BOX PUDDINGS

ALMOND-MACAROON ICEBOX PUDDING

1 cup butter	3 cups macaroons, broken in small pieces
1 cup sugar	
4 eggs	12 ladyfingers
3 tablespoons sherry wine	1 cup chopped blanched almonds
2 cups "boiled custard"	

Cream butter and sugar; add well-beaten eggs. Line mold or bowl with ladyfingers; put in a layer of butter and egg mixture; sprinkle with macaroon crumbs and almonds; cover with a layer of thick "boiled custard"; repeat; cover top with ladyfingers. Chill over night; turn out and serve with whipped cream. Serves 12.

CHOCOLATE ICEBOX PUDDING

2 squares bitter chocolate	4 eggs
2½ tablespoons water	12 ladyfingers
3 tablespoons sugar	1 teaspoon vanilla

Dissolve first three ingredients over hot water; add yolks, one at a time, beating well after each addition; flavor with vanilla; cool; add beaten whites. Put in mold alternating with ladyfingers split in half; chill several hours; serve with whipped cream. Serves 4 to 6.

COFFEE ICEBOX PUDDING

3 eggs
1 cup butter
1 cup sugar
½ cup rum

1 tbsp. powdered coffee dissolved in 1 tbsp. boiling water
½ pound ladyfingers

Cream butter and sugar; add well-beaten eggs; add coffee and rum slowly; split ladyfingers; arrange in layers in mold—alternating with custard mixture; chill until solid, about 6 hours. Turn out and serve with whipped cream. Serves 6 to 8.

FRUIT ICEBOX PUDDING

4 eggs
1 cup sugar
1½ sticks butter

1 teaspoon vanilla
3 cups sliced fruit
12 ladyfingers

Cream butter and sugar. Beat eggs together until light; add butter and sugar, flavor with vanilla. Line loaf pan with lady fingers; fill with mixture, alternating with sliced peaches or strawberries; put rest of ladyfingers over top. Chill overnight; turn out and cover with whipped cream. Serves 8.

ORANGE ICEBOX PUDDING

1 cup milk
3 eggs
½ cup sugar
1 teaspoon flour
1 tablespoon butter

Grated rind and juice of
1 large orange
1 cup double cream
¼ pound ladyfingers

Make a custard of first five ingredients; remove from heat; add orange juice and rind; cool. Split ladyfingers; put in mold, alternating layers of custard with ladyfingers. Chill overnight; turn out and cover with whipped cream. Serves 8.

PINEAPPLE ICEBOX CAKE

4 egg yolks
4 egg whites, beaten stiff
1 cup confectioners' sugar
½ pound butter or margarine
½ cup sliced almonds

1 small can grated pineapple
¼ pound marshmallows
1 package ladyfingers
½ pint whipped cream

Combine pineapple and marshmallows; let stand while making rest of dessert. Cream butter and sugar; add yolks one at a time; beat thoroughly; fold in beaten whites; add nuts and pineapple mixture. Line mold with split ladyfingers; fill with mixture; chill in icebox overnight; turn out; serve with whipped cream. Serves 8.

MACAROON-BRANDY PARFAIT

18 large single macaroons
½ cup peach brandy or wine
½ pint whipping cream

2 egg whites
Sugar

Pour brandy over macaroons to soften; mash well; beat egg whites stiff; add macaroons, sugar to taste and whipped cream; put in refrigerator tray to chill and partially freeze.

MERINGUES

MERINGUE CAKE DESSERT

8 egg whites
¼ teaspoon salt
½ teaspoon cream of tartar

2½ cups sugar
1 tablespoon vinegar

Put salt with egg whites; beat until foamy; add cream of tartar; beat until stiff; add sugar gradually, beating until the meringue is very stiff. Put in spring mold; cook in a very slow oven at 250° until firm to touch; cool; remove from spring mold. This can be served, covered with ice cream or with sliced peaches or strawberries. Serve whipped cream if fruit is used. Serves 8.

MERINGUE RINGS OR NESTS

Make meringue as described in "Meringue Cake," when very stiff, shape into individual rings or nests. These can be filled with ice cream or berries. Bake on lightly oiled cookie sheet, 250° until firm to touch. Rings can be made by using a pastry bag. Nests can be shaped, with a spoon, into desired shapes. For a valentine party, draw hearts on heavy brown paper; shape a spoonful of meringue on each heart, by spreading it to the edges of the pattern. When meringues are baked, place paper over a damp cloth for a few minutes; lift meringues off with a knife.

Meringue rings can be tinted pastel shades if desired. Attractive dessert platter: Vanilla ice cream in center of dessert tray surrounded by pale green meringue nests filled with specimen strawberries.

DATE-ALMOND MERINGUES

4 egg whites
1 cup sugar
¼ teaspoon cream of tartar
1 cup chopped dates

½ cup chopped pecans
1 teaspoon almond flavoring
¾ cup soda cracker crumbs
½ teaspoon vanilla

Beat eggs until frothy; add cream of tartar; beat until very stiff. Add sugar gradually; flavor; add dates, pecans and coarsely ground cracker crumbs. Shape into large meringues on a greased cookie sheet. Bake at 275° until firm. Serve topped with whipped cream. Chocolate wafer crumbs can be substituted for cracker crumbs if desired. Serves 10 to 12.

MACAROON MERINGUE RING

Make a ring of "macaroon pudding No. 1." Use 3 envelopes of gelatin instead of 2, to congeal it. Turn out; cover with a stiff meringue, made of 4 egg whites beaten with ¼ teaspoon of cream of tartar and 8 tablespoons sugar. Cover entire surface and swirl meringue thickly on top of ring. Run in very hot oven for a few minutes, to brown the meringue slightly; take out, cool, fill with vanilla ice cream. Sprinkle chopped crystallized fruits over ice cream if desired. Serves 10 to 12.

PEACH OR STRAWBERRY MERINGUE

Make one recipe for "Meringue Cake," cook in two 9" circle layers in a very slow oven; cool. Peel and slice 2 pounds of peaches, reserving 3 peaches to decorate top of dessert. Sweeten remainder of peaches; put between the two layers of meringue. Decorate around outer edge of top with overlapping slices of peaches; surround dessert with whipped cream. If preferred, the middle layer of dessert can be a thick layer of ice cream with the fruit used on top layer. The whipped cream is not used with this.

For strawberry meringue, roll whole berries in confectioners' sugar and fold into whipped cream; put between layers of meringue. Decorate top layer of meringue with specimen berries. Serves 8.

PEACH-MACAROON MERINGUE

1 can large, firm peach halves	4 egg whites
⅓ pound almond macaroons	8 tablespoons sugar
½ cup chopped pecans	½ teaspoon cream of tartar
Sherry wine	½ teaspoon almond flavoring

Drain peaches; toast and roll macaroons into coarse crumbs; add pecans; bind together with sherry wine; form into balls size of a walnut. Beat egg whites until frothy; add cream of tartar; beat very stiff; add 8 tablespoons sugar gradually; flavor with almond. Cover peaches with meringue; bake until light brown. Vanilla wafer crumbs can be substituted for macaroons. Add a little almond flavoring to wafer crumbs. Serve cold. Serves 6 to 8 (according to peach halves).

PLUM PUDDING

3 eggs, beaten separately	1 cup wine or whiskey
1 stick butter	¼ pound citron
½ cup sugar	½ pound each currants and seeded
½ teaspoon each of cinnamon, nutmeg,	raisins
mace, and allspice	1 cup blanched almonds
¼ teaspoon powdered cloves	1 cup flour

Wash currants; roll between palms of hands; dry carefully; cut raisins in small pieces; slice citron thin and cut in small pieces; slice almonds; flour fruits. Cream butter and sugar; add beaten egg yolks; alternate beaten whites and flour; mix fruit into batter, alternately with wine and nuts. Oil a pudding mold; put batter in mold; fit lid on carefully. Be sure no water can get into mold. Put in a kettle; cover with boiling water; cook 3 hours, keeping covered with boiling water the entire time. This can be made days ahead of time. When ready to serve, cover again with boiling water; cook for one hour; turn out. Serve hot with hard sauce. If preferred, this recipe can be cooked in 2 baking powder cans and sliced in circles when ready to serve. Serves 8.

PUDDING SAUCE

Cream a half cup of butter until fluffy; gradually add one cup of confectioners' sugar; flavor to taste with whiskey or brandy; grate nutmeg over sauce.

ORANGE CHIFFON DESSERT

Split an orange chiffon cake in 3 sections; put orange filling between each layer; cover with whipped cream. Orange filling: 3 beaten eggs, ½ cup butter, 1 cup sugar, ½ cup undiluted frozen orange juice, juice of 1 lemon, 3 tablespoons cornstarch, 3 tablespoons grated orange rind. Cook butter, beaten eggs, cornstarch and sugar in double boiler until thick; add juice; cook 3 minutes more, stirring constantly.

ORANGE PUDDING

1 cup orange juice
½ pound marshmallows
1 pint cream
½ pound macaroons

Dissolve marshmallows in orange juice in double boiler; cool; when perfectly cold, fold in whipped cream. Toast and grind macaroons; put a layer in mold; cover with pudding; add rest of crumbs; chill.

RED RASPBERRY CHIFFON CAKE DESSERT

1 orange chiffon cake
1 box frozen raspberries
1 pint whipping cream
Sugar to taste
1 tablespoon lemon juice
1 tablespoon unflavored gelatin
¼ cup cold water

Drain berries; add lemon juice and enough water to make 1 cup of liquid to berry juice; heat to boiling; soak gelatin in cold water; add to hot juice; stir until dissolved; chill; when almost set, beat mixture until frothy; add drained raspberries and whipped cream. Sweeten to taste. Split cake in 3 layers; put raspberry mixture between each layer; fill center with any that remains. Ice with whipped cream; chill until ready to use. Strawberries can be substituted if desired.

SNOWBALL DESSERT

2 small angel food cakes
Twice recipe for "White Icing"
1 pound of fresh grated cocoanut

Rub the crumbs from the outer surface of cakes. Place one cake on a platter with small end down. Cover top of this with a thick layer of icing and sprinkle with six tablespoons of the cocoanut. Now cover the larger end of the remaining cake and place it, icing side down, over the cocoanut. You now have a cake which is small at top and bottom and larger through the center. Trim the cake into a perfectly round ball using scissors to snip off the excess cake. Combine some of the snipped off cake with several spoons of icing and pack down into the hole at the center of the cake. Cover the ball with the remaining icing and sprinkle thickly with cocoanut to resemble snow. Decorate the top with a spray of holly, using green and red icing. Cut the cake in wedges and pass "Eggnog" to pour over it as a sauce. Serves ten or twelve. The hostess should serve this dessert from the table. It is especially beautiful at Christmas time.

SUMMER DELIGHT

Arrange pale green lime or mint sherbet on a chilled silver tray; at either end of tray put fruits in season, arranged on galax leaves. Use unpeeled apricots, blue and red plums and little bunches of dark red cherries. The different colors of the fruit blend well with the light green sherbet and the darker green galax leaves. Allow one of each variety of fruit for each person to be served.

SNOW PUDDING—LEMON VELVET SAUCE

1 package lemon flavored gelatin   2 egg whites
1½ cups hot water

Dissolve gelatin in hot water; let congeal until almost set, beat until very frothy and add stiffly beaten egg whites. Congeal in flat pan; cut in squares; cover with ground graham cracker crumbs. Serve with Lemon Velvet Sauce.

LEMON VELVET SAUCE

2 egg yolks   2 tablespoons lemon juice
½ cup cream, whipped   4 tablespoons melted butter
⅓ cup sugar   Grated rind of one lemon

Beat egg yolks with sugar; add lemon juice, melted butter and lemon rind; fold in whipped cream. Serves 6.

STRAWBERRY TORTE

1 quart sliced strawberries   1 teaspoon baking powder
4 egg yolks   1 teaspoon vanilla
½ cup sugar   4 well-beaten egg whites
1 stick butter   8 tablespoons sugar
4 tablespoons milk   ½ teaspoon vanilla
⅔ cup flour   Whipped cream

Cream butter and sugar; add well-beaten yolks; sift flour and baking powder together; add alternatingly with milk; flavor with vanilla. Pour batter into two 8 inch cake pans, that have been greased and floured. Cover uncooked batter with meringue, made of 4 egg whites, 8 tablespoons sugar and ½ teaspoon vanilla. Bake in 325° oven about 20 minutes. Test with straw; remove from pans; cool with meringue side up. Put together with a thick layer of berries between layers. Keep meringue outside. Garnish with whipped cream and a few reserved, whole berries. Packaged yellow cake mix can be substituted for cake batter.

STRAWBERRY-PINEAPPLE DESSERT

A combination of fresh pineapple, cut in bite-size pieces, and specimen strawberries makes a refreshing, simple dessert. Sweeten with confectioners' sugar and serve with hot muffin cakes.

TRIFLE

4 cups milk	½ pound ladyfingers
8 egg yolks	1 cup almonds, blanched and sliced
8 tablespoons sugar	1 pint jar red raspberry jam
1 teaspoon vanilla	Sherry wine
½ pound macaroons	

Make a boiled custard of first four ingredients; chill. Put a layer of ladyfingers in large flat pan; dribble sherry wine over them; spoon some custard over them; cover with a layer of macaroon halves; put chopped blanched almonds in any cracks you can find; dribble sherry wine over the macaroons; cover with a thin layer of red raspberry jam; alternate remaining custard and the cakes until dish is full. Refrigerate several hours. Serve in compotes topped with whipped cream. Serves 10. This is a favorite with men.

VIENNA CAKE

Bake a sponge cake in 3 thin layers, or buy a bakery sponge cake and slice into 3 layers. Put together with custard filling. Use chocolate custard for the middle layer; cover the other two layers, and sides of cake with plain custard; sprinkle crushed nut brittle over top. Serve with whipped cream. For the filling make a custard of:

3 egg yolks	⅓ cup flour
1 pint milk	⅓ cup sugar
1 cup butter or margarine	

To one third of the custard add 1 square of bitter chocolate that has been melted over hot water. Serves 6.

WASHINGTON CREAM PIE

1 box yellow cake mix	2 cups milk
2 whole eggs	½ cup flour
1 cup sugar	1 teaspoon vanilla

Bake yellow cake in loaf pan; cool; split in half and fill with thick custard made of remaining ingredients; cover with whipped cream. Serves 8.

MOLDED DESSERTS

BAVARIAN CREAM

1 cup milk	1 teaspoon vanilla
2 whole eggs	1 envelope gelatin
½ cup sugar	¼ cup cold water
½ pint whipping cream	

Make custard in double boiler, of milk, sugar and well-beaten eggs. Soak gelatin in cold water; dissolve in hot custard; chill; add whipped cream and vanilla. Pour into ring mold that has been rinsed in cold water. When ready to serve, turn out on platter, fill center with red or black raspberries; surround with extra whipped cream. Serves 6.

CARAMEL BAVARIAN CREAM

1 pint milk	2 envelopes gelatin .
⅔ cup sugar	½ cup cold water
2 eggs	1 teaspoon vanilla
1 pint double cream	

Soak gelatin in cold water; scald milk; add well beaten eggs. Melt sugar in heavy iron skillet until it turns a light caramel color, stirring constantly; reduce heat; add milk and egg mixture slowly; add gelatin, stirring until dissolved. Chill until thick; add whipped cream and vanilla. Turn into mold that has been rinsed in cold water; chill until firm; serve with "Date-wine Sauce." Serves 6 to 8.

COCOANUT BAVARIAN CREAM

1 pint milk	1 pint double cream
¾ cup sugar	1 teaspoon vanilla
2 tablespoons gelatin	½ pound fresh grated cocoanut

Soak gelatin in ½ cup of the milk; heat the rest; dissolve sugar and gelatin in hot milk. Chill until thick and ropy; add whipped cream. Put in mold to congeal; turn out; cover thickly with fresh cocoannt. Serve with "Butterscotch Sauce." Serves 8.

COFFEE BAVARIAN CREAM

Follow directions for plain "Bavarian Cream"; add 1 tablespoon of instant powdered coffee to hot custard and congeal in ring mold. Fill center with sweetened whipped cream, strongly flavored with rum.

GINGER BAVARIAN CREAM

1 pint whipping cream	1 tablespoon gelatin
3 eggs, beaten separately	½ cup cold water
3 tablespoons chopped preserved ginger	⅛ teaspoon salt
2 tablespoons ginger juice	Sugar if needed

Soak gelatin in cold water; dissolve over hot water; beat yolks; add salt, chopped ginger and ginger syrup. Cool gelatin until lukewarm;

beat into yolks; add whipped cream at once; fold in beaten whites. It will probably be sweet enough but if not, add a little sugar. Serves 8.

STRAWBERRY BAVARIAN CREAM

1 quart strawberries
¾ cups sugar
2 cups double cream

2 tablespoons gelatin
¼ cup cold water

Grind strawberries; strain off ½ cup of the juice; heat. Soak gelatin in cold water; dissolve in hot juice; add sugar and rest of strained strawberries. Put in refrigerator until thick and ropy; add whipped cream; pour in mold. Serve with extra whipped cream; decorate platter with large strawberries. Serves 6 to 8.

CHARLOTTE RUSSE

1 quart double cream
⅔ pound confectioners' sugar
2 tablespoons gelatin
¼ cup cold water

4 egg whites
1½ dozen ladyfingers
2 teaspoons vanilla

Soak gelatin in cold water; dissolve over hot water; whip egg whites; add sugar slowly; add whipped cream and flavoring; stir in gelatin which has been cooled to lukewarm. Pour into bowl lined with split ladyfingers; decorate top with ladyfingers. Serves 8.

CHARLOTTE RUSSE CAKE

Make half recipe for "Charlotte Russe No. 2," add 1 pint sliced strawberries to it. Cut center from large angel food cake, leaving an inch wall. Form a bottom to cake with some of the cake that has been removed. Fill with Charlotte mixture. If there is any Charlotte left, put it over top of the cake. Chill several hours. When ready to serve cover with whipped cream and decorate with a few specimen berries.

Charlotte Russe (2)

1 pint milk
1½ pints double cream
1 cup sugar

2 tablespoons Knox gelatin
¼ cup cold water
1 teaspoon vanilla

Soak gelatin in cold water. Heat milk; add sugar and gelatin; stir until dissolved; chill until thick; add whipped cream and vanilla. Pour in bowl lined with ladyfingers. Serves 6 to 8.

EGGNOG CHARLOTTE RUSSE

3 eggs
¼ cup sugar
½ cup whiskey
2 cups double cream

1 tablespoon gelatin
4 tablespoons cold water
Ladyfingers

Soak gelatin in cold water; dissolve over hot water. Beat yolks and sugar; add whiskey, gelatin and whipped cream; fold in beaten whites; pour in serving bowl; decorate with ladyfingers. Serves 6.

DESSERTS AND ICES

GOLDEN CHARLOTTE RUSSE

6 egg yolks	½ cup more of cold milk
1 cup sugar	12 large ladyfingers
1 pint milk	1 teaspoon vanilla
1 pint double cream	Sherry wine to taste
2 envelopes gelatin	

Soak gelatin in half cup of cold milk. Make custard of eggs, milk and sugar; dissolve gelatin in custard; cool; flavor with vanilla and sherry to taste; fold in whipped cream. Put in bowl lined with split ladyfingers; decorate top of bowl with ladyfingers. Serves 8 to 10.

MARRON CHARLOTTE

4 egg yolks	¼ cup cold water
1 cup sugar	¼ cup boiling water
3 cups double cream	1 cup sherry wine or
2 envelopes gelatin	½ cup whiskey
1 cup marrons, cut fine	

Soak gelatin in cold water; dissolve with the boiling water. Beat yolks until thick and lemon colored, then add whiskey or wine (this cooks the egg yolks); add dissolved gelatin; fold in whipped cream and marrons. Congeal in mold. Serve with additional whipped cream. Serves 6 or 8.

CHARLOTTE RUSSE RING-WINE JELLY TOP

1 package lemon flavored gelatin	½ cup sherry wine
1 cup hot water	

Dissolve gelatin in one cup hot water; add wine; pour in bottom of ring mold; when congealed pour Charlotte Russe, made as follows, over wine jelly.

CHARLOTTE RUSSE PART

1 pint double cream, whipped	¼ cup cold water
2 egg whites	1 teaspoon vanilla
¾ cup confectioners' sugar	¼ pound macaroon crumbs
1½ tablespoons gelatin	

Soak gelatin in cold water; dissolve over hot water; beat egg whites; add sugar and whipped cream; then slowly stir in gelatin, which has been cooled to body heat; test with finger tip; flavor; stir in macaroon crumbs; pour over wine jelly. Turn out when ready to serve; fill center with more whipped cream. Serves 8.

RUM CHARLOTTE RING

6 egg yolks	½ cup cold water
1 scant cup sugar	½ cup rum
1½ tablespoons gelatin	1 pint cream, whipped

Soak gelatin in cold water, dissolve over hot water. Beat eggs and sugar together; add rum and gelatin; fold in whipped cream. Line mold with split ladyfingers; using 12 to 18 according to size; congeal; turn out on platter; fill center with additional whipped cream. Serves 10. Twice recipe fills 2 eight inch ring molds.

CHERRY-SHERRY RING

2 packages cherry flavored gelatin
2 large cans black Bing cherries, seeded and drained

2½ cups cherry juice
1 cup sherry wine

Heat juice; pour over gelatin powder; stir until dissolved; cool; add cup of wine; let congeal until very thick; add cherries; put in large ring mold and congeal. Turn out; serve with whipped cream. Serves 10.

CHOCOLATE PUDDING

1 quart milk
4 squares chocolate
3 eggs
1 cup sugar
1 tablespoon flour

2 tablespoons gelatin
½ cup cold water
1 cup sliced blanched almonds
2 cups marshmallows, cut fine

Make custard of milk, egg yolks, sugar and flour; add grated chocolate; add gelatin that has been soaked in cold water; stir until dissolved; cool. Add beaten whites, almonds and marshmallows when almost congealed. Put in mold that has been rinsed in cold water; congeal. Turn out and serve with whipped cream. Serves 6 or 8.

CHRISTMAS DESSERT

1 large angel food cake
1 quart double cream
4 tablespoons confectioners' sugar
18 to 20 marshmallows, cut fine
1 cup almonds, sliced

1 tablespoon gelatin
¼ cup cold water
½ pound crystallized cherries, pineapple and green citron mixed
Vanilla or sherry wine to flavor

Soak gelatin in cold water; dissolve over hot water; cool; add to sweetened and flavored whipped cream; fold in marshmallows and almonds. Fill center of cake with part of cream and ice top and sides with rest. Cut fruits in strips and then in small pieces. Completely cover the surface with the chopped fruit, being careful to alternate the three colors of the fruit as you put it on. Send to the table whole to be served by the hostess. Serves 10.

DAFFODIL DESSERT

1 small sunshine or orange chiffon cake
6 eggs
1¼ cups sugar
1 cup orange juice

Grated rind of 2 oranges
2 envelopes gelatin
½ cup cold water

Break cake in inch pieces. Beat yolks with half the sugar; add orange juice; cook over hot water until thick. Soak gelatin in cold water; dissolve in egg mixture; cool; chill until it is thick and ropy; add orange rind. Beat egg whites stiff; add rest of sugar; fold into the chilled mixture. Rinse a ring mold with cold water; put in an inch layer of the mixture; cover with small pieces of cake; alternating cake and custard mixture until mold is full. Congeal; turn out; serve with whipped cream. Ladyfingers can be substituted for cake. Serves 8.

MACAROON PUDDING

1 pound almond macaroons, broken in bits
1 cup sherry wine
6 eggs
¼ cup sugar
2 envelopes plain gelatin
½ cup cold water

Soak macaroons in wine. Soak gelatin in cold water; beat egg yolks with sugar; cook over hot water until thick; dissolve gelatin in mixture; cool; when almost congealed, fold in the stiffly beaten egg whites and macaroons. Congeal in ring mold; turn out; serve with whipped cream. This makes a large ring and will serve 10.

Macaroon Pudding (2)

1 tablespoon gelatin
¼ cup cold water
2 cups milk
3 eggs
⅓ cup sugar
2 cups macaroon crumbs

Soak gelatin in cold water; make custard of egg yolks, sugar and milk; dissolve gelatin in hot custard; add macaroon crumbs; chill. When very thick, fold in beaten whites. Put in mold and congeal. Serve with whipped cream. Serves 6.

MOCHA CAKE

1 large sunshine cake
1 pint cream, whipped
2 tablespoons confectioners' sugar
1 tablespoon gelatin
¼ cup cold water

Soak gelatin in cold water; dissolve over hot water; cool; add to sweetened whipped cream. Split cake and use cream as a filling. Ice with "Mocha Icing" made as follows: 1 pound confectioners' sugar, sifted, 6 to 8 tablespoons double strength coffee, 2 tablespoons melted butter. Beat until thick, add more sugar if necessary. Ice cake; cover with ground, salted almonds and stick whole almonds around edges. Surround cake with spoonfuls of whipped cream. Serves 8 to 10.

ORANGE JELLY

2 cups orange juice
¼ cup lemon juice
¾ cup sugar
2 envelopes gelatin
¼ cup cold water
1 cup boiling water

Add sugar to fruit juice; let stand until dissolved. Soak gelatin in cold water; dissolve in boiling water. Combine ingredients; cool; strain through cheese cloth and congeal.

RUM CHIFFON PIE

1 crumb pie crust
5 egg yolks
1 cup sugar
½ cup rum
2 cups whipping cream
1 tablespoon gelatin
¼ cup water
2 tablespoons boiling water

Beat egg yolks until light; add sugar; beat well; add rum. Soak gelatin in cold water; add boiling water; stir over hot water until dissolved. Add gelatin to egg mixture; cool. Fold in whipped cream; put in pie crust. When ready to serve, sprinkle top with curls of semi-sweet chocolate. Serves 6.

SUNSHINE MOCHA DESSERT

6 egg yolks	1 tablespoon gelatin
¾ cup sugar	¼ cup cold water
3 tablespoons double-strength hot coffee	1 medium-sized sunshine or orange chiffon cake
1 pint double cream	
1 teaspoon vanilla	½ pound peanut brittle

Soak gelatin in cold water; dissolve in hot coffee; beat egg yolks until light; add sugar; cook until thick in double boiler; add coffee; cool; chill until very thick; add vanilla and whipped cream. When it begins to set, spread between layers cut from Sunshine or Orange Chiffon cake. Ice top and sides of cake with mixture. Sprinkle with crushed peanut brittle; serve with additional whipped cream. Coffee can be made of instant coffee. Serves 8.

WINE JELLY

Two packages lemon flavored gelatin. 2½ cups hot water. 2 cups sherry wine. Dissolve gelatin in hot water; add wine and congeal. Serves 6 to 8. This is an easy way to make a delicious wine jelly.

Wine Jelly (2)

2 tablespoons gelatin	2 cups boiling water
1 cup cold water	1½ cups sherry wine
3 lemons (juice of)	1 cup sugar

Soak gelatin in cold water; add boiling water and remaining ingredients; boil a few minutes with beaten white of an egg to clarify. Remove from heat; let stand two minutes and strain.

FROZEN DESSERTS

ANGEL FOOD TOAST WITH ICE CREAM MOLDED EGGS

Buy an angel food cake that has been baked in Pullman shaped loaf; cut in half inch slices and toast them lightly; put 2 halves of molded ice cream egg on each slice of cake; pass "wine sauce."

CANTALOUPE ALASKA

3 small cantaloupes	1½ cups sugar
1 quart vanilla ice cream	½ teaspoon cream of tartar
6 egg whites	

Cut cantaloupes in half; remove pulp and chop fine; pour a mixture of half cup of wine, 1 tablespoon lemon juice and 2 tablespoons sugar over pulp. When ready to use, replace cantaloupe in shells; pack hard frozen ice cream over pulp; cover with meringue, letting it come to edges of cantaloupe, completely sealing off all air. Set cantaloupes in large pan, filled with cracked ice; put in oven; bake at 500° until meringue has browned; watch carefully. To make meringue, beat egg whites until foamy; add cream of tartar; beat stiff; add sugar gradually. Serves 6.

GRAPEFRUIT ALASKA

Cut grapefruit in half; remove sections carefully; take out all of inside skin possible; put grapefruit sections back in the shell; sprinkle with sugar and sherry wine; fill with firmly frozen ice cream; seal over completely with meringue. Put grapefruit on a bed of cracked ice and run into oven heated at 500° until the meringue is slightly browned. Use small grapefruit for this. For 4 grapefruit halves use 1 quart of vanilla ice cream, and meringue made of 4 eggs, 1 cup sugar and ½ teaspoon of cream of tartar. Commercial ice cream can be bought already sliced and is easier to handle; it must be frozen very hard.

ORANGE ALASKA

Buy the largest oranges available (size 90 to the box, if possible). Slice off tops; scoop out, leaving a little pulp inside. Buy vanilla ice cream already sliced; cut each slice in 4 pieces and pack down in orange shells until they are completely filled. The ice cream should be frozen very hard and the oranges filled at the last minute. Cover the top completely with meringue, taking care to seal out all the air. Put oranges on a bed of cracked ice in a large pan; slip in a very hot oven, at 500° for a few minutes, until meringue is firm. Serve at once, putting each orange on a galax leaf. 3 egg whites and 6 tablespoons sugar will make meringue to cover 6 oranges.

PINEAPPLE ALASKA

1 No. 2½ can sliced pineapple
1 quart vanilla ice cream
8 egg whites

16 tablespoons sugar
½ teaspoon cream of tartar
Pound cake

Arrange pineapple slices far apart in large flat pan; cover each slice with a thin slice of pound cake. Trim cake to fit over pineapple. Buy ice cream in round cartons; slice in eight round slices; put in ice box tray to keep as hard as possible until ready to use. Just before serving, put ice cream circles over cake; completely covering with meringue, being careful that the meringue seals out all air. Bake in oven at 500° for 3 minutes. Serve at once. Make meringue by beating egg whites very stiff with cream of tartar and adding sugar slowly. Serves 8. Bakery pound cake loaf can be used for this.

PLAIN BAKED ALASKA

1 layer of cake—8 or 9 inches
3 pints of ice cream
6 egg whites

1½ cups sugar
½ teaspoon cream of tartar

Make a stiff meringue of egg whites, cream of tartar and sugar, added gradually. Put the cake on a silver or an oven proof tray; cover cake with ice cream that has been frozen as hard as possible. Cover ice cream completely with the meringue, taking care to seal out all of the air. Put the tray on a sheet of asbestos or over a biscuit pan that has been filled with cracked ice. Run in a very hot oven preheated to 500°, bake 3 to 5 minutes, watching carefully as it will burn quickly. Any combination of cake and ice cream can be used, yellow cake with vanilla or fruit ice cream, chocolate cake with chocolate or coffee ice cream or spice cake with vanilla ice cream are good combinations. A heaping teaspoon of powdered coffee used in the meringue is good with chocolate or coffee ice cream and a tablespoon of grated orange rind added to meringue for spice cake is also a good combination. This will serve 8 to 10. A half cake layer can be used for a smaller crowd.

ALASKA PIE

1 quart strawberries
6 individual baked pastry pie shells
½ cup sugar
1 quart vanilla ice cream

4 egg whites
8 tablespoons sugar
½ teaspoon cream of tartar

Cover capped berries with ½ cup sugar; stir lightly; let stand, while making a stiff meringue of beaten whites, cream of tartar and sugar. Put berries in individual pastry shells; over each one put a slice of vanilla cream frozen hard (this can be bought already sliced). Cover shells entirely with meringue; let it cover entire surface; sealing in the contents. Run in very hot oven, 500°; let brown lightly; serve at once. Serves 6.

BISCUIT TORTONI

1 cup milk
2 eggs
¾ cup sugar
1 tablespoon lemon juice

1 pint whipping cream
½ cup maraschino cherries
12 large macaroons, rolled into fine fine crumbs

Toast macaroons until dry; roll into crumbs. Make custard of eggs, sugar and milk; cool; add whipped cream and rest of ingredients. Freeze, stirring once or twice. Serves 6.

CRANBERRY FRAPPÉ

4 cups cranberries
1 quart water
¾ cups sugar or to taste
½ cup lemon juice

½ cup orange juice
¼ cup sherry wine
1 tablespoon gelatin
¼ cup cold water

Cook cranberries and water until berries are soft; strain; add sugar and gelatin, that has been soaked in cold water. Chill; add fruit juices and wine; freeze in electric refrigerator, stirring several times. Serves 8.

FROZEN CANTALOUPE

2 cups sieved, ripe cantaloupe
2 tablespoons lemon juice
8 tablespoons sherry wine

Sugar to taste (6 to 8 tablespoons)
Pinch of salt

Combine ingredients; freeze, stirring once or twice. Serve on sections of honeydew melon; garnish with mint sprays. Serves 6 or 8.

FROZEN ALMOND PUDDING

1 pint milk
4 tablespoons sugar
3 eggs, beaten together
1 tablespoon gelatin
¼ cup cold water
3 cups cream, whipped

10 marshmallows, cut fine
3 tablespoons sugar
1 cup almonds, sliced thin
½ cup maraschino cherries, chopped
½ cup wine
½ cup chopped preserved ginger

Soak fruit in wine. Soak gelatin in cold water. Make custard of milk, eggs and 4 tablespoons sugar; add gelatin; dissolve; chill. Whip cream; add 3 tablespoons sugar. Fold in fruit; add almonds, and marshmallows, and ginger, freeze, stir twice while freezing. Serves 8 to 10.

FROZEN EGGNOG

1 pint cream
4 egg yolks
1 cup sugar

1 tablespoon gelatin
2 tablespoons cold water
Whiskey to taste

Soak gelatin in cold water. Beat egg yolks and sugar until thick; put in double boiler with a small amount of cream. When hot add gelatin; dissolve; chill; add rest of cream that has been whipped. Flavor with whiskey, but remember that too much alcohol will keep the cream from freezing. Serves 6.

FROZEN LEMON PIE

4 eggs
⅓ cup lemon juice
¾ cup sugar

½ pint double cream, whipped
6 large graham crackers, rolled into crumbs

Grate rind of 1 lemon. Beat yolks, add sugar and lemon juice; cook until thick in double boiler; cool; add stiffly beaten whites, lemon rind and whipped cream. Line refrigerator tray with half of the graham cracker crumbs; add lemon dessert; cover with remaining crumbs; freeze; cut in squares. Serves 6.

FROZEN PEACHES

Peel peaches; put through meat grinder or chop fine; sweeten to taste; put in ice tray; stir several times while freezing. Serve with whipped cream.

FROZEN MACAROON—PINEAPPLE PUDDING

1 can grated pineapple (large size)
2 cups whipping cream
1 tablespoon gelatin

24 macaroons
½ cup sugar

Drain pineapple. Soak gelatin in ¼ cup pineapple juice. Heat remaining juice; add sugar. Dissolve gelatin in hot juice; cool and let almost congeal. Whip cream; add pineapple and gelatin mixture; put in refrigerator dessert tray, in layers with crumbled macaroons, freeze; turn out and slice. Serves 8.

FROZEN PUDDING

1 pint milk
3 egg yolks
½ cup sugar
1 tablespoon gelatin
¼ cup cold water

1 pint cherry preserves
1 cup blanched almonds, sliced thin
1 cup raisins, cut fine
½ cup sherry wine
3 pints cream, whipped

Pour wine over raisins. Soak gelatin in cold water. Make custard of milk, eggs and sugar; dissolve gelatin in hot custard, chill; add whipped cream and rest of ingredients. Freeze, stirring several times. Serves 12 to 15.

Frozen Pudding (2)

1 quart commercial vanilla ice cream
12 macaroons

1 cup mixed crystallized fruits
¼ cup sherry wine

Toast and crumble macaroons. Soak fruit in wine. Cut fruit in small pieces. Soften ice cream slightly; combine; refreeze ice cream. Serves 6 to 8.

FROZEN STRAWBERRY ICEBOX CAKE

1 quart strawberries (slice half of them)
2 cups whipping cream
1 cup confectioners' sugar

1 tablespoon gelatin
½ cup milk
12 large ladyfingers

Soak gelatin in milk; dissolve over hot water; cool. Whip and sweeten cream; add gelatin; put half of mixture in refrigerator dessert tray; cover with a layer of split ladyfingers, then a layer of sliced strawberries; add more split ladyfingers; top with rest of cream; freeze. Turn out; decorate with whole berries. Serves 8.

APRICOT ICE CREAM

1 large can apricots
1 small can grated pineapple
2 large oranges (juice of)
1 lemon (juice of)

1 quart cream, whipped
Sugar to taste, about 1 cup
1 envelope gelatin

Drain fruit; soak gelatin in fruit juices, dissolve over hot water. Mash apricots; add pineapple and combined fruit juices and gelatin. Whip cream; add fruit mixture and sugar; freeze, stirring one or twice. The amount of sugar used will depend upon the acidity of the fruit. Serves 8 to 10.

CHOCOLATE ICE CREAM

1 cup sugar
⅛ cup hot water
4 tablespoons cocoa

2 cups coffee cream
2 cups whipping cream
2 teaspoons vanilla

Combine sugar, water and cocoa; cook until dissolved; cool; add coffee cream; chill; freeze. Take out, beat; add whipped cream. Diced marshmallows can also be added if desired. Return to refrigerator and continue to freeze. Serves 6 to 8.

LEMON ICE CREAM

1 cup milk
1 cup double cream
½ cup sugar
1 cup white Karo syrup

2 eggs, beaten together
4 tablespoons lemon juice
Grated rind 1 lemon

Stir Karo syrup into milk until completely dissolved; beat eggs and sugar together; add lemon juice and rind; combine with whipped cream. Put in freezing tray; stir once while freezing. Serves 4 to 6.

LOTUS ICE CREAM

1 pint whipping cream
2 cups orange juice, unstrained
1 lemon—juice of
4 egg yolks

1¾ cups sugar (more or less)
2 tablespoons gelatin
½ cup cold water
1 teaspoon grated orange rind

Soak gelatin in cold water. Heat fruit juice; dissolve gelatin in hot juice. Beat yolks until thick; add sugar and gelatin mixture; chill until thick; add whipped cream; freeze, stirring once. If oranges are not sweet, more sugar may be needed. Serves 8.

GREEN MINT ICE CREAM

Make "vanilla ice cream"; tint with green fruit coloring; flavor with essence of mint instead of vanilla.

PEACH ICE CREAM

1 cup mashed peaches
¼ cup sugar or to taste
3 tablespoons light Karo syrup

1 teaspoon gelatin
1 tablespoon cold water
½ pint cream

Soak gelatin in cold water; dissolve over hot water, adding 1 tablespoon hot water to the gelatin. Add sugar to peaches; pour gelatin into peach mixture. When it begins to thicken, add cream, whipped stiff. Freeze, stirring once. Serves 4 to 6.

PECAN ICE CREAM

1 pint milk
1 pint double cream
1½ cups dark Karo syrup

1 cup broken pecans
1 teaspoon vanilla

Stir Karo syrup into milk until completely dissolved; add whipped cream and nuts; freeze until mushy; beat well and return to ice box until completely frozen. Serves 6 to 8.

PEPPERMINT CANDY ICE CREAM

½ pound peppermint stick candy
2 cups milk
2 egg yolks

2 tablespoons white Karo syrup
1 pint whipping cream
Few drops mint essence

Beat yolks; add Karo and milk; heat; dissolve crushed candy in custard mixture; cool; add whipped cream and essence of mint to taste, tint deeper pink with a few drops of vegetable coloring. Freeze until mushy; beat; freeze again. Serves 6 to 8.

131

PINEAPPLE ICE CREAM

1 tall can evaporated milk
1 lemon (juice)

No. 2 can crushed pineapple
Sugar as needed

Chill milk in refrigerator tray; add lemon juice; whip in electric mixer; add pineapple and juice; sweeten to taste. Freeze. A box of frozen strawberries or red raspberries can be substituted for pineapple. Serves 6 to 8.

BLACK RASPBERRY ICE CREAM

1 pint black raspberries

Once vanilla ice cream recipe

Mash berries through a fine wire sieve; sweeten; add to vanilla ice cream recipe; freeze as directed. Serves 8.

RED RASPBERRY ICE CREAM

2 boxes frozen raspberries
1 tablespoon gelatin
¼ cup cold water

1 lemon (juice of)
1 quart whipping cream
Sugar to taste

Defrost berries; drain and mash. Soak gelatin in cold water. Heat raspberry juice; dissolve gelatin in hot juice; cool; add to berries and lemon juice. When thickened, add whipped cream; sweeten to taste. Freeze in electric refrigerator, stirring once. Serves 10 to 12.

STRAWBERRY ICE CREAM

1 quart strawberries
1 tablespoon gelatin
2 tablespoons cold water

½ pint coffee cream
1 pint XX cream
Sugar to taste

Put strawberries through meat grinder. Soak gelatin in cold water; dissolve over hot water; add strawberries and juice, which have been sweetened with about 1 cup of sugar. Combine the XX cream and coffee cream; whip together; add to the berries; sweeten to taste, turn into refrigerator tray; beat when partially frozen; return to refrigerator until frozen. Serves 8.

VANILLA ICE CREAM

1 pint cream, whipped
1 pint coffee cream

1 cup sugar
1 teaspoon vanilla

Heat coffee cream; dissolve sugar in cream; chill; add vanilla and whipped cream; freeze until mushy; remove from tray; beat well; return to refrigerator to freeze. Serves 6 to 8.

FRENCH VANILLA ICE CREAM

2 cups milk
5 egg yolks, beaten
1 cup sugar

1 pint double cream
1½ teaspoons vanilla

Make custard of milk, egg yolks and sugar; cook in double boiler until thickened. Cool; fold in whipped cream and vanilla; freeze, stirring several times. Serves 8.

COFFEE MOUSSE

1 cup double strength coffee	4 egg yolks
¾ cup sugar	2 cups double cream
1 tablespoon gelatin	⅓ pound macaroons
¼ cold water	1 teaspoon vanilla

Soak gelatin in cold water. Toast, and grind macaroons. Beat eggs. Cook coffee and sugar to a syrup; dissolve gelatin in hot coffee; stir into beaten eggs, beating constantly; add whipped cream and vanilla when cool. Line refrigerator tray with half of macaroon crumbs; and coffee mixture; cover with remaining crumbs; freeze without stirring. Cut in blocks. Serves 6 to 8.

GINGER MOUSSE

½ cup sugar	1 pint cream, whipped
1 cup milk	1 cup marshmallows, cut up
2 egg yolks	½ cup preserved ginger

Make custard of egg yolks, sugar and milk; chill; add whipped cream, ginger and marshmallows; freeze—stirring twice. Serve with toasted almonds sprinkled over each serving. Serves 5 or 6.

GRAPE MOUSSE

1 cup grape juice	1 tablespoon lemon juice
20 marshmallows	2 cups cream, whipped

Heat grape juice; dissolve marshmallows in hot juice; add lemon juice; chill; add whipped cream. Freeze. Serves 6 to 8.

MAPLE MOUSSE

3 eggs	1 cup toasted almonds or pecans, ground
1 pint double cream	1 cup macaroon crumbs
¾ cup maple syrup	

Cook yolks and syrup in double boiler until thick, stirring constantly; add beaten whites while hot; cool; add nuts, macaroons and whipped cream. Freeze without stirring. Serves 6 to 8.

MINT MARSHMALLOW MOUSSE

10-ounce bag marshmallows	1 pint whipping cream
1 cup milk	Essence of peppermint

Dissolve marshmallows in milk, over hot water; cool and freeze to a mush; add whipping cream; flavor with mint and tint light green. Return to refrigerator and freeze without stirring. Serve with chocolate sauce. Serves 6.

MAPLE PARFAIT

4 eggs, beaten separately	1 cup rolled macaroon crumbs
1 cup maple syrup	½ cup sherry wine
1 cup chopped pecans	1 quart cream, whipped

Beat yolks; add sugar; cook in double boiler until thick; add beaten whites while hot; cool; add macaroons, nuts and cream. Freeze until mushy; beat and add wine; continue freezing. Serves 8 to 10.

133

LIME SHERBET

1 cup sugar	8 limes (juice of)
1½ cups water	2 egg whites
1 tablespoon gelatin	1 lemon (juice of)
¼ cup cold water	

Make syrup of sugar and water. Soak gelatin in ¼ cup cold water; add to syrup; stir until dissolved; chill. Add fruit juice; tint with green vegetable coloring; freeze to a mush. Add beaten whites; mix well. Return to icebox; freeze. Serves 6.

MINT SHERBET

1 quart water	2 egg whites
1⅓ cups sugar	Few drops green coloring
6 tablespoons lemon juice	Large handful fresh mint

Make syrup of sugar and water; pour over crushed mint (mint extract can be used if desired). Let stand until cooled; strain; freeze until mushy; add beaten egg whites; color green; continue freezing; stir once more and freeze.

ORANGE SHERBET

4 cups orange juice	1½ cups sugar
½ cup lemon juice	½ cup water
Grated rind 2 oranges	1 tablespoon gelatin
2 egg whites	

Soak gelatin in lemon juice. Make syrup of sugar and water; dissolve gelatin in syrup; add orange juice and rind. Freeze until mushy; add beaten egg whites; continue freezing; stir once more; freeze. Serves 8.

ORANGE ICE

Follow recipe for orange sherbet, omitting the egg whites. Stir several times while freezing.

RASPBERRY—PINEAPPLE SHERBET

1 pint fresh raspberries	1 cup sugar
1 smallest can grated pineapple	2 egg whites
1 cup lemon juice	4 tablespoons white Karo syrup

Crush berries; put through sieve; add pineapple, lemon juice and Karo syrup. Put in refrigerator, freeze to a mush; add meringue made of beaten whites and sugar; mix well; freeze again. Serves 6 to 8.

STRAWBERRY SHERBET
With Ice Cream Circles

1 package strawberry flavored gelatin	1 lemon, juice of
3 cups water	2 cups ground strawberries
1 cup sugar	1 quart vanilla ice cream

Grind berries. Boil sugar in 1 cup of the water 5 minutes; add gelatin powder; stir until dissolved; add rest of water, 1 lemon juice and berries; cool. Freeze, stirring several times. Put sherbet in center of chilled serving tray, surround with circles of vanilla ice cream that have been dipped on both sides in macaroon crumbs. Decorate between slices with large strawberries. Buy vanilla ice cream in round cartons and slice into 7 slices. Serves 6 or 7.

Strawberry Sherbet (2)

2 cups sugar	½ cup cold water
1 cup water	1 quart strawberries, ground
2 tablespoons gelatin	1 lemon

Grind berries, make syrup of sugar and water, add gelatin that has been soaked in cold water; chill; add berries and lemon juice. Freeze. If berries are very acid, add more sugar. Serves 6.

WE THREE SHERBET

1 cup orange juice	1 cup water
1 cup pineapple juice	½ cup sugar
1 cup sieved canned apricots	½ cup cream
2 egg whites, beaten	1 tablespoon gelatin

Cook sugar and water to syrup for 3 minutes; add gelatin that has been soaked in ¼ cup cold water. Cool; add fruit and freeze to a mush, add beaten whites and cream. Freeze. Serves 8.

CORN FLAKE CARAMEL RING FOR ICE CREAM

4 cups corn flakes	1 cup butter
1½ cups chopped pecans	½ teaspoon vanilla
2 cups brown sugar, packed	

Cook brown sugar and butter slowly, in iron skillet, until it bubbles (soft ball stage). Put corn flakes and pecans in large bowl; pour syrup over them, mix well. Pack into 8 or 9 inch ring mold that has been generously covered with softened (not melted) butter and put in icebox for several hours ahead of time. Turn out in 10 or 15 minutes. Do not put back in icebox. Fill with vanilla ice cream; serve with "Butterscotch Sauce." Serves 8.

PECAN CRISP CUPS FOR ICE CREAM

1 cup brown sugar (sifted)	4 tablespoons flour
½ cup butter	1 teaspoon vanilla
½ cup ground or chopped pecans	1 pinch salt
2 eggs, beaten together	

Cream butter and sugar; add beaten eggs; combine with other ingredients. Put spoonfuls of batter, far apart, on greased cookie sheet. Cook two at a time for 8 minutes at 325°; take up carefully, with a spatula; shape over custard cups or small individual pie pans, while warm. They will be uneven looking like big brown leaves. Fill cups with vanilla ice cream. Serve with "Butterscotch Sauce." Serves 8.

CHOCOLATE CORN FLAKE CUPS FOR ICE CREAM

6 cups corn flakes

2 packages semi-sweet chocolate bits

2 squares unsweetened chocolate

1 cup finely chopped pecans

Melt chocolate over hot (not boiling) water. Put corn flakes in a large bowl; add pecans; pour chocolate over them. Form into cups on waxed paper, or press into individual ring molds, that have been oiled. Turn out on waxed paper; chill until ready to use; fill with vanilla ice cream. This will make 12 cups.

BAKED STUFFED EGGS—CHEESE SAUCE

6 hard-boiled eggs
1 pint fresh mushrooms (or 1 small can)
3 tablespoons butter
1 tablespoon Worcestershire sauce
Salt and red pepper to taste

1½ cups milk
3 tablespoons flour
3 tablespoons butter
½ cup grated Swiss cheese

Wash mushrooms; grind coarsely through meat chopper; sauté in butter; add Worcestershire sauce. Split eggs lengthwise; remove yolks; mash; add mushrooms and seasoning; stuff back into egg whites. Make cream sauce of rest of ingredients; add grated cheese; stir until melted. Arrange eggs and sauce in buttered casserole; cover top with buttered crumbs. Bake. Serves 6 to 8.

CRAB MEAT OMELET

1 small can crab meat
4 eggs
2 tablespoons butter
½ teaspoon salt

1 teaspoon chopped parsley
1 teaspoon grated onion
2 tablespoons tomato catsup
2 tablespoons lemon juice

Flake crab meat; beat eggs separately; add seasoning and crab to yolks; fold in stiffly beaten whites. Heat butter in skillet; pour in omelet; cook over low heat until brown. Crease down center with knife blade; fold over and serve at once. Grated ham can be added instead of crab if preferred. Serves 4 to 6.

CREAMED EGGS ON TOAST

6 hard-boiled eggs
8 rounds of toast
2 cups milk
½ cup cream
4 tablespoons flour

4 tablespoons butter
1 tablespoon Worcestershire sauce
¼ teaspoon salt
1 dash cayenne pepper

Chop egg whites in small pieces; add to highly seasoned cream sauce made of other ingredients. Put on rounds of buttered toast; sieve egg yolks over top. Put a dash of paprika at the center of each piece. Garnish with parsley. Serves 8. This recipe can be varied by chopping the whole eggs and adding them to cream sauce, with a half cup of coarsely chopped cashew nuts. Serve on toast.

CREAMED EGGS, SWISS CHEESE SAUCE

6 hard-boiled eggs
2 cups milk
3 tablespoons butter

3 tablespoons flour
1 cup grated Swiss cheese
Salt and red pepper to taste

Cut eggs in half lengthwise. Make a cream sauce; season with salt and red pepper; add Swiss cheese. Cook in double boiler until the right consistency; add eggs. Serve on a round platter, surrounded by clear fried apple rings; slip a broiled breakfast sausage through the center of each apple ring. Nice for a breakfast dish. Serves 6.

CREOLE EGGS

9 hard-boiled eggs
"Creole Sauce" (once recipe)

1½ cups medium "Cream Sauce"

Slice eggs; put in layers, alternate with cream sauce and creole sauce. Put creole sauce on top, sprinkle with buttered crumbs; bake only long enough to heat. Serves 8.

CREOLE OMELET

6 eggs
6 tablespoons milk

"Creole Sauce"
¼ teaspoon salt

Beat yolks and whites separately; add milk and salt to yolks; fold in beaten whites. Butter an omelet pan well; have it very hot. Pour omelet in; cook over flame until it begins to brown. Slip in the oven for 5 minutes to dry slightly. Run a knife all around edges of pan and fold omelet over. Slip omelet out; cover with creole sauce. A few mushrooms can be added if desired. Serve at once. If you do not have an omelet pan, cook in a well-greased skillet, cut in half and fold over. Serves 5 or 6.

CURRIED EGGS

8 eggs
2 large Spanish onions
2 tablespoons butter
1 can bouillon
½ cup cold water
2 tablespoons flour
1 teaspoon curry powder or to taste
1 cup cream

4 cups boiled rice
            (Condiments)
Parmesan cheese, grated
Chutney
Peanuts, ground
Bacon, crumbled
Fresh cocoanut, grated
Green peppers, minced

Grind onions; cook in butter until clear; but not brown. Smooth flour and curry powder with cold water; add to the onions; add bouillon and simmer slowly for fifteen minutes; add cream; season to taste with salt and cayenne pepper. Boil eggs 20 minutes; plunge in cold water 3 minutes; shell; cut in quarters; put in sauce long enough to heat well. Pass rice first; pour eggs over it, then pass dishes of condiments named in list of ingredients. Serves 6 or 8.

DEVILED EGGS

6 hard-boiled eggs
½ teaspoon salt
1½ tablespoon mayonnaise
1 tablespoon vinegar

½ teaspoon salt
1 teaspoon prepared mustard
1 pinch cayenne pepper
¼ teaspoon sugar

Hard boil eggs about 20 minutes; plunge into cold water for a minute; peel while warm. When cold, halve eggs lengthwise; remove yolks and sieve; add seasoning, mayonnaise and vinegar; stuff back into white shells and sprinkle with paprika. Garnish each egg with a parsley bud. Cover eggs with waxed paper; chill in refrigerator until ready to use.

HOT DEVILED EGGS

Prepare stuffed "Deviled Eggs"; press 2 halves together and hold in place with a toothpick; keep over hot water until ready to serve. Broil large mushroom caps. Stand an egg upright in each mushroom cap. Put on flat platter and pour "Hollandaise" or "Cheese Sauce" around them. Garnish top of each egg with a parsley bud. Remove tooth picks.

EGG CUTLETS

6 hard-boiled eggs	½ teaspoon grated onion
1 cup milk	½ teaspoon chopped parsley
4 tablespoons flour	1 tablespoon Worcestershire sauce
2 tablespoons butter	

Make a thick cream sauce; add seasoning and finely chopped eggs. Chill; shape into cutlets; roll in beaten egg and bread crumbs and fry. Serve with creamed peas or tomato sauce. Serves 6.

FLUFFY OMELET

6 eggs	6 tablespoons milk
½ teaspoon salt	

Beat eggs separately; put milk and salt into yolks; fold in beaten whites. Pour in well-greased omelet pan. Put over low heat until puffy and browned underneath. Then put in the oven 350° for five minutes, to dry out. Loosen edges of omelet; turn one half over the other; slip off onto a warm platter. Grated cheese can be added just before folding omelet if desired. Serves 6.

HOLLANDAISE EGGS

6 servings of ham	¼ teaspoon cream of tartar
6 eggs	6 tablespoons grated cheese

Separate eggs carefully; beat whites stiff with cream of tartar; season with salt. Put ham slices on a greased baking sheet; make a nest of the whites on each slice of ham; hollow out space at the center of each nest; slip an egg yolk into the nest; sprinkle salt and cheese over yolks. Bake in slow oven. Pass "Hollandaise Sauce." Baked ham is best, but boiled or broiled sugar cured ham can be used. Serves 6.

EGGS WITH SHRIMP HOLLANDAISE

6 eggs	"Hollandaise Sauce" (once recipe)
6 slices tomato	6 rounds toast
1 5-ounce can shrimp	1 tablespoon minced parsley

Clean shrimp; add shrimp and parsley to "Hollandaise Sauce." Broil tomato slices. Poach eggs. Put slice of tomato on buttered toast; top with poached egg and cover with hot sauce. Serves 6.

GOLDEN ROD EGGS

8 eggs, hard-boiled	3 tablespoons butter
2 cups milk	½ teaspoon salt
3 tablespoons flour	1 dash red pepper
1 tablespoon Worcestershire sauce	

Make a cream sauce; add 1 tablespoon Worcestershire sauce; season.

Rice eggs; add to cream sauce. Put in buttered casserole; cover top with crumbs and bits of butter. Several slices of cooked breakfast bacon can be crumbled into eggs if desired. Serves 6 to 8.

STUFFED EGGS

Hard boil six eggs, cooking them for twenty minutes. Plunge them in cold water and then remove shells. When cool, cut them in halves, lengthwise, remove yolks and force them through a sieve. Add any of the following ingredients with enough mayonnaise to bind them together and make a firm filling to stuff into the whites. Season to taste, fill the egg whites and garnish the tops with a parsley bud, a slice of stuffed olive or a rolled anchovy. A pinch of sugar often improves the taste of the filling when vinegar is used.

1. 3 teaspoons of caviar, 1 tablespoon lemon juice, season to taste.
2. 1 tablespoon capers, 1 tablespoon chopped parsley, 1 teaspoon grated onion, salt and red pepper to taste.
3. ½ cup boneless sardines, mashed, 1 tablespoon lemon juice, season to taste.
4. 12 stuffed olives, 2 tablespoons finely minced celery, 1 tablespoon Worcestershire sauce, 1 teaspoon onion juice.
5. 4 tablespoons minced crab or shrimp, 1 tablespoon lemon juice, salt and red pepper to taste.
6. 1 tablespoon grated or deviled ham, 1 tablespoon pickle relish, ½ teaspoon prepared mustard.
7. 1 teaspoon anchovy paste, 1 teaspoon lemon juice, season to taste.
8. 2 tablespoons finely chopped ripe olives, 1 tablespoon finely chopped nuts, 1 tablespoon vinegar, pinch of sugar, season to taste.

STUFFED EGGS WITH NEWBERG SAUCE IN SHELLS

6 hard-boiled eggs	2 cups cooked rice
4 tablespoons butter	¼ cup sherry wine
4 tablespoons flour	3 tablespoons grated or deviled ham
¼ teaspoon grated onion	Salt and red pepper to taste
2 cups milk	

Split hard-boiled eggs lengthwise; remove yolks; mash them; combine with ham and a very little grated onion. Bind together with melted butter. Stuff egg whites. Make a cream sauce of butter, flour and milk; add sherry. Put 2 tablespoons rice in each individual shell; cover with 2 halves of stuffed eggs; pour cream sauce over all; press eggs down into rice; use as much sauce as possible for each shell. Cover with grated Italian cheese; bake until heated through. Serves 6.

LITTLE OMELETS

4 eggs, beaten separately	4 tablespoons milk
¼ teaspoon salt	¾ cup sharp grated cheese

Add milk and salt to beaten yolks; fold in beaten whites. Grease hot baker with butter and pour omelet out in rounds like you would a batter cake. Sprinkle a little sharp cheese on half of the rounds. When they are brown, slip them into the oven for 2 minutes to dry out slightly, then with a batter-cake turner take up a plain round and turn it over carefully on top of a cheese covered round. This makes attractive individual omelets. One baker rarely accommodates over 4 rounds, or 2 complete servings. They should be about 3½ inches in diameter. Serves 4 to 6.

OMELET WITH CHICKEN LIVERS

Make a 6-egg fluffy omelet. Broil 6 chicken livers and 1 teaspoon grated onion in butter; mince livers. Cook omelet; put livers over half of the omelet; fold over the other half; slip out on a warmed platter. Serve at once. Serves 6.

CHEESE BALLS

3 egg whites	2 tablespoons flour
1 pound sharp cheese	Salt and red pepper to taste

Grate cheese; beat egg whites very stiff; add cheese, seasoning and flour. Form into balls 1½ inches in diameter; roll in egg and crumbs; fry in deep fat. Drain on unglazed paper. Serve hot. Good with a salad. Makes 8 to 10 balls.

CHEESE FONDUE

½ pound sharp cheese, grated	1 teaspoon salt
1½ cups milk	4 eggs
2 cups cooked rice	

Beat egg yolks and whites separately. Combine other ingredients; add to yolks; fold in whites. Put in buttered casserole; set in pan of hot water; bake in moderate oven until done. Serves 8.

CHEESE PUDDING

6 slices of bread	1 teaspoon salt
3 eggs	2 cups grated sharp cheese
3 cups milk	

Cut crusts from bread; butter, and cut in small squares. Beat eggs; add milk and salt. Put bread in buttered casserole; pour egg mixture over it; bake at 400° for 20 minutes. Run under flame to brown before serving. Serves 6 to 8.

CHEESE SOUFFLÉ

4 eggs	1 cup sharp cheese, grated
1 cup milk	½ teaspoon salt
2 tablespoons butter	1 tablespoon Worcestershire sauce
3 tablespoons flour	

Make cream dressing; add grated cheese; stir until melted; add beaten egg yolks and seasoning; fold in beaten egg whites last. Bake in casserole in slow oven 325° for one hour. Serve at once. Serves 6.

141

CHEESE SOUFFLÉ RING

3 tablespoons butter
3 tablespoons flour
1½ cups milk
Pinch red pepper

6 eggs
½ teaspoon salt
½ pound grated sharp cheese

Make cream sauce of milk, flour and grated cheese; add eggs to this one at a time; beating well after each addition. Pour in well-greased 9 inch mold; put in pan with a little water in it; cover with waxed paper; cook slowly about 45 minutes at 325° or until firm. This is good to use, filled with creamed sweetbreads or shrimp. It does not "fall." Serves 8.

CHEESE SOUFFLÉ IN GREEN PEPPERS

Make soufflé as described in "Cheese Soufflé Ring"; fill scooped out bell peppers ¾ full, put in oven with a little water around peppers; cook about 20 minutes. Serves 8.

CHEESE STRATA

10 slices of bread, buttered
4 eggs
5 slices sharp cheese

2½ cups milk
½ teaspoon salt
1 tablespoon Worcestershire sauce

Remove crusts from bread; butter; make into 5 sandwiches with the cheese. Cut each sandwich in half; fit them in a well-buttered oblong, flat casserole. Pour milk, to which beaten eggs and salt have been added, over the sandwiches. Put in refrigerator for five or six hours. Bake at 350° for three quarters of an hour. Serve at once. Serves 8 to 10.

WELSH RAREBIT

1 pound sharp cheese
2 eggs, beaten together
2 tablespoons butter
1 cup beer or milk

1 tablespoon Worcestershire sauce
1 teaspoon dry mustard
1 teaspoon cornstarch
Salt and cayenne pepper

Melt butter in double boiler; add beer; when hot add grated cheese. Beat eggs; add seasoning and cornstarch; pour some of it slowly into cheese mixture; stir constantly; add remainder; serve on toast or crackers. Serves 6.

CREAMED CRAB MEAT WITH AVOCADOS

3 avocados
1 6-ounce can crab meat (best grade)
4 tablespoons butter
2 tablespoons lemon juice
4 tablespoons flour
Parmesan cheese

½ teaspoon salt
2 tablespoons chutney, chopped
1 dash red pepper
1½ cups milk
½ cup cream

Make cream sauce; season; add flaked crab meat and lemon juice; cook until thick; add chutney. Peel and split avocados lengthwise; remove seed; pile crab meat in center; sprinkle buttered crumbs and Parmesan cheese over top. Put in shallow pan with ½ inch of hot water in it; bake 15 or 20 minutes. Serve as a luncheon meat. Serves 6.

DEVILED CRABS

1 pound crab meat
5 tablespoons butter
3 tablespoons flour
4 hard-boiled eggs
2 tablespoons lemon juice
1 tablespoon chopped parsley
1 tablespoon Worcestershire sauce

½ teaspoon dry mustard
¾ teaspoon salt
⅛ teaspoon cayenne pepper
½ onion, chopped fine
1 cup milk
½ cup cream

Cook onion in half of the butter until tender, but not brown; add seasoning; mustard, and lemon juice. Make cream sauce of milk, cream, flour and rest of butter; stir slowly into the onion mixture; taste and correct seasoning if necessary. Flake cooked crab meat; chop eggs; add both to sauce; put in shells; cover with buttered crumbs; bake until top is browned. Serves 6.

CRAB OR TUNA FISH STUFFED POTATOES

6 baked potatoes (large)
½ cup milk
½ onion grated
1 diced tomato

1 egg
Salt and red pepper
1 tablespoon butter
1 small can of crab or tuna fish

Scoop out baked potatoes, mash well; season with salt, pepper and grated onion; add milk, tomato and well-beaten egg. Flake fish; add to potatoes. Put back in shells; run in the oven 5 or 10 minutes. Serves 6.

CRAB MEAT SOUFFLÉ

1 pound crab meat
3 eggs
1 cup grated cheese
1 cup milk

2 tablespoons flour
Salt and pepper to taste
2 tablespoons butter
¼ cup wine

Make cream sauce of milk, flour and butter; season highly; add beaten yolks and cheese. Shred crab meat, cover with wine; let stand 20 minutes;

combine with sauce; fold in beaten whites. Bake in buttered casserole in medium oven 375° for 45 minutes. Serve at once. Serves 6.

CREAMED CRAB WITH RICE

2 cans crab meat
1½ cups cooked rice
1½ cups milk
4 tablespoons butter
4 tablespoons flour

6 tablespoons dry white wine
1 tablespoon lemon juice
1 teaspoon salt
⅛ teaspoon red pepper
1 pinch nutmeg

Make a cream sauce of milk, butter, flour and seasoning; add wine, flaked crab meat, and dry cooked rice. Cover with crumbs and heat. Serve in shells or in a casserole. Serves 8.

CRAB SUPREME

1 can best grade crab meat (6 ounces)
1 small can mushrooms
1 pimento
1 cup milk
2 tablespoons butter

2 tablespoons flour
½ teaspoon salt
Buttered crumbs
Dash of cayenne pepper

Make cream sauce; add chopped pimento, mushrooms and flaked crab meat; put in shells and sprinkle with buttered crumbs. Heat for 10 minutes. Serves 4.

FISH CUTLETS

2 cups flaked fish (red snapper, salmon, crab, or lobster)
1 cup milk
4 tablespoons butter

4 tablespoons flour
½ teaspoon salt
Red pepper to taste
1 tablespoon lemon juice

Make thick cream sauce; add flaked fish; chill for several hours; form fish into cutlets; dip in crumbs, then in slightly beaten egg and in crumbs again. Let stand a few minutes; fry in deep hot fat. Drain on unglazed brown paper. Serve hot with "Tartar Sauce." Serves 6.

FISH-POTATO PUFF

1 can salmon
2 cups mashed potatoes
1 teaspoon minced onion

3 eggs. beaten separately
1 tablespoon lemon juice
2 pimentos, chopped fine

Mince salmon, add potatoes, onion, pimentos, beaten yolks and lemon juice. Fold in beaten whites; bake in buttered casserole for thirty minutes 375°. Serves 6.

FROG LEGS

Scald frog legs 5 minutes in boiling water; plunge in cold water with a little lemon juice and salt in it. Cool; take out and dry thoroughly. Prepare for frying by seasoning with salt and pepper and rolling in crumbs, then in beaten eggs and again in crumbs. Let stand a few minutes; fry in deep fat. Drain on absorbent paper; serve garnished with parsley and lemon slices.

Frog legs are usually sold "skinned and cleaned" at the market. If they are not previously prepared, skin them before scalding. The hind legs only are used.

FISH WITH CHEESE SAUCE

2 cups flaked whitefish	2 cups "Cheese Sauce"
1 tablespoon Worcestershire sauce	1 teaspoon lemon juice

Combine ingredients; put in casserole; cover top with crumbs and grated cheese. Bake until cheese melts, and fish is heated.

CREAMED FISH—SHRIMP SAUCE

2 pounds red snapper	½ pound cleaned, cooked shrimp
1 pint milk	¼ cup sherry
4 tablespoons flour	Salt and pepper to taste
4 tablespoons butter	1 egg yolk
1 small can mushrooms	2 tablespoons lemon juice

Put red snapper in 1 quart boiling water with two tablespoons lemon juice, large pinch of salt, ½ onion and 2 ribs of celery; simmer until the fish is firm. Remove from fire. Take fish from bones in large flakes; put on flat platter; scatter mushrooms over the fish; add sherry to cream sauce; combine with shrimp. Pour sauce over fish; garnish platter with parsley and lemon wedges. Serves 6.

FISH PUDDING WITH ALMONDS

Make once recipe for "Fish Pudding"; add 1½ cups blanched, sliced almonds; bake in ring mold. Serve with potato balls in center of ring and pass "Tomato Cream Sauce." This is a nice variation from usual fish pudding. Serves 6.

FISH PUDDING

2 cups ground, cooked fish (red snapper preferred)	⅛ teaspoon red pepper
	2 eggs, beaten together
1 cup milk	1 tablespoon each onion and lemon
2 tablespoons flour	juice
2 tablespoons butter	1 tablespoon Worcestershire sauce
½ teaspoon salt	1 teaspoon chopped parsley

Make cream sauce; add seasoning, parsley, fish, and beaten eggs, pour in a well-oiled ring mold, put waxed paper over top; set in shallow pan of water; bake 20 minutes. Unmold; put lemon cups filled with tartar sauce around it; alternating with "Cucumber and Radish Garnish," garnish with parsley. Fill center with potato balls sprinkled with melted butter and parsley. This makes a small ring mold—once and a half this recipe an 8 inch mold and twice the recipe a large fish mold. Serves 6.

JAMBOLAYA LOBSTER

2 small cans lobster	2 large tomatoes, chopped
1½ cups rice, unwashed	3 ribs celery, chopped
3 onions, chopped	Salt and cayenne pepper
2 tablespoons butter	½ cup sherry or Madeira wine
2 or 3 cups boiling water (as needed)	

Cook onions and celery in butter until tender; add raw rice; fry until brown; add chopped tomatoes and hot water as needed; cook ten minutes;

add lobster and season well. Cook until the rice is tender and the liquid is absorbed. Add more water if needed to prevent burning. When rice is tender, add wine; serve at once. Serves 7 or 8.

ROCK LOBSTER TAILS—BROILED

If lobster tails are frozen, thaw them first, then cut the under shell around the edge and remove that part. Now hold the tail in both hands and bend backwards to crack it until it will not curl up while cooking. Be sure it is well cracked. Arrange the tails, shell side up, in the broiler pan; cook at 375° about 5 inches from the flame for 5 to 7 minutes; turn them flesh side up, snip the flesh in several places with scissors. Spread with melted butter and lemon juice and broil for about 10 minutes, more or less, according to size. Pour additional melted butter and lemon juice over them. Garnish with lemon wedges and parsley.

LOBSTER NEWBERG

2 cups cooked flaked lobster	3 tablespoons flour
4 tablespoons sherry wine	1/8 teaspoon nutmeg
1½ cups cream	Salt and red pepper to taste
½ stick butter	1 egg yolk

Soak lobster in sherry. Make cream sauce in double boiler; add beaten egg and lobster. Do not boil. Serve in pastry cones or toast boats. Serves 6.

FRIED OYSTERS

Pick over oysters; drain and pat dry between cloths. Sprinkle with salt and pepper; roll each oyster in bread crumbs; dip in beaten egg and again in crumbs. Let stand 20 minutes. Cover the bottom of a frying basket with oysters; plunge into deep, hot fat. Cook until brown, which takes about 1½ minutes; drain on unglazed brown paper; serve hot with "Tartar Sauce," garnish with lemon slices and parsley.

Two dozen large oysters require 2 eggs diluted with 1 tablespoon of water, 1 teaspoon of salt, ¼ teaspoon pepper and 3 cups toasted crumbs.

DEVILED OYSTERS

1 quart oysters (selects)	1 tablespoon Worcestershire sauce
1 celery bunch	1½ stick butter
1 teaspoon salt	1 pint toasted bread crumbs or more
½ teaspoon black pepper	as needed
1 tablespoon onion, minced very fine	

Pick over and drain oysters, then pat between cloth until all moisture is absorbed—put celery in skillet with melted butter and onion and cook until tender but not brown, add seasoning, fill casserole with alternate layers of oysters, crumbs, and celery and onion mixture, letting crumbs form top layer. If necessary, use a few more crumbs for this. Dot with butter and bake until heated thoroughly. The secret of this dish is to have the oysters completely dry. This dish has been served for many years at our New Year receptions and it is a great favorite with all the men who are guests on that day. We also use it in our little individual oyster loaves which are served for morning coffees. Do not wash oysters, and do not overcook or they will be watery.

LUNCHEON OYSTER LOAVES

6 long French rolls	1 tablespoon Worcestershire sauce
1 pint oysters	1 tablespoon lemon juice
2 cups milk	½ teaspoon salt
3 tablespoons flour	¼ teaspoon red pepper
3 tablespoons butter	

Cut the tops off rolls; remove soft inside part; brush with melted butter; dry out in oven for 5 minutes. Cook oysters in 2 tablespoons water until edges curl; remove from sauce pan; drain; season with salt, pepper and lemon juice. Divide the oysters into the 6 loaves; smooth the flour and butter in the liquid where the oysters were cooked; add milk and seasoning. Pour two tablespoons of this sauce over each roll; replace the tops; brush with melted butter and toast in oven for 10 minutes. Serves 6.

CREAMED OYSTERS

2 cups milk	1½ pint oysters
4 tablespoons butter	2 egg yolks
4 tablespoons flour	1 tablespoon lemon juice

Make cream sauce in double boiler; add egg yolks just before ready to serve; simmer oysters 5 minutes in their juice; drain; add to sauce. Serve on buttered toast points. A small can of "Broiled in Butter Mushrooms" can be added if desired. Serves 6.

MOBILE SUNDAY NIGHT OYSTERS

1 quart oysters, drained and patted dry	1 stick of butter
2 small bunches green onions	2 tablespoons flour
Salt and pepper to taste	

Slice onions thin; cook slowly in butter until tender; add flour, drained oysters and seasoning; stir over slow heat until oysters curl. They will make their own sauce. Serve at once on toast. Serves 6 to 8.

MINCED OYSTERS

1 quart oysters	1 teaspoon salt
2 hard-boiled eggs	1 teaspoon black pepper
2 whole raw eggs	1 tablespoon Worcestershire sauce
1 small minced onion	¼ teaspoon cayenne pepper
1½ cups toasted bread crumbs	1 lemon, juice of
1 stick butter	2 ribs minced celery

Pick over oysters and chop. The sharp edges of a baking powder can, may be used for the chopping. Add minced celery, oyster liquor, raw eggs, beaten together, onions and seasoning. Melt butter in iron skillet; cook oyster mixture 5 minutes; stir in lemon juice, hard-boiled eggs and crumbs. Heat thoroughly; put in shells. Cover with buttered crumbs; bake in medium oven 20 minutes. Fills 6 shells. These are delicious.

SEA FOOD CASSEROLE

3 cans lobster (6 ounces)
3 small cans shrimp
1 8-ounce can mushrooms (pieces and stems)
3 cups milk

1 stick butter
6 level tablespoons flour
¼ cup wine
2 egg yolks
Salt and pepper to taste

Clean shrimp; pick over lobster; sauté mushrooms in part of the butter; soak seafood for an hour in sherry wine; combine with highly seasoned cream sauce made of milk, butter and flour. Cook over hot water; add beaten egg yolks a short while before serving. Do not boil. Put in casserole or shells; cover with buttered crumbs. Bake in medium oven until bubbly and hot. Serves 12.

Sea Food Casserole (2)

1 can tuna fish
1 can crab meat
1 can lobster
1 small can pimentos

8 hard-boiled eggs
4 cups "Medium Cream Sauce"
Sherry wine to taste

Scald and drain tuna fish; flake crab, lobster and tuna fish. Pour ¼ cup sherry wine over fish; let stand while making cream sauce; chop eggs and pimentos; add to fish. Combine with sauce. Serve in large flat casserole covered with buttered crumbs. Serve 12 or 14. It is best to plan this dish for a large crowd, since three cans of fish have to be used. Half the recipe can be made for a small crowd, and the rest of the fish saved for a salad.

SHRIMP WITH CHEESE SAUCE

1 pound cooked shrimp
2 cups milk
3 tablespoons flour
3 tablespoons butter
1 dash red pepper

1 cup grated cheese
1 tablespoon Worcestershire sauce
½ teaspoon prepared mustard
1 teaspoon salt

Make cream sauce; add seasoning; cheese, mustard; combine with shrimp; serve on toast. If cheese thickens the sauce too much add a few tablespoons of cream. Garnish with parsley. Serves 6.

CREOLE SHRIMP

1 large can tomatoes (2½ size)
4 ribs celery
2 bell peppers
2 onions
1 small can tomato paste
1 tablespoon Worcestershire sauce

1 stick butter
3 cups cooked shrimp
½ teaspoon salt
2 tablespoons horse-radish
1 pinch salt

Clean shrimp; cook chopped onions, peppers and celery in butter until tender; add tomatoes and seasoning, simmer until thick; add soda to tomato paste. Combine; add shrimp. Serve over hot fluffy rice. Serves 8 to 10.

CURRIED SHRIMP

1 pound cooked shrimp	6 tablespoons flour
2 tablespoons butter	1 tablespoon curry powder or to taste
3 cups milk or light cream	Salt and cayenne pepper to taste
6 tablespoons butter	½ cup dry white wine

Clean shrimp; sauté in 2 tablespoons of butter for 5 minutes; smooth curry powder in this; add the wine; simmer 5 minutes; add cream sauce made of 6 tablespoons butter, 6 tablespoons flour, and 3 cups milk; season with salt and cayenne pepper to taste. Serve in rice ring. Serves 6.

SHRIMP JAMBOLAYA

1½ cups rice, unwashed	½ cup tomato sauce
2 tablespoons butter	Salt and cayenne pepper to taste
2 cans shrimp	½ bay leaf
1 cup water	1 teaspoon onion juice
2 cups cream or milk	1 teaspoon Worcestershire sauce

Fry rice in butter until brown; add water; tomato sauce, milk and seasoning; cook ten minutes; add cleaned shrimp; simmer until liquid is absorbed. A pound of cooked fresh shrimp can be substituted for canned shrimp if preferred. Serves 8.

SCALLOPED SHRIMP

3 cups cooked shrimp	4 tablespoons butter
1 large bunch celery	4 tablespoons flour
6 onions	½ teaspoon salt
1 can condensed tomato soup	¼ teaspoon cayenne pepper
2 cups milk	Buttered bread crumbs

Slice onions thin; dice celery; boil in salted water until very tender; drain thoroughly. Make cream sauce; add condensed soup; combine with other ingredients; put in casserole; cover top with buttered bread crumbs; bake. This fills a large casserole and will serve 10.

This is a delicious luncheon dish and you are not even aware of the onions in it.

SHRIMP SEA SHELLS

3 eggs, hard-boiled	30 large shrimp
1 small can deviled ham	⅛ teaspoon cayenne pepper
1 pint milk	3 tablespoons sherry
4 tablespoons butter	3 tablespoons Parmesan cheese
4 tablespoons flour	¼ teaspoon salt

Make cream sauce. Split eggs lengthwise; season and mash yolks, add deviled ham. Put back into egg whites. Put a half egg in each large baking shell at the upper edge; arrange cleaned, cooked shrimp around the egg; cover with cream sauce which has been seasoned with sherry wine, salt and red pepper; sprinkle Parmesan cheese over each shell; run in the oven to heat. Makes 6 shells.

SHAD ROE BALLS

1 oblong can of shad roe	1 tablespoon lemon juice
2 cups milk	½ teaspoon salt
4 tablespoons flour	⅛ teaspoon cayenne pepper
4 tablespoons butter	

Make cream sauce; season; mash shad roe; add to sauce, chill several hours in refrigerator. Form into balls; roll in fine crumbs, dip in slightly beaten egg and roll again in crumbs. Fry quickly in deep fat; drain. Makes 8 large balls or 10 small ones. Serve each ball on a slice of lemon. Use as a garnish around soufflé ring filled with sweetbreads, for a formal breakfast. Can also be served with breakfast bacon.

FRIED SCALLOPS

1 quart scallops	Bread crumbs
2 teaspoons French dressing	Parmesan cheese
Salt and pepper	2 eggs

Drain scallops; let stand in French dressing one hour; drain again. Mix Parmesan cheese with bread crumbs; dip scallops in crumbs, then in beaten egg and again in crumbs; fry quickly in deep fat; drain on unglazed paper. Serve hot with "Tartar Sauce."

SCALLOPS IN NEWBERG SAUCE

Boil scallops five minutes; drain and cut in small pieces. For every two cups of scallops, make "Newberg Sauce" as described in "Lobster Newberg." Serves 6.

SALMON LOAF

1 can salmon	½ cup fine bread crumbs
4 eggs, beaten together	¼ cup melted butter
1 teaspoon lemon juice	1 teaspoon minced parsley

Mash salmon to a paste; add eggs, butter and crumbs; season to taste; add lemon juice and parsley. Pour in buttered mold; steam one hour; turn out; serve with hot "Mustard Sauce." Serves 5 or 6.

TUNA CASSEROLE

2 cans tuna fish	½ teaspoon salt
1 medium bag potato chips	1 tablespoon Worcestershire sauce
1 small can mushrooms	Dash of red pepper
1½ cups milk	3 tablespoons flour
3 tablespoons butter	

Make cream sauce; season highly; scald, drain and flake tuna fish; add to sauce with mushrooms. Put in casserole in alternate layers with crushed potato chips. Serves 6 to 8.

TUNA FISH CREOLE

1 can tuna fish	2 tablespoons flour
1 small can mushrooms	Salt and red pepper to taste
1 small can peas	2 tablespoons butter
1 cup tomato puree	1 tablespoon Worcestershire sauce
1 pinch soda	1 large onion, minced
1 cup milk	3 ribs celery, minced

Pour hot water over tuna fish; drain and flake. Put a pinch of soda in tomato puree; cook celery and onion in a little butter until tender. Make cream sauce; add tomato puree; combine with the other ingredients. Serve over crisp Chinese noodles. Serves 6.

TUNA SHELLS

2 cans tuna fish	Scant tablespoon dry mustard
1 pint milk	½ teaspoon salt
1 cup buttered bread crumbs	Pinch of red pepper
3 tablespoons flour	1 avocado
3 tablespoons butter	1 tablespoon Worcestershire sauce

Pour hot water over tuna fish; drain and flake. Put in shells, alternating fish, diced avocado, and crumbs. Make cream sauce, season and pour carefully over each shell, be sure to get enough on each to keep it from being dry. Put crumbs on top and bake 20 to 30 minutes at 375°. Serves 8.

APPLE COMPOTE

2 cups sugar
2 cups water
1 orange (juice and grated rind)

½ lemon (juice and grated rind)
6 apples, cored, peeled and quartered

Cook syrup until it threads; add apples; cook carefully until tender, turning several times. Remove each piece at it gets tender. Cook syrup a few minutes after apples are done; pour syrup over apples. Serves 8.

MINTED APPLES

6 medium-sized Winesap apples
2 cups water
2 cups sugar

4 drops essence of peppermint
Green coloring

Peel and core apples. Boil sugar and water until a syrup; add peppermint and coloring. Cook apples in syrup until tender. Cook slowly and turn often. These are pretty to serve as a plate garnish filled with a spoon of "Cranberry Relish." Nice with turkey. Serves 6.

APPLE SAUCE RING

2 cans apple sauce
2 tablespoons sugar
2 tablespoons gelatin
½ cup water

1 teaspoon lemon extract or a few drops essence of mint
5 drops green vegetable coloring

Soak gelatin in ½ cup water; dissolve over hot water; combine with apple sauce and other ingredients; tint light green; put in 8 or 9 inch ring mold which has been rinsed in cold water. Turn out on tray and garnish with fresh mint. This can be served with large honeydew or watermelon balls in the center. Nice to serve as a side dish with cold sliced turkey or ham. Serves 8. This is attractive molded in a melon mold.

APPLES STUFFED WITH MINCE MEAT

Cut an inch slice from the tops of large red apples; remove core and most of the apple pulp; do not peel apples. Stuff with mince meat; pour a tablespoon of sherry on top of each. Bake in slow oven. Nice with meats.

CLEAR APPLE RINGS (Fried)

Core and cut large winesap apples in half-inch rings; put in a large biscuit pan; sprinkle each slice well with both brown and white sugar; dot generously with butter. Put a small amount of water around the apple slices and cook in oven, turning the slices once or twice until clear. This is a good way to fry apples. They are especially nice to serve at a breakfast. Small, cooked, breakfast sausages can be slipped through the center of each slice, just before serving, or small pats of cooked sausage can be put on top.

CINNAMON APPLES

8 Winesap apples, cored and peeled
2 cups water
1½ cups sugar
½ cup red cinnamon drops

Make syrup of sugar, water and cinnamon drops; cook five or ten minutes, or until drops dissolve; add apples; cook slowly until tender; turn and baste with the syrup until they are a pretty red color and clear in appearance. If the cinnamon drops do not seem to color the apples enough, add a few drops of vegetable coloring to the syrup. Remove from heat; pour syrup around apples. Serve cold, as a plate garnish with meat course. Spoon the red, jellied syrup into the center of each apple.

CLEAR APPLES WITH ORANGE MARMALADE

6 Winesap apples, peeled and cored
1 cup sugar
1½ cups water
Orange marmalade

Make a syrup of sugar and water; cook apples in syrup until clear, turning once or twice. Remove from syrup; fill centers with a stiff orange marmalade; put in a flat pan; pour the syrup they were boiled in around them. Run in stove; baste once or twice. Cook just long enough to glaze. If desired, a little more marmalade may be put on top of them at serving time. Nice to serve with meats.

STUFFED APPLES

8 large Winesap apples
1½ cups sugar
1 tablespoon lemon juice
½ cup pecans, chopped
½ cup crystallized cherries
½ cup sherry wine
1 cup water

Core apples, being careful not to go all the way through; scrape out the apple, leaving a ¼ inch shell. Cook apple pulp, sugar and water until the apples are soft and clear. Soak cherries and nuts in sherry wine When apples have cooked down, add lemon juice, nuts and cherries. Fill apple shells. Sprinkle a few more grated nuts over the top of apples; run in oven to heat again just before serving. This is nice to serve as a side dish. Can also be served cold. Serves 8.

APPLES STUFFED WITH SAUSAGE

6 apples
½ pound sausage meat
2 tablespoons brown sugar
2 tablespoons water

Scoop out the apples, leaving a half inch wall; chop the scooped out apple. Combine it with the sugar and water and cook until tender. Fry out the sausage; drain off fat; crumble it into cooked apples. Use this to stuff the apple shells. Bake for about 10 or 15 minutes in a moderate oven.

It will be a good idea to chop an extra apple if the sausage seems to have much fat in it. Serves 6.

APRICOT AND GREENGAGE PLUM COMPOTE

1 2½-sized can apricots   1 2½-sized can greengage plums

Put in casserole; add a little sugar and lemon juice to fruit juice and cook to a syrup. Pour over apricots and plums. Serve hot as a side dish. Serves 8.

BAKED BANANAS

Put six firm bananas, peeled and split lengthwise, in a flat casserole; squeeze the juice of a lemon over them; sprinkle with brown sugar and bits of butter. Bake 15 minutes or more at 375°. If desired, several table-spoons of rum can be dribbled over the fruit. Serve as a side dish. Serves 6 to 8.

CRUSTY FRIED BANANAS

3 large bananas   2 tablespoons water
1 egg slightly beaten   Dry grated bread crumbs

Cut bananas in half cross-wise; dip in egg mixture and then in dry grated bread crumbs; fry in deep fat, just long enough to brown. Serve with meats. Serves 6.

CANTALOUPE POND LILIES

Select rather small cantaloupes for this; wash them. Draw five deep pointed V shaped sections around the melon with a sharp pencil; letting the pointed ends stop about one inch from the base of the melon on each side, as you go along. Hold the melon up and cut along the lines you have drawn with a sharp paring knife; pull the melon apart and you will have 2 pieces, each cut in deep petals. Now take the knife and cut the rind away from each petal stopping at the base of each V, pull this back gently and let it lay flat on the plate with the golden lily standing, intact, on top of it.

CANTALOUPE RINGS FILLED WITH FRUITS

Cut a medium sized cantaloupe in 3 or 4 rings; pare all the outside rind away from the cantaloupe; fill with melon balls, red, green and yellow, that have been sprinkled with salt. Pile them up and garnish with a spray of mint. They can be soaked in "Orange Marmalade Sauce" if preferred or they can be topped wtih green mint sherbet—nice first course.

CRANBERRIES—JELLIED

1 quart cranberries   2 cups sugar
1 cup water

Cover berries with water and simmer in a covered vessel about 8 min-utes or until soft. Run through a collander and add sugar. Bring to a boil, reduce heat and let simmer about 10 minutes. Turn into mold rinsed in cold water and let set. Should be refrigerated.

CRANBERRY RELISH

4 cups cranberries
1 large orange

2 cups sugar

Grind cranberries and sliced unpeeled orange together; add sugar; stir several times. A large spoon of this relish put on a slice of orange makes a pretty plate garnish.

MAMMY'S CRANBERRIES

2 cups cranberries

1 pound sugar

Wash berries; do not use any water except the water that clings to the berries; put sugar over berries; let stand a few minutes. Stir sugar around in berries; put over very slow heat; when it reaches a boil let it cook only 3 to 5 minutes. Mammy, who was our colored cook for fifty-three years, made these look like beautiful crystallized cherries. A large, flat sauce pan is best to use for these.

FIG AND GINGER COMPOTE

2 cans whole figs
¼ pound crystallized ginger, cut fine
1 lemon (juice of)

½ teaspoon powdered ginger
1 teaspoon cornstarch

Drain figs. Add powdered ginger, cornstarch and lemon juice to fig juice; cook until slightly thickened. Put figs in casserole; sprinkle crystallized ginger over them; cover with thickened juice, and put in oven until heated through.

FRUIT COMPOTE WITH MELBA SAUCE (DESSERT)

3½ cups sugar
2½ cups water
6 fresh pears

8 fresh peaches
12 red plums

Cook sugar and water 5 minutes; poach fruit in this syrup, a few pieces at a time, until tender. Arrange fruit around the outer edge of a flat, round platter. Sieve a pound of cottage cheese; sweeten slightly with confectioners' sugar; add a few spoons of cream if necessary. Put in center of platter. Cook fruit syrup until it thickens; pour over the fruit; cover with "Melba Sauce." Serve as a dessert with hot toasted crackers. Canned fruit can be used for this dessert if desired. Serves 8.

FROSTED GRAPES

Use firm red or white grapes; cut small bunches from the stem with scissors; wash and drain well. Dip each little bunch in slightly beaten egg whites; roll in coarse, granulated sugar; put on waxed paper in refrigerator. These can be served as a first course, with fruit juice. Put each little bunch on a galax leaf. The red grapes are especially nice with cranberry juice cocktail and the white ones are good with grapefruit-pineapple cocktail, tinted light green. They can also be used on honeydew or cantaloupe sections as a first course. Large black cherries, on stems can be used instead of grapes if desired.

FRUITS ON THE HALF SHELL

Cut rather small, ripe pineapples in halves lengthwise, leaving on the green top leaves and hull. Scoop out a well at the center of each piece and fill with fresh fruit. In the summer, use balls of honeydew, watermelon and cantaloupe, that have been soaked in sherry wine or "Lime Mint Sauce." Pile high and top with a sprig of mint. The pineapple that has been removed can be chopped, sweetened, and put in the bottom of the pineapple before putting in the balls. In the winter use whatever fruit you wish. For a bride, we often tie a tiny bunch of sweet peas or other small flowers, with a fluffy bow of green ribbonzine to the pineapple handle. At Christmas time we tie a sprig of red holly berries and their leaves with red ribbonzine; however, it makes a lovely first course without other decoration than the fruit. Each guest is served a pineapple half.

FROZEN FRUIT COCKTAIL

Add 1 can of fruit cocktail (large 2½ size) to a quart bottle of ginger ale; freeze in refrigerator tray until mushy. Beat and freeze again to a thick mush. Garnish with mint. Serve as first course. Serves 8.

FRUIT FRENCH BOUQUETS

Fruit cocktails, encircled by lace paper frills, make a lovely first course for a spring luncheon. They closely resemble little French bouquets. To make the little bouquet holders, you will need some six inch lace paper doilies and some nine ounce paper cups. Cut eight slits in the paper doilies, radiating from the center to within 1½ inches of the outer edges. Now cut an inch deep rim from the top of each paper cup. Discard the bottom part of cups. Use these rims to protect the lace paper from the dampness of the fruit. Force the rim through the slits in the center of the doilie and pull the lace mat out around it to resemble the outer edge of a paper French bouquet holder. Fit these into small, individual glass compotes and fill cups with balls cut from cantaloupe, honeydew and watermelon. Fill the cups almost full; then make a top layer by putting a cantaloupe ball at the center, encircled with watermelon balls. Put a row of honeydew balls on the outer edge. Pull single mint leaves from stems and encircle the bouquet with leaves, letting them extend over the lace paper frill. The holders are very simple and easy to make, but it is possible to buy tiny, three-inch paper, French bouquet holders from the florists. These can be fitted into the glass compotes and filled with fruit balls.

FRESH FRUIT PLATE

This can be served as a first course or as a dessert. Assemble as many fresh fruits as the market affords, the more the merrier as this has many possibilities. I use a ring cut from small honeydew melon as a container for the fruit, or perhaps a ring cut from a large cantaloupe. Several pieces of each of the following fruits can be put in the container, arranging them so that each bright color can be seen; fresh pineapple, peaches, pears, bananas, apricots, blue, red and yellow plums, white and red grapes, watermelon, cantaloupe and honeydew balls, big dark bing cherries and anything else you might find, makes a lucious plate. Pour "Mint-Lime Sauce" or "Wine Sauce" over the fruit. Peel melon ring, peaches and pears, but leave skins on plums, grapes and cherries.

HOT FRUIT COMPOTE

2 cans of "fruits for salad"   1 small bottle of preserved ginger
1 small bottle of marrons

Drain juices off fruits; add ginger syrup and enough sugar to sweeten, for a syrup; cook until it thickens; add 2 tablespoons lemon juice and 2 tablespoons of rum. Put fruits in a large flat pan, with chopped ginger and marrons. Pour syrup over fruit; put in oven just long enough to heat the fruit. Serve, spooned out into a silver vegetable dish as a side dish. If preferred, any combination of canned fruits can be used to make an equal amount of fruit. Do not use canned fruit cocktail for this, however. Serves 10.

Hot Fruit Compote (2)

1 can apple sauce   1 can pineapple cut in pieces
1 can blue plums   2 sliced bananas
½ cup pecans, grated   3 tablespoons brown sugar

Combine, in layers, in a casserole; cover the top with brown sugar and grated nuts. Bake until heated through. Serve as a side dish. Serves 10.

GRAPEFRUIT HALVES WITH MAPLE SYRUP OR CRYSTALLIZED- GINGER

Cut grapefruit in half; remove center and loosen fruit, nick around edges in small points. Fill hole at center with several spoons of maple syrup or with chopped crystallized ginger. Put grapefruit on galax leaf when ready to serve. Chill well before serving.

GRAPEFRUIT MAY BASKETS

Cut grapefruit in half and remove all fruit and membrane with very sharp knife; cut a ⅜ inch band around top of grapefruit shell stopping on each side of the grapefruit for a space of 1 inch; bring the slit bands on each side up and fasten them together to form a handle—tie them together with a fluffy bow of ribbonzine. Fill the baskets with mixed fruits; orange and grapefruit sections, pineapple, bananas, strawberries, etc., that have been sweetened to taste with "Mint-Lime Sauce" or sweetened and flavored with sherry wine.

HONEY DEW GRAPE BUNCHES

Cut balls from honeydew melons with two sizes of ball cutters; make a foundation for the bunch of grapes from the larger balls by starting with four balls in a line, under this line put 3 balls; then two balls, and then one. Over this framework pile the smaller balls to simulate a bunch of grapes. Break the stem from a galax leaf and put a 2 inch piece at the top of the bunch, for a stem; tuck the galax leaf under the side of the bunch of grapes. Just before sending to the table dribble a thick syrup over the grapes to glaze them. Make the syrup of 1 cup of sugar and ½ cup water cooked to a thick syrup; flavor with fresh lemon or lime juice. Cool before putting on the fruit. The grape bunches are assembled on individual plates. Nice first course for a breakfast or luncheon.

HONEYDEW SECTIONS WITH MELON BALLS

Cut honeydew melon in 6 or 8 sections, remove balls from the sides of each section and replace them with watermelon and cantaloupe balls. Put honeydew balls which have been removed with more watermelon and cantaloupe balls, on top of honeydew sections; garnish with mint sprays. Drizzle "Mint-Lime Sauce" over the fruit or serve with a slice of fresh lime—nice first course.

ORANGE CHRYSANTHEMUMS WITH MOLDED FRUIT SALAD

Use thin skinned oranges. Cut down 4 ways almost to the bottom; peel back and remove orange meat, leaving the peel intact. Cut each section of the peel into four petals, like a chrysanthemum; cover them with damp cloth until ready to use. These can be made a day ahead of time. When ready to serve, hold petals apart and fill cup with molded fruit salad, top with a spoon of Philadelphia cheese that has been smoothed with a small amount of French dressing. Use this instead of mayonnaise. This is used as a first course. Orange jello, with orange sections and pineapple in it, is nice to use in the "Chrysanthemum"—arrange orange peel petals around salad to look like a flower.

ORANGE AND GRAPEFRUIT FLOWERS

Allow 4 pieces each of grapefruit and orange sections for a serving. Overlap the 4 grapefruit sections until a 4 inch circle has been made of the fruit. This constitutes the outside of the flower. Inside the circle make an overlapping circle of the orange sections, and in the center, put a ball cut from avocado pear. This can be made with a melon ball cutter. Arrange the flower on lettuce hearts; serve with French dressing, for a first course salad. Nice to use at a luncheon with yellow color scheme.

BAKED PEACHES

Peel large fresh peaches; cut in half; put them in oven, in a flat pan, with just enough water to prevent them from burning; sprinkle with a mixture of white and brown sugar; dot with butter; bake slowly: I serve these as a side dish at a breakfast.

CRUSTY PEACHES

Drain and wipe off canned peach halves; roll in corn flakes; bake until corn flakes are very crisp. Put a large spoon of red or black variety of jelly in each peach. Serve as a plate parnish, or around meat platters. These are pretty served around a ring of chicken pudding.

STUFFED PEACHES

Fill large, firm, canned peach halves with sliced bananas; cover thickly with brown sugar and bits of butter; top with shredded cocoanut. Bake in slow oven. Serve as a plate garnish or around a meat platter.

RIPE JAPANESE PERSIMMONS

Slash a big ripe persimmon across the top, both ways; pull the four points back to resemble a flower; put on a galax leaf; serve very cold as a first course. It should be eaten with a spoon. Care should be taken to have the fruit very ripe.

GINGERED PEARS

12 cooking pears   2 cups sugar
2 cups water   2 pieces ginger root

Cut ginger in several pieces; make a syrup of sugar, water and ginger root. Peel and quarter pears; cook slowly in the syrup until clear.

PEAR GARNISH FOR MEATS

1 can large, firm pear halves   8 tablespoons mayonnaise
Grated cheese

Fill pear halves with a spoon of stiff, homemade mayonnaise; cover with grated yellow cheese; run in oven until cheese melts and browns. Serve at once.

BROILED GRAPEFRUIT

Cut grapefruit in half; remove center; loosen sections; sprinkle with sugar; let stand a short while. Sprinkle again with sugar; put a spoonful of rum or sherry in the center of each. Run in oven; cook until slightly brown. Serve hot.

BROILED PINEAPPLE AND BACON

Wrap pineapple fingers with a strip of breakfast bacon; put on wire rack so that excess fat will drain off; broil or bake in oven until bacon is crisp and brown. Nice to serve as a breakfast dish.

GRILLED PINEAPPLE SLICE

Grill slice of pineapple in browned butter. Nice to serve as a breakfast dish with a large cooked prune or a pat of cooked sausage on it.

PINEAPPLE POINTS

Score around one of the "eyes" of a large ripe pineapple with a sharp paring knife; pull the section out with prongs of a fork. It will come out in a pointed section. The rest of the pineapple can be removed in the same manner. Do not peel pineapple. Arrange on individual plates with pointed ends of sections to the center of the plate. Arrange a mound of confectioners' sugar in the center of the plate; garnish each plate with several large strawberries, caps left on. Nice for first course of either luncheon or breakfast. Pineapple sections and berries can be picked up by fingers.

PINEAPPLE QUARTERS WITH FRUIT GARNISH

Select large, ripe pineapple; cut through hull, stem and leaves in 4 lengthwise sections; slice hard core from center with a sharp knife; separate fruit from hull, but leave it in place on the hull. Now slice down in 6 or 8 verticle slices, so that the fruit can be easily removed. Decorate across the top of each section with either a small bunch of frosted grapes, orange sections, large strawberries or black bing cherries. Garnish with mint. Serve each guest a pineapple section, with a small mound of confectioners' sugar to one side. Makes a nice first course.

PINEAPPLE CHRISTMAS WREATHS

Cut inch slices from a ripe pineapple, without removing the outside hull; now cut the fruit away from the hull, leaving a ½ inch border of the pineapple attached to the hull. This makes a ring shaped container for a fruit cocktail. Dice the pineapple that has been cut from the center of the rings, put to soak with a little sherry wine and sugar. Add any other fruits available; drain and put fruit in rings. A small sprig of holly berries and leaves and a fluffy red ribbon bow can be stuck at the top of the ring so that it resembles a Christmas wreath. Use as first course.

WATERMELON BALLS ON GREEN ICE

Chip ice very fine; just before serving, put a few drops of green coloring over it; spoon into individual compotes, covering the bottom of the glass to the depth of one inch; over this pile watermelon balls, that have been sprinkled with salt; top with a sprig of mint. This is pretty and refreshing on a hot summer day as a first course.

CABBAGE SPOOK-HEAD CONTAINERS

A container for olives, celery and radishes can be made of a large, smooth head of white cabbage, to resemble a spook head. Each eyeball is fashioned from a 1½ inch slice of onion, which in turn has a smaller slice of unpeeled radish over it. The eyebrows are cut in arched pieces from green bell peppers and a mouth is shaped from a piece of red bell pepper. A section cut from the small end of a small bell pepper is used for a nose. All are pinned in place by toothpicks. A slice is cut from the top of the spookhead and the center is scooped out to form the container for olives, celery, etc. A spook hat is put on the head and removed as each guest is served. These hats can be fashioned from sheets of black or orange paper although they are usually available in 10 cent stores at the Halloween season of the year.

PURPLE CABBAGE FLOWER

Pull the outer leaves of a head of purple cabbage down carefully to form a foundation ruffle for the center that is left. Scoop out this center and fill with 2 inch celery sections that have been fringed on the end and put in ice water to curl. The outer edge of the cabbage can be stuck with radish roses; ripe and stuffed olives, and carrot flowers put on with colored toothpicks.

CARROT FLOWERS

Scrape large carrots; slice in thin circles, slightly overlap 3 of these circles along the outer edge, catch them together with a toothpick. Let this point be the center of the flower; covering the protruding edge of the toothpick with a small round cut from black ripe olive to make flower center.

CHEESE CARROT OR CRAB APPLE

Grate yellow cheese; season with Worcestershire sauce and red pepper. Take a spoonful of the mixture and form into small carrots or crab apples; dust with paprika. Put parsley bud stems on the carrot. Put a plain stem at top of the apples and a clove at the other end. Chill. These can be used to garnish salad trays.

CHEESE AND PEPPER RINGS

1 pound yellow cheese, grated	1 small bottle stuffed olives, sliced
2 green bell peppers, cut fine	2 hard-boiled eggs, chopped
1 pimento, chopped	2 sweet cucumber pickles, chopped

Combine ingredients; knead together until well mixed; stuff into scooped out bell peppers and pack down firmly. Chill in refrigerator overnight. Slice with sharp knife. Serve cheese filled rings as salad garnish.

CHEESE AND OLIVE ROSE GARNISH

Remove pimento from medium sized stuffed olives; cut olives in 5 points to resemble the calyx of a rose. Make rose buds of a yellow cheese spread, forming cylinders of the cheese and shape each end to a point. Chill these until they are firm; insert them into the olives, molding the cheese to resemble a rose bud. Chill again. When ready to serve, stick real rose stems, with leaves on them, into the bottom of the olives. Small stems from a running rose are the best kind to use. Place on a plate with tomato juice or fruit cocktail, as a garnish.

CHEESE PUMPKIN GARNISH

Grate cheddar cheese and season with red pepper and a little Worcestershire sauce. Knead well. It should be the right consistency without adding anything else, but a little cream can be added if you find it necessary. Roll into small balls about an inch in diameter; chill; make indentations with back of a silver knife blade to resemble the lines of a pumpkin. Put a clove in one end and a bit of parsley stem in the other end. If preferred you can use a jar of yellow cheese spread to make the pumpkins. Chill until ready to use as a garnish.

CHEESE GARNISHES

Cut yellow cheese 1/4 inch thick then cut garnishes from each slice in any desired shape with cookie cutters. At Christmas time a star of cheese can top individual mince pies. At Thanksgiving a harvest moon can be used or at Halloween a cheese jack-o-lantern will be especially attractive served on small apple pies.

CHRISTMAS TREE

An attractive addition to the center of a tray of Christmas canapés is a little plastic Christmas tree hung with ripe and stuffed olives, small radish roses and cocktail onions. These little trees are usually used to hold gumdrops and can be found at candy counters in ten cent stores.

COLONIAL DOLL

China colonial doll heads (which are often used to make pincushions) can be put to another use when they are made into a garnish for the center of a tray of salads. Fasten the head securely on top of an egg plant, with toothpicks, put through the little openings at the doll's waist. First cut a slice from the large end of the egg plant so that it will stand on a firm foundation and cut a small piece from the stem end before fastening the doll to it. The egg plant acts as a skirt foundation for the lettuce ruffles that are pinned to it with bits of toothpicks. Start at bottom of edge and pin the first "ruffle" about 3 inches up on the egg plant letting the lettuce leaves overlap as you go around. Overlap another layer of ruffles over the first row and repeat until you get to the top of the skirt. Tiny bits of lettuce hearts can be used to cover waist line connections. A miniature bouquet made of a tiny stuffed olive and cocktail onions can be bordered with parsley and pinned in place with toothpicks at waist line.

CUCUMBER AND RADISH

Peel long slender cucumbers; score down the entire length with the tines of a silver fork. Cut each cucumber in half crosswise then slice each section down, crosswise, into 6 or 8 slices. Slice about ¾ of the way down. Dribble a little French dressing over each section; let stand until ready to use. Put a thin slice of unpeeled radish between each slice, letting the radish extend above the cucumber. This is a nice garnish for a fish platter.

EGG TULIPS

Hard boil eggs; plunge in cold water; shell at once. Color eggs in a solution made of water and fruit coloring. Fix a cup of each color (pink, yellow and lavender) having liquid deep enough to cover an egg. Dip one egg at a time in the liquid. If this does not seem to tint egg the desired color, at once, remove egg and add more fruit coloring. Never add coloring while egg is in liquid as it will streak the egg. When egg tulips are ready, fit them into cucumber sections made as follows: Cut long, slender cucumbers in half, cross ways, cut a slice off of the narrow end so the cucumber stem will sit level and cut the top part of the stem in five points; scoop out enough cucumber so the egg can be fitted into the pointed cup. Arrange 3 colored tulips into a tulip bed at the center of a salad platter. Can be used several times if kept in refrigerator.

EGG POND LILIES

Hard boil eggs; plunge at once in cold water; peel. Roll between palms of hands until they are round. With a sharp paring knife, cut into 5 or 6 petals, starting at the top and stopping about half an inch from the bottom edge of the egg. Force the petals away from the yolks and remove yolks. If it is very hard to remove, leave about half of it, but break it up with a knife point; otherwise grate the yolk and put some of it in the center of each lily. These are rather hard to make, so cook one or two extra eggs. Leaves can be made by cutting ovals from a green pepper and snipping one end to resemble the top of a pond lily leaf. Put a leaf under each lily; use to garnish a salad platter.

EGG APPLES

Hard boil eggs; plunge in cold water; shell at once. While they are still warm, roll gently between palms of hands, until they are perfectly round. Tint one side with diluted red fruit coloring, patting it on lightly with a soft cloth. Put clove at one end and a parsley stem at the other.

PEPPER RING GARNISH

Slice rings from small red or green peppers and put on main course plate. Fill rings with pickle or red pepper relish.

163

PICKLE GARNISHES

Select large firm sour pickles, several inches long. Cut in half crosswise; cut a slice from one end and remove the center with an apple corer. Press a cheese mixture (see cheese pumpkins) into the opening; force it down firmly so that it will be well packed. Chill and slice in thin slices. This makes a nice garnish around a salad platter. I use it on a slice of cucumber just larger than the pickle which is in turn put on a slice of tomato. Score the cucumber down the entire length with the tines of a silver fork to give a scalloped edge to each slice. Pickle fans also make a nice garnish. Use small slender sweet pickles and slice nearly to the end, lengthwise, in 4 or 5 sections. Thin slices of carrots or radishes can be put at the center of each fan.

RED PEPPER FLOWERS

Select small red bell peppers and slice them from the top to within a half inch of the base of the pepper. Each pepper should have 10 or 12 petals. Pull them open and cut out any of the center that is unsightly. The seeds often make a pretty center and can be left in place. Arrange one or two flowers in parsley at one end of a vegetable or salad platter.

RADISH ROSES

Use large round radishes. Remove stems. Make 5 incisions around radish, starting at the top or root end, cut down three fourths of the way. Run a knife point under each section of the skin. Cut down through the white part of the radish to make additional petals. Put in icewater to open.

ROSE APPLE AND CHEESE

Fill little bright red pimento rose apple cups with a stiff mixture of yellow cheese that has been kneaded together with tomato catsup. Make balls of this and stuff peppers, packing the cheese down and mounding it up at the top edge. Put in the oven just long enough to heat through. This makes a colorful garnish for meats. Canned Rose Apples are available.

SQUASH GARNISH

Little yellow geese made from yellow squash, in graduating sizes make an attractive garnish for the center of a large canapé or salad tray. Let them march through a path bordered by parsley buds, down the center of the tray, with the largest goose leading the procession. Cut a slice from the bottom of the squash so it will have a firm foundation; let the small end be the head of the goose. The green tip forms the bill and 2 cloves or carpet tacks can be used for eyes. It will surprise you how life-like they are and you will have fun selecting the ones that will have the most quizzical look.

TURNIP-CALLA LILY

Select very large firm turnips, peel and cut in thin slices. Trim a stick of carrot so that it will look like a lily stamen; fold two of the turnip slices around the carrot stamen, overlapping them at the lower edge and holding them in place with toothpicks. Put in ice water to crisp.

TURNIP-NARCISSUS

Peel large firm turnips until they are smooth; cut in thin slices; snip with scissors from the outer edge to the center, leaving a small space at the center that is not cut. Cut six petals to each circle; snip little slanting sections from the sides of each petal section and trim in petal shape. Stick a toothpick through the center of this; anchor a thick slice of scraped carrot on the toothpick to form the flower center.

JELLIES

APPLE JELLY

Wash apples; cut in quarters without removing seeds or skin; barely cover with water; cook until tender. Put in jelly bag to drain; do not squeeze. Measure juice; to every pint of juice allow 2 cups of sugar. Boil 20 minutes or until jelly sheets from the spoon.

BLACK RASPBERRY JELLY

Allow 1 cup of water to every quart of berries. Mash berries; heat slowly with water; boil for 5 minutes; strain in jelly bag; measure juice; to every pint of juice add 2 cups of sugar; boil 20 minutes or until jelly sheets from spoon; strain; pour into jelly glasses and cover with melted paraffin. If berries are very ripe cook with a few green apples.

BLACKBERRY JELLY

Blackberries do not make a firm jelly if the berries are ripe. For that reason it is wise to have some partially ripe berries along with the ripe ones. If this is not possible, add some sour green apples to the berries before they are cooked. Use the same recipe as the above one for black raspberry jelly.

CRAB APPLE JELLY

Wash crab apples; take out stems; cover with water; cook until soft; strain. Allow a pint of juice to a pound of sugar; bring to a boil and cook 15 or 20 minutes depending upon the acidity of the apples. Pour into glasses and seal with paraffin.

SPICED CRAB APPLE JELLY

3 quarts of juice
1 quart vinegar
3 quarts sugar

1 tablespoon cloves
2-ounce stick cinnamon

Tie spice in a bag. Boil juice and vinegar 20 minutes with spices; add sugar and boil until it sheets from the spoon. Remove spice bag. Pour into glasses; when cool seal with melted paraffin.

GRAPE JELLY

Only half ripe grapes should be used for this as ripe grapes will not jell. Pick the grapes from the stem and crush. To every five pounds of grapes add about 2 cups of water; cook the mixture to a pulp; press through a sieve; put to strain in a cloth bag; do not squeeze. Measure the juice and to every pint allow 2 cups of sugar; heat the juice; add sugar; boil for 20 minutes or until it sheets from a spoon. Pour in jelly glasses; cover with melted paraffin. Cook a small quantity at a time and skim well while cooking.

MINT JELLY

2 gallons tart green apples	Green food coloring
Sugar	Oil of peppermint

Slice and core apples; cover with water and cook until mushy; strain in a cloth bag. To every pint of juice allow 2 cups of sugar. Boil and skim until it sheets from the spoon; 15 to 20 minutes according to the acidity of the apples. When done, color a pretty green with fruit coloring and add a few drops of oil of peppermint. Pour into glasses and seal with melted paraffin.

PLUM JELLY

The most delicious plum jelly is made from the small hard plums that are found in wild plum thickets. They are very acid and make a beautiful, firm jelly. Partially ripe, cultivated plums can be used if the wild plums are not available. Boil until tender in water to come two thirds of the way up on the plums; strain in a cloth bag. Do not squeeze bag. To every two pints of juice measure two pounds of sugar. Boil until the jelly sheets from a spoon—15 to 20 minutes. Pour in glasses; seal with melted paraffin.

RED RASPBERRY JELLY

2 quarts red raspberries	Sugar
1 gallon tart green apples	

Slice apples; cover with water; boil until mushy; add berries and boil until the berries are quite soft. Strain through a jelly bag. Measure two pints of sugar to two pints of juice. Boil 20 minutes or until it jells.

QUINCE JELLY

18 quince	2 quarts cranberries
24 apples	Sugar

Cut quince and apples in quarters; add cranberries; cover with water; let strike a boil; reduce heat and simmer until the fruit is very soft; strain through a cloth bag, but do not squeeze. Measure juice; to each pint of juice add 1 pint of sugar; boil until it jells, 20 minutes or less. Skim well. Cook a small amount at a time for best results. Strain into glasses at once and seal with melted paraffin. This combination makes a beautiful jelly.

GUAVA JELLY

Slice sour guavas, cut up and cover with water; boil until the guavas are tender (or about 20 minutes) stirring occasionally; strain while hot.

To every pint of juice allow 2 cups of sugar; heat slowly until sugar dissolves, then boil until it sheets from a spoon. If the guaves are not sour, add juice of half a lemon to each pint of guava juice before cooking. Cook a small amount of jelly at a time. Skim, strain and pour in glasses while hot. Cover with melted paraffin.

PICKLES

SPICED CANTALOUPE BALLS

6 cups cantaloupe balls	2 cups water
1½ cups sugar	2 teaspoons whole allspice
1½ cups vinegar	2 sticks cinnamon

Tie spice in bag; cook with sugar, vinegar and water to a syrup; add melon balls; reduce heat; cook half hour; pour in glasses and seal.

CHERRY PICKLE

Seed and weigh cherries; set aside the same weight in sugar for future use; cover cherries with vinegar; leave overnight. The next morning drain them; discard vinegar; add sugar, that was set aside, to cherries. Add some sticks of cinnamon and a few whole cloves. Do not cook, but stir for several days until the sugar has dissolved; put up in jars. I serve this as a plate garnish by putting a spoonful of pickle on a slice of orange or by filling a large canned peach half with the pickle.

CHILI SAUCE

1 peck ripe tomatoes	2 quarts vinegar
12 bell peppers	4 tablespoons salt
4 hot red peppers	1 nutmeg, broken in pieces
8 large onions	2 tablespoons allspice
1 cup horse-radish	1 tablespoon whole cloves
1½ cups brown sugar	1 teaspoon garlic buds (optional)

Scald and skin tomatoes; cut in pieces. Grind peppers, discarding seeds of all but one bell pepper; slice onions. Put spices in a bag; combine all ingredients. Cook in a large kettle for 2 hours, stirring frequently as it burns easily. This makes about 12 pints.

CRANBERRY RELISH

4 cups cranberries	2 oranges
2 cups sugar	

Slice oranges, remove seed; put through meat grinder with cranberries; add sugar, stir several times. Will keep some time in refrigerator.

CHOW CHOW PICKLE

½ peck green tomatoes
½ peck green cucumbers
12 large bell peppers (green)
12 large onions
2 large heads cabbage
12 bundles celery
1 pint silver skinned small onions
1 pint grated horse-radish
1 pint tiny cucumber pickles

1 quart pickled small onions
5 pounds brown sugar
½ pound white mustard seed
¼ pound ground mustard
2½ ounces ground black pepper
1 ounce celery seed
½ ounce powdered cinnamon
2 ounces tumeric
1½ gallons apple vinegar

Chop cabbage and green tomatoes fine; cut celery and cucumbers in small pieces; grind large onions and peppers; add handful of salt; put in bags and let drip overnight. In the morning squeeze dry. Put ½ gallon of the vinegar on with the spices and let come to a hard boil. Mix mustard with sugar; sprinkle over the vegetables; pour boiling vinegar over them. Heat half gallon remaining vinegar the next morning, and pour over pickle. Repeat on the third morning. When done, add pickled onions and tiny cucumber pickles and bottle. Always keep pickle covered with vinegar, when putting it up.

CRISP CUCUMBER RINGS

1 dozen large, firm sour pickles
1 pound white sugar
Spices, garlic, powdered alum

1 pound brown sugar
½ cup tarragon vinegar

Slice pickles in inch pieces; soak in ice water 20 minutes, drain. Put a layer of the sliced pickle in a large stone crock; sprinkle a tiny bit of powdered alum over it, on the point of a knife; cover with a layer of mixed white and brown sugar. Over this put a sprinkle of pickling spice, a little powdered ginger, and a few broken pieces of stick cinnamon. Repeat until the pickles are all used. Pour the tarragon vinegar over all. Stir for several days until sugar is dissolved. Several buds of garlic can be sliced very thin and added if desired.

CUCUMBER AND ONION PICKLE

4 pound cucumbers, weighed after they
    have been peeled and sliced
2 pounds onions, sliced
6 large red bell peppers, sliced
2 quarts vinegar
2 tablespoons celery seed

6 cups brown sugar
3 tablespoons olive oil
2 tablespoons white mustard seed
2 tablespoons grated horse-radish
1 tablespoon tumeric

Put a small handful of salt over the green vegetables; let stand overnight. Next morning pour a glass of cold water over them; let drain. Combine the vinegar, sugar and spices with the vegetables; cook until it reaches a boil; remove from fire; add olive oil when cold.

169

SPICED GRAPES

7 pounds Concord grapes (weighed after stemming)
4½ pounds white sugar
1 pint vinegar

1 tablespoon powdered cinnamon
1 tablespoon powdered allspice
½ tablespoon powdered cloves

Separate pulp from hulls of grapes. Cook pulp until soft enough to put through collander to remove seeds. After removing seeds add hulls to the pulp. Mix spices with sugar; combine with pulp and vinegar, cook slowly until thick.

MUSTARD PICKLE

1 pint sliced green tomatoes
1 large bunch celery, cut fine
1 large head cauliflower, broken into flowerettes
3 green bell peppers, sliced thin
4 red bell peppers, sliced thin
1 quart button onions
1 quart sour cucumber pickles, cut one-inch lengths
3 tablespoons white mustard seed

3 tablespoons celery seed
1 quart very small cucumber pickles
1 cup salt
1 quart vinegar
1 quart water
2½ cups white sugar
2 cups flour
½ cup dry mustard
1 tablespoon tumeric
3 more pints vinegar for dressing

Sprinkle salt over green vegetables; let stand overnight; Next morning, scald in the brine and drain; wash in cold water and drain again. Cover with quart of vinegar and quart of water; and boil until tender; drain thoroughly; let drip dry in a thin cotton bag. Make a dressing of tumeric, flour, mustard, and sugar mixed into a paste with part of the 3 pints of vinegar; add the rest of the vinegar slowly. Cook until thick; add vegetables; cook 5 minutes more. Remove from fire; add mustard and celery seed.

SPICED PEACH PICKLE

14 pounds peaches (freestone Elbertas)
8 pounds sugar
2 quarts vinegar
2 tablespoons allspice

4 sticks cinnamon
2 teaspoon whole cloves
2 teaspoons celery seed
2 tablespoons mace

Put spices in a muslin bag; cook 15 minutes with vinegar and sugar. Weigh peaches after peeling; drop a few at a time into the syrup; cook until they can be pierced with a straw. Spread on flat platters until all are done; boil syrup until fairly thick; remove spice bag; put pickles in warmed jars; pour hot syrup over them; seal. Peaches should not be too ripe.

PEAR RELISH

5 pounds pears after peeling and coring
2 pounds onions
2 pounds bell peppers, green
1 pound bell peppers, red
6 large sour pickles
2 scant teaspoons mustard

1 cup salt
3 cups vinegar
1 teaspoon tumeric
1 teaspoon celery seed
2 cups sugar
4 tablespoons flour

Grind first five ingredients; sprinkle cup of salt over them; add water to cover; soak overnight. The next morning; pour fresh water over them; drain well. Combine sugar, flour and spices, add one cup of vinegar, stir till smooth; add rest of the vinegar; cook five minutes. Combine all ingredients. Cook five minutes more.

SPICED PEARS

1 gallon small Seckel pears	8 sticks cinnamon
8 cups sugar	2 tablespoons allspice
1 quart vinegar	½ teaspoon whole cloves

Tie spices in a bag. Peel pears, leaving stems on. Cover with water; boil 10 or 15 minutes; drain. Add to syrup made of sugar, vinegar and spices; boil gently until pears are tender. Leave overnight. Remove pears from syrup and pack in jars the next day; cook syrup until it thickens; pour over pears.

RED PEPPER RELISH

24 large red bell peppers	6 cups sugar
1 quart vinegar	2 tablespoons salt

Remove seeds and tough part inside of peppers; grind, add salt. Put on with sugar and vinegar; boil until the consistency of jam.

RELISH

2 quarts green tomatoes	1½ pounds sugar
12 red bell peppers	1¼ teaspoons tumeric
12 green bell peppers	¼ cup mustard seed
12 onions	¼ cup celery seed
1 head cabbage	1 cup horse-radish
¼ cup of salt	1½ pints vinegar

Put vegetables through food chopper; add salt; let stand overnight. Pour a cup of cold water over them the next morning and drain thoroughly. Boil sugar, vinegar and spices for five minutes; add vegetables; cook 15 or 20 minutes; remove from fire; stir in horse-radish and bottle.

TOMATO CATSUP

2 pecks ripe tomatoes	1 tablespoon mustard
2 cups chopped onions	1 tablespoon celery seed
6 cups vinegar	2 tablespoons black pepper
1 cup horse-radish	1 teaspoon red pepper
4 bell peppers, chopped	4 tablespoons salt

Scald tomatoes; peel and slice; boil until thick and soft; strain through sieve. This should measure about one gallon of pulp. Add rest of ingredients. Boil until thick, stirring constantly to prevent burning. Bottle and seal while hot.

GREEN TOMATO PICKLE

1 gallon green tomatoes, sliced	4 cups sugar
1 gallon onions, sliced	1 teaspoon tumeric
1 cup chopped hot green peppers	2 tablespoons pickling spice, tied in cloth
2 quarts vinegar	bag
1 cup salt	

Put cup of salt over sliced vegetables; let stand for 3 hours; drain and put in a cloth sack to drip overnight. In the morning squeeze out excess juice; put in a large pan with vinegar, sugar and spices; cook half an hour after it reaches a boil.

WATERMELON PICKLE

1 large watermelon (rind only)	1 teaspoon whole cloves
1 cup light brown sugar	3 pieces mace
1 cup white sugar	2 cups vinegar
1 small box stick cinnamon	

Peel melon rind; cut in half inch thick pieces, in any desired shape. Cover with brine that is strong enough to float an egg; let stand several days. Drain; cover with hot water; add one teaspoon of powdered alum; let stand several days. At the end of that time, boil melon rind in the same water until tender. Drain; chill in refrigerator for several hours. Combine vinegar; sugar and spices which have been tied in a bag; cook to a syrup; add melon rind and cook until it is clear.

PRESERVES

BLACKBERRY JAM

Weigh berries. Set aside an equal amount of sugar. Put berries through meat grinder. Combine berry pulp and juice with sugar. Let come to a boil, then cook fifteen to twenty minutes. Put in jars while hot. Do not cook over two quarts at a time. You will find that grinding the berries is the secret of a perfect jam.

CHERRY PRESERVES

Stone cherries; cover with an equal amount of sugar; let stand a short while. Stir and heat slowly until it strikes a boil; let boil hard 20 minutes, skimming the top as you cook it. Cool overnight; put in jars; pour melted paraffin over top of the preserves.

DAMSON-ORANGE CONSERVE

5 pounds damsons	1 pound raisins
4 pounds sugar	1 pound shelled pecans, cut coarsely
3 oranges	

Remove seeds from damsons and cut in half. Slice oranges; remove seed; grind in coarse blade of food chopper. Save juice and use that also. Put all together, except nuts, and cook until thick; stir to keep from burning; add nuts a few minutes before taking from stove. Cool several hours; put in glasses and seal with paraffin.

DAMSON PRESERVES

Seed damsons if they are the freestone variety, otherwise skim the seeds off as you cook the preserves. To every 2 quarts of fruit add 1 cup of water; heat slowly until the juices seem to be extracted; add 2 quarts of sugar; boil 20 minutes, skimming off the seeds and foam. Pour into a bowl; let stand overnight. Put up in jars; seal with paraffin.

FRUIT CONSERVE

2 quarts peaches (peeled)	4 oranges
2 dozen blue plums (freestone), skins left on	¾ pound almonds
	8 cups sugar
1 pound grapes—white seedless	2 lemons

Slice oranges and lemons with skins left on; cut into little strips; cut grapes in half; dice peaches and plums; blanch almonds and slice. Save all juice that accumulates and add water to make 2 cups of liquid. Put on with sugar and cook slowly to a syrup; add fruit and cook until thick. Add almonds when done; put in glasses; cover with melted paraffin.

ORANGE MARMALADE

3 oranges	6 pints of water
1 lemon	4 pounds sugar

Slice oranges and lemons; remove seeds; put through the coarse blade of a meat grinder. Put the water over this; let stand 24 hours. The next morning boil 1 hour; skim constantly; stir in the sugar just before removing from the stove. Let stand another 24 hours; return to stove; boil slowly until thick. The syrup should congeal when tested by putting a little on ice, in a saucer. Put on while hot.

PEAR MARMALADE

1 peck of pears	2 lemons
6 oranges	Sugar

Peel and core pears; remove seed from oranges and lemons; slice but do not peel them. Run all fruit through a meat chopper. To each pint of pulp allow 1½ cups of sugar; boil until thick, heating slowly at first to dissolve sugar.

PEAR PRESERVES

4 pounds cooking pears	1 piece ginger
3 pounds sugar	1 piece mace
1 pint hot juice	

Cover fruit with water; boil until tender. Take out of water and put in sauce pan with the sugar, spices and 1 pint of the juice they were boiled in. Cook until clear.

STRAWBERRY PRESERVES

Two pounds washed capped berries, two pounds sugar. Heat very slowly until the sugar dissolves; do not use any water. When it strikes a boil, cook for 20 minutes; skim well; let stand overnight. By that time the syrup has thickened and the berries do not come to the top when put in jars. Seal with paraffin.

TUTTI-FRUITTI

1 quart fine grain alcohol or brandy	Sugar
1 quart strawberries	1 quart diced blue plums
1 quart diced peaches	1 quart raspberries, both black and red
1 quart diced pears	1 quart diced pineapple
1 quart seeded cherries	1 quart fresh diced apricots

Put alcohol in stone crock; add each fruit, with an equal amount of sugar, as it comes in season. Stir several times after each addition. In the fall add sliced almonds and pecans if desired. Any other fresh fruit can be added as it comes in season with the same amount of sugar. Serve on ice cream.

SIMPLE TUTTI-FRUITTI

A very good sauce for ice cream can be made by this recipe which is very easy. Pour rum over a variety of cut crystallized fruit, such as fruit cake mix of pineapple, cherries and citron. Pack fruit in a quart jar and fill up cracks with rum. Let soak several weeks. Use as necessary.

HOT AVOCADOS STUFFED

Cut pears in half, lengthwise, remove seed; fill with well-seasoned cooked sweetbreads, crab or chicken, in thick cream sauce; cover with Parmesan cheese and bits of butter; brown in slow oven.

CURRIED BRAINS AND EGGS

1 pound calf brains	Salt and red pepper to taste
4 hard-boiled eggs, riced	½ teaspoon curry powder or to taste
1½ cups milk	Some may prefer more curry
3 tablespoons flour	1 tablespoon water
4 tablespoons butter	

Parboil brains; plunge in cold water; drain when cold; break in small pieces. Make cream sauce, season highly; add curry powder smoothed with 1 tablespoon water; add eggs and brains; put in casserole or shells; cover with crumbs; bake until heated thoroughly. This will fill 5 shells or a small casserole. For large casserole to serve 8, use once and a half recipe. This is a delicious dish and everyone wants the recipe.

BRAIN CUTLETS

1 pound calf brains	1 tablespoon Worcestershire sauce
2 cups very thick "White Sauce"	Salt and red pepper to taste
2 egg yolks	

Beat egg yolks; add to thick white sauce; cook over low heat, in double boiler 10 minutes. Parboil brains; cool; chop; add to white sauce. When cold, put in flat dish in refrigerator until mixture is stiff; form into cutlets, dip in bread crumbs, then in beaten egg, and again in crumbs; fry in deep fat. Makes 8 cutlets.

BRAINS WITH MUSHROOM SAUCE

Scald and remove membrane from brains; boil in salted water, but do not overcook. Sprinkle with salt; roll in bread crumbs; dip in beaten egg; roll again in crumbs. Let dry a few minutes; fry. Serve with "Mushroom Sauce." Have each section of brains large enough to look like a large croquette.

BRUNSWICK STEW

1 chicken (4 pounds)	2 cups chopped potatoes
3 cups corn, cut from cob	1 stick butter
2 cups butter beans	Salt, red and black pepper
1 cup okra, cut in small pieces	3 strips breakfast bacon, cut fine
1 No. 2½ can tomatoes	Light bread to thicken
4 onions, sliced	

Disjoint chicken; cover with water; cook until it falls from bones; add tomatoes, bacon, seasoning and vegetables; cook until all are tender.

175

Cover; let simmer a short time, being careful not to burn. Thicken with a little fresh light bread, broken up and soaked in hot water. Add this as needed. It should be very thick. Remove as many chicken bones as possible. Serves 8 to 10.

CHICKEN A LA KING

6 cups diced cooked chicken	4 cups "Medium Cream Sauce"
2 cups mushrooms (buttons)	4 egg yolks
1 pimento, chopped	Salt, red pepper and sherry wine to
1 teaspoon onion juice	taste

Make cream sauce in double boiler; add mushrooms, chicken, onion juice and pimento. Just before serving; add beaten yolks; cook a few minutes. Do not let water under mixture boil at any time. Season to taste with salt, red pepper and sherry wine. Serves 10 to 12.

BARBECUED CHICKEN

Split two chickens (2 pounds each) up the back; flatten, rub chickens, inside and out, with salt and pepper; brown both sides lightly in butter; pour 2 cups of water and ½ cup vinegar around them; add a pod of red pepper and a sliced onion; cover; steam for ½ an hour; remove cover; put in slow oven. Begin basting the chickens with "Barbecue Sauce," and continue doing so every 10 or 15 minutes until they are very tender and brown. Be sure to baste often enough to keep the chickens from drying out. It will take from 1 to 2 hours, as it should cook slowly, but the result is well worth the trouble. Serves 4 to 8.

CHICKEN BREASTS IN MUSHROOM SAUCE

Parboil 6 whole chicken breasts in salted water with 2 carrots, 2 onions and a little parsley. Remove skin and small bones from inside of breasts; flatten breasts. Put ½ pound mushrooms and 1 onion through food chopper; cook in butter until tender, 5 or 10 minutes; add ½ pint sour cream, ½ pint sweet cream, salt and red pepper to taste. Put chicken in this, breasts down; cover; simmer until done, in slow oven. If necessary, more sweet cream can be added to the sauce. Serve a whole breast to a person, putting a little sauce over each portion. Canned mushrooms can be used if desired. Serves 6.

CHICKEN BREASTS IN MUSHROOM SOUP

3 large chicken breasts, cut in half	1 cup milk or cream
1 stick butter or margarine	1 can mushroom soup

Remove bones with sharp knife. Broil the chicken breasts in butter until well browned; remove from skillet; arrange side by side in a flat oblong casserole; pour a can of condensed mushroom soup into skillet where chicken has cooked; stir slowly until soup and butter are combined; thin with milk or cream; pour over chicken. Cover casserole; bake in a slow oven for about an hour or until chicken is very tender. Be sure to keep the cover on the entire time. Serves 6.

CHICKEN BREASTS WITH WHITE WINE

4 large chicken breasts, cut in half
¼ pound butter
6 shallots, chopped
½ pound fresh mushrooms, sliced

½ cup dry white wine
2 tablespoons chopped parsley
Salt
Pepper

Remove bones with sharp knife. Rub chicken with salt and peppeı, broil both sides until brown; add shallots; lower heat; cover skillet; cook slowly for half an hour. Five minutes before taking off, add choppea mushrooms; cook 5 or 6 minutes longer. Remove chicken to a platter; add wine and parsley to mixture in skillet; stir well, pour over chicken. Serves 8.

CHICKEN CHOP SUEY

1 5-pound hen, boiled aṛd cut in slivers
2 cups celery, cut in slanting slivers
2 medium onions, sliced thin
1 can mushrooms
1 can bean sprouts
1 cup water chestnuts

1 cup bamboo shoots
3 cups chicken broth
3 tablespoons brown sauce
2 tablespoons Worcestershire sauce
3½ tablespoons cornstarch
1 teaspoon salt (scant)
Red pepper to taste

Cook onions, celery and mushrooms in butter; add chicken broth and seasoning, thicken with cornstarch; add chicken and rest of ingredients. Serve with fried Chinese noodles. Serves 8 to 10.

CREAMED CHICKEN

3 cups boiled chicken
1½ cups "Medium White Sauce"
1 canned pimento, chopped

1 tablespoon Worcestershire sauce
Salt, red pepper to taste

Make cream sauce in double boiler; add other ingredients; keep over hot water until ready to use; do not let water boil. Serve in pastry cones. Wine can be added to sauce if desired. Serves 6.

CREAMED CHICKEN IN NOODLE RING

Make once recipe for "Creamed Chicken" and serve it in noodle ring made by following recipe:

1 package of noodles (8 ounces)
1 tablespoon butter
¼-pound package pimento cheese

4 tablespoons tomato catsup
2 tablespoons Worcestershire sauce
3 well-beaten eggs

Melt cheese and butter in double boiler; add tomato catsup, Worcestershire sauce, and beaten eggs; combine with boiled and drained noodles; put in well-buttered 8 inch mold; set in pan of hot water; bake at 350° until done (about ¾ hour). Serves 6 to 8.

CREOLE CHICKEN

1 hen, boiled and cut in rather large cubes
1 can tomatoes (2½ size can)
2 onions, ground
1 bell pepper, ground

4 ribs celery, chopped
1 can tomato paste
2 tablespoons Worcestershire sauce
1 tablespoon horse-radish
Salt and red pepper to taste

Cook onions, celery and pepper in butter until tender, but not brown; add tomatoes, seasoning, and tomato paste. When tomatoes have cooked to pieces, add chicken; simmer over low heat for a half hour. Serves 8.

CURRIED CHICKEN

4 or 5 cups chicken, cut in blocks
3 cups rich "Medium Cream Sauce"
1 tablespoon Worcestershire sauce
1 tablespoon curry powder (more or less)
2 tablespoons water

1 onion
2 apples
2 tomatoes
4 tablespoons butter
6 hard-boiled eggs, cut in blocks

Chop onion, apples and tomatoes; cook in butter until tender. Smooth curry powder with water until lumps disappear; add to cream sauce; add chicken, tomato mixture and eggs. Serve with boiled rice or Chinese noodles. Serves 10.

CHICKEN INDIAN-CURRY

Make recipe for "Curried Chicken"; put in large bowl, on buffet, next to large bowl of dry, fluffy rice. Around this have small bowls containing following condiments; grated Parmesan cheese, grated ham, grated toasted peanuts, grated cocoanut, raisins, crumbled, crisp breakfast bacon, Chinese noodles, crisp fried onion rings, English chutney and crumbled sardines (optional). Guests serve themselves to a large portion of rice, generously covered with curried chicken and a spoonful of each of the condiments. This is, of course, a complete meal. Will serve 12.

CHICKEN CURRY MEXICAN

Saw small cocoanuts in half, crosswise; wipe shells off carefully; scrape about half of the cocoanut meat away from each piece; add this cocoanut meat to the recipe for our "Chicken Curry"; fill each half of the cocoanut shells. Sprinkle grated cocoanut over tops and put in a pan containing a little hot water; cover; bake slowly at 300° for half hour.

CHICKEN HAWAIIAN

Use "Chicken Mexican" recipe, substituting "Creamed Chicken" for "Curried Chicken"; add 4 slices of canned pineapple, cut in small pieces, and the cocoanut to chicken. Bake in cocoanut shells.

CHICKEN CUTLETS

1 5-pound hen, boiled and chopped
3 cups milk
8 tablespoons flour
6 tablespoons butter

1 tablespoon lemon juice
1 tablespoon Worcestershire sauce
1 tablespoon onion juice
Salt and red pepper to taste

Make thick cream sauce; add seasoning and chopped chicken; cool, chill for several hours in refrigerator. When firm, form into cutlet shape; dip in crumbs and egg, again in crumbs, and fry in deep fat. Chicken can be ground if preferred. This should make 10 to 12 cutlets. Serve with mushroom or tartar sauce.

DEVILED CHICKEN

2 broiling chickens, cut in half
1 stick butter
1 teaspoon salt
1 tablespoon dry mustard

1 tablespoon paprika
2 tablespoons vinegar
1½ cups grated fresh bread crumbs

Mix dry ingredients to a paste with vinegar; add to butter that has been creamed until soft. Cook broilers, breasts down in skillet, in additional butter, for 10 minutes; remove from fire, rub chickens with creamed butter mixture; put in skillet, breasts up; sprinkle with bread crumbs; add a little water (about 1 cup) and cover skillet; put in oven; bake until chickens are very tender; basting occasionally; add more water if necessary. Remove top to brown crumbs; baste again before serving. Serves 4.

CHICKEN AND RICE CASSEROLE

1 5-pound hen, boiled and cut in cubes
1 cup raw rice
1 cup sliced almonds
3 cups "Medium Cream Sauce"

1 small can pimento, cut fine
Wash rice and boil for 15 minutes in some of the stock that the hen was boiled in.

Cut hen in cubes; put in layers with cooked rice, pimento, cream sauce and almonds. Put sauce on top; sprinkle with buttered crumbs. Have plenty of sauce so that the dish will not be too dry. Sauce can be made of 2 cups milk and 1 cup of chicken stock instead of all milk, if desired. Serves 10.

CHICKEN LIVERS, MUSHROOMS, WILD RICE RING

1 pound chicken livers
1 can (8-ounce) or 1 pound fresh mushrooms

1 onion
1 pound wild rice
Salt and red pepper to taste

Boil livers until nearly done; chop; sauté with mushrooms and onion in butter for 5 or 10 minutes; pour off excess grease. Boil wild rice until done (about half an hour); drain thoroughly; add other ingredients; season; mix together with 2 forks; put in greased mold; set in pan of hot water; bake at 350° for about half an hour. Turn out on platter; put ¼ inch wide strips of pimento across the ring at 2 or 3 inch intervals, spacing them evenly around the ring. Fill mold with peas or creamed celery; garnish with parsley. Serves 8.

CHICKEN RING

1 hen cooked until tender, and ground
1 pound sweetbreads, cooked and broken
   in pieces
1 8-ounce can mushrooms, sliced and
   broiled
2 cups milk

3 tablespoons flour
3 tablespoons butter
2 eggs, beaten separately
1 tablespoon Worcestershire sauce
½ cup bread crumbs

Make cream dressing of butter, flour, and milk; season well; add beaten yolks. Put half of the mushrooms with this; save the other half for sauce. Add crumbs and sweetbreads, fold in beaten whites; put in greased mold; cover top of mold with waxed paper; set in pan of hot water to bake for about half an hour at 350°. Make "Mushroom Sauce"; add a few sliced olives. Turn out chicken ring; put a bowl of mushroom sauce in the center of ring; garnish ring with "Pear Garnish for Meats" and parsley. Serves 10 to 12.

CHICKEN AND SHRIMP IN TOAST BOATS

1 large hen, boiled, cut in large cubes
2 cups cooked and cleaned shrimp
1 pound fresh or 8-ounce can mushrooms,
   broiled and sliced

¼ pound chipped beef, broiled
3 cups "Medium Cream Sauce"
Salt, red pepper and sherry wine to
taste

Frizzle chipped beef in butter until crisp; crumble, add to mushrooms that have also been broiled in butter; add other ingredients. Season to taste with sherry wine, salt and red pepper and serve in "Toast Boats" with paprika on top. Garnish with parsley. Serves 12.

CHICKEN PUDDING RING

1 5-pound hen, boiled and ground
2 cups milk
⅛ cup butter
4 tablespoons flour
1 tablespoon Worcestershire sauce

1 teaspoon parsley
1 cup pecans, chopped
1 teaspoon onion juice
4 eggs, beaten separately
Salt and red pepper to taste

Make cream sauce of milk, butter and flour; add seasoning and beaten yolks. Combine with chicken and nuts; fold in beaten whites; put in well-oiled ring mold; steam in a pan of hot water for about ¾ of an hour or until firm. Turn out on platter; garnish with parsley. Put a bowl of "Mushroom Sauce" in center of ring. Serves 8 to 10.

CHICKEN VALENCIANA

1 5-pound hen
1 bunch celery, chopped
1 tablespoon horse-radish
3 large onions, chopped
1 tablespoon Worcestershire sauce
1 bell pepper, chopped

1 can tomatoes, 2½ size
1 can tomato paste
1 can mushrooms
Salt and pepper to taste
1 can peas
1½ cups raw rice, boiled until tender

Boil hen; season stock highly and save. Cook onions, celery and pepper in butter until tender; add 2 cups chicken stock; cook 15 minutes; add tomatoes and tomato paste; simmer slowly until the tomatoes have cooked to pieces and you have a thick creole sauce. A half hour before serving, add chicken that has been shredded in rather large pieces, boiled rice, and mushrooms; add more chicken stock if necessary; let cook until rice has practically absorbed the moisture; add peas 10 minutes before serving. Put on platter; garnish with hard-boiled eggs cut in quarters, alternating with small Vienna sausages and parsley. Serves 12 to 14.

CHICKEN OR TURKEY DIVAN

1 package frozen broccoli (2-pound size)
3 cups rich cream sauce
Sliced chicken or turkey breast
4 tablespoons grated Parmesan cheese
½ cup sherry wine

Cook broccoli until tender in salted water; drain; spread out on large flat platter; cover with slices of turkey or chicken, drizzle sherry wine over surface and completely cover with the sauce to which 4 tablespoons of cheese have been added. Sprinkle surface with more Parmesan cheese and put in oven until brown and bubbling. Sharp yellow cheese can be substituted for Parmesan cheese if preferred. Serves 8.

CHICKEN SUPREME

1 hen, boiled and sliced
1 pound mushrooms or 8-ounce can
3 cups "Cheese Sauce"
1 tablespoon Worcestershire sauce
1 teaspoon onion juice
1 tablespoon grated horse-radish
1 teaspoon (or to taste), curry powder

Broil mushrooms in butter; slice hen; add seasoning to cheese sauce; put chicken on toast in layers with cheese sauce; let sauce be top layer; sprinkle with additional grated cheese; put under broiler flame until cheese melts. Use only breast of the chicken. A slice of baked ham can be put under the slice of chicken if desired. Serves 6 to 8.

CHICKEN WITH SAUSAGE BALLS

1 large hen, boiled and cut in large cubes
1 pound mushrooms or 8-ounce can
1 pound sausage
1 pint chicken broth
1 pint milk
6 tablespoons flour
6 tablespoons butter
Salt and red pepper to taste

Boil hen in salted water, with celery and onion to season, until tender; cut in cubes. Make small balls of sausage; fry; drain well. Sauté mushrooms in butter. Add all the above to sauce made of milk, broth, flour and butter, highly seasoned. Pass with fluffy, dry rice. Serves 12.

SMOTHERED CHICKEN

Spilt a 2½-pound chicken up the back; brown on both sides in butter; season well with salt and pepper; rub with butter creamed with a little flour; put a cup of milk and a cup of cream in skillet around chicken, add 1 rib of celery, 1 tablespoon chopped parsley, ½ of a bay leaf and a sliced onion. Cover tightly and simmer over low heat for an hour. Strain gravy; thicken if necessary.

Chicken can also be prepared by above recipe, put on rack in a covered roaster with 2 cups of boiling water in bottom of roaster, and steamed for an hour over low heat. Additional water can be added if necessary to make gravy. Season gravy with butter, salt and pepper. Remove top from roaster the last 15 minutes of cooking and put in oven for additional browning. Serves 3 or 4.

CHICKEN TETRAZINNI

1 large hen, boiled and cut in shreds
½ pound spaghetti
1 small bottle stuffed olives
½ pound sharp cheese, grated
1 cup broken pecans
1 pint chicken stock

1 can mushroom soup (condensed)
6 ribs celery, chopped
2 onions, chopped
3 tablespoons butter
1 tablespoon Worcestershire sauce
Salt and red pepper to taste

Cook celery and onion in butter until tender; add chicken stock and seasoning; simmer 15 minutes; add slowly to mushroom soup; add cheese. Boil and blanch spaghetti; add to the stock. Let stand an hour; add chicken and olives; put in long, flat casserole 9x15 inches. Sprinkle chopped pecans over top; put in oven until heated thoroughly. Serves 12 to 15.

CHICKEN TURNOVERS

1 hen, boiled and cut in cubes
6 tablespoons flour
6 tablespoons chicken fat or butter
3 cups chicken stock

2 egg yolks, beaten
1 tablespoon Worcestershire sauce
1 teaspoon onion juice
Salt and red pepper to taste

Make sauce of stock, fat, flour and seasoning; add chicken. Just before making turnovers, add beaten egg yolks; cook over hot water until thickened; add more seasoning if necessary. Make pastry; cut out circles, using saucer as a guide; put some of the chicken mixture on half of the circle; fold the other half over in turnover shape; seal the edges with tines of a fork and bake. Serve with "Mushroom Sauce" or with more of the chicken stock made into a thick gravy. Do not put too much of the sauce inside the turnover. If there seems to be excess sauce, drain it off to use in the gravy. Serves 8.

CHICKEN TERRAPIN

1 hen (5-pound) boiled
¾ cup chicken stock
¾ cup sherry wine

1¼ cups "Thick White Sauce"
2 hard-boiled eggs

Use all the chicken except the drumsticks. Dice chicken; cover with ¾ cup of seasoned stock and simmer 5 or 10 minutes. Add sherry, gradually to "White Sauce"; fold in chicken and riced yolks of eggs; cook in double boiler 10 minutes. Serve in "Toast Boats," garnish with riced whites and parsley.

BAKED HAM

This recipe does not apply to tenderized ham, which should be cooked according to directions on the ham.

A country ham should be washed, scraped and put to soak overnight. The next morning, put in large kettle with several ribs of celery, 2 onions, a handful of parsley, a few cloves and blades of mace and a cup of sugar;

add water to cover the ham. Bring to a boil; reduce heat; simmer until tender and the bone is loosened. Allow 25 minutes a pound at least for this simmering. Remove from heat; when cool enough to handle, pull off skin; cover top of ham with mixture of cup and a half brown sugar, half cup ground dry bread crumbs, and 2 teaspoons dry mustard, moistened with a little ham fat. Put in oven with a cup or two of ginger ale or cider around it; bake at 400° for about ½ to ¾ hour, basting with the liquid occasionally. If a glazed ham is preferred, do not use crumb mixture, but cover ham with as much jelly as you can spread on it. It will melt and run off into the liquid; continue putting it back and basting it. You will have a beautiful glaze when ham is done. Cover with waxed paper; put in refrigerator. A cold ham slices to much better advantage than a hot one does. Slice in thin slices, being careful to always cut across grain of meat; put a tablespoonful of "Creole Crumbs" over each slice of ham. Garnish with parsley. A 15-pound ham should serve 30.

CREOLE CRUMBS OR STUFFING FOR HAM

2 cups dry bread crumbs	1 tablespoon celery seed
2 cups India Relish	½ teaspoon black pepper
2 cups brown sugar	1 teaspoon dry mustard

Bind together with enough cream to make a fairly dry mixture. Sprinkle these crumbs on individual slices of baked ham, when ready to serve garnish with parsley. Can also be used as stuffing for boned, baked ham; however, I like to put the crumbs on each slice as served.

Baked Ham (2)

This method of baking a ham is preferred by many, as it does not boil away so much of the substance of the ham. If followed carefully, this recipe will always be successful. Completely cover a large ham with hot water (use a lard stand with top on it for this). Put can on stove. When it begins to boil the steam will come from under the top and you should begin to time the boiling from that minute. Let boil for only 20 minutes longer. Take from fire; put can with top still on it in a large tub lined heavily with newspaper. Turn the paper up around can; cover entirely with heavy blanket; leave for 24 hours; take ham out and bone it; remove skin; wrap ham as tightly as possible in cloth; tie it up. When cool, store in icebox (still wrapped) overnight. The next day unwrap it; cover top with mixture of crumbs, brown sugar, black pepper and mustard; run in oven for 5 minutes; cool, store again in icebox until ready to slice.

HAM A LA KING

3 cups cooked ham, diced	1 onion, chopped
3 hard-boiled eggs, diced	2 ribs celery, chopped
1 pint white sauce (medium)	2 tablespoons butter
1 green pepper, chopped	

Cook onion, celery and pepper in butter until tender; add to cream sauce; combine with ham and eggs. Serve on toast or pastry. Serves 6 to 8.

HAM CROQUETTES

2 cups ground ham
1 cup mashed Irish potatoes
1 tablespoon butter

2 beaten eggs
1 teaspoon grated onion
Salt and red pepper to taste

Mix together; chill; shape into croquettes; roll in crumbs, then in egg, again in crumbs; fry in deep fat. Makes 8 large croquettes.

SPICE ROUND—HOW TO COOK

Spice round, so far as I know, originated (in this country) in Nashville, Tennessee. The recipe was brought over from the old country by an ancestor of a man who now makes it. It is a traditional Christmas meat and is served sliced, cold. It can be bought already cooked in Nashville, but I usually buy the uncooked spice round and boil it myself in the following manner: Soak round in cold water 1 hour; tie in a cloth bag; cover with cold water; add cup of sugar; let come to a boil; reduce heat; simmer 15 minutes for each pound of meat, add water to cover as needed. Let cool in water it is cooked in, and, although it looks greasy, leave the bag around the meat until ready to slice. Keep in the refrigerator. When ready to serve it, cut a large wedge from the round; turn it on the side; slice thin slices with a very sharp knife. The meat is a beautiful deep pink color and each slice is dotted with small pieces of white fat surrounded by black spices. Care should be taken to slice it correctly. It is usually used as an interesting substitute for baked ham. Be sure to slice it very thin.

BAKED CANADIAN BACON

1 piece Canadian bacon, 3 pounds
¾ cup brown sugar

¾ teaspoon dry mustard
¾ cup ginger ale or pineapple juice

Spread seasoning over bacon; bake an hour; baste occasionally with juice. This is nice to serve sliced, in hot biscuits, at informal buffet suppers.

HAWAIIAN BAKED HAM

Have 2 center slices of ham cut ¾ inches thick. Rub with a mixture of 1 tablespoon dry mustard, ½ teaspoon black pepper and 4 tablespoons brown sugar. Cover with canned pineapple, cut in small pieces. Pour pineapple juice around ham; bake in covered vessel 350° for an hour and a half. Remove cover, to brown, the last 15 minutes. Baste occasionally.

STUFFED LAMB CHOPS

8 lamb chops, double thickness
1 cup mushrooms, ground
½ onion

1 teaspoon chopped parsley
Salt and black pepper to taste
1 cup ground bread crumbs, toasted

Have butcher cut double lamb chops; remove 1 of the bones, and split chop to bone to allow a space for stuffing. Sauté mushrooms and onions in butter until tender; season; add parsley and bread crumbs. This should be the right consistency for a stuffing, but if it should need

184

more liquid to bind it together, use a little cream. Stuff chops; skewer together with toothpicks; broil both sides until brown; put in oven at 350° for about 20 minutes in covered skillet. These are nice to use as a meat for a party breakfast. Serves 8.

BROILED SWEETBREADS WITH TOMATO SAUCE

3 pairs sweetbreads	2 tablespoons chopped onion
1 cup tomato puree	3 tablespoons lemon juice
3 eggs (yolks)	Salt and red pepper to taste
2 tablespoons chopped bell peppers	3 tablespoons butter

Soak, clean and parboil sweetbreads 20 minutes; put in cold water for 10 minutes; drain; brown in butter. Make sauce by cooking onion and pepper in 3 tablespoons butter until tender; add tomato puree, lemon juice and well-beaten egg yolks; season. Cook until thick. Serve sweetbreads on toast points or thin slices of ham; cover with sauce. Serves 6.

SWEETBREADS—CREAMED

2 pairs sweetbreads	2 tablespoons sherry
2 cups "Medium Cream Sauce"	

Soak sweetbreads in cold water for 20 minutes; drain; place in saucepan with salted water to cover them. Add juice of 1 lemon; boil for 20 minutes. When done, plunge sweetbreads in cold water to harden; remove skin and membrane; break in small pieces; combine with cream sauce; add sherry wine. Serves 6 to 8.

SWEETBREADS, BACON AND PINEAPPLE

Parboil sweetbreads, which have been soaked in acidulated water, for 20 minutes; plunge in cold water to harden; drain; break into sections about 3 inches in diameter; dip in ground bread crumbs; egg, and again in crumbs; fry in deep fat. Broil large slices of lean Canadian bacon in butter; grill large slices of canned pineapple in butter; top pineapple with bacon; place the sweetbreads on top of the bacon. Garnish each serving with parsley and half a slice of lemon. A pound of sweetbreads should serve 4 or 5.

SWEETBREAD CASSEROLE

3 cups cooked diced sweetbreads	2 tablespoons butter
¼ pound dried chipped beef	1 pint "Medium Cream Sauce"
1 cup mushrooms	

Sauté mushrooms in butter; add chipped beef which has been dusted with flour; cook 5 minutes. Add more butter if necessary. Pour cream sauce into skillet with beef and mushrooms; add the sweetbreads. If the mixture seems too dry, add a little cream. Put in casserole; cover with buttered crumbs; bake until crumbs are brown. Serves 8 to 10.

SWEETBREADS IN CUCUMBER BOATS

6 unpeeled cucumbers, 5 inches in length
1 onion, chopped
   Salt and red pepper to taste
2 pairs sweetbreads

3 ribs celery, chopped
2 tablespoons butter
1 pint "Thick Cream Sauce"

Scoop out cucumbers to make boat-shaped containers; soak and boil sweetbreads; plunge in cold water; drain; break in pieces. Cook the scooped out part of cucumbers with onion and celery in a little salted water; drain thoroughly; add sauce; combine with sweetbreads. Put in the cucumber boats that have been steamed lightly; cover with crumbs and bits of butter; bake until brown on top. Serves 6.

SWEETBREAD CUTLETS

1 pound sweetbreads
1 cup finely chopped chicken (white meat)
2 cups thick cream sauce

½ onion, grated
2 teaspoons chopped parsley
   Salt and red pepper to taste

Soak sweetbreads in cold salted water; cook in acidulated water for 20 minutes; blanch in cold water when done. Remove; chop; add to white sauce with chicken and seasoning; cool and chill in refrigerator for several hours. Form into cutlets, dip in bread crumbs, then in beaten egg and again in crumbs; fry in deep fat. Serve garnished with parsley and lemon wedges. Makes about 10 cutlets.

SWEETBREADS, MUSHROOMS AND CHICKEN

1 pound sweetbreads
1½ cups chopped chicken breasts
1 cup mushrooms
2 beaten eggs

2 cups highly seasoned, thick white sauce
   Salt and red pepper to taste
½ cup sherry wine, or to taste

Soak sweetbreads in salted, cold water; remove membrane; boil in acidulated water for 20 minutes; drop in cold water; remove; cut in small pieces. Sauté mushrooms in butter; add to cream sauce with sweetbreads and chicken; season; add well-beaten eggs. Put in casserole; cover with buttered bread crumbs; put in moderate oven; cook until brown. This can be served in pastry cases if preferred. Serves 8.

BAKED STUFFED SQUAB OR CORNISH HENS

Stuff 6 squabs; rub breasts with a mixture of butter, pepper and salt, dust with flour; brown in oven; pour a little water around them; add a stick of butter, juice of 2 oranges and the grated rind. Cover vessel; bake slowly inside oven, basting often with liquid in pan.

STUFFING No. 1: 4 cups of bread crumbs, lightly browned, ½ cup seeded raisins, 3 tablespoons chopped onions, 2 tablespoons butter, 3 tablespoons chopped celery, salt and pepper to taste.

STUFFING No. 2: 2 cups cooked wild rice, 1 tablespoon minced onion, 1 cup chopped mushrooms, giblets of the 6 squabs, boiled and chopped, salt and pepper. Fry giblets slowly in butter with onions and mushrooms; add to rice; add melted butter as needed.

ITALIAN SPAGHETTI

1 pound package spaghetti
1 pound round steak, ground
1 large can tomatoes, 2½ size
1 can tomato paste
2 large onions, chopped fine
1 small bunch celery, chopped
2 bell peppers, chopped

1 tablespoon Worcestershire sauce
1 tablespoon horse-radish
6 ounces Parmesan cheese
1 pod garlic
1 bay leaf.
1 cup dried mushrooms

Soak dried mushrooms for several hours in water to cover; take out; chop fine. Save water for future use. Make a creole sauce by cooking onions, celery and pepper in butter until tender; add tomatoes and tomato paste; simmer; add mushrooms and water they were soaked in which will look dark. Cook steak until brown in butter; add to the creole; season. Boil spaghetti in salt water until tender; blanch in cold water; drain; add to creole sauce; let heat and serve with grated Parmesan cheese. The dried mushrooms make this especially delicious. Serves 10.

SWEDISH MEAT BALLS

½ pound beef (from loin)
¼ pound veal
¼ pound pork
¾ cup finely ground crumbs
½ cup cream
½ cup bouillon
  Yolk of 1 egg

2 tablespoons finely chopped Bermuda
  onion
⅔ tablespoon salt
⅛ teaspoon black pepper
¾ tablespoon butter
1 pinch allspice

Grind meat together several times. Soak bread crumbs in cream and bouillon. Fry onions in butter until tender, but not brown; add to ground meat with seasoning, soaked bread crumbs, and egg yolk; make into small balls; fry. Remove balls; make gravy of some of the fat with a little flour added; brown flour; add water; pour over balls. Serve with a border of French fried onions. Serves 6.

BEEF STROGANOFF

2 pounds beef tenderloin
1 pound fresh mushrooms or 8-ounce can
2 small onions, grated

½ pint sour cream
3 tablespoons tomato paste
Salt and pepper to taste

Have butcher cut tenderloin in finger-length strips and flatten. Sauté mushrooms and onion in butter; add tomato paste, seasoning and sour cream. Sauté beef in 2 tablespoons butter until brown, add to sauce and simmer for 15 or 20 minutes. Do not let mixture boil. Serve with fluffy rice. Serves 4 to 6.

BAKED TURKEY

Have butcher draw turkey for you; hold it under running water to wash it out thoroughly, before you begin to stuff it. Cut neck off close to body; leave a flap of neck skin; remove the windpipe and crop; rub inside of turkey well with salt. After it has been thoroughly washed and dried, fill body and neck cavity loosely with "Southern Style Turkey Stuffing"; close opening by inserting skewers or toothpicks and crisscross a cord across them. Turn neck flap over the back; fasten it with a skewer. Fold wings across back; tie ends of legs together with cord. Rub turkey with Wesson oil; put in open roaster. Cover the body and legs well with a cloth dipped in Wesson oil; roast in a slow oven at 300° until tender. Allow 25 minutes per pound for a small turkey and 20 minutes per pound for a large one. Baste turkey every half hour with a mixture of hot water, melted butter and a little salt and paprika. Remove cloth a short while before serving, but continue to baste turkey. While turkey is cooking, boil liver, gizzard and neck until tender in about a quart of water; remove liver and gizzard; chop fine. Strain drippings from turkey and remove excess fat; add the stock from cooking giblets and enough water to make 6 cupfuls. Blend about ¾ cup of flour with some of the fat; slowly add the liquid to this; season with salt, red pepper and a little Kitchen Bouquet. Add giblets; cook until right consistency.

SOUTHERN STYLE TURKEY STUFFING

4 cups corn meal	2 eggs
4 teaspoons baking powder	3 cups buttermilk
½ teaspoon soda	2 teaspoons salt

Make egg bread of above ingredients; bake in quick oven until light brown; when cool, crumble thoroughly and add to it:

1½ cups minced celery	1 teaspoon salt
1 tablespoon chopped parsley	1 teaspoon black pepper
2 cups dry bread crumbs, grated	Poultry seasoning to taste

Bind together with 8 tablespoons melted butter and a little turkey broth made by boiling the neck in a little salted water. Chestnuts or oysters can be added to dressing if desired.

Baked Turkey (2)

A new method of baking turkey is to completely incase the fowl in aluminum foil. Prepare the stuffed turkey as described in method No. 1, brush well with melted fat; wrap it securely in a length of wide aluminum freezer foil or fold 2 pieces of the narrow width foil together and seal edges over turkey. Place in an open roaster on rack in oven, preheated to 400°. Cook small turkeys 18 to 20 minutes per pound and larger ones 15 minutes per pound. During the last 45 minutes of baking, remove foil or fold it back, so that juices can run into the roaster to be used for gravy. Baste turkey during this period with melted fat to make it brown evenly. No basting is done at any other time. I usually allow a little extra time in cooking a turkey to be sure it is perfectly tender. Turkeys slice to better advantage when cold, so it is wise to cook them a day ahead of time when a large crowd is to be served. They can be sliced in uniform slices, white and dark meat put in separate pans, and reheated with a little turkey broth poured over them. The pans should be covered while the turkey is heating. When ready to serve, put the dark meat in the center of a large silver tray, surrounded with large slices of white meat. Put individual pats of turkey dressing on outer edge of the platter. Garnish with parsley. Pass gravy. If plates are to be served from the pantry, cover a pat of dressing with some dark meat and put a large slice of white meat on top. Pour gravy over surface. Garnish with parsley and a slice of orange covered with cranberry sauce.

HALF TURKEY ROASTED

Rub the turkey half inside with salt; brush the outside with melted butter or Wesson oil; dip a cloth in Wesson oil and water combined; put over turkey. Baste with this mixture several times while turkey cooks, so that cloth is never entirely dry. Roast at 325° until tender, half an hour to each pound. When turkey is half done; put dressing on a piece of aluminum foil or waxed paper slightly larger than the turkey; pile dressing to the center; cover with the turkey. Continue cooking. Remove cloth to brown. Make dressing and gravy by recipe for whole turkey, using half the amount.

TURKEY OR CHICKEN HASH

Boil fowl until tender with 2 onions, a bunch of celery, salt and pepper. Reserve stock and strain, skimming off some of the excess fat. When turkey is cool, cut into small squares, using all of the turkey except the drum sticks. Make hash, using the stock that turkey was cooked in for gravy. Thicken with flour; season with salt, pepper and butter. A few drops of kitchen bouquet will keep the gravy from looking too white, be sure to add it slowly as only a very little will be needed.

Have gravy thick so that hash can be served in center of large or individual grits or rice rings.

A 20 pound turkey will serve 35 people. This recipe is used for a party breakfast; hash for home use can be made of left-over baked turkey.

TURKEY BALLS

4 cups ground cooked turkey
2 cups "Thick White Sauce"
2 tablespoons chopped parsley
½ onion, grated
Salt and red pepper to taste

Add turkey to cream sauce and seasonings; chill mixture; form into large balls (instead of cutlets); roll in crumbs; dip in slightly beaten egg; roll in crumbs again and fry, as you would cutlets. Drain on brown paper to absorb grease. Serve on round pats of baked turkey dressing with "Mushroom Sauce," using turkey stock as liquid for sauce. This is economical way to serve turkey as a 15 pound turkey will make 30 turkey balls.

WILD DUCKS

Wild ducks should be hand picked; never scalded. Draw them; wipe inside and out with wet towel (washing destroys the flavor); rub inside and out with salt and pepper; put a turnip and a lump of butter inside each duck; pin a strip of breakfast bacon across top of duck with toothpick. Put in open roaster with 2 cups of water in bottom; bake 45 minutes at 400°; baste frequently with a mixture of orange juice, melted butter and water. The turnip absorbs some of the wild taste of the duck. If preferred, the duck can be stuffed with wild rice and the turnip omitted. Make gravy of drippings in pan. Do not let ducks cook long enough to be dry.

BROILED QUAIL OR DOVES

Rub birds with salt and pepper; split down backs and flatten out. Put a large slice of butter in an iron skillet; let brown; add birds, breasts down; put a flat tin top over birds and weight down so the birds will be perfectly flat. (I use an old flatiron as a weight.) Let birds brown nicely; add about a cup of water; cover; cook over very low heat until they are tender; add more water if necessary. Put birds on toast; if gravy has cooked away, add more water, butter and seasoning. Scrape any dry crust from the skillet; stir into gravy and pour over birds. Serve with orange slices topped with plum jelly.

ROASTED QUAIL

Rub birds, inside and out, with butter, salt and pepper. Stuff them with a mixture of seasoned, cooked, wild rice to which a few plumped raisins have been added. Wrap each bird in aluminum foil; bake at 400° for 20 minutes. Fold back foil, baste with melted butter and bake 10 or 15 minutes or until brown and tender. Baste once or twice during the browning period. Serve on buttered toast garnished with orange slices. Put a spoonful of cherry pickle or jelly on each slice.

ROASTED WILD GOOSE

A wild goose is cooked very much like a tame one; in both cases a young goose makes a finer dish. Rub goose inside and out with salt and pepper; steam an hour with celery and onion inside; let cool slightly so it can be handled. Remove celery and onion; stuff with "apple and potato" stuffing. Rub breast of goose with Wesson oil; cover bottom of roaster with a sprinkling of flour. Put goose in roaster; cook in hot oven until flour has browned and the goose has begun to brown; baste with a mixture of butter, water, salt and pepper; lower heat; cover breast with a cloth saturated in Wesson oil; baste through cloth every 15 minutes. When the goose is tender, remove cloth; continue to baste until brown. It will take 3 to 4 hours to cook an average sized goose. Make gravy from water in which goose was steamed; skim off excess fat. The stuffing can be one usually used for turkey, but the following dressing is especially suitable for roast goose:

APPLE AND SWEET POTATO STUFFING: 6 apples, peeled, cored and sliced; 4 ribs of celery, cut small; 4 onions peeled and sliced. Combine ingredients; cover with water; cook until tender; drain; mash thoroughly; add to cup and a half of sweet potatoes (mashed). Season with a little poultry seasoning, salt, pepper and melted butter; add 2 beaten egg yolk and ½ cup chopped pecans. The water that has been used to steam the goose can be used as liquid to baste it and also as part of the gravy. Skim off excess fat when making the gravy; thicken with more flour if necessary. Serve the goose with thick apple sauce.

ROASTED WILD TURKEY

Prepare wild turkey as you would a domestic fowl. Stuff with any desired dressing. Wild rice stuffing (No. 2) which is used for "Baked Stuffed Squab" is especially nice for this. "Southern Stuffing," with a pint of oysters (cut in pieces) added, can also be used. Roast by either method described for "Baked Turkey." Be sure to baste carefully.

PASTRY ☆

PASTRY AND PIE CRUSTS

PASTRY

3 cups flour
1 cup shortening

¾ cup ice water
1 pinch salt

Cut shortening into flour with a pastry blender. Half lard and half butter is a good combination for the shortening. Add water very slowly; do not knead pastry. Chill.

HOT WATER PASTRY

1 cup Snowdrift
½ cup boiling water

1 large pinch salt
3 cups flour

Cream lard; add boiling water; whip thoroughly; combine flour and salt; work into the lard. Chill before using. This is a very simple recipe and exceptionally good.

FLAKE PASTRY

2 sticks butter
2 tablespoons lard
4 cups flour

1 teaspoon salt
Ice water

Cream butter well; add lard; chill several hours. Sift salt and flour; mix half of the butter into a dough with flour and ice water; roll to half inch thickness; spread with remaining butter, fold over; roll out, repeat this several times. Chill before using.

PHILADELPHIA CHEESE PASTRY

1 3-ounce package Philadelphia cheese
¼ pound butter

1 cup flour
¼ teaspoon salt

Melt butter; sift salt with flour; rub the cheese into the butter; add the flour. Chill before using. Nice to use as pastry for tiny cherry preserve turn-overs.

ALMOND PASTRY

Add ½ cup of coarsely ground almonds to recipe for "Pastry." This is especially nice to use for pastry cornucopias; serve creamed sweetbreads, ham, or chicken in them.

CHEESE PASTRY
1 cup flour   ½ pound grated cheddar cheese
½ cup butter

Cream butter; work grated cheese and flour into it. Chill before using. This is delicious used for little mincemeat (bite-size) turn-overs.

CHICKEN FAT PASTRY
1½ cups flour   ½ teaspoon salt
½ cup chilled chicken fat   4 tablespoons milk

Cut chicken fat into flour and salt; add milk to combine. Chill well before using. Roll out; line pie pan; brush over raw pastry with well-beaten white of egg before filling.

GRAHAM CRACKER PIE CRUST
1½ cups graham cracker crumbs   ⅛ cup powdered sugar
¼ cup butter

Cream butter and sugar; add cracker crumbs; pat into pie pan. This is nice to use for uncooked pies.

PASTRY CORNUCOPIAS
Make pastry; roll out in 10 inch circles; cut each circle in 4 sections; roll each section around little cornucopias made of heavy paper; trim off excess pastry to use again. Bake on the paper foundations; slip them off when they are done. Use a sheet of heavy typewriter paper, folded in half crosswise, to make the cornucopia forms; fold them in shape; pin together; trim off edges. Serve creamed chicken, sweetbreads or sea food in pastries.

VANILLA OR GINGER WAFER PIE CRUST
2 cups vanilla wafer crumbs   ¼ cup sugar
½ cup butter, melted

Add sugar to wafer crumbs; combine with melted butter; pat into pie pan; chill for half hour. Ginger wafer crumbs can be substituted for vanilla wafer crumbs if desired.

TINY CHEESE MINCEMEAT TURNOVERS
½ pound Cheddar cheese   ½ cup butter
1 cup flour

Make "Cheese Pastry" by grating cheese, and working it with butter and flour. Roll thin; cut in small circles; put mincemeat, strongly flavored with wine, on half of the circle; fold over into turnovers; press edges together with tines of a silver fork; bake; serve hot. These can be made a day ahead and reheated, when needed. Nice for morning coffees.

CHEESE STRAWS
1 pound cheese, grated   2 cups flour
1 stick butter   1 large pinch red pepper

Cream butter; add cheese; cream together by hand; add flour gradually.

Roll up; put in cooky press; grind out in 3 inch lengths; cut off. Bake in slightly greased pan 5 or 10 minutes. These can be ground out of the cooky press with a circular motion into cheese wheels if preferred. They can also be cut with a pastry wheel into little squares or strips.

PASTRY TID-BITS

Make tiny pastry shells by fitting rounds of pastry into very small muffin pans; bake; fill with cherry preserves, lemon or rum fillings; topped with whipped cream. To be served as a sweet at morning coffee or afternoon tea.

LEMON OR RUM FILLING: Combine 3 eggs beaten together, ½ cup butter, 1 cup sugar and 1 tablespoon cornstarch; cook 5 minutes in double boiler; add ½ cup lemon juice or ¼ cup rum; cook 3 minutes more.

CALLA LILY PASTRIES

Make "Philadelphia Cheese Pastry"; cut in circles; fold around small cones in calla lily shape. Bake; put in a bit of orange marmalade in center of each one. These can be pinched into shape on cooky sheet, if preferred.

ROQUEFORT CHEESE PASTRIES

Make "Philadelphia Cheese Pastry"; cut in small rounds and bake. Put 2 of these together with a bit of creamed "Roquefort Spread"; reheat. Serve hot.

CHEESE WAFERS

½ pound butter   1 cup flour
½ pound Cheddar cheese, grated

Cream butter and grated cheese together; add flour; form into roll and wrap in waxed paper; chill several hours; cut very thin; bake with ½ pecan on top of each. These can also be made into slightly flattened balls, topped with a pecan half, and baked.

PIES

BUTTERSOTCH PIE

3 eggs   ½ cup pecans
3 tablespoons flour   1 cup milk
1 cup brown sugar   1 pinch salt
3 tablespoons water   ½ teaspoon vanilla
2 tablespoons butter

Beat egg yolks; add sugar and flour; put in double boiler with rest of ingredients, except nuts and butter. Cook until thick; add butter and nuts. Put in baked crust; cover with meringue made of whites of eggs, ½ teaspoon of cream of tartar and 6 tablespoons sugar.

CHESS PIES

9 egg yolks
2½ cups sugar
1 tablespoon flour
1 cup butter

1 pinch salt
1 teaspoon grated nutmeg
⅔ cup milk
1 teaspoon vanilla

Cream butter and sugar; add beaten eggs, flour, flavoring and milk. Bake in pastry lined, individual, pie pans very slowly. Makes 12. These are delicious. The yokes left from angel food cake can be used to good advantage for these pies.

CHESS PIE WITH JELLY

4 eggs—yolks only
1 cup butter

2 cups sugar
½ glass jelly (plum or crab apple best)

Cream butter and sugar; add beaten eggs; chop jelly into small pieces and add. Bake a pastry shell slightly; pour in filling. Bake slowly. This is delicious.

JULIENNE CHESS PIE

1½ cups sugar
6 egg yolks
½ cup butter
1 cup citron, pineapple and cherries
mixed

4 tablespoons sherry wine
2 teaspoon powdered cinnamon
½ teaspoon powdered nutmeg

Soak fruit and spices in wine while making the pie. Cream butter; add sugar and yolks that have been well beaten; add fruit and wine. Bake in uncovered pastry shell in slow oven.

CHOCOLATE PIE

3 eggs
1 cup sugar
1½ cups milk
2 cups grated cocoanut

2 squares Baker's chocolate
2 tablespoons flour
1 teaspoon vanilla

Make custard of egg yolks beaten well with sugar, flour, butter and hot milk; cook in double boiler until very thick. Melt chocolate and add to custard. Remove from heat, beat well, chill. Pour in baked pastry shell; cover with meringue made of whites of 3 eggs beaten stiff with ½ teaspoon cream of tartar and 6 tablespoons sugar. Bake in slow oven until meringue is firm.

COCOANUT PIE

2 cups milk
2 cups grated cocoanut
½ cup sugar

1 tablespoon butter
3 eggs

Beat yolks; add butter and sugar creamed together, cocoanut and milk. Pour in pastry shell that has been brushed with melted butter and dusted with flour. Bake. Cover with meringue made of 3 egg whites, ½ teaspoon cream of tartar and 6 tablespoons sugar. Bake until light brown. Canned, moist cocoanut can be substituted if fresh is not available.

195

MINCEMEAT PIE

2 cups mincemeat   ¼ sherry wine or whiskey

Soak mincemeat in wine for 2 hours. Line pie pan with pastry; fill with mincemeat; cover top of pie with latticed strips of pastry; bake at 450° for 20 to 30 minutes. Serve with cheese, hard sauce or a ball of eggnog ice cream on each portion. "Cheese Pastry" is also good to use with mincemeat pies.

MINCEMEAT AND CHEESE CHRISTMAS TREES

Make these like cheese pastry turn-overs only cut the pastry in the shape of a little tree. Cover with mincemeat and then with another pastry tree. Seal edges with the tines of a fork; cut three little slanting slashes on the top of either side of each tree, using a very sharp knife. Bake until golden brown. Little tree shaped cookie cutters are available in 10 cent stores.

PECAN PIE

1 cup sugar	2 tablespoons butter
½ cup Karo syrup	¼ teaspoon nutmeg
2 eggs, beaten together	½ cup pecans
½ teaspoon vanilla	

Cream butter and sugar; add beaten eggs and Karo syrup; flavor. Pour in unbaked pastry shell; bake in slow oven. When half done cover top with pecan halves.

RAISIN PIE

2 cups sugar	3 teaspoons vinegar
½ cup butter	4 eggs
1 cup chopped pecans	1 teaspoon powdered nutmeg
1 cup chopped raisins	½ teaspoon powdered cinnamon

Cream butter and sugar; add spice, beaten yolks, vinegar, pecans and raisins, add beaten whites last. Bake in pastry crust in very slow oven.

SHARKY CUSTARD

1 cup sugar	5 eggs
½ cup butter	1 cup blackberry jam
1 cup buttermilk	

Make custard of beaten yolks, sugar and milk in double boiler; cook until thick; add butter and jam; cool; pour in pastry shells and cook slowly until done. Cover with meringue made of egg whites, ½ teaspoon cream of tartar and 10 tablespoons sugar; brown lightly. Cherry preserves can be used instead of jam if preferred.

196

FRUIT PIES

APPLE PIE

6 apples, cored and sliced thin
¾ cup sugar
½ cup water

¼ teaspoon grated nutmeg
¼ teaspoon cinnamon
2 tablespoons butter

Cook apples, sugar and water over moderate heat for half hour; add butter and spices; cook 3 minutes; put in unbaked pastry shell that has been brushed with unbeaten egg white. Put criss cross pastry over top; bake until crust is brown. 350°.

Apple Pie (2)

4 grated Winesap apples
¼ cup orange juice
¼ cup lemon juice

1 teaspoon cornstarch
½ cup sugar
2 teaspoons melted butter

Make "Chicken Fat Pastry"; line pan; cover raw pastry with the beaten white of 1 egg; sprinkle a little sugar over the egg white before putting in filling. Combine ingredients; put in pastry shell; cover filling with pastry strips; sprinkle a little sugar over top of pie. Bake in hot oven 10 minutes; reduce heat; bake at 350° twenty minutes.

BANANA PIE

2 egg whites
1 cup sugar
¼ teaspoon cream of tartar

3 ripe bananas
½ teaspoon almond extract
1 teaspoon lemon juice

Make stiff meringue of the first 3 ingredients; add flavoring and bananas which have been thoroughly mashed through a sieve. Bake in pastry shell, in slow oven, about 15 to 20 minutes. Chill. When ready to serve spread whipped cream over the top.

BLACKBERRY PIE

1 quart blackberries
1 cup sugar

¼ cup flour
1 tablespoon butter

Mix sugar with berries; put in an unbaked pastry shell that has been brushed with unbeaten egg white. Sift flour over top of berries, put bits of butter over flour. Cover with top crust. Bake 10 minutes in a hot oven; reduce heat; cook at 350° for 25 to 30 minutes.

BLUEBERRY PIE

1 quart blueberries
1½ cups sugar
2 tablespoons flour

2 tablespoons butter
¼ cup water

Brush unbaked pastry shell with unbeaten egg white; fill with 3 cups of the berries mixed with a cup of sugar; sprinkle 2 tablespoons flour over berries, dot butter over top; cover with top crust; slit in several places.

197

Bake in hot oven for ten minutes; reduce heat; bake at 350° for half hour. Cook the other cup of berries, half cup of sugar and ¼ cup of water to a syrup; serve with pie; thicken it slightly with flour if too juicy.

CHERRY PIE

1 quart cherries
¾ cup sugar

2 tablespoons flour
2 tablespoons butter

Pit cherries, saving all juice; cover with sugar; let stand 1 hour; stir and drain off juice; smooth flour in juice; cook until thick; add butter. Put cherries in unbaked pastry shell, brushed with unbeaten egg white; pour thickened juice over cherries; put pastry on top. Bake in hot oven 10 minutes. Reduce heat to 350° and bake until crust is brown.

LEMON PIE

2 cups sugar
2 lemons
2 level tablespoons flour

1 cup water
4 eggs
1 pinch salt

Beat yolks; add sugar, flour, water and lemon juice; cook in double boiler until thick, cool. Put in pastry shells; cover with meringue made of 4 egg whites, ½ teaspoon cream of tartar and 8 tablespoons sugar. Cook until lightly brown. This will make 2 small pies.

LIME ICEBOX PIE

1 can condensed milk
3 eggs, beaten separately

4 limes
1 tablespoon sugar

Chill milk; whip until fluffy; add beaten yolks, sugar, unstrained lime juice and 1 tablespoon grated rind. Put in "Vanilla Wafer Crust"; cover with meringue made of whites beaten with 6 tablespoons sugar. Cook until meringue browns, at 425°. Chill in icebox. If desired, filling can be tinted green, with vegetable coloring.

ORANGE NUT PIE

3 eggs
1 cup sugar
2½ tablespoons flour
1 cup orange juice

2 tablespoons grated orange rind
1 tablespoon butter
½ cup pecans

Make custard of egg yolks beaten with sugar, flour, orange juice, and grated rind. Cook until very thick; add butter and nuts. Bake in partly baked pastry shell. Cover with meringue made of 3 egg whites, ½ teaspoon cream of tartar and 6 tablespoons sugar. Bake at 350°.

PEACH COBBLER

3 pounds fresh sliced peaches
1½ cups sugar
2 pieces mace

2 tablespoons butter
6 tablespoons whiskey

Combine peaches and sugar; cover; let stand until syrup begins to form; add mace; put over low heat; bring to a boil; cook 15 or 20 minutes; add butter; cook 3 minutes. Take off fire; add 6 tablespoons whiskey; put in a small deep casserole lined with pastry; cover top with pastry; cook in hot oven 10 minutes; reduce heat, bake at 350° for half hour or until pastry is well done. Serve with "Whiskey Sauce."

PINEAPPLE PIE

1 can grated pineapple	½ cup flour
2 eggs	1¼ cups sugar

Combine 1 cup of the sugar with flour; beat yolks; add sugar mixture, pineapple and juice. Cook until thick in double boiler. Cool, pour in prebaked pie shell; cover with meringue made of the rest of the sugar, egg whites and ½ teaspoon cream of tartar. Bake at 350° until meringue is firm.

TROPICAL PIE

1 cup orange juice	4 egg yolks
1 cup water	2 tablespoons grated orange rind
1 cup sugar	2 tablespoons lemon juice
5 tablespoons cornstarch or flour	¾ cup cocoanut
1 pinch salt	

Beat egg yolks; combine with sugar, flour and salt. Heat water and fruit juice; add to egg mixture. Cook in double boiler until very thick, remove from heat; add orange rind and ½ cup cocoanut. Cool. Put in baked pie shell; cover with meringue made of stiffly beaten whites of egg, and 8 tablespoons sugar, flavored with ½ tablespoon almond extract. Sprinkle remaining cocoanut over meringue; bake until firm at 350°.

TARTS

BANBURY TARTS

Cut rich pastry in 3 inch squares; put a teaspoon of filling on each; fold over in triangle shape; moisten edges slightly with fork tines dipped in cold water; press together; prick with fork; bake until brown.

FILLING FOR TARTS:

1 cup dates	1 cup yellow sugar
1 cup raisins	1 egg, beaten together.
¾ cup chopped pecans	1 lemon, juice and rind
1 tablespoon flour	

Chop raisins and dates; add other ingredients; cook in double boiler until thick; add chopped nuts. Cool. These are nice for morning coffees and afternoon teas.

CHERRY TARTS

1 can cherries	1 teaspoon lemon juice
1 cup sugar	2 tablespoons cornstarch or flour

Boil sugar, cherry juice, lemon juice and cornstarch until thick; add.

cherries and cook a short while. Cool. Make "Philadelphia Cheese Pastry" into tart shells; bake shells and fill with cherries; top with whipped cream.

CHOCOLATE TARTS

Make tart shells of "Philadelphia Cheese or Plain Pastry." Fill them with recipe for "Chocolate Pie." Cover with meringue swirled high on the tart and bake until lightly brown.

LEMON TARTS

Make tart shells of "Philadelphia Cheese or Plain Pastry"; fill them with the lemon filling used for "Pastry Tid-Bits." Cover with meringue made of 4 egg whites and 8 tablespoons sugar. Flavor the meringue with ½ teaspoon of almond extract. Swirl the meringue high on the tarts and bake until lightly brown.

☆ SALADS AND SALAD DRESSINGS ☆

SALAD PLATTER SUGGESTIONS

SALAD PLATTER SUGGESTION

Arrange a grapefruit in the center of a large round platter; stick as full as possible with large shrimp, impaled on colored hors d'oeuvre picks. Around this put lettuce cups, with halves of avocado in each. Fill avocados with "Frozen Tomato Mayonnaise." At intervals, around the edge of tray, put halves of stuffed eggs, large stuffed olives and ripe olives, alternate these with pepper rings, stuffed with cheese. (See "Cheese in Bell Pepper Rings.") Garnish tray with parsley. This makes a beautiful platter as the frozen mayonnaise is a lovely shrimp color, which make a pleasing contrast to the green of the pears and the other colorful items on the tray.

Salad Platter Suggestion (2)

In the center of salad platter put a large ring of "Molded Chicken Salad with Aspic Top" surrounded by lettuce hearts; border with halves of "Stuffed Eggs," ripe olives and bunches of parsley.

Salad Platter Suggestion (3)

Put a ring of "Stuffed Eggs in Tomato Aspic" in the center of salad platter; fill center of ring with chopped vegetable salad; border with lettuce hearts. On the outer edge of tray, put slices of cold, boiled, smoked tongue; garnish with parsley and radish roses.

Salad Platter Suggestion (4)

At the upper edge of a large round salad platter, put a fish mold of "Salmon Mousse." Spoon green "Cucumber Aspic" around the fish; border tray with lettuce hearts; garnish with "Egg Pond Lilies." (See Garnish.)

Salad Platter Suggestion (5)

In center of salad platter put a ring of "Lamb Mold" salad; fill center of mold with potato salad; surround it with lettuce cups. In each lettuce cup, put a slice of tomato, on top of which put a thin slice of cucumber. On top of the cucumber put a slice of pickle that has been stuffed with cheese. (See "Cucumber Pickle and Cheese Appetizer.") Put "Stuffed Eggs," ripe olives and small bunches of parsley on outer edge of the platter.

Salad Platter Suggestion (6)

In center of salad platter, put a large ring mold of "Jewel Salad," place a bowl of Philadelphia cream cheese, thinned with French dressing, in middle of the salad ring. Surround with lettuce hearts. On the outer edge of the platter put thin slices of cold, sliced turkey. Garnish with parsley.

Salad Platter Suggestion (7)

Put a large mold of "Crab Salad with Cucumber Aspic Top" in the center of platter; surround with lettuce cups, filled with "Tomatoes Stuffed with Cheese" which have been slightly frozen. Put a bowl of mayonnaise in center of the platter.

Salad Platter Suggestion (8)

In the center of large salad platter, put slices of cold baked chicken or turkey; surround with lettuce cups filled with a variety of fresh fruits. Peaches, pears, melon balls, pineapple, cherries and grapes make a beautiful combination. Serve poppy seed dressing with this.

SALADS

GREEN ASPARAGUS AND EGG SALAD

For each serving, put 4 stalks of green asparagus on lettuce hearts; arrange a half "Deviled Egg" on either side of the asparagus. Serve with "Russian Dressing."

AVOCADO SALAD

Cut avocados lengthwise; remove seed; marinate in French dressing. When ready to serve, place avocado, cut side down, on lettuce; slice down in thin slices, leaving them in place. Serve with French or "Poppy Seed Dressing."

STUFFED AVOCADO

2 large avocados	1 teaspoon onion juice
2 packages Philadelphia cheese	½ cup chopped pecans
1 tablespoon Worcestershire sauce	1 envelope gelatin
1 tablespoon mayonnaise	¼ cup cold water

Cut avocados in half crosswise; pull part; remove seed. Soak gelatin in cold water; dissolve over hot water, adding 1 tablespoon of hot water to gelatin. When cool, add to combined cheese and mayonnaise; add nuts and seasoning; pack into avocado halves. Dip in lemon juice; wrap in waxed paper. Put in icebox overnight, or until thoroughly chilled. Slice with very sharp knife; serve several slices on lettuce, with French dressing. Serves 6.

CHICKEN SALAD

4 cups cooked chicken, cut in pieces
2½ cups chopped celery
1 cup almonds, cut in pieces

1 cup boiled salad dressing
½ cup whipped cream
Mayonnaise as needed

Add whipped cream to salad dressing, combine ingredients; add enough mayonnaise to make the salad the right consistency. Serves 8.

CRAB SALAD IN AVOCADO PEARS

2 large avocados, cut lengthwise
1 can crab meat (5 ounces)

1 cup minced celery
Russian dressing

Peel avocados; marinate in French dressing; drain; fill very full with crab meat that has been shredded and combined with celery and a little mayonnaise. Serve with Russian dressing. Serves 4.

CRAB SALAD IN TOMATOES

2 cans crab meat
2 avocados, chopped
1 cup chopped celery
8 tomatoes

8 artichoke hearts, marinated in French dressing
6 hard-boiled eggs, riced
1 head lettuce, shredded

Pick over crab meat; add avocado and celery; bind together with mayonnaise; stuff tomatoes with mixture. On top of each tomato, put an artichoke heart, pulled open to represent a flower; put tomatoes on shredded lettuce; arrange a circle of riced eggs around each tomato; serve with "Anchovy Mayonnaise." Serves 8.

GRAPEFRUIT AND ASPARAGUS SALAD

Allow 4 segments of large grapefruit and 4 stalks of asparagus for each serving. Put on shredded lettuce; cover with "Red Dressing."

GRAPEFRUIT WITH AVOCADO

Peel avocado; split in half, lengthwise; remove seed; marinate in French dressing. Allow four or five grapefruit sections for each avocado half; arrange them in fan shaped effect, inside avocado; garnish with parsley; serve with French dressing. Wedges of avocado alternating with grapefruit sections can also be used for a salad.

GRAPEFRUIT AND BLACK GRAPE SALAD

Allow 4 sections of grapefruit and 3 narrow strips avocado for each serving. Arrange sections close together alternating with strips of avocado. Surround with large, black grapes, which have been seeded, stuffed with Roquefort cheese spread, and pressed back in original shape. Allow four or five grapes for each serving. Serve with French dressing.

GRAPEFRUIT SALAD WITH CHEESE CAMELLIA OR GARDENIA

Allow a half grapefruit for each serving. Remove seeds; cut out center; separate sections from skin with a sharp knife. When using the Cheese Camellia or Gardenia on this, remove 4 sections from the top, bottom and each side of the grapefruit, equal distances apart; put these cut out sec-

203

tions in the space from which the seeds have been removed. Fill each of the cut out spaces with a wedge of avocado to represent the green leaves of the gardenia, and over these, at center of the grapefruit, put a gardenia, made of Philadelphia cheese. Season cheese with salt and a little scraped onion, soften with a little cream, so that it can be used in decorating tube. Make a cone of a double thickness of heavy typewriter paper; cut an inverted V from the tip of cone; fill with cheese mixture; bending over top edges to keep cheese in cone. Force out 5 petals of cheese by pressing the upper edge of the cone; place them in circular shape to resemble the outer petals of a gardenia. To do this, hold the cone in horizontal position in front of you as you work. Now make 2 short petals at the center of the flower which should stand up, rather than lie flat, as the outer petals do. Elevate your cone to do this, until it is in a vertical position. Make petals around center until gardenia takes shape. With a little practice these can be made to look life-like. Make gardenias on waxed paper, which is spread on a tray; put in refrigerator. Gardenias should chill and harden for several hours. Pink Camellias can be made in the same manner by tinting the cheese light pink. When ready to serve, remove cheese flowers from the waxed paper and put in place at center of grapefruit. Put grapefruit halves on lettuce, on individual salad plates. Serve with French dressing.

GRAPEFRUIT WITH CHEESE JONQUILS

When jonquils are in season, substitute cheese jonquils for the gardenias. Tint the Philadelphia cheese a light yellow. Make the flat outer petals much the same way as gardenia petals. The jonquil cups, however, are molded by hand, using a sandwich spread of Old English or Vera Sharp cheese. One glass of cheese will make 15 to 18 centers. It should be thoroughly chilled before trying to mold it. These centers are put in refrigerator and are not put in place until ready to assemble the salad. This is a deep yellow cheese and contrasts somewhat with the color of the outer petals which are made of the Philadelphia cheese.

When using cheese jonquils do not remove any sections from the grapefruit half. A wedge of avocado can be put in the space at the center of the grapefruit so that the jonquil will sit level over the center. The leaves are cut in narrow strips, lengthwise of the avocado, and laid in place along the side of the jonquil.

GRAPEFRUIT—POMEGRANATE SALAD

Allow 4 segments of large, pink-meat grapefruit for each serving. Circle segments to form a nest, overlapping the sections so that a small space is left in center of the circle. In this space put a fairly large cheese ball, that has been highly seasoned with onion juice, Worcestershire sauce, salt and red pepper. Roll the ball in pomegranate seed before putting it in place; sprinkle a few more seed over the salad. Serve with French dressing.

GRAPEFRUIT SALAD WITH CUCUMBER DRESSING

Soak peeled cucumber in ice water 10 minutes; grate and drain; add to oil mayonnaise or boiled dressing, just before serving. Serve over sections of grapefruit in lettuce cups.

EASTER RABBIT SALAD

Allow one fresh pear for each serving. Core pears, leaving an uncored space at bottom of pear. Fill opening with guava jelly. Soften Philadelphia cheese with milk to spreading consistency; season highly with salt, cayenne pepper, onion juice and a small amount of Worcestershire sauce. Butter pears with cheese; sprinkle with fresh grated cocoanut to resemble rabbit fur. Cut marshmallows in half; tint cut edges with pink vegetable coloring; insert toothpicks in each section; stick on either side of top of pear to make rabbit ears. Make eyes of cinnamon drops, nose of a clove, and whiskers of bits of shredded wheat biscuit. Cut other marshmallows in half; roll into ball shaped tails. Hold in place at bottom of pear with toothpick. Stand upright in a nest of shredded lettuce. Serve with mayonnaise.

LOBSTER, SHRIMP OR CRAB SALAD

Three cups of lobster, shrimp or crab meat. Marinate fish for an hour in French dressing; drain; combine with 2 cups chopped celery; add mayonnaise to bind together. It will take about a cup of mayonnaise for this. Garnish with sections of hard-boiled eggs. The eggs can be chopped and added to the salad if preferred. Serves 8.

POTATO SALAD

3 pints diced, boiled potatoes	1 pint chopped celery
2 onions, minced	1 tablespoon chopped bell pepper
Cooked dressing or mayonnaise	

Combine ingredients; season highly with salt, and red pepper. 1 cup of diced cucumber can be added if desired or 3 hard-boiled eggs chopped. Serves 10 or 12.

LOUISIANA SHRIMP SALAD

3 cups cooked shrimp	1 cup French dressing
6 shallots, chopped fine	2½ tablespoons creole (horse-radish)
2 tablespoons chopped parsley	mustard
2 hard-boiled eggs, chopped	

Clean shrimp. Add mustard to French dressing; combine with other ingredients. Let stand several hours in refrigerator before serving. Serves 6.

SLAW

2 cups finely chopped cabbage	3 tablespoons sugar
1 green pepper, chopped fine	⅛ teaspoon red pepper
⅓ cup vinegar	1 teaspoon celery seed
½ teaspoon salt	

Heat vinegar with seasonings; cool; pour over cabbage and pepper.

Slaw (2)

2 cups shredded cabbage, 2 hard boiled eggs. Put cabbage in ice water until crisp; drain and dry between towels. Chop hard-boiled eggs; combine with cabbage and "Slaw Dressing."

SWEETBREADS AND CUCUMBER SALAD

1 pound sweetbreads	1 cucumber, diced and drained
1 small onion, grated	1 chopped pimento
1 small bunch celery, diced	2 hard-boiled eggs, chopped
1 lemon	½ cup sliced almonds
Mayonnaise	Salt and red pepper

Soak sweetbreads for half an hour in cold acidulated water; put on to boil in salted water; cook 20 minutes. Put in cold water to blanch; drain; remove membrane; break into small pieces; marinate in French dressing. Add other ingredients; bind together with highly seasoned mayonnaise with a little whipped cream added. Serve on lettuce hearts or stuff tomatoes with salad. Serves 6.

TOMATO-CHEESE-ARTICHOKE SALAD

Sprinkle a firm slice of peeled tomato with a little salt. Marinate artichoke bottom in French dressing; put on top of tomato slice; fill artichoke bottom with a large spoonful of Philadelphia cheese, highly seasoned with onion juice, salt and red pepper. On top of cheese put an artichoke heart; open artichoke heart carefully to resemble a flower; serve on lettuce with French dressing.

STUFFED TOMATOES-EGG GARNISH

Scald and peel tomatoes; chill. Cut tomatoes, two-thirds of the way down in six sections and spread apart to resemble a flower; fill with chicken, crab or sweetbread salad. Slice hard-boiled eggs in quarter inch slices and carefully place a slice between each cut section of the tomato. Top the salad with additional mayonnaise; dust with paprika.

TOMATO-CHEESE ROSES

Four small, firm tomatoes, two packages Philadelphia cheese (3 ounces). Grate a small amount of onion juice into the cheese, soften with a little cream; tint pink or yellow. Scald, peel and remove hard part from stem end of tomatoes; dry thoroughly with a soft cloth. Hold tomato in left hand; with a small teaspoon take up some of the cheese, scrape it across the top of the bowl to smooth it level; press it against the top edge of tomato and draw the spoon down away from tomato, leaving a cheese petal. Continue making these petals around the top of tomato. Make a second row of petals below the first row, slightly overlapping each row; repeat until tomato is covered with petals. Fill space at top carefully with riced yolks of hard-boiled eggs. Put in lettuce cups. Serves 4.

TOMATO-CHEESE LAYER SALAD

Dip firm tomatoes in boiling water for 1 minute; skin. Chill until ready to use. Remove stem end with sharp knife and slice tomato into 3 equal sections. Spread a half inch layer of cheese mixture between tomato slices; using two layers of cheese and 3 slices of tomato for each serving. Wipe tomato off carefully with a soft cloth or a paper napkin to remove excess cheese. Serve on lettuce leaf with either mayonnaise or French dressing. One half pound of riced drained, cottage cheese combined with one 3 ounce package of Philadelphia cheese, a little onion juice, salt and red pepper, will fill 4 large tomatoes.

VEGETABLE SALAD PLATE

Arrange shredded lettuce on individual salad plates and cover with a thin layer of "Russian Dressing"; over this put shredded carrots, diced cucumbers, sliced spring onions and sliced radishes. Cover with a generous serving of the dressing and garnish with additional carrots and radishes. Around the outer edge of the salad alternate two rye bread and cheese sandwiches, cut in triangle shape, with two sandwiches made of white bread and tongue. Place large olive and halves of deviled eggs between sandwiches.

TOMATO-EGG AND CAVIAR SALAD

Dip firm tomatoes into boiling water for 1 minute; chill; skin; cut slice from stem end; scoop out inside; sprinkle with salt and invert until ready to stuff. Hard boil eggs, allowing an egg and a half for each tomato; rice yolks and whites separately; add half of riced whites to riced yolks; bind together wtih mayonnaise. Add $\frac{1}{2}$ teaspoon of caviar for each egg, a little lemon juice, salt and red pepper to taste. Stuff tomatoes with this mixture; sprinkle remaining whites over top. Serve on lettuce with mayonnaise. Domestic caviar can be used for this.

TOMATO SANDWICH SALAD

Spread a slice of Holland rusk with anchovy paste; cover with a thin slice of baked ham. Over this put a slice of cooked chicken breast; cover with a large slice of tomato; sprinkle tomato with salt; put 2 halves of stuffed egg on tomato, flat side down. Over all of this pour a generous portion of "Russian Dressing." Completely cover salad. On top of salad put an opened artichoke heart or a large stuffed olive, flanked on either side by tiny whole sardines. Serve this salad on shredded lettuce and you will have a complete meal. When planning for a small group, you can buy a large chicken breast and several slices of baked or boiled ham from your butcher. Frizzle this variety of ham in butter before using; boil and slice chicken breast.

CHOPPED VEGETABLE SALAD

1 head of lettuce, shredded	1 bunch celery, chopped fine
1 cucumber, chopped fine	$\frac{1}{2}$ bell pepper, chopped fine
1 bunch spring onions, sliced thin	2 hard-boiled eggs, chopped (optional)
1 bunch radishes, sliced thin	2 carrots, grated or sliced thin

Combine chopped vegetables and chill; just before serving, toss with French dressing. Crumble a small amount of Roquefort cheese over salad if desired. Serves 6 to 8.

MOLDED SALADS

APRICOT NECTAR SALAD

1 can apricot nectar, 12-ounce size
Water to make one pint

1 lemon, juice of
1 package lemon Jello

Combine lemon and apricot juice; add water to make one pint; heat and pour over lemon Jello. Can be served plain or have one can of combined grapefruit and orange sections added. Pour into individual molds and congeal. Serves 4 to 6.

APRICOT MOLDED SALAD

1 can apricots, 2½ size
2 lemons
1 orange
1 package orange flavored gelatin

1 package Philadelphia cream cheese (3 ounces)
1 tablespoon Worcestershire sauce
½ cup chopped almonds

Drain apricots. Combine fruit juices; heat; pour over orange gelatin; dissolve; chill. When very thick, stir in sieved apricots. Put in juice from apricots also. Let partially congeal. Soften cheese with milk; season with Worcestershire sauce; add chopped almonds; form into small balls. Arrange apricot mixture and cheese balls in small oiled molds. Serves 6.

MOLDED ASPARAGUS SALAD

1 can white asparagus tips, drained and sieved
1 cup mayonnaise, highly seasoned
1 cup cream, whipped
1 cup asparagus, liquid, heated
1½ tablespoons gelatin

¼ cup cold water
Salt and red pepper
1 teaspoon onion juice
1 teaspoon Worcestershire sauce
1 pimento, minced fine

Soak gelatin in cold water; dissolve in heated asparagus juice; chill. When very thick, add to combined mayonnaise and whipped cream; add rest of ingredients; season highly. Arrange additional asparagus tips around bottom of well-oiled mold, radiating like spokes of a wheel, tips toward outer edge; put salad over tips; congeal. Turn out on platter; garnish with tomato wedges and lettuce hearts. Serves 6 to 8.

AVOCADO SALAD RINGS

1 avocado, sieved
1 package lemon flavored gelatin
1 cup boiling water

1 tablespoon lemon juice
½ cup mayonnaise
1 cup cream, whipped

Dissolve gelatin in hot water; add lemon juice; cool; chill until thick. Add sieved avocado and mayonnaise to whipped cream; fold in partially congealed gelatin. Put in oiled rings; congeal. Turn out on shredded lettuce; fill center with grapefruit sections. This makes 8 to 10 individual rings.

BING CHERRY GRAPEFRUIT SALAD

2 packages lemon flavored gelatin   2 No. 2 cans grapefruit
1 No. 2½ can black Bing cherries

Drain cherries; combine juice with water to make 2 cups liquid; drain grapefruit; repeat process. Heat separately; add 1 package of lemon gelatin powder to each; dissolve; chill until partially set; add cherries to cherry gelatin powder; fill oiled tea cups half full of mixture; put in ice-box to set. Add grapefruit sections to grapefruit gelatin; chill until partially set; pour over cherry gelatin; congeal. This makes a salad with dark top and lighter gelatin bottom. Fills 10 to 12 cups, according to size.

CHEESE RINGS

1 pound cottage cheese
2 packages Philadelphia cream cheese
1 small onion, grated
½ cup stuffed olives, chopped fine

1 tablespoon horse-radish
1 tablespoon gelatin
¼ cup cold water
Salt and red pepper to taste

Drain and sieve cottage cheese; add to Philadelphia cheese, slowly (an electric mixer is a great help for this); season; soak gelatin in cold water; dissolve over hot water; chill until it has begun to thicken slightly; combine with cheese and olives; mold in individual rings. Serve with centers filled with grapefruit sections and balls cut from avocados. Serves 6.

ROQUEFORT CHEESE RING

2 packages lemon flavored gelatin
2 cups hot water
1 lemon (juice of)
1 can crushed pineapple, drained

½ pint whipping cream
2 packages Philadelphia cheese, 3 ounces
1 large point (about 6-ounce size) Roquefort or bleu cheese

Dissolve gelatin in hot water, add lemon juice; chill until very thick. Mash cheese; mix to smooth paste with gelatin mixture; add drained pineapple; chill until almost set; fold in whipped cream; put in large ring mold to congeal. Turn out; surround with lettuce; fill centers with grapefruit or any combination of fruits. Serve with "Poppy Seed Dressing." Serves 10.

CHEESE AND CUCUMBER MOLDED SALAD

1 tablespoon gelatin
¼ cup cold water
2 packages Philadelphia cream cheese
1 cup mayonnaise
Salt and red pepper to taste

2 tablespoons lemon juice
1 tablespoon grated onion
2 small cucumbers, chopped fine and drained

Soak gelatin in cold water; dissolve over hot water, cool. Mix mayonnaise with cheese until smooth; add gelatin; cucumber and seasonings; mold in small individual molds. Turn out on slices of tomato; garnish with lettuce hearts. Serves 6.

CHEESE AND PINEAPPLE ASPIC

1 package orange flavored gelatin
1 cup hot water
1 cup pineapple juice

1 cup drained, crushed pineapple
Salt and red pepper to taste
1 cup riced cottage cheese

Dissolve gelatin in hot water; add pineapple juice; chill until very thick; add drained pineapple and cheese; mold. Serves 6.

BING CHERRY SALAD

2 packages cherry flavored gelatin
1 large can Bing cherries
2 cups juice from cherries
1 can pineapple, drained

1½ cups boiling water
½ cup sherry wine
1 cup almonds

Dissolve gelatin in boiling water; add cherry juice and wine; chill and partially congeal. Seed cherries; put an almond in each one. Add cherries and pineapple cut in small pieces. Fills ten small molds.

CHICKEN CURRY MOLD

2 cups chopped chicken
1 cup chopped celery
½ bell pepper, chopped
1 pimento, chopped
1 teaspoon onion juice
Salt and pepper
1 tablespoon Worcestershire sauce

5 hard-boiled eggs, chopped
1 cup mayonnaise
1 cup whipped cream
1 cup chicken broth, heated
2 tablespoons gelatin
½ to 1 teaspoon curry powder
½ cup cold water

Soak gelatin in cold water; dissolve in hot chicken stock; chill. When partially congealed, add curry powder, mayonnaise and whipped cream; season highly. Smooth curry powder with a little cream before adding it to the mixture. Add other ingredients; put in an oiled mold or in individual molds. This will serve 10 to 12.

JELLIED CHICKEN

1 5-pound hen
1 onion
Celery tops
Salt and pepper
3 tablespoons gelatin
4 cups chicken stock

¾ cup cold water
1 small stalk celery, cut fine
2 tablespoons capers
1 pimento, chopped
6 large stuffed olives

Boil hen until very tender, in water to cover, with celery tops, sliced onion, salt and pepper. Remove chicken; refrigerate stock when cool. Pull chicken from bones in shreds. The next day, skim all fat from chicken broth; put on to boil with the shell and beaten white of an egg, to clarify the stock. Reduce to 4 cups. Measure; add gelatin that has been soaked in cold water; strain; chill until partially congealed. Put a small mount of aspic in bottom of an oiled ring mold; decorate with slices of stuffed olives; then put in a layer of chicken, a little chopped celery, capers and pimento. Cover with more aspic; alternate chicken, celery, pimento, capers and aspic until mold is filled. Serve surrounded by sliced tomatoes with Philadelphia cheese and artichoke heart on top of each slice. Serves 10 to 12.

MOLDED CHICKEN SALAD

2 cups diced chicken
1 cup diced celery
½ cup chopped almonds
1 cup mayonnaise or boiled dressing

1 cup cream, whipped
1 tablespoon gelatin
¼ cup cold water

Soak gelatin in cold water; dissolve over hot water; cool; add to combined mayonnaise, and cream; add chicken, nuts and celery; mold. Serves 6.

CHICKEN MOUSSE MOLDED

2 cups ground chicken
1 cup chicken stock
1 onion
2 ribs of celery

1 cup whipped cream
1 tablespoon gelatin
¼ cup cold water
Salt and pepper

Heat chicken stock with celery and onion for fifteen minutes, over slow heat. Add gelatin that has been soaked in cold water; dissolve; strain; chill. When it is partially congealed beat into whipped cream; add ground chicken; congeal. Serve with "Russian Dressing." Serves 6.

CHICKEN SALAD MOLDED WITH TOMATO ASPIC TOP

3 cups tomato juice
2 celery ribs
2 slices onion
1 tablespoon Worcestershire sauce
Salt and pepper (red) to taste
2 tablespoons gelatin
½ cup cold water

3 cups chopped chicken, white meat
2 cups finely chopped celery
2 cups boiled dressing or mayonnaise
1 cup cream, whipped
1 tablespoon gelatin
¼ cup cold water

Make tomato aspic of first seven ingredients; strain; pour in bottom of a large ring mold; congeal. Soak one tablespoon gelatin in ¼ cup cold water; dissolve over hot water; cool; add to combined mayonnaise and whipped cream; add chicken and celery. Put chicken salad over tomato aspic. Congeal. Serves 12 to 14. This can be molded in tea cups, if preferred, with the aspic tops.

CHICKEN-VEGETABLE MOLDED SALAD

4 or 5 cups chopped chicken
2 cups chopped celery
1 cup chopped almonds
2 cups peas
2 pimentos
2 hard-boiled eggs
1 cup chicken stock, heated

2 tablespoons Worcestershire sauce
1 teaspoon onion juice
Salt and red pepper to taste
2 cups boiled salad dressing
1 cup cream, whipped
2 tablespoons gelatin
¼ cup cold water

Soak gelatin in cold water; dissolve in heated chicken stock; add seasonings; chill. When thick add combined salad dressing and whipped cream, add rest of ingredients; put in oiled ring mold, or in individual molds. This will fill 14 cup-sized molds or a large ring. One large hen will make the correct amount of chicken.

TWO-TONED CHRISTMAS SALAD

Make once the recipe of "Molded Grapefruit Salad"—tint a deep green. Make half the recipe for "Bing Cherry Salad"—add a little red coloring. First put a layer of green jelly in bottom of tea cups. Let the green part congeal in the refrigerator; when set, put a layer of "Bing Cherry Salad" over the green part. The layer should be the same depth, so that the completed salad is half green and half red. Serves 10.

CHRISTMAS WREATH SALAD

2 packages lemon flavored gelatin	"Emeraldettes"
1 lemon (juice of)	Pimento
1 large can "Fruits for Salads"	1¾ cups each fruit juice and water

Heat the combined fruit juice, lemon juice and water, dissolve gelatin, chill; when almost congealed, add fruit, cut very fine. Put a little of the gelatin mixture in bottom of individual, oiled, ring molds; decorate with red and green emeraldettes. These come in bottles and are nice for Christmas decoration; if they are not available, substitute red and green marischino cherries, cut fine. Fill molds with remaining gelatin; congeal. Turn out on shredded lettuce. Cut pimento around in long narrow strips; use to form bowknots at the top of each ring. Serves 10.

CRAB MEAT SALAD MOLDED

1 can crab meat (5½ ounces)	½ lemon (juice of)
2 tablespoons chopped olives	Salt and red pepper to taste
½ cup chopped celery	1 tablespoon gelatin
2 tablespoons chopped green pepper	¼ cup cold water
¾ cup mayonnaise	

Soak gelatin in cold water; dissolve over hot water; cool; add to mayonnaise. Pick over crab meat and shred; add mayonanise and chopped vegetables. Congeal in individual molds. Serve with anchovy mayonnaise. Serves 6.

CRAB SALAD WITH CUCUMBER, ASPIC TOP

Make twice the recipe for "Crab Salad Molded." Put half-inch layer of "Cucumber Aspic" in bottom of a large ring mold; when almost congealed, put "Crab Salad" on top. Congeal. Serves 12.

CRANBERRY-PINEAPPLE SALAD

4 cups red cranberries	3 cups water
1 small can pineapple, diced	2 envelopes gelatin
1 cup blanched almonds, cut in half	1 cup sugar
1 cup Tokay grapes, cup in half	

Soak gelatin in half cup of water. Cook the other 2½ cups water with sugar, cranberries and juice drained from the pineapple. Boil until berries have cooked to pieces; add gelatin and dissolve; cool; chill until it begins to thicken. Add fruit and nuts; pour in molds. More sugar can be added if desired. Serves 8.

CUCUMBER ASPIC

1 package lemon flavored gelatin	Green coloring
1 cup boiling water	3 small cucumbers
3 tablespoons lemon juice	

Dissolve gelatin in boiling water; cool. Peel and grate cucumbers; press through sieve until you have a half cup of juice; add with lemon juice to gelatin; tint green with vegetable coloring; congeal in individual ring molds. Turn out on shredded lettuce; fill centers of rings with crab, shrimp or lobster salad. Serves 4 or 5.

FISH MOLDED IN CUCUMBER ASPIC LAKE "POND LILY GARNISH"

Make twice recipe for both "Cucumber Aspic" and Salmon or "Crab Mousse." Congeal mousse in fish mold. Mold cucumber aspic in flat pan. When ready to serve, unmold fish on flat platter; spoon green cucumber aspic around it. This looks best on a white china platter. Surround with tiny lettuce hearts and pond lilies made of eggs. (See "Garnishes.")

FROSTY SALAD RINGS

1 package lime flavored gelatin	2 tablespoons horse-radish
1 cup hot water	1 cup cottage cheese
2 tablespoons lemon juice	

Drain and sieve cottage cheese, measure 1 cup, beat until smooth, in electric beater; add horse-radish. Dissolve gelatin in hot water; add lemon juice; chill. When almost set, beat until frothy; stir in cheese; mold in individual ring molds. Turn out on shredded lettuce; fill centers with grapefruit sections and avocado pear balls or with seafood salad. Serves 6.

MOLDED FRUIT ASPIC

2 packages lemon flavored gelatin	1 can pears (No. 2 can)
1 can sliced pineapple (No. 2 can)	1 lemon
1 can Queen Anne cherries (No. 2 can)	

Drain fruit; add juice of lemon to syrup; add water if necessary, to make 4 cups of liquid. Heat juice; dissolve gelatin in hot juice; chill until thick and ropy. Dice pineapple and pears; seed cherries. When aspic has almost congealed, add fruit; put in individual molds. Serves 10 to 12.

MOLDED FRUIT SALAD

1 cup Queen Anne cherries	1 cup cream, whipped
1 cup diced pineapple	1 tablespoon gelatin
1 cup orange segments or apricots as de-desired	¼ cup cold water
1 cup cooked dressing or mayonnaise, highly seasoned	

Soak gelatin in cold water; dissolve over hot water; cool; add to mayonnaise. Add whipped cream; fold in fruits. This is a delicious molded salad, and it can also be frozen. Serves 8.

GINGER ALE SALAD

2 packages lemon flavored gelatin
½ cup lemon juice
1 cup pineapple juice
2 cups ginger ale

1 small bunch celery
4 eating apples, medium size
1 pound white grapes
1 No. 2 can pineapple, drained

Heat fruit juice; dissolve gelatin in hot juice; cool; add ginger ale; chill until partially congealed. Seed grapes; cut in half. Cut celery, apples and pineapple in small pieces. Add fruit to gelatin mixture; put in molds; congeal. This will make 12 individual molds or 1 large ring mold.

GOLDEN SALAD

1 package orange flavored gelatin
1 No. 2 can crushed pineapple
2 carrots, grated

2 oranges
1 lemon

Grate carrots. Remove segments from oranges; save juice. Drain pineapple. Combine juices of pineapple, orange, lemon. This should make nearly 2 cups of liquid. Heat juice; dissolve gelatin in hot juices; chill. When it begins to congeal, add carrots, pineapple and orange segments. Pour in mold. Serves 6.

MOLDED GRAPEFRUIT SALAD

1 package lemon flavored gelatin
1 cup hot water
¾ cup grapefruit juice

2 tablespoons lemon juice
1 large grapefruit

Dissolve gelatin in hot water; add fruit juice; chill until partially congealed. Break grapefruit sections in half; put in individual molds; pour gelatin over them; congeal. Turn out on lettuce; surround with honeydew balls, cut with a large size ball cutter. Allow 6 balls to a serving. Serves 5 or 6.

MOLDED GRAPEFRUIT AND PINEAPPLE SALAD

1 box lemon flavored gelatin
1 lemon (juice of)
1 small can pineapple, diced

1 grapefruit
1 cup celery
½ cup almonds, cut in half

Drain pineapple; combine lemon and pineapple juice with enough water to make two cups; heat; dissolve gelatin in hot juice; chill. When almost congealed, add grapefruit segments cut in half, diced pineapple, celery and almonds. Congeal in individual molds. Serves 6.

HAM MOUSSE

2 cups ground baked or boiled ham
1 tablespoon minced green pepper
1 teaspoon minced onion
1 tablespoon horse-radish
1 cup milk, heated

1 teaspoon mustard
1 tablespoon gelatin
1 tablespoon vinegar
¼ cup cold water

Soak gelatin in cold water; dissolve in hot milk. Add vinegar, mustard and horse-radish. Chill until partially congealed; add rest of ingredients. Put in mold to congeal; turn out on lettuce; serve with Russian dressing. Serves 6.

HAWAIIAN SALAD

2 packages lime flavored gelatin
½ pound Philadelphia cream cheese

1 large can crushed pineapple
1 cup seedless white grapes

Drain pineapple; save out several tablespoons of juice. Add enough water to remaining juice to make 3½ cups liquid. Heat; dissolve gelatin in hot juice; chill; color deep green with vegetable coloring; congeal until quite thick. Fold in fruit; put in oiled molds. Soften Philadelphia cream cheese to the consistency of mayonnaise, with pineapple juice saved for the purpose. It should stand up in peaks. Put a spoon of this on top of each mold. Use cheese instead of mayonnaise. Serves 10 or 12.

JEWEL SALAD

2 boxes lemon flavored gelatin
3 cups water, heated
1 cantaloupe
½ honey dew melon
¼ watermelon

Scoop balls from melons
1 No. 2 can Bing cherries
1 cup Thompson seedless white grapes
½ pound Philadelphia cream cheese
French dressing

Pour boiling water over gelatin; chill and partially congeal. When quite thick, add fruit balls, cherries and grapes, putting them in so that the colors will be evenly distributed. Mold in a large ring mold; congeal. Turn out on platter; garnish with lettuce hearts. Thin Philadelphia cheese to mayonnaise consistency with French dressing. Serve in center of salad ring. It is not necessary to serve mayonnaise with this salad. Serves 10 to 12.

LAMB MOLD

3½ cups ground cooked lamb
1 small onion, minced
½ cup chopped olives
½ teaspoon salt
2 envelopes gelatin

½ cup cold water
2 cups bouillon, heated (diluted canned
 bouillon will do)
1 tablespoon lemon juice

Soak gelatin in cold water; dissolve in hot bouillon; chill. When thick, add rest of ingredients. Pour in ring mold; congeal. Turn out on platter; fill with chopped vegetable salad or potato salad; garnish with tomato wedges and lettuce hearts. Serves 6 to 8.

MOLDED LOBSTER SALAD

1 small can lobster (5 or 6 ounces)
3 ribs celery, diced
1 small cucumber, diced
3 tablespoons French dressing

1 package lemon flavored gelatin
2 tablespoons lemon juice
1½ cups hot water
4 tablespoons mayonnaise

Dissolve gelatin in hot water; cool; add lemon juice; let partially congeal. Fold into mayonnaise; add lobster that has been pulled to pieces. Marinate cucumber and celery in French dressing; drain; add to lobster and mayonnaise. Put in small molds to congeal. Serves 6.

JELLIED PEAR SALAD

1 can pears, preferably a small-sized pear
½ cup pecans (
2 packages Philadelphia cream cheese
1 lemon (juice of)

1 small can pimentos
2 packages lemon flavored gelatin
3 cups hot water and pear juice mixed

Drain pears; add enough water to juice to make 3 cups of liquid. Heat; dissolve gelatin in hot juice, add lemon juice, pour a small amount in bottom of tea cups; congeal. Season cheese highly, with a little salt, red pepper and onion juice; moisten with a little cream or mayonnaise; add nuts to cheese. Make the required number of cheese balls. Put a ball in each pear half; outline the ball with a narrow strip of pimento; put face down over gelatin in cup, press down slightly; fill cup with rest of gelatin. Serves 8.

PERFECTION SALAD

1 package lemon flavored gelatin
1 lemon (juice of)
1½ cups hot water
½ cup shredded cabbage

1 cup chopped celery
1 pimento
2 tablespoons red and green bell peppers

Dissolve gelatin in hot water; add lemon juice; chill until almost set; add vegetables; put in individual molds. Serves 6.

PINEAPPLE CHEESE SALAD

1 can (No. 2 size) crushed pineapple
1 cup boiled salad dressing
½ cup sliced almonds
1 cup grated yellow cheese

1 cup cream, whipped
2 tablespoons gelatin
¼ cup cold water

Drain pineapple. Heat pineapple juice; soak gelatin in cold water; dissolve in hot juice; chill. When partially congealed, add to combined cream and salad dressing; fold in cheese; pineapple and almonds. Congeal in a ring mold or individual molds. Serves 6 to 8.

PINEAPPLE CUCUMBER ASPIC

1 can pineapple (size 2½)
1 cucumber, chopped fine
1 orange

1 lemon
1 package lemon flavored gelatin

Drain and dice pineapple; add juice of the orange and lemon to juice from the pineapple. Heat juice; pour over the gelatin; stir until dissolved; chill; add pineapple and cucumber when aspic begins to jell. Makes 6 tea-cup size molds or 8 small ones.

POTATO SALAD MOLDED

Make "Tomato Aspic"; pour a small amount in bottom of 8 tea cups; congeal. Let rest of aspic congeal until very thick. Make "Potato Salad" of 2 cups of finely cut potatoes, 1 grated onion, 1 cup celery chopped fine, one tablespoon minced bell pepper, salt and red pepper, bound together with boiled dressing; let stand several hours. Put in cups over layer of tomato aspic. Put salad in center of the cups, leaving a space around sides and filling the cups until they are ¾ full; then carefully pour the rest of the thickened tomato aspic around potato salad. Congeal; turn out in lettuce cups; arrange on platter; surround by slices of smoked tongue, stuffed eggs and olives. Serves 8.

RUSSIAN SALAD MOLDED

1 package lime flavored gelatin
1 cup boiling water
1 lemon (juice of)
1 cup Tokay grapes (seeded)
1 cup finely cut eating apples

1 cup finely cut celery
1 cup mayonnaise, highly seasoned
1 cup cream, whipped
1 tablespoon gelatin
¼ cup cold water

Dissolve lime gelatin in boiling water; add lemon juice; cool; pour in bottom of a large ring mold; congeal until almost set. Soak gelatin in ¼ cup cold water; dissolve over hot water; cool; add to the combined mayonnaise and whipped cream. When it thickens, add apples, celery and grapes; pour over the congealed lime gelatin. Serves 8 to 10.

SEAFOOD IN SALAD RINGS

4 egg yolks
1 cup vinegar
¾ cup sugar
½ teaspoon salt

4 teaspoon dry mustard
2 tablespoons gelatin
½ cup cold water
1 cup whipping cream

Soak gelatin in cold water. Beat egg yolks with seasonings and sugar. Heat vinegar and pour over egg mixture. Cook in double boiler until thick; add gelatin and dissolve. Chill, and when cold add cream which has been whipped. Put in oiled, individual ring molds. Unmold on shredded lettuce and fill with flaked crab or shrimp that has had an equal amount of minced celery added and is bound together with a very little mayonnaise. The salad ring furnishes most of the dressing needed. Canned figs stuffed with cottage cheese can also be used in these salad rings— allow four figs to each ring. Fills 10 or 12 individual rings.

SALMON MOUSSE

2 tablespoons gelatin
½ cup cold water
2 tablespoons lemon juice
2 tablespoons Worcestershire sauce
½ teaspoon salt
1 cup boiling water

1 onion, grated
2 tablespoons vinegar
2 cups red salmon, flaked
1 cup mayonnaise
1 cup whipping cream
2 cups chopped cucumber or celery

Soak gelatin in cold water; dissolve in hot water; add lemon juice and vinegar; cool. When thick add to combined mayonnaise and whipped cream; add other ingredients; pour in a large, oiled fish mold; congeal. Turn out on platter; surround with lettuce hearts; put olive slice in place for fish eye. Serves 10 or 12.

JELLIED SHRIMP SALAD

3 cups canned tomatoes
1½ cups water
1½ teaspoons salt
3 cloves
1 bay leaf
1 grated onion
1 teaspoon mustard

1 tablespoon sugar
2 tablespoons gelatin
½ cup cold water
2 cups shrimp
1 cup diced celery
1 diced green pepper
4 hard-boiled eggs, sliced

Cook tomatoes, water and seasoning until tomatoes are quite soft; strain; add soaked gelatin; chill. When thick, add shrimp, celery and pepper; congeal in ring mold, alternating layers of gelatin mixture with sliced eggs. Serves 8 to 10.

SWEETBREADS AND ASPARAGUS RING

1 pound sweetbreads
1 small onion
1 can asparagus tips, cut in pieces
2 cucumbers, diced
2 pimentos
2 tablespoons Worcestershire sauce
¼ cup sugar

1 teaspoon salt
1 cup whipping cream
1 tablespoon gelatin
¼ cup cold water
1 cup chopped celery
½ cup vinegar

Soak sweetbreads half an hour, in cold water, with tablespoon of vinegar added. Boil with onion for 20 minutes in salted water. Plunge in cold water; drain; remove membrane; break into small pieces. Soak gelatin in cold water; dissolve in vinegar which has been heated with salt, sugar and Worcestershire sauce; chill; when thick add to whipped cream. Fold in sweetbreads, pimentos, drained cucumber, asparagus and celery. Put in oiled ring mold. Serves 8.

TOMATO ASPIC

2 pints tomato juice
Juice 1 small lemon
3 tablespoons sugar
2 ribs celery
1 small onion, sliced

½ bay leaf
Salt and red pepper to taste
2 tablespoons gelatin
½ cup cold water

Soak gelatin in cold water. Combine other ingredients; cook over slow heat for 10 or 15 minutes. Pour over gelatin and stir until dissolved; strain; pour in molds. Makes 8 small molds.

Tomato Aspic (2)

1 can red ripe tomatoes (2 cups)
1 onion, sliced
3 ribs celery
1 teaspoon salt
1 tablespoon sugar

1 tablespoon Worcestershire sauce
1 tablespoon lemon juice
2 tablespoons gelatin
¼ cup cold water
Cayenne pepper to taste

Soak gelatin in cold water. Simmer rest of ingredients until tomatoes are thoroughly softened. Strain over gelatin. Serves 6 or 7.

TOMATO-AVOCADO ASPIC

Make "Tomato Aspic No. 1"; add 1 cup each of finely chopped celery and avocados, when the aspic is partially congealed. The avocado can be scooped out with a small ball cutter or diced. Mold in small tea cups. Serve with mayonnaise, to which a can of flaked crab meat has been added. Serves 8 to 10.

TOMATO ASPIC WITH ARTICHOKE HEARTS

Open artichoke hearts; press seasoned Philadelphia cream cheese into each one. Pour a small amount of "Tomato Aspic" in bottom of each small individual mold; let congeal until almost set; put an artichoke heart, cheese side down, into each mold; pour more partially congealed tomato aspic around artichoke hearts, completely filling mold with aspic. Minced celery can be added to aspic if desired.

TOMATO ASPIC CHEESE RING

Make once recipe for "Tomato Aspic No. 1"; pour half inch layer of aspic in bottom of an oiled 9 inch ring mold; let congeal; cover with the following mixture: 1 pound cottage cheese, sieved and drained thoroughly, 1 cup diced cucumber, 1 cup diced celery, 1 chopped onion, combined with remainder of the tomato aspic, to which ½ cup of stiff mayonnaise has been added when partially congealed. Serves 8 to 10.

TOMATO ASPIC WITH SHRIMP

Simmer 2 cups tomato juice, highly seasoned, 2 slices of onion and 2 celery ribs for 5 minutes. Soak 1½ tablespoons gelatin in cold water, dissolve in hot juice; strain. Congeal until beginning to set; then add 1 cup chopped celery and 1 cup of shrimp. Serves 6.

TOMATO ASPIC RINGS WITH STUFFED EGGS

Make "Tomato Aspic"; pour in individual ring molds; congeal. Prepare "Eggs Stuffed with Caviar"; cut eggs crosswise to stuff; allow half an egg for each serving. Peel avocados and slice in half-inch circles: dip in French dressing. Unmold aspic rings on shredded lettuce; put stuffed egg half, encircled with ring of avocado, in center of each ring. Serve with mayonnaise.

STUFFED EGGS IN TOMATO ASPIC

4 cups tomato juice	¾ cups cold water
Salt and red pepper	6 hard-boiled eggs
2 ribs celery	2 tablespoons caviar
1 onion	1 tablespoon lemon juice
1 bay leaf	2 tablespoons chopped ripe olives
3 envelopes gelatin	

Combine tomato juice, celery, onion and bay leaf; simmer for 10 minutes. Soak gelatin in cold water; add to tomato juice; stir until dissolved; strain; chill; pour about 1 inch of aspic in bottom of ring mold. Cut hard-boiled eggs crosswise; remove yolks; mash; add lemon juice, caviar and olives; season well. Put yolks back in egg whites; press 2 halves together. Arrange eggs over the layer of aspic, spacing them evenly around mold. Pour rest of aspic over eggs; congeal. Serve this salad ring with chopped vegetables, tossed lightly in French dressing in center of mold. If preferred, the aspic can be made of bouillon instead of tomato juice.

JELLIED TONGUE

2½ cups bouillon
2 envelopes gelatin
½ cup cold water
2 cups cooked smoked tongue, chopped

½ cup chopped celery
1 tablespoon green pepper
1 small onion, grated
2 hard-boiled eggs, chopped

Soak gelatin in cold water; dissolve in hot bouillon; chill and partially congeal; add rest of ingredients; mold in individual ring molds. Fill centers of rings with mayonnaise when ready to serve. Serves 8.

JELLIED TUNA FISH SALAD

1 can tuna fish
1 cup cooked dressing with whipped cream added

½ cup chopped celery
1 tablespoon gelatin
¼ cup cold water.

Soak gelatin in cold water; dissolve over hot water; chill until thick; add to dressing. Pick over tuna fish; chop celery; combine with dressing. Mold. Serves 6.

MOLDED VEGETABLE SALAD

1 package lemon flavored gelatin
1 lemon (juice of)
1½ cups hot water
1 cup celery, cut fine
½ cup thinly sliced radishes

1 small onion, minced
½ cup chopped cabbage
½ cup grated or chopped carrots
½ cup chopped cucumber

Dissolve gelatin in hot water; add lemon juice; chill until partially congealed; add vegetables; put in ring mold or individual molds. Serves 6 or 7.

WATERMELON SLICE SALAD

Cut grapefruit in half; remove fruit and as much of the white, inner skin as possible, leaving a perfectly clean shell. Soak these shells for a half hour in water colored a deep green. The outer skin will not absorb the color but the inside will be green. Take shells from water and pat the inside until dry. Make "Tomato Aspic No. 1," using 3 tablespoons of gelatin instead of 2, as the aspic should be very firm. Congeal until very thick and spoon into the grapefruit shells. Slice small blanched almonds crosswise in thin slices. Put a few of these into the aspic very carefully. When aspic has congealed, slice each grapefruit section in half, then slice each of those sections, lengthwise, in half again. These sections will resemble little slices of watermelon with almonds for seed. Serve two slices to each person, on lettuce hearts.

FROZEN SALADS

FROZEN CHEESE AND GRAPEFRUIT SALAD

½ pound Roquefort cheese
3 ounces Philadelphia cream cheese
2 cups heavy cream

1 teaspoon onion juice
Salt and cayenne pepper to taste

Mash cheese; whip cream; combine. Add onion and season; freeze, cut in squares; surround by grapefruit sections; serve with poppy seed dressing.

FROZEN CREAM CHEESE AND JELLY SALAD

6 packages (3 ounces) Philadelphia cream cheese	1 cup blanched almonds, sliced
1 cup mayonnaise	1 teaspoon onion juice
1 cup whipping cream	1 tablespoon Worcestershire sauce
	1 large glass guava or currant jelly

Mash cheese; combine with whipped cream, mayonnaise and almonds. Put a layer of this in refrigerator tray; cover with a layer of jelly; on top of jelly put rest of cheese; freeze. Cut in small squares; put on lettuce; surround each square with grapefruit segments, allowing 3 or 4 segments for each serving. Serve with French dressing. This is very rich and only a small square of cheese is needed for each person. Serves 10.

FROZEN FRUIT SALAD

1 can apricots, cut in pieces	2 cups cream, whipped
1 can peaches, cut in pieces	1 cup almonds cut in half
1 can pineapple, cut in pieces	3 oranges (segments cut in half)
1 can Queen Anne cherries	2 cups mayonnaise, highly seasoned
½ pound marshmallows, cut in quarters	

Drain fruit. Combine cream and mayonnaise; add fruit, marshmallows and almonds; freeze. This can also be served without freezing, if preferred. Let stand in refrigerator several hours before using. Serves 20.

Frozen Fruit Salad (2)

1 can "Fruits for Salad," cut fine	1 tablespoon gelatin
1 small can pineapple, cut fine	¼ cup cold water
2 bananas, sliced thin	"Fruit Salad Dressing"

Soak gelatin in cold water; dissolve over hot water; add to once recipe for "Fruit Salad Dressing"; combine with fruits; freeze in ice tray. Serves 8 to 10.

FROZEN FRUIT AND CHEESE SALAD

Make like "Frozen Pear and Cheese Salad No. 1" substituting 1 large can of "Fruit for Salad" for pears.

FROZEN SPICED GRAPE SALAD

2 cups canned spiced grapes	1 tablespoon gelatin
½ cup mayonnaise	¼ cup juice from grapes
1 cup cream, whipped	1 teaspoon salt
1 package (3-ounce size) Philadelphia cream cheese	2 avocados

Soak gelatin in grape juice; dissolve over hot water; cool; add slowly to combined mayonnaise and whipped cream. Mash cheese; work to a paste with a small amount of mayonnaise mixture; gradually add remaining mixture and the grapes; freeze. Peel avocados; cut crosswise in rings; dip in lemon juice; put a large spoon of frozen salad on each pear ring. Serve French dressing with salad. Serves 8.

FROZEN PEAR AND CHEESE SALAD

5 cakes (3-ounce) Philadelphia cream
cheese
1 cup condensed tomato soup, heated
1 cup highly seasoned mayonnaise
1 cup cream, whipped
1 large can pears, cut in quarters, lengthwise
French dressing

Marinate pears in French dressing; drain. Mash cheese; smooth with heated tomato soup; cool; add whipped cream and mayonnaise. Put in layers in refrigerator trays with alternating layers of pears. Freeze; cut in squares. Serves 12.

FROZEN TOMATO-MAYONNAISE SALAD

1 pint tomato juice
1½ cups stiff mayonnaise
1 tablespoon Worcestershire sauce
1 tablespoon grated onion
1 tablespoon horse-radish
1 tablespoon gelatin
1 tablespoon sugar
Salt and red pepper to taste
2 tablespoons tomato paste
½ cup cream, whipped
½ cup stuffed olives, sliced

Soak gelatin in ¼ cup tomato juice. Heat rest of juice with seasonings. Dissolve gelatin in hot juice; congeal until thick and ropy; fold in mayonnaise, whipped cream and olives; freeze in refrigerator tray. Marinate avocado pear halves with French dressing; fill with frozen salad. It is not necessary to use any other dressing with salad. Serves 8 to 10.

FROZEN TOMATO-VEGETABLE SALAD

4 cups diced peeled tomatoes
2 cups chopped celery
1 cup chopped cucumber
1 onion, grated
1 bell pepper, chopped fine
½ pint whipping cream
1 tablespoon gelatin
1 large carrot, grated
1 cup boiled salad dressing, highly seasoned with red peppers, Worcestershire sauce and horse-radish
Salt to taste
¼ cup water

Soak gelatin in ¼ cup cold water; dissolve over hot water; cool; add to cooked dressing; fold in whipped cream. When it begins to thicken, stir in the drained vegetables; freeze. Serves 10.

FROZEN SWEETBREAD SALAD

1 pound sweetbreads
1 bunch celery (small), chopped
2 cucumbers, diced
1 cup green peas
1 cup pecans, chopped
1 cup mayonnaise
½ cup cream, whipped
½ cup vinegar
1 teaspoon grated onion
2 tablespoons sugar
1 teaspoon salt
1 tablespoon gelatin
¼ cup cold water
Cayenne pepper to taste

Soak sweetbreads ½ hour in acidulated water; boil in salted water for 20 minutes; blanch in cold water; drain; break in small pieces. Soak gelatin in cold water; dissolve in vinegar which has been heated with salt, onion and sugar; chill. When thick, add to combined mayonnaise and whipped cream. Add sweetbreads, pecans and vegetables. Correct seasoning. Put in refrigerator tray; freeze slightly for about 2 hours. Serves 10.

FROZEN STUFFED TOMATOES

8 small tomatoes
1 pound cottage cheese
1 tablespoon grated onion

1 cup finely minced celery
2 heaping tablespoons mayonnaise

Sieve cheese; drain thoroughly; combine with other ingredients. Scald, skin, and scoop out tomatoes from stem end; sprinkle with salt; invert to drain. Stuff with cheese mixture; put in freezing unit of refrigerator for 2 hours, or until frozen lightly. These are nice to serve in hot weather around a mold of jellied chicken. Serves 8.

FROZEN TREASURE SALAD

1 can firm peach halves
2 packages (3-ounce) Philadelphia cream cheese
½ cup chopped almonds
Salt and cayenne pepper to taste

1 cup mayonnaise
1 cup cream, whipped
1 tablespoon lemon juice
1 teaspoon onion juice

Add lemon and onion juice to mayonnaise; season highly. Smooth cheese with whipped cream; add mayonnaise and almonds. Place peach halves side by side in small refrigerator tray. Pour cheese mixture over and around peaches so that peaches are covered with the mixture. Freeze. Cut in squares, allowing a peach half covered with cheese for each portion. Serves 6 to 8.

SALAD DRESSINGS

ANCHOVY MAYONNAISE

1 cup mayonnaise
½ teaspoon anchovy paste
1 teaspoon tarragon vinegar

2 tablespoons plain vinegar
1 tablespoon chili sauce

Smooth anchovy with vinegar; combine with other ingredients.

AVOCADO MAYONNAISE

1 avocado, thoroughly mashed
1 package Philadelphia cheese (3 ounces)

½ cup stiff mayonnaise
Salt and red pepper to taste

Mash cheese with mayonnaise; add pear. This is especially good on tomato aspic.

BOILED SALAD DRESSING

4 yolks or 2 whole eggs, well beaten
1 cup vinegar
2 tablespoons butter
2 tablespoons flour

⅔ cup whipping cream
2 teaspoons dry mustard
Salt and red pepper
4 tablespoons sugar

Add dry ingredients to beaten eggs. Heat vinegar; combine with other ingredients; cook in double boiler until thick. Add whipped cream when cold.

CELERY SEED DRESSING

1 tablespoon celery seed
½ cup sugar
½ teaspoon salt
1½ tablespoons dry mustard
2 teaspoons dry tarragon (optional)

⅛ teaspoon red pepper
2 cups salad oil
1 cup tarragon vinegar
½ teaspoon onion juice
1 clove garlic

Boil the first 6 ingredients with vinegar for 5 minutes. Cool; add oil, onion juice and garlic very slowly, beating until thick. Remove the garlic after an hour. Serve on head lettuce.

CRAB MEAT MAYONNAISE DRESSING

1 pint mayonnaise
1 tablespoon lemon juice

1 6-ounce can crab meat, shredded

Combine. Especially good with tomato aspic.

FRENCH DESSING

2 cups olive oil or Wesson oil
⅔ cup vinegar
2 tablespoons lemon juice
1½ teaspoons salt

¼ teaspoon cayenne pepper
1 tablespoon paprika
1 tablespoon sugar

Combine all ingredients. Put in a jar with an onion sliced in half. Use as needed. Stir well, before serving.

SWEET FRENCH DRESSING

1 cup French dressing
⅓ cup sugar

⅓ cup tomato catsup

Make French dressing according to recipe; add sugar and catsup.

TOMATO-FRENCH DRESSING

2 cups salad oil
½ cup vinegar
1 lemon (juice of)
½ cup tomato catsup
1 onion, grated
1 egg, beaten

½ cup sugar
½ teaspoon mustard
1 teaspoon salt
1 teaspoon paprika
¼ teaspoon black pepper

Combine dry ingredients. Add oil gradually to beaten egg alternating wih onion juice; combine with other ingredients.

FRUIT SALAD DRESSING

1 cup pineapple juice
1 lemon
½ cup sugar

2 tablespoons flour
2 eggs
1 cup whipping cream

Beat eggs; add sugar and flour. Heat fruit juice; pour over the mixture. Cook in double boiler until quite thick. Chill; add whipped cream when ready to serve.

Fruit Salad Dressing (2)

2 eggs
2 teaspoon cornstarch
½ cup sugar
1 lemon

1 orange
1 lime
½ cup pineapple juice
1 tablespoon butter or magarine

Add sugar to cornstarch. Beat eggs until well mixed; add sugar mixture.

Heat juices in double boiler; when hot add the egg mixture and cook over hot water until thick. Add butter when done. Whipped cream can also be added if desired.

FROZEN MAYONNAISE

1 cup mayonnaise
½ cup chili sauce
2 hard-boiled eggs, riced

1 chopped pimento
1 tablespoon Worcestershire sauce

Combine. Season highly and freeze, not too hard. Serve in tomatoes.

MAYONNAISE

2 egg yolks
½ teaspoon salt
¼ teaspoon cayenne pepper

1 teaspoon dry mustard
1 pint olive or Wesson oil
Juice lemon

Beat yolks until very thick; add salt, mustard and pepper; pour oil into mixture a few drops at a time until it begins to thicken; gradually increase additions of oil, alternating with lemon juice. Eggs and oil should both be the same temperature. If mayonnaise should curdle, it can be reclaimed by beating an egg yolk in another bowl and gradually adding the curdled mixture.

JIFFY MAYONNAISE

This is an easy recipe, if an electric mixer is available. Use the same ingredients listed above. Beat yolks five minutes; add oil, a fourth cup at a time, alternating with lemon juice. Add seasoning last. This is important, as the seasoning thins the consistency of beaten yolks when added first, and the oil has to be added more slowly. I have never known this method to curdle.

POPPY SEED DRESSING

½ cup sugar
⅓ cup honey
1 teaspoon onion
6 tablespoons tarragon vinegar
3 tablespoons lemon juice

1 cup salad oil
1 teaspoon dry mustard
1 teaspoon paprika
¼ teaspoon salt
2 teaspoon poppy seed

Soak poppy seed 2 hours in water; drain through cheese cloth. Mix dry ingredients; add honey, vinegar, onion, and lemon juice. Pour oil in very slowly, beating constantly; add drained poppy seed. Best made in electric mixer. It should be very thick.

RED DRESSING

1 bottle chili sauce
½ cup Wesson oil

1 cup chopped celery
¼ cup lemon juice or vinegar

Combine ingredients.

ROQUEFORT CHEESE DRESSING

1 cup French dressing
2 eggs, hard-boiled and chopped fine

1 point Roquefort cheese

Smooth cheese with part of the French dressing; add rest of dressing and eggs. Serve over shredded lettuce; sprinkle crumbled breakfast bacon over the salad just before serving.

Roquefort Cheese Dressing (2)

1 small can evaporated milk
1 pint mayonnaise
½ pound Roquefort cheese (ground)

3 tablespoons lemon juice
½ pod garlic, minced very fine or crushed in garlic press

Chill milk; add lemon juice; beat until thick; add other ingredients.

RUSSIAN DRESSING

2 cups mayonnaise
½ onion, minced fine
1 tablespoon bell pepper, minced fine
1 cup finely chopped celery

½ teaspoon curry powder (optional)
1 tablespoon Worcestershire sauce
½ cup tomato catsup or chili sauce

Combine ingredients.

SLAW DRESSING

1 cup water
1 cup vinegar
¾ cup sugar
½ cup flour

1 teaspoon salt
1 tablespoon dry mustard
½ cup butter or margarine
4 beaten eggs

Beat eggs; add dry ingredients. Heat vinegar and water; pour over eggs. Cook until thick, in double boiler. Add butter just before taking off stove.

Slaw Dressing (2)

3 eggs, beaten together
½ cup vinegar
½ cup sugar
1 tablespoon melted butter
1 teaspoon salt

2 tablespoons cornstarch
1 tablespoon dry mustard
Red pepper to taste
1 cup milk or cream

Beat yolks; add dry ingredients and vinegar. Add milk to this and cook over hot water until thick.

SOUR CREAM DRESSING

½ pint sour cream
½ lemon
1 tablespoon wine vinegar
1 tablespoon horse-radish
Cayenne pepper to taste

1½ teaspoon salt
1 teaspoon dry mustard
½ teaspoon paprika
1 teaspoon onion juice

Combine ingredients. Use commercial sour cream if possible, as it is very thick and makes a better dressing.

THOUSAND ISLAND DRESSING

1 cup oil mayonnaise
4 tablespoons tomato catsup
2 tablespoons chili sauce
1 tablespoon Worcestershire sauce

4 tablespoons finely minced celery
2 hard-boiled eggs, riced
1 tablespoon horse-radish, drained

Combine ingredients in the order given.

VEGETABLE SALAD DRESSING

3 ribs celery
1 onion
1 small bell pepper
2 cloves garlic
1 cup olive or Wesson oil

2 lemons (juice of)
½ cup sugar
1 teaspoon salt
1 cup tomato catsup
2 tablespoons Worcestershire sauce

Chop the vegetables fine and combine with the other ingredients. Take garlic out after it has stood for several hours; store dressing in refrigerator. This is good on head lettuce or on grapefruit salad.

WINE DRESSING

¼ cup sherry wine
¼ teaspoon salt

½ cup lemon or lime juice
⅛ cup sugar

Combine ingredients. This is nice to serve on "Fresh Fruit Salad."

OPEN FACED ANCHOVY AND CHEESE SANDWICH

Mix 2 packages of Philadelphia cream cheese with 1 teaspoon, more or less, of anchovy paste; add a scraping of onion juice; spread on small circles of rye bread; top with an olive slice.

ASPARAGUS AND CREAM CHEESE SANDWICH

Cut white asparagus very fine; squeeze in a clean napkin; add this to Philadelphia cream cheese with some highly seasoned mayonnaise; scrape a little onion juice into it. Spread on whole wheat bread buttered with mayonnaise.

ROLLED ASPARAGUS SANDWICH

Cut crusts from sandwich bread; spread with mayonnaise. Roll a white asparagus tip, that has been sprinkled with French dressing, in each slice of bread, cornerwise; hold together, with a toothpick. When ready to serve, remove toothpick, put a parsley bud at the tip of each sandwich; arrange on platter like spokes of a wheel. These can also be used as a toasted sandwich by brushing with melted butter, toasting, and serving hot. A bit of anchovy paste can be added to the mayonnaise before spreading the sandwiches, for a different flavor.

AVOCADO SANDWICHES

Mash ripe avocados through a sieve; add a scraping of onion juice and a French dressing made of 2 tablespoons olive oil and 1 tablespoon of lime juice; season with salt and red pepper. Spread on crisp circles of toast.

ANCHOVY AND SHRIMP SANDWICH

Grind one small can of shrimp; add 1 tablespoon lemon juice, 1 tablespoon anchovy paste and mayonnaise to bind together. Peel one cucumber; slice very thin, marinate in French dressing fifteen minutes; drain. Cut bread in fancy shapes; spread with mayonnaise. On one-half of each sandwich put one or two cucumber slices; spread the other half with shrimp mixture and put together in pairs.

BROWN BREAD AND CRYSTALLIZED GINGER CIRCLES

Cut crusts from Boston brown bread by using a cutter slightly smaller than the slice of bread; spread with creamed butter that has been mixed with finely chopped crystallized ginger. Put two slices together; remove small round sandwiches from the center of each large sandwich with a small cutter. Put these in the center of the tray and surround by the ring shaped sandwiches.

BOSTON BROWN BREAD WEDGES

Cut Boston brown bread and white bread circles with a cutter just smaller than round slices of canned brown bread. Spread bread lightly with butter. Put together in stacks, with a "Sharp Cheese Sandwich filling," alternate two slices of each kind of bread. The cheese filling should be fairly thick. When they have been assembled, cut each stack in half and then in quarters, making four "wedges" of each stack.

CALLA LILY SANDWICHES

Cut crusts from thin slices of bread; snip off three corners, so they will have a slightly rounded effect. Spread to the edges with a highly seasoned mixture of Philadelphia cream cheese and a little onion juice. Make rolls of yellow, "Old English Spread" cheese, about $2\frac{1}{2}$ inches long and $\frac{3}{8}$ inch in diameter for stamen of lily. Place in icebox until firm; put on the slices of bread, diagonally, with one end of the cheese roll at the untrimmed corner of the bread. Pinch bread together at this end overlapping the cheese roll; hold together with a small section of toothpick; cover toothpick with a parsley bud. Radiate the lilies around sandwich tray, with parsley buds at the center.

CELERY SANDWICHES

Mince celery very fine. To every cup of celery add one-half cup of chopped pecans; bind together with boiled salad dressing; spread between rounds of whole wheat bread that have been previously buttered with mayonnaise.

CARROT SANDWICHES

Grate carrots; grate a little onion over them; put in collander. Spread scalloped rounds of whole wheat bread with mayonnaise. When ready to serve add some chopped black olives and mayonnaise to carrots. Fill sandwiches.

CHEESE SANDWICHES

1 8-ounce package sharp cheese	½ grated onion
12 stuffed olives, chopped	2 tablespoons melted butter
2 hard-boiled eggs, cut fine	2 tablespoons lemon juice
½ cup chopped celery	

Grate cheese; add the other ingredients. Spread on bread that has been buttered with mayonnaise.

Cheese Sandwiches (2)

1½ cups grated sharp cheese	1 tablespoon mayonnaise
2 tablespoons tomato catsup	2 tablespoons celery, minced
1 tablespoon Worcestershire sauce	1 tablespoon minced parsley
Rye bread	1 teaspoon minced onion

Combine ingredients. Spread on rye bread that has been buttered with mayonnaise.

Cheese Sandwiches (3)

1 cup grated cheese	3 strips crisp breakfast bacon, crumbled
6 minced olives	1 tablespoon horse-radish
3 pieces minced celery	1 tablespoon mayonnaise

Combine ingredients. Spread on rounds of bread that have been buttered with mayonnaise.

CHEESE AND ANCHOVY SANDWICH

1 cup Philadelphia cream cheese	1 cup celery, chopped
1 tablespoon anchovy paste	½ cup chopped stuffed olives
½ cup pecans, chopped	

Combine ingredients. Cut whole wheat bread in fancy shapes; spread with mayonnaise then with cheese mixture.

CHEESE AND BACON OPEN FACED SANDWICHES

1 cup raw breakfast bacon, cut fine with scissors	2 tablespoons prepared mustard
1 cup grated sharp American cheese	1 teaspoon onion juice
	2 teaspoons mayonnaise

Combine cheese, bacon and seasoning. Toast rounds of bread on one side; spread the untoasted side with the cheese mixture, put in oven until cheese melts and bacon cooks. Serve at once.

CHEESE DREAMS

Grate sharp American cheese; add Worcestershire sauce and red pepper to taste; put a flattened ball of cheese between two rounds of bread. Do not let it extend to the edges of the bread; but have it rather thick at the center; brush with melted butter and toast. These can also be rolled from corner to corner and held in place by a toothpick until toasted.

CREAM CHEESE AND GUAVA SANDWICHES

Cut sandwich bread in star shape; brush with melted butter; toast on both sides. On top of each star, put a spoon of Philadelphia cream cheese, that has been softened slightly with cream; make an indentation at the center; put a small spoon of guava jelly into the indentation. Best made shortly before serving.

CHEESE, LILY OF THE VALLEY SANDWICH

Cut small rounds of bread; cover first with mayonnaise and then with highly seasoned Philadelphia cream cheese, which has been tinted a pretty green color and flavored slightly with onion juice. Let the cheese extend to the outside edges of the bread and smooth it on carefully. This is used as a base for a lily of the valley spray, which is arranged on the green cheese. Stems and leaves are cut from bell peppers and lily bells are made of the very tiny French pearl onions. Use a pair of eyebrow tweezers to put these little onions in place along the stems. Cut stems as narrow as possible and curve them slightly. The leaves are cut wider. Trim off inside of pepper from stems and leaves.

CHEESE WITH OLIVE FLOWER SANDWICH

Spread rounds of bread with "Roquefort Spread" cheese, tinted yellow. Arrange flower stems and leaves, cut from green bell peppers, on top of the cheese; make flowers from slices of very small stuffed olives.

PHILADELPHIA CHEESE AND MINCEMEAT SANDWICHES

Cut bread with a scalloped cutter. From the top half of each sandwich, remove a circle, with a small round sandwich cutter; spread with mayonnaise. Cover top half of sandwich with Philadelphia cheese, that has been softened to spreading consistency with cream or milk. Spread the bottom half with mincemeat; put together. If commercial mincemeat is used, season with a little sherry wine.

CREAM CHEESE-ORANGE MARMALADE SANDWICHES

Cut bread in rounds; spread with mayonnaise. On half of the sandwich put Philadelphia cheese, that has been mixed with cream or milk to spreading consistency; on the other half sandwich spread "Orange Marmalade." Put together.

CHEESE AND ORANGE MARMALADE TOAST

Toast rounds of bread; spread with melted butter; top with a rather stiff orange marmalade; cover marmalade with grated American cheese; put under broiler. Serve hot.

CHEESE OLIVE-CAVIAR SANDWICHES

½ pound Philadelphia cream cheese	1 tablespoon caviar
1 cup chopped ripe olives	1 tablespoon lemon juice

Combine ingredients; moisten with enough cream to make a spreading consistency. Spread fingers of toast with mayonnaise; cover with a thin layer filling and decorate with a slice of stuffed olive.

CHEESE AND STUFFED OLIVE SANDWICHES

Put a small bottle of stuffed olives through meat grinder; drain; add this to four cakes Philadelphia cream cheese; blend well. More cheese can be added if desired. Cut bread in heart shape; from the center of the top half of the sandwich, cut a heart with tiny heart shaped cutter. Fill the space with a pimento heart, cut with same cutter. Spread sandwiches with mayonnaise; fill with cream cheese mixture. Sets of very tiny cutters, to be used for canapés and sandwich decoration, can be bought from stores carrying a good line of kitchen gadgets.

CHEESE AND POPPY SEED OPEN FACED SANDWICHES

1 pound Cheddar cheese	½ pound butter

Cream together and spread on toast rounds. Sprinkle with poppy seed and toast in moderate oven.

CHEESE PUFF SQUARES

Cut day old, unsliced bread into 1½ inch square blocks, cover all sides, except the bottom, with the following: 1 cup of butter creamed with 2 cups grated cheese, a dash of cayenne pepper. Toast just before using. If cheese mixture spreads when toasted, trim edges of puffs with scissors; serve at once.

BACON WRAPPED CHEESE ROLLS

Make or buy finger rolls 2½ to 3 inches long. Stuff, by making a slit on one side and packing "Cheese Dream" mixture inside the roll. Cut breakfast bacon in half lengthwise; wrap these strips around and around the roll; tuck bacon on underneath side; put on a wire rack; cook in oven until bacon is crisp. Serve hot.

RUSSIAN CHEESE SANDWICHES

Grate one pound sharp cheese; mix to spreading consistency with tomato catsup; add two tablespoons Worcestershire sauce, one small grated onion, one cup finely minced celery and one minced bell pepper. Remove crusts from rye bread; cut in finger lengths; butter with mayonnaise and spread with cheese mixture.

SWISS CHEESE AND RYE BREAD

Grate one pound of Swiss cheese; chop one large green bell pepper fine; knead with several tablespoons of mayonnaise to spreading consistency. Cut rounds of rye bread; spread with mayonnaise and then with cheese mixture. Remove a circle from the top half of each sandwich and when the sandwich is assembled, put a pickle slice into the cut out space. If preferred, plain round sandwiches can be made; brushed with melted butter and toasted to make delicious cheese dreams.

CHEESE AND RIPE OLIVE SANDWICHES

1 pound cheese, grated   1 tablespoon chopped bell pepper
¾ cup chopped ripe olives

Combine; add enough cream or mayonnaise to make spreading consistency; put on rounds of toasted bread.

SNAPPY CHEESE SANDWICH

1 cup sharp grated cheese   2 slices crisp breakfast bacon, crumbled
6 stuffed olives, chopped   2 pieces celery, cut fine
1 hard-boiled egg, chopped

Combine with mayonnaise to make sandwich filling.

CHEESE AND CRYSTALLIZED FRUIT SANDWICHES

Smooth half pound of Philadelphia cheese with orange juice; add 1 cup chopped, mixed, crystallized fruit; ½ cup chopped pecans and 1 teaspoon grated orange rind. Spread between buttered rounds of brown bread.

CHEESE AND WATER CRESS SANDWICHES

Soften cream cheese with a little cream; season with salt, cayenne pepper, and a few drops of onion juice; strip off leaves of water cress; add to cheese. Use as many as you like as the cheese is merely a base to hold the cress together. Use as filling for finger shaped sandwiches, which have been previously spread with mayonnaise.

CHEESE WHEELS

Cut rounds of bread. With a smaller cutter, take circles from the centers of each round; toast on one side; spread the other side with melted butter; cover thickly with grated Parmesan cheese. Toast; serve cold. Can be made a day ahead.

CHEESE WHEEL CHRISTMAS WREATHS

Make "Cheese Wheels," just before serving, arrange tiny parsley buds and bits of pimento around the circle, at intervals. Put two bits of pimento on each parsley bud to resemble holly. The pimento bits are cut about an 1/8 of an inch across; put them in place with a pair of eyebrow tweezers.

CHICKEN SALAD SANDWICHES

1 hen, boiled and ground
1 stalk celery, minced fine
1 cup sliced almonds (optional)
1/2 cup cooked dressing
1/2 cup whipped cream
1/2 cup (more or less) of
Oil mayonnaise to make a spreading consistency

Combine ingredients. Cut bread in fancy shapes; spread with mayonnaise; fill with the chicken mixture. Heart shaped sandwiches, with a tiny heart removed from the center (which is replaced with a pimento heart of the same size), are especially attractive looking.

THIS SAME FILLING can be used to fill tiny toast cups or 1½ inch cream puff shells; put parsley bud garnish on top of each.

CHICKEN AND MUSHROOM OPEN FACED SANDWICHES

Melt three tablespoons butter in skillet; add 1 tablespoon minced onion; cook until tender. Smooth two tablespoons flour with onion and butter; add half cup of milk and two tablespoons grated cheese. Stir in one cup each of ground chicken and minced mushrooms; season to taste. Spread on rounds of buttered toast; sprinkle with grated Parmesan cheese; toast and serve hot.

CHICKEN-TONGUE-HAM SANDWICHES

1 cup ground chicken
1/2 cup ground ham
1/2 cup ground tongue
1/2 cup "Cream Sauce—Medium"
1/2 cup mayonnaise with
1/2 teaspoon of curry powder in it

Combine ingredients. Toast circles of bread; cover with the mixture; sprinkle with grated cheese; bake until cheese is melted.

CINNAMON TOAST SANDWICHES

Spread trimmed slices of bread with a paste made of 1 cup of brown sugar, 2 tablespoons melted butter and 1 teaspoon powdered cinnamon. Roll, point to point, to make open-end rolled sandwiches; brush with melted butter; toast carefully, as they burn easily. Serve hot. These can be made a day ahead, brushed with melted butter and kept covered in the refrigerator until ready to toast.

CINNAMON TOAST STICKS

Slice bread half inch thick; cut in half inch wide finger length; dip in melted butter; roll in cinnamon sugar; toast on all sides on greased baking sheet. Allow one teaspoon of cinnamon to one cup of granulated sugar.

CRAB MEAT SANDWICHES

1 can (5 ounces) crab meat
2 hard-boiled eggs, chopped fine

4 ribs celery, chopped fine
Mayonnaise or cooked dressing

Pick over crab meat and chop; add eggs and celery; bind together with dressing. Cooked dressing is especially nice with seafood, but mayonnaise can be used with a little lemon juice added to the mixture. Spread rounds of sandwich bread with mayonnaise before adding the filling. The same mixture can be used on toasted rounds, for open faced sandwiches; decorate these with slice of stuffed olive.

CUCUMBER AND ONION SANDWICHES

Grate cucumbers; add salt and a little grated onion. Drain and pat dry between cloths. Add mayonnaise to make spreading consistency. Cut whole wheat bread in fancy shapes; spread with mayonnaise; fill with cucumber mixture. These should be assembled just before they are to be served.

CUCUMBER SANDWICHES

Marinate thinly sliced cucumbers with French dressing; let stand for half on hour; drain. Just before serving, put between slices of whole wheat bread, that has been spread with mayonnaise.

CUCUMBER AND ALMOND SANDWICHES

3 cucumbers, chopped fine and drained (this should make about two cups); marinate with French dressing for half hour; drain; add 1 cup chopped salted almonds. Spread whole wheat bread with mayonnaise; put cucumber mixture between layers.

CUCUMBER AND CHEESE SANDWICHES

Chop or grate one cucumber very fine; add to six 3 ounce cakes of Philadelphia cream cheese; season with salt, red pepper and a little Worcestershire sauce. Butter petal-shaped sandwiches of whole wheat bread with mayonnaise; spread with the cheese mixture.

CUCUMBER AND TONGUE SANDWICHES

1 cold, boiled, smoked tongue
½ cup minced celery
½ cup chopped and drained cucumber

1 tablespoon minced green pepper
1 tablespoon minced onion

Bind ingredients together with cooked dressing. Cut sandwiches in fancy shapes; butter with mayonnaise before spreading with filling.

DATE NUT SANDWICHES

1 package dates	1 cup orange marmalade
1 cup pecans	1 lemon (juice of)

Grind pecans and dates together; add marmalade and lemon juice; make into small scalloped sandwiches; using buttered white bread for one side and whole wheat for the other.

DATE GINGER SANDWICHES

Grind one pound of dates with one cup English walnuts; add a half cup of chopped, preserved ginger, 1 tablespoon lemon juice and a few tablespoons of cream. Mix to a smooth paste. Spread on buttered brown bread.

EGG AND ALMOND SANDWICHES

6 hard-boiled eggs	½ teaspoon sugar
½ cup blanched almonds	1 teaspoon vinegar
¼ teaspoon prepared mustard	Salt and pepper to taste

Chop eggs and blanched almonds very fine; add seasoning and enough cooked dressing to bind together; spread between rounds of bread that have been buttered with mayonnaise; decorate top centers with slices of stuffed olive. A little chopped celery can be substituted for the almonds if desired.

EGG AND ANCHOVY SANDWICHES

6 hard-boiled eggs, chopped fine or grated	2 tablespoons chopped bell pepper (op-
2 tablespoons anchovy paste	tional)

Bind ingredients together with mayonnaise. Spread circles of bread with mayonnaise; fill with egg mixture. If desired these can be brushed with melted butter and toasted.

HALLOWEEN SANDWICHES

Slice Boston brown bread in thin slices, then, with a round cutter, a fraction smaller than the bread slices, cut out sandwiches. Cut jack-o'-lantern faces from half of the circles, with a sharp, pointed knife. Use these for the top half of the sandwiches. Spread the lower half with a sharp yellow cheese filling, putting it on thickly; top with the jack-o'-lantern face; press down until the cheese is forced up into the cut out spaces.

HAM OR CHEESE POCKET BOOK ROLLS

Use any good roll dough; cut in circles; brush with melted butter; put grated ham or cheese over each round; fold over like pocket book rolls, brush with melted butter; bake; serve hot.

HAM AND OLIVE SANDWICHES

1 cup ground ham	1 cup grated Swiss cheese
1 cup chopped olives	1 small onion grated

Combine ingredients. Put on buttered toast rounds; sprinkle with Parmesan cheese; toast until cheese melts.

HAM SQUARES

Trim crust from a day old loaf of unsliced bread; cut into 1½ inch slices, then into 1½ inch squares. Trim out center of each square, in a box effect, with walls ¼ inch thick (use scissors to do this). Brush with melted butter; toast all except the top of the squares, turning the boxes as they toast. Fill with a mixture of grated Cheddar cheese and grated ham, kneaded with enough mayonnaise or tomato catsup to bind them together; press filling down into boxes; run into oven and toast. Serve hot.

MOCK PATÉ DE FOIE GRAS SANDWICHES

1 pound calf liver	6 tablespoons melted butter
½ teaspoon salt	1 tablespoon lemon juice
1 teaspoon prepared mustard	1 dash red pepper

Boil liver until tender; put through meat grinder; work to a paste with butter and seasoning. Use as spread on whole wheat sandwiches that have first been spread with mayonnaise.

TOASTED MUSHROOM SANDWICHES

2 8-ounce cans mushrooms	2 tablespoons flour
1 onion	¼ teaspoon salt
2 canned pimentos	1 pinch cayenne pepper
2 tablespoon butter	

Grind mushrooms, onion, and pimentos. Cook mixture in butter five minutes; add flour and seasoning; cook until slightly thick. Put between bread rounds; brush with melted butter and toast. These can be filled, brushed with butter, and kept overnight in refrigerator, covered with a damp cloth. Toast just before serving.

INDIVIDUAL OYSTER LOAVES

Make very small pocketbook rolls; brush with melted butter; bake. When ready to serve, open top of each roll; put in one "Deviled Oyster" (sea foods).

RIPE OLIVE AND NUT SANDWICH

1 cup finely ground black olives	3 tablespoons cooked dressing or enough
½ cup pecans, ground, or cut fine	to make spreading consistently

Butter bread with mayonnaise before spreading with olive mixture. Especially good on whole wheat bread.

ORANGE TOAST

1 cup brown sugar	Enough orange juice to make a very
Grated rind of 1 orange	stiff paste
1 tablespoon melted butter	

Spread on buttered toast and run in the oven until it bubbles. The secret of this is a stiff paste.

PIN WHEEL SANDWICH

Trim crusts from unsliced day-old bread; slice lengthwise in thin slices. Spread with any good cheese mixture (green-tinted cheese used for ribbon sandwiches, pimento cheese, or cheese used for Roquefort sandwiches can be used). Roll tightly from end to end; hold in place with a toothpick; wrap in waxed paper; cover with damp cloth; chill in refrigerator several hours. Slice with a very sharp knife in ½-inch slices when ready to use. If desired, several small pickles or stuffed olives can be laid end to end across the small end of the bread and rolled up with it to form the center of the pin wheels. Bread can be flattened with a rolling pin before it is filled. This facilitates rolling the bread.

TINY CREAM PUFF SHELLS WITH CHICKEN SALAD OR SEA FOOD

Make puff shells from "Cream Puff" recipe, put small teaspoons of batter on baking sheet; bake until crisp and brown. When cold, remove tops with a sharp-pointed knife; fill with chicken salad; top with parsley bud.

CREAM PUFF SHELLS WITH CHEESE

Make tiny cream puff shells. Remove tops with pointed knife; fill with desired cheese mixture. A combination of cream and Roquefort cheese or equal parts of a heavy cream sauce and sharp grated cheese are especially good. The latter should be topped with more grated cheese and heated.

RIBBON SANDWICHES

1 loaf sandwich bread, sliced	2 pimentos, chopped
2 cakes (3-ounce) Philadelphia cream cheese	8 stuffed olives, chopped
2 tablespoons cream	½ pound package spreading cheese (yellow)
½ small onion, grated	

Soften Philadelphia cheese with milk; add onion and pimentos. Add olives to spreading cheese with enough milk to soften. Trim crusts off bread; spread slices with mayonnaise; then spread one slice with Philadelphia cheese; top with second slice which has been spread with yellow cheese; top that with a third slice. Cover stacks with damp cloth and put in refrigerator until ready to serve. Chill several hours; cut in ½-inch slices. If desired, the middle slice can be whole wheat bread.

OTHER RIBBON SANDWICHES can be made by coloring the seasoned cheese with green vegetable coloring. Use this filling with three slices of white bread to make ribbon sandwiches.

ROQUEFORT SANDWICHES

3 ounces Philadelphia cream cheese	1 teaspoon onion juice
3 tablespoons Roquefort cheese	1 teaspoon Worcestershire sauce
2 tablespoons butter or cream	½ tablespoon paprika
½ teaspoon salt	3 tablespoons chopped celery

Cream first three ingredients together; add seasoning and finely chopped celery; spread between rye bread crescents that have been spread with mayonnaise.

SARDINE SANDWICHES

1 small can sardines
1 teaspoon prepared mustard

⅛ large sour pickle, chopped fine
2 teaspoons lemon juice

Mash sardines and add seasonings. Butter toast circles with mayonnaise and put a thin layer of sardine mixture on each. Top with a slice of stuffed olive.

Sardine Sandwiches (2)

6 sardines
6 anchovies
4 hard-boiled eggs

2 tablespoons melted butter
Lemon juice

Grate eggs; mince sardines and anchovies; combine with melted butter; add lemon juice and smooth to a paste. Spread small rounds of bread with mayonnaise; put together with filling; decorate with olive slices.

HOT SARDINE BISCUIT

Fill small baking powder biscuit with a paste made of 1 stick of creamed butter to one box of good sardines, mashed fine.

SAUSAGE TURNOVERS

Cook smoked sausage; chop fine; use as a filling for tiny pastry turnovers; serve piping hot.

SHRIMP OVALS

Cut ovals from sandwich bread with a petal-shaped sandwich cutter; brush with melted butter; toast; cover with shrimp paste; top with ¾-inch circles of toast placed in center of oval; flank with parsley bud. To make the shrimp paste, marinate a pound of cooked, cleaned shrimp in French dressing for one hour; drain and grind; add a cup of finely minced celery and enough mayonnaise to bind together. A pinch of curry powder in the mayonnaise gives a good flavor.

SPRING SANDWICHES

3 firm tomatoes
1 bunch celery
1 cucumber

1 onion
1 bell pepper
Mayonnaise

Peel and chop tomatoes; chop other vegetables in very small pieces; add salt to taste; put in colander to drain. Just before serving the sandwiches, stir several spoons of mayonnaise into the mixture; put in a colander to drain again. Cut whole wheat bread with a scalloped cutter and spread with mayonnaise; fill with vegetable mixture; serve at once.

TOAST CUPS WITH CREAMED CRAB AND MUSHROOMS

Cut bread in circles; brush with melted butter; fit into tiny muffin tins and toast. Fill these little cups with the following mixture: 1 cup of rich, thick cream dressing, 1 cup of flaked crab meat and ½ cup of chopped mushrooms; season highly; flavor with sherry.

TOMATO SANDWICH

Scald and skin firm tomatoes; slice thin; sprinkle with salt; scrape a little onion juice over them. Place slices in large colander and leave until ready to make sandwiches. Cut bread with round or scalloped cutter. From center half of the rounds cut a small circle; use these for top half of sandwich. Spread with mayonnaise before filling with tomato. Another attractive way to cut tomato sandwiches is to use a circle of bread for the bottom of the sandwich and a crescent-shaped piece for the top; put a parsley bud at the inner edge of the crescent on the tomato slice.

TOASTED TOMATO SANDWICH

Toast rounds of bread on both sides; spread one side with mayonnaise. Make open-faced sandwiches by putting a slice of tomato on each toasted round; scrape a little onion juice over the surface of the tomato; sprinkle with salt; cover with ½ slice of crisp breakfast bacon. Sprinkle grated Parmesan cheese over the surface and toast until cheese melts.

TOMATO PASTE SANDWICH

Mash Roquefort cheese, or "Roquefort Cheese Spread," with a can of tomato paste; season to taste with salt, red pepper and onion juice; add more cheese if necessary; spread on open-face toasted circles, or heart-shaped pieces of toast; decorate outer edges with tiny pearl onions.

TONGUE OLIVE SANDWICH

1 boiled, smoked tongue, ground
2 cups pecans, cut fine

2 cups stuffed olives, chopped
Cooked dressing

Bind ingredients together with cooked salad dressing; spread bread with mayonnaise before filling with tongue mixture.

HOT TOMATO SANDWICH

Remove crusts from large slices of bread; toast; butter with mayonnaise. Cover toast with slice of tomato, grating of onion and sprinkle of salt. Lay several crisp slices of breakfast bacon over tomato and cover completely with hot "Cheese Sauce" or with "Welsh Rabbit."

TOWER OF PISA SANDWICH

Allow 5 rounds of bread in graduating sizes, for each sandwich. The first round should be as large as possible and the last one about an inch and a half in diameter. Spread the largest round with mayonnaise; cover with a slice of baked chicken breast; sprinkle with salt. The other rounds should be buttered on both sides with mayonnaise; cover chicken breast with the next size smaller round; on top of that put a slice of tomato. Grate a suspicion of onion over the tomato and sprinkle with salt. Cover tomato with next size slice of bread; spread this round with grated egg and almond mixture; (see "Egg and Almond Sandwich"); sprinkle egg with minced breakfast bacon. Cover the next round with a fish mixture. This can be crab, shrimp, lobster or caviar (see "Fish Sandwiches"). Spread the last round with seasoned Philadelphia cream cheese and top with a spoon of guava jelly. Serve this on lettuce with additional mayonnaise. This is a complete meal.

CHICKEN-EGG BREAD SANDWICH

2 cups meal
3 eggs, beaten together
2 cups milk
4 teaspoon baking powder
1 teaspoon salt
2 tablespoons melted shortening

2 tablespoons chicken fat
2 tablespoons minced celery
2 tablespoons grated onion
1 can condensed cream of mushroom soup
3 cups chicken broth
Salt and red pepper to taste

Make egg bread of first 6 ingredients; pour in hot greased pan; cook at 400° for 25 minutes; cut in large squares; split and butter. Make sauce of remaining ingredients. Cook celery and onion in chicken fat until tender. Add soup, broth, salt and pepper. Put a large slice of baked chicken between corn bread; cover completely with sauce.

TRICORNE TOASTS WITH CHERRY PRESERVES

Cut 3-inch circles from fresh sandwich bread; pinch into tricorne shape by dividing the circles in thirds and pinching the bread together at the 3 intervals. This makes a little container which can be brushed with melted butter and toasted. When this is filled with thick cherry preserves, it will resemble a little George Washington hat. A little pointed, green leaf (such as cherry laurel) can be stuck at one side as a cockade.

TUNA FISH SANDWICH

1 can tuna fish
3 tablespoons cooked dressing
1 teaspoon Worcestershire sauce

1 teaspoon lemon juice
½ cup chopped celery

Mince tuna fish; add other ingredients; spread bread with mayonnaise before filling sandwiches.

THREE DECK TURKEY SANDWICH

Use 3 slices of bread, cut in rounds, for each sandwich. Butter the bread and put the three slices together, using sliced turkey breast for the top and bottom layers and a ¼-inch slice of canned cranberry jelly for the central layer. I use a round sandwich cutter which is the same diameter of the can of cranberry sauce. The sandwiches have to be eaten with knife and fork unless they are cut in half crosswise before they are served.

TURKEY SANDWICHES (CRANBERRY JELLY GARNISH)

Make turkey salad, following recipe for chicken salad. Turkey breast cut in thin slices and trimmed the same size as the sandwich can be used instead of salad. Use a 2½-inch round cutter for sandwich. From the top of each sandwich cut a 1-inch circle. With the same small cutter take circles from sliced cranberry jelly and insert in the top of each sandwich. When using turkey salad, spread the sandwiches first with mayonnaise. Use softened butter if turkey breast is used. Nice at Christmas time.

VALENTINE SANDWICHES

Cut bread with a heart-shaped cutter; toast on both sides; spread with mayonnaise. Make highly seasoned tomato aspic, using a little more gelatin than usual. Congeal about ½-inch thick in a flat pan; cut hearts from aspic with smaller cutter. Place on toast; cover margin with riced white of egg.

NEW ORLEANS PO' BOY SANDWICH

Poor boys, in old New Orleans made a favorite sandwich of long rolls filled with any leftovers of meat or vegetables and these sandwiches are a glorified copy of the original "Po Boy" Sandwich. Get twin loaves of "Bake and Serve" French bread. The smallest sized loaves available should be used. Split these lengthwise before baking. Brush with melted butter and bake—open up and spread generously with mayonnaise. Make a filling of sliced chicken, sliced ham or tongue, crisp breakfast bacon, lettuce hearts sliced tomato, slivers of Swiss cheese and onion rings if desired. Replace tops and skewer at either end with cocktail picks. Put a stuffed olive on each pick. If small loaves of bread are not available the larger loaves can be cut in half diagonally. However a whole loaf is preferable. Serve with additional mayonnaise which can be used if desired. The old fashioned Durkee dressing is especially good with these sandwiches. Each person is supposed to have a whole loaf or sandwich.

WIENER AND CHEESE ROLLS

Split and butter wiener rolls; cut wieners in half lengthwise and put on rolls. Then put on a long narrow slice of cheese to cover the wiener and toast under flame or in hot oven until the cheese melts.

ANCHOVY SAUCE

¼ cup butter
1 pinch red pepper
1 teaspoon anchovy paste

1 teaspoon onion juice
1 tablespoon lemon juice

Cream butter with anchovy paste; add seasoning and lemon juice. This is especially good spread over broiled Spanish mackerel.

BARBECUE SAUCE

½ pound butter
½ cup vinegar
½ cup water
¼ cup lemon juice
1 cup tomato catsup
2 tablespoons Worcestershire sauce

1 pod red pepper
2 tablespoons prepared mustard
2 tablespoons grated horse-radish
1 large onion, grated
1 teaspoon salt

Melt butter; add other ingredients; cook 10 minutes. This makes enough sauce to barbecue several chickens.

BECHAMEL SAUCE

1 cup chicken stock
1 cup cream
4 tablespoons butter
4 tablespoons flour

¼ teaspoon salt
1 pinch red pepper
1 pinch of nutmeg

Melt butter; add flour; stir until smooth; add rest of ingredients; cook in double boiler, stirring often until thick.

CHEESE SAUCE

1 cup "Medium Cream Sauce"
¾ cup sharp grated cheese

1 tablespoon Worcestershire sauce

Combine ingredients.

Cheese Sauce No. 2

2 cups milk
2 tablespoons butter

2 tablespoons flour
1½ cups grated Cheddar cheese

Make cream sauce of milk, butter and flour; add grated cheese.

Cheese Sauce No. 3

Another sauce that is frequently used instead of the usual cheese sauce is in reality nothing but "Welsh Rarebit." This is especially good used over hot sandwiches.

CREAM SAUCE

	THIN	MEDIUM	THICK
Butter	1 tablespoon	2 tablespoons	4 tablespoons
Flour	1 tablespoon	2 tablespoons	4 tablespoons
Salt	½ teaspoon	½ teaspoon	½ teaspoon
Milk	1 cup	1 cup	1 cup

Melt butter in double boiler; add flour; add milk slowly; stir until smooth; cook over hot water for five minutes or until thick; stir constantly; add salt and a pinch of cayenne pepper.

COCKTAIL SAUCE

1 cup tomato catsup
½ cup lemon juice
½ teaspoon salt
1 cup finely chopped celery

1 tablespoon Worcestershire sauce
1 tablespoon horse-radish
Few drops Tabasco sauce

Combine ingredients. To be used for shrimp or oyster cocktail.

CREOLE SAUCE

1 2½-pound can tomatoes
1 large bell pepper
1 large onion
2 tablespoons butter
4 ribs celery

2 tablespoons Worcestershire sauce
1 small can tomato paste
1 teaspoon (or less) sugar
2 tablespoons horse-radish
Salt and cayenne pepper to taste

Grind onion and pepper; chop celery fine; cook in butter until tender, but not brown; add tomatoes, seasoning and tomato paste; simmer slowly until thick. Add pinch of sugar if too acid.

CUCUMBER SAUCE

1 cucumber, chopped fine and drained
¼ teaspoon salt
1 pinch cayenne pepper

½ cup whipping cream
2 tablespoons vinegar

Whip cream; season; add vinegar gradually; fold in drained cucumber.

Cucumber Sauce (2)

1 cup heavy cream
2 tablespoons chopped and drained cucumber

¼ teaspoon salt
2 tablespoons vinegar
1 pinch red pepper

Whip cream stiff; add seasoning and cucumber. Good with salmon mousse.

CURRY SAUCE

3 cups chicken stock
1 cup coffee cream
5 tablespoons flour
1 tablespoon curry powder
1 tablespoon cold water

½ cup chopped onion
½ cup chopped apple
2 firm tomatoes, chopped fine
1 stick butter

Cook onion, apple and tomato in part of butter until tender. Smooth curry powder with cold water; add to sauce made of remaining butter, flour, stock, and cream. Season with salt and red pepper. Add the onion mixture.

SAUCES

EGG SAUCE
(For Fish Pudding)

2 cups milk
3 tablespoons flour
3 tablespoons butter
2 egg yolks

½ teaspoon salt
¼ teaspoon cayenne pepper
2 tablespoons lemon juice
1 teaspoon Worcestershire sauce

Make cream sauce; add beaten yolks; season. Do not boil.

HOLLANDAISE SAUCE

3 egg yolks
½ cup melted butter

1 tablespoon lemon juice
Salt and red pepper to taste

Beat eggs until very thick; put in double boiler over hot (not boiling) water; add 2 tablespoons butter, gradually, beating constantly. Then alternate the rest of the butter with the lemon juice, adding it slowly. Season and cook a few minutes longer. Remove from heat. Never let the water boil under the sauce as it will curdle. If this should happen add 2 tablespoons of boiling water and beat.

COLD HORSE-RADISH SAUCE

½ cup mayonnaise
½ cup cream, whipped
2 tablespoons horse-radish
1 teaspoon prepared mustard

1 tablespoon lemon juice
Salt, red pepper and grated onion to taste

Combine ingredients.

FROZEN HORSE-RADISH SAUCE

1 cup mayonnaise
½ pint cream, whipped
1 tablespoon lemon juice

¾ cup horse-radish
Salt and cayenne pepper
1 teaspoon prepared mustard

Whip cream; add to mayonnaise; combine with other ingredients and freeze.

HOT HORSE-RADISH SAUCE

1 cup "Medium Cream Sauce"
4 tablespoons grated horse-radish

1 tablespoon onion juice
1 teaspoon minced parsley

Combine ingredients.

LEMON BUTTER SAUCE

1 stick butter or margarine
1 lemon (juice of)

Salt and red pepper to taste
2 tablespoons minced parsley (optional)

Melt butter; add strained lemon juice and seasoning.

LOBSTER, SHRIMP OR CRAB MEAT SAUCE

1 cup "Medium Cream Sauce"
1 cup flaked fish

2 tablespoons lemon juice
1 teaspoon Worcestershire sauce

Combine ingredients.

SAUCES

MINT SAUCE

1 cup chopped mint leaves
½ cup sugar

1 cup vinegar

Heat vinegar; add sugar; dissolve; pour over mint while hot. Let stand several hours. When cold serve with lamb.

NEWBERG SAUCE

3 egg yolks
2 tablespoons butter
Salt and cayenne pepper to taste

¼ cup sherry wine
1 cup cream

Beat egg yolks; heat cream and butter; pour over yolks; add seasoning and sherry; cook in double boiler until thick. A mock Newberg sauce can be made of cream sauce flavored with sherry.

MOCK HOLLANDAISE SAUCE

3 tablespoons butter
2 level tablespoons flour
¾ cup hot water
½ teaspoon salt

¼ teaspoon cayenne pepper
1 lemon, juice of
2 egg yolks

Melt butter in top of double boiler; add flour; add water gradually; season. Leave over slow heat until ready to use, then add the beaten egg yolks and lemon juice; cook 3 minutes. If too thick, this can be thinned with boiling water. This is about as good as Hollandaise and is "fool proof."

MORNAY SAUCE

2 cups "Medium Thick Cream Sauce"
1 cup grated Parmesan cheese

1 cup grated Swiss cheese

Make cream sauce; add grated cheese; cook over hot water until cheese has melted.

MUSHROOM SAUCE

3 tablespoons butter
3 tablespoons flour
1 cup milk
1 cup chicken stock (more or less)

1 teaspoon onion juice
½ teaspoon Kitchen Bouquet
1 pound fresh mushrooms or
1 can of mushrooms, 8 ounce size

Make cream sauce; add seasoning. Broil mushrooms; add to sauce. If chicken stock is not available, use chicken bouillon cubes.

Mushroom Sauce (2)

¾ cup butter
½ pound fresh mushrooms
1 pint chicken stock
½ cup cream
4 tablespoons flour

1 teaspoon salt
Red pepper to taste
2 egg yolks
1 tablespoon lemon juice

Cook mushrooms in part of the butter for 5 minutes; put the rest of butter in double boiler; smooth flour in butter; gradually add stock; season; beat the egg yolks; add to cream; pour slowly into stock, stirring constantly; add mushrooms and lemon juice.

SAUCES

MUSTARD SAUCE

1½ cups cream
4 egg yolks
1 cup vinegar
½ cup sugar

1 tablespoon flour
1 teaspoon salt
4 level tablespoons dry mustard
⅛ teaspoon red pepper

Make a paste of mustard, sugar and vinegar; heat in top of double boiler; add beaten yolks; add cream and cook until thick.

POULETTE SAUCE

1 tablespoon butter
1 tablespoon flour
1 cup chicken broth
2 egg yolks
4 tablespoons lemon juice

6 tablespoons cream
⅛ teaspoon nutmeg
1 tablespoon minced parsley
Salt and cayenne pepper

Melt butter; add flour; combine with chicken broth; season. Beat egg yolks; add cream. When ready to serve, add lemon juice to sauce very slowly; add egg and cream mixture. Serve at once. This is apt to curdle if allowed to stand. Especially good to serve with chicken or sweetbreads.

ORANGE SAUCE FOR MEAT

½ cup currant jelly
¼ cup orange juice

2 tablespoons grated orange rind

Beat jelly; add orange juice and rind; melt over hot water. Good with duck or squabs.

RAISIN SAUCE

1 cup seedless raisins
1 cup sugar
4 tablespoons vinegar
4 tablespoons lemon juice

1 glass grape jelly
1 teaspoon grated lemon rind
¼ teaspoon cloves
1 stick cinnamon

Plump the raisins in hot water; drain; tie spices in bag. Combine ingredients; simmer very slowly about an half hour; remove spice bag. Serve hot with ham.

RIPE OLIVE SAUCE

1 cup ripe olives, chopped
1 cup diced celery
¼ cup chopped onion
1½ tablespoon butter
2 tablespoons flour

½ teaspoon salt
½ cup undiluted canned bouillon
¾ cup milk or cream
1 large pinch curry powder

Cook onion and celery in butter until tender. Mix dry ingredients; smooth into the butter mixture; add the combined cream and bouillon; stir until thickened. Add olives last.

SHRIMP SAUCE

4 tablespoons butter
4 tablespoons flour
2 cups milk

Salt and cayenne pepper to taste
½ pound cooked shrimp, cleaned

Make cream sauce in double boiler; season highly; add shrimp. If this should be too thick, thin with a little cream.

TARTAR SAUCE

1 cup mayonnaise, highly seasoned
1 teaspoon onion juice
1 tablespoon capers

1 tablespoon chopped sour pickle
1 tablespoon chopped parsley

Combine ingredients.

HOT TARTAR SAUCE

1 cup milk
2 tablespoons butter
2 tablespoons flour
2 tablespoons chopped cucumber pickle

Salt and red pepper to taste
1 cup mayonnaise
1 small onion, grated

Make cream sauce of first 3 ingredients, season, add the rest of ingredients. Nice with fish.

TOMATO CREAM SAUCE

2 cups milk
4 tablespoons butter
4 tablespoons flour

¼ to ½ can condensed tomato soup
1 tablespoon Worcestershire sauce
1 teaspoon grated onion

Make a cream sauce of milk, butter and flour; add other ingredients.

TOMATO SAUCE

1 No. 2 can tomatoes
1 onion
½ bay leaf
2 ribs celery
1 teaspoon salt

1 pinch red pepper
1 tablespoon sugar
3 tablespoons butter
2 tablespoons flour
1 tablespoon Worcestershire

Slice onion; cut celery in pieces; cook with tomatoes and seasoning
until tomatoes are soft. Strain; thicken with butter and flour creamed
together.

VINAIGRETTE SAUCE

2 hard-boiled eggs
1 bell pepper, chopped fine
2 sour cucumber pickles, chopped fine

1 onion, chopped fine
1 tablespoon chopped parsley
1½ cups French dressing

Chop the eggs very fine; run peppers and onion through food grinder;
combine ingredients. This is good on asparagus, cauliflower or broccoli.

SWEET SAUCES

BUTTERSCOTCH SAUCE

2 cups sugar
1 cup butter

1 cup coffee cream
1 teaspoon vanilla

Melt butter and sugar in heavy iron skillet; cook until deep tan, lower
heat and pour cream in slowly. Cook 2 minutes after adding cream; add
vanilla.

Butterscotch Sauce (2)

½ cup white Karo syrup
1½ cup sugar
1 stick butter

½ pint cream
Pinch of salt
1 teaspoon vanilla

Cook syrup, sugar and half of the cream to soft-ball stage (238°); add butter, salt and remaining cream and cook again until it reaches soft-ball stage. Flavor with vanilla. Cook in double boiler or in heavy saucepan which has been greased around top edge to prevent boiling over.

CARAMEL SAUCE

1½ cups sugar
1 tablespoon butter

½ cup milk

Caramelize ½ cup of the sugar. Put the other cup on to cook with the milk; mix slowly when both are bubbling; add butter. This is especially good served with creamed sweet potatoes.

CHERRY JUBILEE SAUCE

1 No. 2 can Bing cherries
1 tablespoon cold water

½ teaspoon cornstarch
3 ounces brandy or rum

Drain cherries; heat the juice; thicken with cornstarch, smoothed in cold water. Add cherries and heat. Add 3 ounces of warm brandy or rum; set ablaze just before serving. To be used over vanilla ice cream. If you have difficulty in making sauce blaze, dip several lumps of sugar in lemon extract until thoroughly soaked. Put sugar lumps in top of bowl of sauce and put a lighted match to them.

CHOCOLATE SAUCE

2 cups sugar
¼ cup cream or milk

4 squares bitter chocolate
2 eggs

Shave chocolate. Beat eggs together; combine with sugar and cream; add chocolate; cook over hot water until thick. More cream can be added if sauce gets too thick.

DATE WINE SAUCE

1 cup sugar
3 cups hot water
2 tablespoons flour
2 egg yolks

½ cup wine
½ lemon (juice of)
1 package dates, cut fine
½ stick butter

Beat eggs, sugar and flour together; add hot water; cook in double boiler until thick; add butter, dates and lemon juice; chill; add wine.

GOLDEN SAUCE

1 cup sugar
½ cup water
2 egg yolks

½ cup heavy cream
Wine to taste

Cook sugar and water until thick; pour slowly over beaten egg yolks; cook a few minutes longer; cool; keep covered until ready to use; add cream that has been whipped; flavor with wine.

HARD SAUCE

½ pound butter   1 pound confectioners' sugar
¼ cup cream

Cream butter well; add sugar and cream. Flavor to taste with whiskey, adding it slowly. Chill until firm. Grate nutmeg on top.

HONEY SAUCE (FOR WAFFLES)

Melt ½ cup of butter; add slowly to 1 cup of strained honey, beating constantly. When it is well blended, serve with crisp waffles. No butter is needed, except that in the sauce.

MAPLE NUT SAUCE

2 cups maple syrup   1 cup broken pecans

Use synthetic maple syrup that is mixed with cane syrup, instead of the pure maple syrup, as it is much thicker and the nuts can be added without any other preparation. This is especially nice to use with ice cream molded into the shape of waffles.

MELBA SAUCE

1 cup red raspberries   1 teaspoon cornstarch
¼ cup sugar   1 lemon

Mash and strain raspberries to remove seeds; cook juice with sugar and cornstarch until thick; add lemon juice, chill.

MINT-LIME SAUCE FOR FRUIT COCKTAILS

1 glass green mint jelly   1 lemon
2 limes   1 orange

Melt mint jelly; beat until smooth; add the juice of the limes, lemon and orange and beat until thoroughly combined. Chill before using.

MINTED MARSHMALLOW SAUCE

1 cup sugar   2 or 3 drops oil of peppermint or
1 cup boiling water   ½ teaspoon of essence of peppermint
20 marshmallows   Green vegetable coloring
2 egg whites

Cut marshmallows in quarters; dissolve in sugar and water that have been cooked to a syrup. Cool; pour over beaten whites; tint light green and add peppermint to taste. Beat.

MOCHA SAUCE

1 cup confectioners' sugar   1½ cup heavy cream
2 tablespoons cocoa   2 tablespoons double strength coffee

Cook sugar, coffee and cocoa until melted and smooth; chill; add to cream that has been whipped.

ORANGE MARMALADE SAUCE

½ cup orange marmalade   1½ cups hot water
Juice of one lemon or lime

Combine and blend thoroughly; chill and use over fruit cocktails.

PECAN SAUCE

1 pound shelled pecans
1 cup sherry wine or rum

2 cups sugar

Dissolve sugar in wine; pour over pecans. Put in quart jar, turn jar occasionally to mix well. Add more wine if needed to fill jar so that nuts will be completely covered. Serve over ice cream.

PLUM PUDDING SAUCE

1 cup sugar
½ cup butter
¼ cup hot water

2 egg yolks
1 cup cream
2 egg whites

Cream butter and sugar; add beaten yolks and water; cook in double boiler until thick; chill; add beaten whites and whipped cream. Flavor with brandy or rum.

RUM SAUCE

2 eggs
1½ cups confectioners' sugar

½ stick butter
⅓ cup, or more, of rum

Beat yolks with sugar; add butter which has been melted; cook in double boiler until thick. Remove from heat; add rum, beating constantly. Pour slowly over stiffly beaten whites. Serve while hot.

SAUCE FOR MELON BALL COCKTAIL

1 cup sugar
⅓ cup water
Grated rind of half a lemon, grated

rind of half an orange
3 tablespoons lemon juice
2 tablespoons lime juice

Combine; boil 5 minutes and chill.

SABAYON SAUCE WITH RUM

3 egg yolks
4 tablespoons cream

2 tablespoons sugar
4 tablespoons rum

Beat yolks and sugar together; add cream; cook in double boiler until very thick. Add rum when cool.

STRAWBERRY SAUCE

½ cup butter
1 cup confectioners' sugar

1 quart strawberries

Cream butter and sugar; crush strawberries; add very slowly, beating constantly.

Strawberry Sauce (2)

Cream 4 tablespoons of butter with 1 cup confectioners' sugar until smooth; add 1 cup of sliced strawberries gradually; beat until they are combined. This must be done carefully so that the sauce will not curdle, but will look like a hard sauce.

WHIPPED CREAM CHOCOLATE SAUCE

½ pint whipping cream
1 square bitter chocolate

½ cup sugar
2 teaspoons boiling water

Melt chocolate in double boiler; add water and sugar; cook until smooth; cool. Whip cream; add chocolate. Serve over vanilla ice cream.

WHISKEY SAUCE

⅔ cup brown sugar
⅛ cup Karo syrup
4 tablespoons water

4 tablespoons butter
1 piece of mace
½ cup whiskey

Cook first 5 ingredients in double boiler until thick; remove from fire; add whiskey.

WINE SAUCE

3 eggs, beaten together
½ cup sherry wine
½ cup sugar
1 tablespoon butter

1 orange (juice of)
1 lemon (juice of)
½ cup heavy cream, whipped

Combine all ingredients except cream; cook in double boiler until thick, chill; add whipped cream. This is delicious served over summer fruits as a first course.

SOUPS

CREAM SOUPS

CREAM OF CAULIFLOWER SOUP

1 medium-sized head of cauliflower
1 pint thin cream
1 pint milk

3 tablespoons butter
2 tablespoons flour
Salt and red pepper to taste

Cook cauliflower half to three quarters of an hour; drain and rub through sieve. Make a cream sauce of milk and cream, thickened with flour and butter; add sieved cauliflower. Serves 8.

CREAM OF CELERY SOUP

2 cups milk
2 bunches celery, cut in pieces
3 cups water
2 slices onion
2 tablespoons butter

2 tablespoons flour
1 cup cream, whipped
Scant teaspoon salt
Dash of red pepper

Simmer onions and celery in the water for an hour; run through a sieve; add to hot milk that has been thickened with flour and butter, creamed together; season to taste. Add whipped cream and serve at once. Serves 8.

CREAM OF CORN SOUP

1 quart sweet milk
2 thick slices onion
1 can cream style corn

Salt and red pepper to taste
3 tablespoons flour
3 tablespoons butter

Combine milk, corn (corn can be run through sieve if desired), onion and seasoning; cook in double boiler half hour over slow heat. Remove onion; add flour and butter, creamed together; cook until thickened; stir constantly. Serve with spoon of whipped cream on top of soup; sprinkle paprika over cream or put a few pieces of popped corn over it. Serves 6 to 8.

CREAM OF MUSHROOM AND ASPARAGUS SOUP

1 10½-ounce can condensed mushroom soup
1 10½-ounce can asparagus soup

1 pint coffee cream or milk
2 tablespoons sherry wine

Combine ingredients and season to taste with salt and red pepper. Heat over hot water. Serves 6.

CREAM OF MUSHROOM SOUP

1½ pounds mushrooms (3 boxes)
3 tablespoons butter
3 tablespoons flour

2 pints of cream
2 pints chicken stock
Salt and red pepper to taste

Chop mushrooms fine; brown in butter; smooth flour into this, adding alternately, with a little of the chicken stock; stir constantly; add remaining stock. Simmer for twenty minutes; add cream and season. On each serving place a spoonful of whipped cream; sprinkle with paprika. Serves 8 to 10.

CREAM OF POTATO SOUP

3 pints sweet milk	1 teaspoon salt
3 Irish potatoes, boiled	1/8 teaspoon cayenne pepper
1 onion, sliced	1 tablespoon flour
1 rib of celery, cut in pieces	1 egg yolk

Cook onion and celery in milk until tender; strain. Boil potatoes and run through sieve; combine with butter, flour, hot milk and seasoning. Cook until thickened (about ten minutes). Just before serving, beat the egg yolk; add half cup of milk; combine with the hot soup; serve with whipped cream on each portion and sprinkle with chopped chives or parsley. Serves 8.

POTATO SOUP WITH SOUR CREAM

3 potatoes	1 cup of water
1 onion	1 pint of sour cream
Salt and red pepper to taste	

Peel and slice potatoes; slice onion; cook in cup of boiling water until tender; press through a sieve; season; add sour cream. Cook till very hot in double boiler; serve sprinkled with chopped chives. Serves 4.

CREAM OF TOMATO SOUP

1 large can of tomatoes	3 pints sweet milk
1/2 large onion, sliced	3 tablespoons flour
1 bay leaf	1/4 teaspoon soda
4 cloves	3 tablespoons butter
Salt and red pepper to taste	

Simmer tomatoes with onion and seasoning for 20 minutes; strain; keep hot; add 1/4 teaspoon soda. Make a cream soup of the milk, flour, and butter; add salt to taste. Just before serving add the tomato mixture. Heat, but do not boil, and serve as soon as possible. Serves 8. Can also be served chilled.

CHILLED SOUPS

CHICKEN CURRY SOUP

3 cups chicken broth	1 tablespoon curry powder
1 cup cream	1 tablespoon flour
4 egg yolks	1 cup chopped almonds

Melt butter; smooth in curry powder and flour; add chicken stock; cook 5 or 10 minutes in double boiler. Beat egg yolks; add cream; combine with chicken broth. Cook over hot, not boiling water. Chill until very cold. Add chopped almonds and serve garnished with minced parsley. Serves 4.

FROZEN CONSOMMÉ WITH SHRIMP

3 10½-ounce cans consommé
1 can tomato juice (No. 2)
½ teaspoon onion juice
1 tablespoon Worcestershire sauce

1 tablespoon gelatin
¼ cup cold water
1 tablespoon lemon juice
Salt and cayenne pepper to taste

Soak gelatin in cold water. Heat consommé; season; add lemon and tomato juice. Dissolve gelatin in hot consommé; chill. Put in freezing tray; freeze until mushy; stir and freeze again until mushy. Serve before it is frozen hard. Put 4 shrimps in each cocktail glass; cover with frozen mixture; garnish with 1 more shrimp and a parsley bud. Marinate shrimp in highly seasoned French dressing for several hours before using them. Serves 6 to 8.

VICHYSSOISE

4 cups chicken broth or water
6 potatoes peeled and sliced
6 leeks, sliced
1 onion, sliced

2 tablespoons butter
1 pint sweet milk
1 pint coffee cream
½ pint whipped cream

Cook onion and leeks in butter until tender, but not brown; combine with broth and potatoes; cook slowly until potatoes are tender. Run through a sieve; add the milk and coffee cream; season with salt and cayenne pepper; chill; when very cold add ½ pint of slightly whipped cream. Serve cold, sprinkled with chopped parsley or chives. Serves 8 to 10.

JELLIED SOUPS

JELLIED BOUILLON

1 can condensed bouillon, 10½ ounces
1 onion, sliced thick
1 rib celery, broken in pieces
1 cup water

1 tablespoon lemon juice
1 tablespoon gelatin, softened in ¼ cup cold water

Simmer bouillon, water, celery, onion and lemon juice for 10 minutes; strain; add softened gelatin; congeal. Serve with slice of lemon, dipped in minced parsley on each serving. Serves 3.

JELLIED CONSOMMÉ

2 cans consommé
½ lemon (juice of)
4 tablespoon sherry wine

1 tablespoon gelatin
½ cup cold water

Soak gelatin in cold water. Heat consommé; dissolve gelatin in hot consommé. Remove from heat; add sherry and lemon juice. Congeal. Serves 4 to 6.

JELLIED TOMATO BOUILLON

2 10½-ounce cans condensed bouillon
2 cans water
1 No. 2½ can tomatoes
Gelatin

½ teaspoon salt
½ teaspoon celery seed
1 tablespoon Worcestershire sauce
1 tablespoon onion juice

Cook together; strain; and to every pint of liquid add tablespoon of gelatin that has been softened in a fourth cup of cold water. Stir until dissolved. Congeal. Serves 8.

JELLIED TURTLE SOUP

2 cans green turtle soup
½ cup sherry wine
1 tablespoon lemon juice

1 envelope gelatin
1 cup water
Salt and red pepper to taste

Soak gelatin in water; heat soup; dissolve gelatin in hot soup; add wine and lemon juice; strain and congeal. Serve garnished with slice of lemon dipped into minced parsley. Serves 4 or 5.

SEA FOOD SOUPS

CRAB SOUP

1 6-ounce can crab meat
1 10½-ounce can condensed tomato soup
1 10½-ounce can condensed green pea soup

1½ cups coffee cream
½ cup sherry wine
Salt and red pepper to taste

Combine soups and cream; add shredded crab meat; heat over hot water. Just before serving add the wine. Serves 8.

CRAB-SHRIMP GUMBO

1 6-ounce can crab meat
1 6-ounce can shrimp (cleaned)
1 large onion, sliced
1 quart water
2 (No. 2) cans tomatoes, cooked until soft

1 tablespoon gumbo filé powder
Salt and red pepper to taste
3 tablespoons butter
2 tablespoons flour

Cook sliced onion in butter until tender, but not brown. Add crab and shrimp; cook 5 minutes over slow heat. Smooth flour into this mixture; add tomatoes, water, and seasoning. Simmer for 15 minutes. Just before serving add 1 tablespoon gumbo filé powder. Serve in soup bowls over fluffy rice. Serves 8.

CLAM CHOWDER

2 small cans minced clams
1 pint milk
2 tablespoons butter

3 potatoes
1 onion
Salt and cayenne pepper

Drain clams. Set aside juice; peel and dice potatoes; slice onion thin; fry onion in 2 tablespoons bacon grease, until golden. Cover potatoes with water; cook until tender; add clam juice, milk, onion, butter and minced clams. Cook 5 minutes. Just before serving add ¼ cup rolled cracker crumbs. Serves 4 to 6.

FISH CHOWDER

1 pound raw red snapper, free from bones	2 slices bacon
2 Irish potatoes	1 quart boiling water
2 onions	1 quart milk
2 pieces celery, cut fine	1 teaspoon chopped parsley
1 clove garlic	3 tablespoons butter
	1 tablespoon flour

Cook first 7 ingredients for 45 minutes; remove pieces of bacon and garlic; add to milk; thicken with butter and flour creamed together; add chopped parsley and serve. Serves 10.

LOBSTER BISQUE

1 can lobster or	4 cups milk
1 pound fresh lobster	3 tablespoons butter
Salt and red pepper to taste	3 level tablespoons flour

Mince lobster; make cream soup of other ingredients. Combine. Sprinkle paprika on top of soup. Serves 6.

OYSTER SOUP

1 quart sweet milk	3 tablespoons butter
1½ pints soup oysters	1 tablespoon flour
Salt and pepper to taste	

Make cream soup of milk, flour and butter; season to taste; add oysters just before serving; let them cook until the edges curl (about 5 minutes). Black pepper gives it an especially good flavor but red pepper can be substituted for party use. Serves 6.

SALMON BISQUE

1 cup canned salmon	3 tablespoons butter
3 cups milk	3 tablespoons flour
1 cup cream	Salt, red pepper to taste

Rub salmon through sieve before measuring. Make cream soup of milk, butter and flour; combine with salmon; season and heat over hot water; serve topped with whipped cream sprinkled with minced parsley. Serves 4.

SHRIMP OR CRAB BISQUE

1 quart milk	2 tablespoons flour
1 pound cooked shrimp or crab meat or 3 small cans	2 tablespoons butter
	Salt and red pepper to taste

Remove black lines from shrimp and grind. Make a cream soup of other ingredients; add the shrimp or crab meat. Sprinkle paprika on top of soup. Serves 6 or 7.

SOUPS

SHRIMP STEW

1 pound cooked shrimp	2 bell peppers
1 pound okra, sliced	2 small onions
1 No. 2 can tomatoes (stewed and strained)	1½ tablespoons butter
	Steamed rice

Cook onion and peppers in butter until tender; add okra, shrimp, and tomatoes. Cook slowly for 15 minutes. Add hot water if necessary, to keep from burning. Serve in soup plates over steamed rice. Serves 6.

SOUPS FROM VEGETABLES

BEET SOUP (BORSCH)

1 quart well-seasoned beef stock	Cooked shrimp
6 grated beets	1 pint sour cream
1 onion, grated	
1 small dish grated cucumber	

Simmer beets and onions in beef stock. Heat cream in another vessel; do not boil; combine at the last minute. Add 2 or 3 shrimp to each service. Pass grated cucumber to put in the soup. Serves 8 to 10. Can also be served chilled.

FRENCH ONION SOUP

6 onions	1 stick butter or margarine
1 quart chicken stock	2 tablespoons flour
Salt and red pepper to taste	

Peel and slice onions; cook in 1 cup of water until water is absorbed. Melt butter; add onions and fry until golden. Smooth flour into onion mixture; add chicken stock; cook slowly in double boiler for 10 minutes. Pour into soup bowls. Put toasted slice of French bread on each serving. Sprinkle toast with Parmesan cheese; put under broiler to brown cheese slightly. Toasted bread and cheese can be heated in oven and put on top of soup if bowls are not oven proof. Serves 4.

TOMATO SOUP

1 quart can of tomatoes	2 tablespoons butter
1 onion, sliced	2 tablespoons cornstarch
1 stick celery	Salt and red pepper to taste
1 bay leaf	1 pint water

Combine tomatoes, onion, celery, bay leaf and water. Simmer for 10 minutes; press through a sieve; add butter, salt and pepper; thicken with cornstarch, moistened with cold water. Cook until clear. Serves 4.

TOMATO BOUILLON

1 can bouillon—10½ ounces	1 sliced onion
1 can (10½ ounces) water	2 sticks celery, cut in several pieces
1 No. 2 can tomato juice	Red pepper and salt to taste

Simmer together for 15 minutes and strain. Serve very hot, with buttered and toasted triscuits. Put a slice of lemon, that has been dipped in minced parsley, in each cup of soup. Serves 6 to 8.

VEGETABLE BOUILLON

2 cans V-8 vegetable juice (12 ounces)   2 cans beef bouillon (10½ ounces)

Combine and heat. Serves 6 or 8.

VEGETABLE SOUP

1 soup bone (full of meat)
1 large can of tomatoes
1 can tomato pureé
3 pieces celery, cut fine
1 pod red pepper
2 carrots, cut in slices

½ pound okra, cut in slices
2 onions, cut in slices
4 ears corn, cut from cobs
½ pound lima or butter beans
1 large potato, cut in cubes
4 quarts water

Cook slowly for an hour or two, being careful that it does not burn or stick to pan. Thicken before serving and season to taste with salt, pepper and Worcestershire sauce. A little broken spaghetti can be added if desired. Serve croutons or toasted ½ inch cubes of bread. Serves 12.

SOUPS FROM POULTRY

CHICKEN CURRY SOUP (HOT)

1 quart Chicken Stock
1 cup cream
2 egg yolks
whipped cream

Salt, Cayenne Pepper and
Curry Powder to taste
2 tablespoons flour

Thicken the hot chicken stock with flour and curry powder, which have been smoothed to a paste with a little cold water. Season well. Just before serving add cup of cream with egg yolks beaten into it. Mix carefully to prevent curdling. Top with whipped cream when ready to serve. The amount of curry powder will depend on your personal taste. Start with teaspoon of curry powder and add more as desired. Always smooth it to a paste with cold water before adding. Serves 6.

TURKEY SOUP

6 cups turkey broth
½ cup rice
1½ teaspoon salt
½ teaspoon red pepper
1 onion, sliced

4 ribs celery, cut in fine pieces
2 tablespoons butter
2 cups milk
1 tablespoon flour
Turkey carcass

Boil turkey carcass in water with onion and celery; remove carcass and flake off any small pieces of meat. Measure 6 cups of this stock; add seasoning and rice; boil slowly until rice is tender. Add flaked turkey, milk, butter and seasoning. Thicken with flour rubbed smooth in 2 tablespoons cold water. Serves 8.

CREAMED ASPARAGUS WITH ALMONDS

1 pint "Cream Sauce (Medium)"
1 cup almonds, cut in half

1 can asparagus, large size

Cut asparagus in 2-inch lengths; combine with cream sauce and almonds; put in casserole; cover with buttered crumbs; bake 20 minutes. Serves 6.

ASPARAGUS IN BELL PEPPERS

2 cans white asparagus
1 cup almonds

8 large bell peppers
1 pint "Cream Sauce, Medium"

Scoop out bell peppers. Cut 2-inch tips from 24 stalks of asparagus and save for decoration. Cut rest of asparagus in 1-inch lengths; add to cream sauce and nuts; fill peppers; put buttered crumbs on top; stick 3 of the tips down around edges of pepper, letting the tips extend about an inch above the pepper. Decorate outside the tips with a long narrow strip of pimento; this should outline the top of the pepper. Put peppers in pan with a little hot water; bake long enough to heat well. Serves 8.

CREAMED ASPARAGUS WITH CHEESE

1 can white asparagus
2 cups milk
4 tablespoons flour

3 tablespoons butter
Salt and red pepper
1 cup grated cheese

Make cream sauce; add grated cheese; stir until smooth; cut asparagus in 1-inch pieces; put in casserole in layers with cheese sauce; cover top with buttered bread crumbs. Bake 20 minutes. Serves 6.

ASPARAGUS AND EGG CASSEROLE

2 cans asparagus tips
6 hard-boiled eggs

2½ cups "Cheese Sauce"
Bread crumbs

Place asparagus in rows in long, flat casserole; cover with a layer of sliced hard-boiled eggs; put the sauce over the entire surface; sprinkle bread crumbs over top. Heat until brown. Serves 10.

Asparagus and Egg Casserole (2)

1 No. 2 can asparagus
4 hard-boiled eggs, sliced
1 pint "Medium White Sauce"

1 cup cheese, grated
1 tablespoon Worcestershire sauce
1 teaspoon onion juice

Add cheese, Worcestershire sauce and onion juice to cream sauce; put asparagus, eggs and sauce in alternate layers in casserole, cover top with sauce sprinkled with buttered crumbs; bake until top is brown. Serves 7 to 8.

ASPARAGUS ON TOMATOES

Cut large tomatoes in 3 slices; sprinkle with salt; arrange several asparagus tips on each slice; cover thickly with grated sharp cheese. Bake at 325° until cheese has melted.

FRIED ASPARAGUS

Drain a can of large, fine canned asparagus, white variety; dip stalks in egg, then in bread crumbs; fry. Serves 6.

ASPARAGUS OR CAULIFLOWER WITH SHRIMP SAUCE

2 cans large green asparagus tips	1 cup grated cheese
4 tablespoons flour	4 tablespoons butter
1½ cups milk	½ pound cleaned and cooked shrimp

Make cream sauce; add cheese and shrimp; pour over hot asparagus or cauliflower. Serves 8.

ASPARAGUS SOUFFLÉ RING

2 cans asparagus tips	1 tablespoon Worcestershire sauce
1 cup milk	1 teaspoon onion juice
3 tablespoons butter	Salt and pepper to taste
2 tablespoons flour	4 eggs, beaten separately

Make cream sauce; combine with beaten yolks and 1 cup of the asparagus tips, cut in short lengths; fold in beaten whites; pour into buttered ring mold; arrange the remainder of asparagus tips around sides and on bottom of mold. Put in pan of hot water; bake until firm. Turn out on platter; put a bowl of "Mock Hollandaise Sauce" (see sauces) in center of ring. Decorate outer edge of ring with a border of parsley. Serves 8.

ASPARAGUS ON TOAST-CHEESE SAUCE

Allow 4 or 5 large stalks of asparagus for each serving. Toast large slices of bread; brush with melted butter. Arrange asparagus on toast and cover with a rich "Cheese Sauce." Serve this with "Molded Grapefruit Salad" for lunch.

BOSTON BAKED BEANS

Soak 1 quart of Navy beans overnight in cold water; drain the next morning; put cup of molasses in bottom of a large bean crock with 2 tablespoons dry mustard, 2 teaspoons salt, ½ teaspoon cayenne and 2 large onions sliced. Add drained beans; cover with hot water. Put 1 pound of lean pork on top of beans; let it also be covered with water for the first few hours of cooking. Cook in slow oven from 9 A.M. until 6 P.M., adding water as necessary. The last hour, spoon into casserole, with pork on top; allow to dry out and brown. Serve buttered and toasted slices of Boston brown bread. Serves 8 to 10. These are delicious and a great favorite for informal buffet suppers. When time is limited, a very good substitute can be quickly made from plain canned baked beans. To each can of beans add a little grated onion, a half teaspoon of mustard, a little cayenne pepper and a tablespoon of molasses. Put in casserole; arrange strips of bacon across top, and bake until bacon is crisp.

CREAMED LIMA BEANS

One pound lima beans, ½ cup milk or cream, 2 tablespoons butter, 1 teaspoon grated onion, salt and red pepper to taste. Boil beans until tender in small amount of salted water; drain thoroughly. Heat milk, onion and seasoning slowly, so that onion will cook slightly; strain; pour over drained lima beans. Serves 6.

LIMA BEANS WITH SOUR CREAM

1 box frozen lima beans
½ cup sour cream
Salt and cayenne pepper to taste

½ onion, minced
½ pimento, chopped

Boil lima beans by directions on box. Do not overcook. Cook onion in 2 tablespoons of butter until tender, but not brown; combine with lima beans, onion, pimento and cream. Season to taste. One pound of fresh lima beans can be used if preferred. Serves 5.

LIMA BEANS AND MUSHROOMS

1 pound fresh lima beans
½ pound mushrooms or
1 can mushroom pieces and stems (8 ounces)
2½ cups milk

4 tablespoons butter
3 tablespoons flour
½ pound Swiss cheese, grated
½ onion, grated

Broil mushrooms and onion 5 minutes in butter. Boil lima beans; drain. Make cream sauce of milk, butter and flour; add grated cheese. Combine ingredients; put in casserole; top with toasted crumbs. Heat. Serves 8 to 10.

GREEN BEANS WITH TOASTED ALMONDS

Heat 2 cans of tiny whole snap beans; drain thoroughly; pour melted butter and lemon juice over them, after arranging on flat platter; cover top with toasted almonds, using about 1 cup. To toast almonds, blanch in boiling water; skin and cut each piece in 3 pieces; put on a flat cooky sheet that has been well greased; brown in a hot oven; shake to turn them as they brown. Serves 8 to 10.

GREEN BEANS IN MUSHROOM SAUCE

1 large can snap beans, drained
1 can condensed cream of mushroom soup
1 tablespoon butter
Salt and red pepper to taste

1 teaspoon flour
1 cup milk or cream
1 teaspoon Worcestershire sauce
½ cup chopped blanched almonds

Make cream sauce of milk, flour and butter; season with salt, pepper and Worcestershire sauce; stir in condensed soup, slowly; beat smooth; add snap beans and almonds; put in casserole and heat through. Serves 6 to 8.

BROCCOLI WITH CHICKEN OR TURKEY

A delicious combination is: broccoli, sliced chicken or turkey breast and cheese sauce. (See "Chicken Divan.")

BROCCOLI RING

2 cups cooked broccoli	½ lemon (juice of)
1 cup thick cream sauce	½ onion, grated
4 eggs, beaten separately	Salt and cayenne pepper

Drain cooked broccoli; put through grinder; measure 2 cups broccoli and broccoli juice; add lemon juice. Add grated onion to very thick white sauce. Beat yolks; add to sauce; combine with broccoli; add beaten whites last. Put in buttered ring mold; set in pan of hot water; bake at 375° for an hour or until firm; turn out on platter; put a bowl of "Hollandaise Sauce" in center of ring. Garnish with parsley. Serves 8.

BROCCOLI CASSEROLE

1 bunch broccoli	1 teaspoon Worcestershire sauce
1 cup milk	½ cup grated cheese
1 tablespoon flour	2 tablespoons sherry wine
3 tablespoons butter	Salt and cayenne pepper to taste

Cook broccoli until barely tender in salted water; drain. Make cream sauce of remaining ingredients. Put in casserole in layers. Sprinkle top with a little grated cheese. Bake until top is lightly browned.

BROCCOLI WITH HOLLANDAISE SAUCE

Select fresh green broccoli with firm heads; split lengthwise; put in boiling salted water; let stalks stand upright, so that heads are out of water, for first part of cooking time; then cover vessel; let heads steam 15 minutes. Cook until tender; drain well; put on flat platter; cover with "Hollandaise Sauce."

CARROT RING

3 bunches carrots	4 eggs, beaten separately
1 cup thick white sauce	Salt and red pepper to taste
1 grated onion	

Scrape carrots; boil until very tender; mash through sieve; add to seasoned white sauce and onion. Add beaten yolks; fold in beaten whites last. Put in well-buttered ring mold; bake in pan of hot water for about 40 minutes at 350°. Turn out on platter; fill center of ring with green peas and chopped pimentos. Garnish with parsley; put close against the outer edge of ring. Cover top of ring mold with waxed paper while cooking. Serves 8 to 10.

GLAZED CARROTS

2 bunches of carrots, scraped and parboiled	½ cup sugar
4 tablespoons butter	4 tablespoons water

Dissolve sugar in water; add butter; cook a few minutes before adding boiled carrots; simmer until they are glazed; carrots can be left whole, cut in inch sections, or in slices before glazing. Serves 8.

CAULIFLOWER WITH CARROT ROSES

Soak a large, perfect head of cauliflower in cold water for 20 minutes; cook, head up, in salted water until tender; drain in colander; put over hot water until ready to use. Scrape carrots; cut in 1-inch lengths; notch around larger end of each section to resemble a flower; trim lower edge to a thick point. Parboil carrot flowers and then glaze in several spoons of melted butter with 2 tablespoons of sugar added. When ready to serve cauliflower, put carrot "roses" in gashes cut in top of cauliflower; arrange to look like a bouquet; about 7 or 8 roses to a cauliflower. Pour melted butter, with a little lemon juice added, over cauliflower; outline with a border of parsley.

CREOLE CAULIFLOWER

2 small cauliflowers	1 can tomatoes
2 bell peppers	Salt and red pepper
1 onion	1 cup thick white sauce
1 small bunch celery	5 hard-boiled eggs, sliced

Parboil cauliflower in salted water; drain; break into flowerettes. Make creole sauce of peppers, onion, celery and tomatoes; season highly. Put alternate layers of cauliflower, eggs, creole sauce and cream sauce in casserole; bake until well heated. This fills a large casserole and will serve 10 to 12. It is especially nice, mixed together, and used as a filling for bright red or green red peppers. Put crumbs on top of peppers or casserole before baking.

FRENCH FRIED CAULIFLOWER

1 box frozen cauliflower	Bread crumbs (sifted)
2 eggs	

Parboil cauliflower until barely tender; drain well; dip in beaten eggs and bread crumbs; fry until brown. Serves 4.

CARROT RICE RING

2 bunches carrots (about 12)	½ pound sharp cheese, grated
1 small onion, chopped very fine	3 eggs, beaten together
2 cups rice	Salt and red pepper to taste

Grate carrots; parboil in salted water; drain; combine with other ingredients; season well; put in oiled ring mold. Bake in pan of hot water for about ½ hours. Turn out on platter; fill center with fresh green peas, creamed celery or mushrooms. This makes a large ring mold; will serve 10. Cover top of ring mold with waxed paper while cooking.

BAKED CAULIFLOWER

1 large cauliflower	Salt and red pepper to taste
1 onion	½ cup cheese, grated
1 pint thick cream sauce	4 eggs, beaten separately

Grind raw cauliflower and onion together; add cream sauce; add cheese and beaten yolks; fold in beaten whites. Bake in greased casserole; put in pan of hot water; cook for ¾ hour, or until firm, at 350°. Serves 8.

CAULIFLOWER WITH CHEESE SAUCE

Boil cauliflower until tender; break off flowerettes. If preferred, you can cook a box of frozen cauliflower, which is already separated. Put in casserole with "Cheese Sauce" (2 cups), cover with buttered crumbs. Bake until brown. Serves 6.

CAULIFLOWER AND MUSHROOMS

2 medium-sized cauliflowers	2 cups rich cream sauce
1 pound fresh mushrooms	⅓ pound grated Swiss cheese

Parboil cauliflower; drain; break into flowerettes. Broil mushrooms in butter; add a scraping of onion juice; combine all ingredients. Put in large casserole; cover top with buttered crumbs. Canned mushrooms can be substituted for fresh if desired. Serves 8 to 10.

CAULIFLOWER SOUFFLE RING

2 medium-sized cauliflowers	½ cup grated cheese
1 cup milk	4 eggs, beaten separately
3 tablespoons flour	Salt and red pepper
3 tablespoons butter	1½ cups "Cheese Sauce"

Cook cauliflower until well done in salted water; drain well; mash or run through sieve. Make cream sauce of milk, flour and butter; season; add grated cheese and beaten egg yolks; add beaten whites and cauliflower. Turn into large, well-greased ring mold. Cook in pan of hot water at 325° until firm; loosen edges carefully; turn out on serving platter. Pour "Cheese Sauce" over ring; sprinkle grated cheese on top of mold; garnish with parsley. Serves 10 to 12.

CAULIFLOWER WITH TOMATO CURRY

Boil a large head of cauliflower in salted water; drain in colander. When ready to serve, cover with "Tomato Sauce" to which a large pinch of curry powder has been added. Garnish with a border of parsley. Serves 6.

SCALLOPED CELERY

5 cups chopped celery	Salt and red pepper to taste
2 cups "White Sauce (Medium)"	Buttered bread crumbs
1 cup grated cheese	

Parboil celery in salted walter; drain thoroughly; put in casserole, alternating celery, cream sauce and grated cheese. Put grated cheese on top layer. Cover with buttered bread crumbs. Bake until crumbs are brown. Serves 6.

CLIPPED CORN WITH PEPPERS

8 ears corn	⅓ cup cream
1 bell pepper	Salt and red pepper to taste
2 tablespoons butter	

Boil corn until just tender; cut corn from cob. Chop green pepper. Add butter and seasoning to cream; pour over corn and peppers. Put over low heat for a few minutes, until the cream almost cooks away. Serves 6 to 8.

MAMMY'S FRIED CORN

6 large ears corn
2 kitchen spoons bacon grease

1½ cups water
½ teaspoon salt

Cut tip ends from kernels and scrape pulp from cobs with back of a knife. Heat bacon grease in an iron skillet; sprinkle salt over hot grease; add corn; rinse out bowl with 1½ cups water; pour over corn. Sprinkle a large pinch of flour over corn; stir up from bottom when it begins to cook; then turn down heat; let the corn cook slowly until done, without stirring. When ready to serve, spoon corn into a vegetable dish; then, with a batter cake lifter, take up the crust that completely covers bottom of skillet; cut crust in half; put on top of the corn so that crust covers top of dish. This is delicious.

CORN FRITTERS

2 cups boiled corn, cut from cob
2 cups flour
½ cup milk
1½ teaspoon salt

3 teaspoons baking powder
1 tablespoon melted butter
2 eggs

Add milk to corn. Sift flour with salt and baking powder; add to mixture; add well-beaten eggs and melted butter; drop by spoonfuls into fat heated to 375°; drain on unglazed paper. This makes about a dozen and a half fritters. Nice to use for a party breakfast. "Corn Fritters No. 2" are not so pretty, but they are delicious for home use.

Corn Fritters (2)

6 ears corn
2 eggs, beaten separately
½ teaspoon salt

1 tablespoon milk
1 tablespoon flour

Shave off top of kernels; scrape out pulp with back of knife; add salt, beaten yolks, milk and flour. Then fold in beaten whites. Fry on a hot skillet, in butter, as you would a batter cake. Serves 6.

CORN PUDDING

10 large ears corn
1 pint milk
2 tablespoons sugar
2 tablespoons flour

3 eggs, beaten separately
1 teaspoon salt
2 tablespoons butter

Shave off tips of corn kernels; scrape pulp from cobs. Melt butter and smooth flour in it; add milk, corn, beaten yolks, sugar and salt; fold in egg whites. Bake in greased casserole at 350° to 375° until firm. Should take about ¾ of an hour. Serves 8 to 10.

CANNED CORN PUDDING

2 cans whole-kernel corn
2 cups milk
3 well-beaten eggs

1 tablespoon sugar
1 teaspoon salt

Drain off liquid and put corn through meat grinder; combine with rest of ingredients; pour into casserole; bake in pan of hot water at 350° until firm. This will require nearly an hour. Serves 8.

CORN TIMBALES ON BROILED TOMATO SLICES

Score, cut and scrape enough corn to make 1 cupful; add 4 well-beaten eggs; ½ teaspoon salt, 2 tablespoons sugar, 1¼ cups milk. Fill generously buttered timbale molds ⅔ full; bake in pan of hot water until firm. Cut around sides of each mold; turn out on a batter cake lifter or on palm of hand. Invert this, so that timbale is placed brown side up, on a slice of broiled tomato. To prepare tomatoes dip in seasoned meal; plunge in deep fat for 2 or 3 minutes. Garnish with parsley. Serves 8.

STEWED CORN

6 ears corn
1 teaspoon salt

1 cup milk
1 tablespoon butter

Shave off tops of kernels; scrape out corn pulp. Add salt, milk and butter; cook in double boiler until done—about ¾ hour. Serves 6.

CORN AND LIMA SUCCOTASH

3 ears corn
½ pound lima beans
1 tablespoon butter

4 tablespoons cream
Salt and red pepper to taste

Boil corn and lima beans separately; cut corn from cob and add rest of ingredients. Simmer a few minutes; serve. Serves 6.

FRIED EGGPLANT

Peel eggplant; cut in slices about ¼ inch thick; sprinkle with salt; stack on a platter. Put a plate over them, with weight on it, to press out excess juice; leave for an hour or so. Dip slices in meal or in egg and cracker crumbs. Fry until brown and crisp. Serves 4 to 6.

EGGPLANT SOUFFLÉ

1 large eggplant
1 cup "Medium Cream Sauce"
½ cup grated cheese
3 eggs, beaten separately
1 onion, grated

1 teaspoon salt
1 tablespoon Worcestershire sauce
2 tablespoons tomato catsup
1 cup dry bread crumbs

Peel, parboil and mash eggplant; add seasonings. Make cream sauce; add grated cheese and beaten yolks. Combine with eggplant; fold in beaten whites. Put in casserole; bake in pan of water at 375° for 45 minutes. Serves 8.

STUFFED EGGPLANT

1 large eggplant
1 onion, chopped
2 ribs celery, chopped
½ bell pepper, chopped
1 tomato, chopped

2 tablespoons butter
½ cup grated ham
Canned pimentos
Salt and pepper to taste

Cut a slice from 1 side of eggplant; scoop out pulp; cook pulp in salted water until tender. Soak eggplant shell in cold salted water. Cook onion, pepper, celery and tomato in butter until soft. Drain and mash cooked eggplant; combine with vegetables; add grated ham or 1 small can of deviled ham. Stuff mixture in eggplant shell; cover top with toasted bread crumbs. Cut long half-inch strips around and around canned pimentos; crisscross these strips over top of eggplant. Decorate spaces between with slices of stuffed olives. Bake until heated through, with a little water in pan around eggplant. Serves 4 to 5.

Stuffed Eggplant (2)

Prepare eggplant as described in "Stuffed Eggplant No. 1"; add either a small can of mushrooms or a can of shrimp instead of ham mixture, before stuffing the eggplant. Serves 4 to 6, according to size of eggplant.

EGGPLANT, TOMATO AND CHEESE

Fry slices of eggplant, according to directions given in "Fried Eggplant"; cover each slice with a slice of peeled tomato; sprinkle salt and a scraping of onion juice over tomato; put an inch and half square of cheese on top of tomato. Run in oven long enough to melt cheese and heat tomato. Serves 4 to 6.

STUFFED MUSHROOMS

Wash large mushrooms; cut off stems; broil mushrooms and stems in butter for about 5 minutes; chop stems; add them to some finely minced celery, onion and a little grated ham; add a little cream to moisten. Stuff mushroom caps with this mixture; cover with buttered crumbs; put in flat pan with a little cream around them; bake long enough to brown the crumbs. Serve several mushroom caps on toast points; pour cream in pan over them. Garnish with parsley.

CREAMED MUSHROOMS

One pound fresh mushrooms, rich cream sauce made of 2 cups of coffee cream, 3 tablespoons butter, 3 tablespoons flour. Wash and slice mushrooms; broil in butter for 5 minutes; season with salt, red pepper and a trace of onion juice; add cream sauce. Just before serving, beat 2 egg yolks and add to mushrooms. Serve in center of a ring of wild rice. Serves 6 to 8.

FRENCH FRIED ONION RINGS

Slice Spanish onions; separate into rings; soak an hour in sweet milk; remove from milk; put in paper bag with salted flour in it; shake until they are well coated, or dip them in a thin waffle batter if preferred. Fry in hot fat until brown and puffed.

STUFFED ONIONS

Peel and parboil white onions that are large enough to stuff. Remove centers of onions and chop; add to them equal parts of ground ham and bread crumbs, with salt, red pepper and melted butter to season. A little cream can also be used to bind the stuffing together. Fill centers of onions with this stuffing; cover with buttered bread crumbs. Set in pan with a little water around the onions; heat until tops are browned. Do not cook too long or have heat too high.

ONIONS STUFFED WITH CELERY

Parboil, in salted water, 10 or 12 Spanish onions; scoop out centers and chop; cook 2 cups finely chopped celery; drain; add to onions; combine with 1 cup of thick white sauce; stuff onions with mixture. Cover with bread crumbs; bake with a little water around onions. Serves 10 or 12.

ONION SOUFFLE

2 cups boiled, chopped onions	2 onions, chopped and browned in butter
2 well-beaten eggs	½ teaspoon baking powder

Combine; cook in buttered casserole; put crumbs on top. Serves 6.

GREEN PEAS FRENCH STYLE

Cook frozen peas according to instructions on box; use only half the amount of water called for, however. Slice half head of lettuce; cook with peas. This furnishes the needed moisture. Also add a small onion. When peas are done, remove onion; season peas with salt, pepper and a large pinch of sugar. Fresh peas can be used if desired.

GREEN PEAS WITH PIMENTOS

To one can of peas, drained, add 1 finely chopped pimento and a little melted butter; stir lightly until mixed.

GREEN PEAS WITH MUSHROOMS

1 can peas	Salt, cayenne pepper
1 small can mushrooms, broiled in butter	1 tablespoon butter
1 small onion	

Heat peas with onion; drain; remove onion; add mushrooms; season to taste. Serves 4 to 6.

GREEN PEAS WITH SWEETBREADS

1 can peas	Salt, cayenne pepper
½ pound sweetbreads	Melted butter
1 onion	

Soak sweetbreads; cook 20 minutes in boiling water; plunge in cold water for 5 minutes; remove membrane and break in small pieces. Heat peas with onion. When ready to serve remove onion and drain; add sweetbreads; season with salt, pepper and add melted butter. Serves 4 to 6.

GREEN PEAS WITH MINT

Add a few sprigs of mint to water in which peas are to be cooked. Boil until tender; remove mint; season with salt, cayenne pepper and melted butter.

GREEN PEA TIMBALES

1 can condensed green pea soup	½ onion, grated
½ can "Thick Cream Sauce"	2 beaten eggs
1 pimento, chopped	Salt and cayenne pepper to taste

Combine ingredients; put in greased timbale molds; cook at 325°

with molds in pan of hot water for 20 minutes or until firm. Turn out on slices of broiled tomatoes. Garnish with parsley. Serves 6.

GREEN PEAS WITH BABY CARROTS

Cook canned or fresh peas until tender; add minced pimentos and season. Put on platter and surround with tiny canned baby carrots radiated around edges of platter with small end of carrots to the outside. Garnish between carrots with small bunches of parsley.

BELL PEPPERS WITH CHEESE SOUFFLÉ

2 tablespoons butter	1 package Old English creamed cheese,
2 tablespoons flour	cut in small pieces
1 cup milk	½ teaspoon salt, red pepper to taste
4 eggs	

Make cream dressing; add cheese; add eggs, one at a time, beating well after each addition. Cut slice from stem end and scoop out peppers; fill ¾ full of this mixture. Put peppers in pan with a little water; bake 15 to 20 minutes at 350°. This will fill 6 to 8 peppers according to size.

STUFFED PEPPERS WITH RICE AND HAM

6 bright red or green bell peppers	2 cups cooked rice
1 onion	1½ cups ham, ground
2 tomatoes	2 tablespoons butter
4 ribs celery	

Cut off stem ends of pepper; remove seeds. Chop ends of peppers, celery and onion; fry in butter until tender. Add chopped tomatoes; cook until soft; add rice and ham; cook until most of the moisture has absorbed. Stuff mixture in peppers; put buttered crumbs on top. Put in pan with a little hot water; bake 10 minutes.

BELL PEPPERS STUFFED WITH CHEESE
AND TOMATO CATSUP

Grate American cheese; add just enough tomato catsup to bind together; knead with hands until thoroughly mixed; stuff cheese mixture into medium size bell peppers with seeds removed. Pack down firmly; run in stove long enough to heat through and slightly toast cheese.

OTHER SUGGESTIONS FOR STUFFED PEPPERS

Stuff with corn pudding; creamed asparagus; clipped corn; creole eggs; Creole cauliflower; cauliflower with cheese sauce; lima beans and mushrooms; creamed oysters or deviled oysters.

STUFFED ROSE APPLE PIMENTO PEPPERS

Rose apples are tiny, firm pimentos and can be bought in cans. My favorite stuffing is the one used for bell peppers, "Cheese and Tomato Catsup." Pack in pimento shells and heat 10 minutes in moderate oven. Use as a plate garnish.

POTATO BALLS

Peel large Irish potatoes; cut balls from them with a large size melon ball scoop; boil in salted water; drain; pour melted butter and minced parsley over them. Do not overcook. These are usually used inside of ring of fish pudding.

IRISH POTATOES AND EGGS IN CREAM SAUCE

6 medium size Irish potatoes	2 canned pimentos
6 hard-boiled eggs	Salt and red pepper to taste
2 cups "Medium White Sauce"	

Peel and dice potatoes; cook in salted water until done but still firm; drain well; chop egg whites; combine with potatoes and white sauce; add finely chopped pimentos. Stir gently until blended. Put on flat platter; sprinkle riced yolks over surface. Border with parsley. Serves 8.

BAKED IRISH POTATOES WITH CRAB OR SHRIMP SAUCE

Bake 4 large Irish potatoes until just tender; cut in halves; press potatoes up in each half; leave in oven a few minutes to let steam escape. Sprinkle salt and melted butter over potatoes; pour over each a liberal serving of crab or "Shrimp Sauce." Allow a pint of cream sauce to a can of crab meat. This can be served as a meat substitute, giving each person 2 halves of potato as a serving. Garnish with parsley. Serves 4.

POTATO-CHEESE PUFF

4 cups seasoned mashed potatoes	½ cup bread crumbs
2 beaten eggs	2 tablespoons melted butter
1½ cups grated cheese	¼ teaspoon salt
½ cup milk	¼ teaspoon paprika

Combine potatoes, beaten eggs, milk, and seasoning. Put in casserole; sprinkle with bread crumbs and melted butter. Bake about 40 minutes at 375°. Serves 6 or 8.

POTATO PANCAKES

2 cups grated potatoes	1 tablespoon flour
2 eggs, beaten separately	1 teaspoon salt

Peel and grate potatoes; beat eggs; add flour and salt to yolks; combine with potatoes. Fold in beaten whites; put on hot, greased griddle by spoonfuls; cook slowly until brown; turn and brown on other side.

BOILED NEW IRISH POTATOES

Select medium size new Irish potatoes of uniform size; wash but do not peel. Scrape off ¼-inch band around center of the potatoes; boil until tender. Drain; leave covered for 5 minutes. When ready to serve, sprinkle with salt, melted butter and finely minced parsley.

NEW IRISH POTATOES IN GARDEN PLATTER

Select small new potatoes. Scrape off skin; boil until tender; drain; keep covered for a few minutes, over low heat, to make them mealy;

sprinkle with salt. When ready to serve, arrange them in a double line slantwise of a silver platter. On one side, put a similar line of tiny red beets; on the other side put a line of glazed carrots; on either end of the platter put lines of green asparagus; pour melted butter over vegetables; sprinkle chopped parsley over the line of potatoes. Now put a row of parsley buds between each row of vegetables, so that each one is distinctly outlined. This is a nice side dish to serve men.

POTATOES AU GRATIN

6 medium size potatoes	1 cup milk
½ pound sharp cheese, grated	2 pimentos, chopped

Parboil potatoes in salted water; peel; cut potatoes in blocks. Butter a casserole; put in alternate layers of potatoes, cheese and pimentos. Pour milk over top; cover with bread crumbs and bits of butter. Bake 30 minutes in moderate oven. Serves 6 to 8.

BAKED POTATOES WITH SHIRRED EGGS

Bake large potatoes; cut a slice from side of each potato and scoop out; cream potatoes with salt, a little grated onion, a large lump of butter and enough milk to make the right consistency; replace in potato shells; make a well in center of each potato; build potato up around outer edge to form a wall. Break an egg into each potato and put in moderate oven until egg is set.

SWEET POTATOES AND APPLE BALLS

4 large sweet potatoes (yellow yams), parboiled	1 cup water
8 Winesap apples	1 cup sugar
	1 stick cinnamon

Scoop balls from peeled apples and also from parboiled sweet potatoes. Make a syrup of sugar, water and cinnamon; remove cinnamon; cook apple balls in this until clear; do not overcook them. Divide syrup; color part of it green and the other part red with vegetable coloring. Return some apple balls to each color syrup—simmer until colored. Cook potato balls in a separate syrup. Drain and combine; put on a flat platter; sprinkle top of balls with fresh grated cocoanut. This makes a pretty Christmas platter. Serves 8.

SWEET POTATO BALLS ON PINEAPPLE SLICES OR PEARS

One can sliced pineapple or large, firm canned pears; 3 or 4 sweet potatoes (yellow yams). Parboil sweet potatoes; cut out balls with a large ball cutter; glaze as directed in "Sweet Potato Balls"; arrange as many as possible on pineapple slices or pear halves. Pour any remaining syrup left from glaze over them; dot with butter; sprinkle with cocoanut; heat a few minutes. Serves 7 or 8.

SWEET POTATO RING

3 pounds sweet potatoes (yellow yams)   ½ cup melted butter
1 cup brown sugar   Pecans, chopped

Boil potatoes; peel and cream them. Butter 8-inch mold; put brown sugar over butter; put a layer of chopped pecans on next. Chill; put creamed potatoes over sugar and nuts. Put mold in pan of hot water; bake about half an hour. Turn out on platter. The center of ring can be filled with colored apple balls if desired. (See "Sweet Potato with Apple Balls.") It will take 8 Winesap apples to make enough balls to fill a ring. Serves 6 to 8.

SWEET POTATOES AND PINEAPPLE

3 cups cooked mashed sweet potatoes   1 egg, beaten
3 tablespoons brown sugar   Pinch salt and cinnamon
1 large can pineapple   2 tablespoons butter

Add beaten egg, sugar, butter and cinnamon to sieved potatoes. Place rings of pineapple on greased cookie sheet; pipe potatoes into a mound on each slice, using a pastry tube; heat through. On top of each, make a spray of holly berries with small bits of crystallized cherries. Use bits of angelica or citron to make holly leaves on each one. Serves 8. This makes a nice garnish for meats at Christmas time.

MAPLE NUT SWEET POTATOES

Parboil 3 large sweet potatoes; peel; slice in halves, lengthwise; put in a pan, flat side down; press pecan halves into the top of the potatoes; cover with a maple sauce of 2 tablespoons butter and 1 cup maple syrup. Baste potatoes with this; cook in slow oven until well glazed. Serves 6.

SWEET POTATOES AND PEAR HALVES

Parboil 8 long, slender sweet potatoes; peel; glaze in syrup made of 1 cup of water, 1 cup of sugar and 2 tablespoons of butter. When clear and glazed, arrange on platter; radiate from center of platter like spokes of a wheel. Between each potato place a heated canned pear half that has been tinted red or green with fruit coloring. (Dissolve coloring in fruit juice.) Decorate center of platter with a bouquet of parsley. Use yellow yams for this dish. Serves 7 or 8.

SWEET POTATO CROQUETTES

3 sweet potatoes   1 cup chopped black walnuts
½ stick butter   1 teaspoon cinnamon
½ cup brown sugar   ¼ teaspoon salt

Boil potatoes until tender; mash through sieve; add other ingredients; cool and chill. Form into cones; roll lightly in flour; dip in beaten eggs, then in crushed corn flakes. Fry in deep fat. When ready to serve, dip loaf sugar in lemon extract; press into top of each potato cone and touch with lighted match. Send to table flaming. Serves 8.

SWEET POTATOES IN ORANGE CUPS

6 oranges
2 cups mashed sweet potatoes
2 tablespoons brown sugar

3 tablespoons melted butter
Cocoanut or grated pecans for topping

Cut slice from top of each orange; cut out as much orange pulp as possible; save orange pulp and juice for further use. Add butter and brown sugar to mashed potatoes; beat in enough orange juice to make right consistency; fold in orange segments; stuff mixture in orange shells. Cover tops either with grated pecans or fresh grated cocoanut; run in oven to heat. Serves 6.

SWEET POTATO SOUFFLÉ

3 cups riced boiled sweet potatoes
2 tablespoons melted butter
2 well-beaten eggs

⅓ cup sherry
Pinch of salt and of nutmeg
½ cup chopped pecans

Combine ingredients. Arrange in circle around a shallow Pyrex dish, leaving a small space at center. Bake about 15 minutes; serve at once, with "Caramel Sauce" in center of potatoes. If preferred, the nuts can be grated and put over top of ring.

SPINACH SOUFFLÉ

2 cups of cooked, drained and mashed
  spinach
1 cup highly seasoned "Thick White
  Sauce"

2 eggs, beaten separately
2 hard-boiled eggs

Put all ingredients, except hard-boiled eggs, in a buttered casserole; cook in pan of hot water until set, about 20 to 30 minutes. Rice hard-boiled eggs; put over top of casserole before serving. Serves 6.

SPINACH IN CHEESE SAUCE

Cook, drain and put spinach through meat grinder; arrange in casserole in alternate layers with hard-boiled eggs and a rich "Cream Sauce"; put sauce on top layer; cover with bread crumbs; bake until brown.

SQUASH RING

5 pounds tender yellow squash
1 small onion, chopped fine
1 teaspoon salt

3 tablespoons butter
4 eggs, beaten separately

Parboil squash; mash thoroughly; drain. Combine ingredients, folding in beaten whites last. Put in greased, 8-inch buttered mold. Cover top of mold with waxed paper while cooking. Bake at 350° in pan of hot water about ¾ of an hour. Turn out carefully on platter. Fill center of ring with tiny buttered green lima beans. Garnish ring with parsley. Serves 8.

FRIED YELLOW SQUASH

Parboil small yellow squash in salted water with a sliced onion; drain; roll squash in crumbs; then in beaten egg and again in crumbs.

Let stand a few minutes; fry a golden brown. Put on platter with small end of squash radiating from center. Put a bouquet of parsley at center of tray.

SQUASH AND EGG CASSEROLE

2 pounds squash, coarsely grated
2 onions, sliced

2 cups thick white sauce
6 eggs, hard boiled, grated

Boil onions and squash separately; drain. Combine cream sauce, eggs and vegetables. Put in casserole with buttered crumbs on top. Bake for 15 minutes. Serves 8.

SCALLOPED SQUASH

4 cups diced, tender green squash
1 large onion, chopped
4 hard-boiled eggs, sliced

2 cups thick, white sauce
1 cup sharp, grated cheese

Cook squash and onion in salted water until tender; drain. Add cheese to white sauce; combine with squash and eggs. Put in casserole and cover top with buttered crumbs. Bake until top is brown. Serves 8.

TINY PATTY PAN SQUASH

Cook tiny green summer squash in salted boiling water. Do not peel squash. Boil until tender; drain; cover with melted butter to which a little heavy cream, salt and cayenne pepper have been added.

STUFFED SQUASH

8 medium size squash
Several small ones extra
1 cup "Thick White Sauce"

2 cups diced chicken or ground ham
1 large onion, sliced
Salt and red pepper to taste

Scoop out squash; cook pulp with smaller squash and onion, in salted water, until tender. Drain; press out excess water; add to cream sauce and diced chicken or ham. Stuff squash shells, which have been parboiled slightly, with mixture; cover tops with buttered crumbs. Bake until brown. Garnish top of each squash with parsley bud. Serves 8.

Stuffed Squash (2)

8 medium size squash
2 extra ones
3 strips breakfast bacon
1 onion, chopped fine

1 large tomato, chopped
1 bell pepper, chopped
½ cup minced shrimp

Scoop out squash; parboil pulp with extra squash. Also parboil hulls slightly. Drain pulp. Cut bacon in small pieces; broil; take out bacon; cook onion and pepper in bacon grease; add tomato and squash. Let moisture cook away before adding cooked bacon and shrimp. Stuff in squash hulls; cover tops with buttered crumbs; bake. Serves 8.

Stuffed Squash (3)

8 squash 3 inches in diameter
1 large onion, sliced
2 tablespoons butter

2 tablespoons cream
2 tablespoons bread crumbs
Salt and red pepper

Boil squash and onion until tender, but firm. Scoop out 6 of them to stuff; mash the other two with scooped out pulp and onion. Put in sieve; let drain. Mash out as much moisture as possible; add butter and cream to drained pulp; fill shells. Sprinkle bread crumbs on top; dot with butter. Put in pan with a little water around them; bake until tops are brown. Serves 6.

BROILED OR FRIED TOMATOES

Cut unpeeled tomatoes in rather thick slices; dip in meal that has been well seasoned with salt and black pepper; fry in deep fat; drain on unglazed paper. The tomatoes should not be too ripe.

TOMATOES WITH DEVILED EGGS

3 large firm tomatoes, cut in half	2 tablespoons melted butter
2 hard-boiled eggs	1 raw egg
½ teaspoon salt	Parmesan cheese
1 teaspoon vinegar	Pinch of sugar and red pepper
½ teaspoon mustard	

Dip slices of tomatoes into seasoned meal; fry in deep fat; drain on unglazed paper. Do this just before you are ready to serve them. Beat raw egg; add vinegar, butter and seasoning; sieve hard-boiled yolks; combine the two. Put in double boiler; cook until thick; add chopped whites. Pile eggs on top of cooked tomato slices; sprinkle with Parmesan cheese. Run in oven long enough to heat. Serves 6.

BROILED TOMATO, CHEESE AND BACON

Put slices of cheese on slices of broiled tomatoes; run under broiler flame until melted. The broiler heat should be turned low. When melted top with a crisscross of previously broiled breakfast bacon.

BAKED STUFFED TOMATOES

6 firm tomatoes, unpeeled	3 ribs of celery
2 onions	1 cup cooked rice
1 bell pepper	

Cut slices from stem end of tomatoes; scoop out inside, leaving a shell to be stuffed. Sprinkle with salt; invert to drain while stuffing is being prepared. Chop onions, peppers and celery fine; fry in butter until tender, but not brown; add tomatoes; simmer until tomatoes are cooked to pieces; add rice; cook until almost dry; stuff into tomatoes; sprinkle crumbs on top. Put in pan with a little water around them and bake for about 15 minutes. A little ground ham can be added to the stuffing if desired. Serves 6.

Baked Stuffed Tomatoes (2)

8 tomatoes	1 cup chicken livers
1 cup cooked wild rice	1 large onion, minced
1 cup mushrooms, sliced	2 tablespoons butter

Cook onion in butter until tender; add mushrooms and livers; cook 5 or 10 minutes. When done, chop chicken livers, add pulp that has been scraped out of the tomatoes; cook until softened. Add rice; simmer until most of moisture has been cooked away; stuff into tomatoes; cover tops with crumbs; put in pan with a little hot water in it; cook 15 or 20 minutes. Decorate top of tomato with parsley buds. White rice can be substituted for wild rice if desired. Serves 8.

BAKED TOMATOES STUFFED WITH MUSHROOMS

8 firm tomatoes, medium size
1 can of mushrooms (8-ounce)
1 cup ground ham
1 onion
Bread crumbs

Cut off stem end of tomatoes; scoop out. Grind onion; cook in butter until tender; add mushrooms; broil 5 minutes; add tomato pulp; cook until tender; add ham. If necessary, add a few toasted bread crumbs to thicken; season highly with salt, red pepper and Worcestershire sauce. Stuff into tomato shells that have been sprinkled with salt and drained. Sprinkle bread crumbs on top; bake in pan with a small amount of water for 15 to 20 minutes. Serves 8.

BAKED CREOLE TOMATOES

Cut tomatoes in halves. Over each section of tomato put 1 tablespoon chopped celery, 1 teaspoon chopped bell pepper and a half teaspoon of minced onion. Sprinkle brown sugar and salt over vegetables and drizzle melted butter over them. Bake in oiled pan for half hour at 350°. Serve on toast circles.

RICE RING

1 cup rice
2 quarts boiling water
2 teaspoons salt

Wash rice; sprinkle in boiling salted water; cook until grains are soft; drain in colander; pour boiling water through rice. Put over hot water for 10 minutes to dry out; pack in generously buttered ring mold. Cook in pan of hot water in moderate oven a half hour. Run a knife around edges when ready to turn out on platter. This can be filled with creamed vegetables or chicken. Makes a small ring to serve 6 or 8.

WILD RICE RING

Steam a cup of wild rice in 3 cups of boiling water and 1 teaspoon of salt for 45 minutes. Let cook in double boiler until tender and water has been absorbed. Let stand a few minutes; lift out with a fork; add ½ pound of fresh mushrooms; ¾ cup chicken livers that have been cut in pieces and cooked in butter until tender with 1 tablespoon of chopped onion. Mix with fork; pack in a well-buttered ring mold; put in pan of hot water and cook at 350° for about a half hour. Unmold and fill with green peas and pimento. If preferred, the rice can be made into a plain ring and filled with creamed mushrooms and livers. Serves 6 to 8.

CREOLE RICE RING

1½ cups uncooked rice
2½ cups tomato juice
1 small onion, chopped fine
1 small bell pepper, chopped fine
4 ribs celery, chopped fine
1 pimento

1 cup ripe olives, cut off seed
½ pound sharp grated cheese
1 teaspoon salt
1 tablespoon Worcestershire sauce
⅛ spoon cayenne pepper

Cook rice and tomato juice with seasonings, until liquid is absorbed and rice is tender. Mix rest of ingredients into hot rice with fork. Pack into greased 8-inch mold; bake about 10 or 15 minutes in moderate oven. Serve with peas, "Creamed Shrimp," or "Eggs and Mushrooms" in center of ring. Serves 8.

GREEN RICE RING

2 cups cooked rice
2 tablespoons minced onion
4 tablespoons finely minced parsley
1 teaspoon salt

1 cup milk
1 cup grated cheese
2 eggs, beaten slightly

Add other ingredients to beaten eggs; mix well. Pour in well-greased 8-inch mold; put in pan with a small amount of hot water; bake 350° until firm. Unmold on hot platter; fill with "Green Peas and Pimento." Serves 6 to 8.

RICE BALLS

1 cup rice, uncooked
4 cups water (boiling)
1 teaspoon salt

1 cup grated cheese
1 egg, beaten together

Cook rice in boiling water until done; drain, do not wash; add beaten egg and cheese. Form into balls; roll first in bread crumbs, then in an egg beaten with a tablespoon of water; roll again in crumbs; fry in deep fat or bake on greased baking sheet at 350°. If preferred the cheese can be cut in squares and the rice and egg mixture put around the cheese to form a ball. Makes 8 to 10 balls.

RISOTTO

1 cup rice
1 quart water
¼ cup butter
1 onion, chopped fine
½ bell pepper, chopped fine

2½ cups chicken broth
1½ cups tomato juice
Salt to taste
1 cup mushrooms, chopped
½ cup Parmesan cheese

Boil rice in quart of water 3 minutes; drain. Cook onion, pepper and rice in skillet in ¼ cup butter until butter has been absorbed; add broth and tomato juice; cook until the moisture has been absorbed again. Stir in cheese and mushrooms that have been sautéed in butter.

WILD RICE

Wash 1 cup of wild rice thoroughly. Boil in 1 quart of water, with 1 spoon salt added, until tender. This should take about 30 to 40 minutes. Drain rice and keep over hot water until ready to use. Pour melted butter over rice.

BIG HOMINY CROQUETTES

2 cups big hominy (cooked)	2 egg yolks
1 cup milk	1 teaspoon salt
1 cup grated cheese	4 tablespoons butter
1 small onion, grated	4 tablespoons flour

Chop hominy. Make a cream sauce of milk, flour and butter; add grated cheese and beaten yolks; add seasoning and chopped hominy. Put on a flat platter; chill. When it can be handled, make into croquettes; roll in egg and bread crumbs; fry until golden brown. Serves 8.

GRITS RING

1 cup hominy grits	2 tablespoons butter
5 cups water	3 eggs, beaten separately
Salt to taste	

Cook grits in double boiler with water until done and very thick; cool; add salt, butter and beaten yolks. Fold in beaten whites; put into generously buttered ring mold; place in pan with a little water; cook until done (an hour or more). Fill with chicken hash. Serves 8 to 10. This can be put in individual ring molds if preferred.

NOODLE RING

1 package noodles (8 ounces)	1 tablespoon Worcestershire sauce
1 tablespoon butter	4 tablespoons tomato catsup
1 small cake pimento cheese	3 well-beaten eggs

Cook noodles in boiling salted water for 10 minutes; drain. Melt butter and cheese in top of double boiler; add eggs and seasoning; stir well. Pour this over drained noodles; stir until thoroughly mixed. Butter 8- or 9-inch mold; put mixture in mold. Set in pan containing a little hot water and bake at 350° degrees for 45 minutes. Unmold; fill ring with creamed chicken or sweetbreads. Serves 8.

NOODLE NESTS

A good imitation of the little noodle nests (which are usually available at large groceries) can be made at home by the following recipe: Boil very fine noodles in salted water; drain, but do not wash away the starch. Grease little individual pie pans thoroughly and form nests in them with noodles, as if you were making a pie crust. Chill overnight. Remove carefully from tins with point of knife. Fry in deep fat until brown on both sides. Fill with "Chicken Curry."

Supplement

New recipes are being constantly concocted in our Club kitchens, and kind friends contribute new ideas too, which have given us quite a few items to offer since the first printing of my cook book. At the request of many of my readers I am adding a supplement to this edition with the hope that they will enjoy the extra suggestions.

APPETIZERS

BITE-SIZE BEEF STRIPS IN WINE

2½ pound sirloin tip
½ stick butter or margarine
1 teaspoon grated onion
2 level tablespoons flour
1 10 ounce can beef bouillon
1 cup burgundy wine

½ teaspoon thyme
½ teaspoon salt
¼ teaspoon black pepper
   Dash Tabasco and Worcestershire
   sauces
6 parsley sprigs

Have butcher cut beef into narrow bite-size strips about ½ x 2 inches. Melt butter in skillet and sauté onion until clear. Remove from skillet and add beef strips. Brown on all sides and remove beef also. In the same butter make a roux with 2 tablespoons flour. Add more butter if necessary. Stir bouillon into this and cook until smooth. Add wine and seasonings, parsley, sautéed onion and beef. Simmer covered for 1 hour or until beef is tender. Remove parsley, correct seasoning and put the beef and sauce in chafing dish to keep warm. Serve in little sesame bun bites.

COCKTAIL DIP

½ pound Philadelphia cream cheese
¼ cup milk
1 tablespoon mayonnaise
1 teaspoon Worchestershire Sauce

½ teaspoon paprika
½ teaspoon garlic salt
½ lemon (juice)
1 teaspoon mustard horse-radish

Thin cheese with milk until smooth; add other ingredients. Serve with giant Fritos or potato chips.

ARTICHOKE CANAPÉS

Spread small rounds of bread with well seasoned Philadelphia cheese that has been softened with milk and had a little Worchestershire Sauce and onion juice beaten into it. Pull the petals off of small canned artichoke hearts and use them to form the petals of a flower on top of the canapé. Put a slice of the smallest sized stuffed olive at the center of each flower.

STUFFED CELERY

A nice substitute for stuffed celery hearts is Paschal celery cut in 3-inch lengths. Cut one end of each section in a point, and with a pastry tube make a large cheese flower at the other end. Any cheese spread, highly seasoned with Worcestershire sauce and grated onion can be used. Soften cheese with a little milk if necessary so that it can be forced through the pastry tube.

HOT CHEESE PUFFS

2 eggs	¼ teaspoon salt
1½ cups grated cheese	14 rounds bread (2½ inch)
1 teaspoon dry mustard	

Beat eggs separately until very thick and stiff; combine; add seasoning and freshly grated yellow cheese. Put a heaping teaspoonful on dried out rounds of bread. Toast at 450 deg. until puffy. Serve at once.

CHEESE FONDUE

1 pound Swiss cheese, grated	Dash nutmeg
1½ tablespoons flour	Dash cayenne pepper
1 clove garlic	French bread
1½ cups dry white wine	

Toss grated cheese with flour. Rub inside of fondue pot with cut garlic clove; discard garlic. Pour wine into pot and heat, but do not boil it. Add cheese, a quarter of it at a time. Stir constantly each time until melted before adding another portion of cheese. When all cheese has been added, serve at once.

Have ready French bread slices cut into bite-size pieces, leaving part of crust on each piece. Guests spear these on forks or skewers, and dip into fondue pot with them. If the cheese gets too thick, add a little more warmed wine. Never let fondue boil. Serves 5 or 6.

OLIVES IN CHEESE PASTRY

1 small bottle (5 ounces) pimento-stuffed olives	1 teaspoon paprika
1½ cups flour	½ cup soft margarine
¼ teaspoon salt	½ pound sharp cheese, grated

Drain olives. Sift flour with salt and paprika; cut in cheese and soft butter; knead with hands until a soft dough is formed. Pinch off small sections of dough and wrap a thin coating of pastry around each olive. Put in freezing compartment until ready to cook. Bake unthawed olives at 400° for 15 or 20 minutes, or until light brown. Let stand a few minutes before serving warm.

CHICKEN LIVERS IN WINE

1 pound chicken livers	Salt and pepper
1 tablespoon grated onion	3 tablespoons dry sherry wine

Cook onion in a little butter until clear. Add livers which have been rolled in flour and seasoned with salt and pepper; cook until livers are brown. Add sherry and simmer until most of the wine has cooked away. Serve hot over a candle warmer on cocktail picks.

CHICKEN LIVERS WRAPPED IN BACON

Wash and thoroughly dry the chicken livers. Cut each liver in half; wrap in a half slice of breakfast bacon; secure bacon with a cocktail pick; grill inside of oven on a wire rack and serve very hot.

CANNED BAKED HAM

When only a small amount of baked ham is needed for a cocktail party, the canned boned hams are best to use, since there is no waste. They should be heated, however, even when labeled "Ready To Eat". The directions are on the can.

A small canned ham is usually baked about an hour in a 325° oven. Glaze the top of ham by basting every 15 minutes with the following:

Combine 4 tablespoons brown sugar and ½ teaspoon dry mustard. Add 4 tablespoons white Karo syrup and juice of 1 orange. When the last of the glaze is put on add 2 tablespoons orange marmalade to it, and bake 15 minutes before removing from fire. Cool and refrigerate so it will slice better.

BAKED CANADIAN BACON

Another nice baked meat to use at cocktail parties (to make your own sandwiches) is Canadian bacon. Get a 3-pound piece and spread over it a combination of ¼ cup brown sugar and ½ teaspoon dry mustard. Bake uncovered for 1 hour, basting it at 15-minute intervals with ½ cup ginger ale or orange juice. Cool and chill. This can be served whole on a buffet table with sharp knife nearby or sliced very thin and put on a platter. Nice with buttered and warmed Party Rye Bread circles.

COCKTAIL PARTY DRUMSTICKS

Sprinkle well the desired number of drumsticks from 2½-pound chickens with meat tenderizer. Dip in melted butter flavored with a little garlic salt, and then roll in a combination of crushed cornflakes and grated Parmesan cheese, using 1 cup of cornflakes to ¼ cup of the cheese. Place in greased flat casserole, not touching. Dribble more melted butter over drumsticks and bake for an hour or until tender at

325°. Serve hot with a bowl of the following sauce used to dunk them. The sauce can be served hot or cold. Small plates and paper napkins should be nearby. This sauce will be sufficient to dunk 20 drumsticks. If paper frills are available put one on the end of each drumstick.

SAUCE: Grind 1 onion, 1 bell pepper and 1 cup celery in meat chopper and cook in ½ stick butter until tender, but not brown. Add a pinch of baking soda to 1 pound tomato purée, combine with 1 tablespoon horseradish, 1 tablespoon Worcestershire sauce, 1 teaspoon prepared mustard, and 1 small can tomato paste, and mix with the ground vegetables. Simmer about 10 minutes. Season to taste with salt and red pepper. Add a speck of sugar if the mixture seems too acid.

HOT CRAB CIRCLES

1 6 oz. can crab meat	¼ teaspoon salt
½ cup undiluted celery soup	2 tablespoons sherry
1 chopped pimento	½ cup dried grated bread crumbs
½ green pepper chopped	2 tablespoons Parmesan cheese

Mince crab meat and mix with other ingredients, reserving bread crumbs and cheese to be sprinkled over circles. Toast doughnut shaped rounds of bread and pile crab around circles. Sprinkle with combined cheese and crumbs. Run under broiler until browned. Makes 20 circles.

PARMESAN POTATO CHIPS

Sprinkle large potato chips with grated Parmesan cheese. Heat at 350° until chips are golden brown.

DEVILED PECANS

Mix 2 tablespoons melted butter with 1 tablespoon Worcestershire sauce and a dash of Tabasco sauce. Put 1 pound of large pecan halves on cookie sheet and dribble butter mixture over them. Stir to coat the pecans. Put in 300° oven until crisp. Drain on absorbent paper.

IMPROMPTU PIZZAS

Split English muffins and brush each half lightly with olive oil. Cover with a slice of mozzarella cheese. Over this pour a spoonful of canned or bottled pizza sauce. Cover with grated Parmesan cheese. Drizzle with a little more olive oil and bake at 350° until cheese melts and is toasted. Decorate tops with sliced stuffed olives, anchovies, or sliced sausage rings. A pinch of marjoram can be added if desired. (Another good topping can be found under "Pizza Appetizers.")

PIZZA APPETIZERS

1 No. 2½ can tomatoes	1 cup dried beef
1 cup blocked cheese	Black pepper

,Pour boiling water over beef and drain until dry then cut into small pieces. Cook tomatoes until very thick; add other ingredients. Season with pepper and add salt if needed. The dried beef will probably furnish enough salt. Pile on toast rounds and sprinkle with a little grated Italian cheese. Heat in slow oven and serve hot—makes about 18 small appetizers.

SAUSAGE BALLS IN CHEESE PASTRY

2 or 3 tablespoons beef or chicken bouillon
1 pound "hot" pork sausage
¾ cup dry bread crumbs

¼ teaspoon poultry seasoning
Large pinch nutmeg

Make bouillon with bouillon cube and water. Combine with other ingredients, adding more liquid if necessary to hold ingredients together. Form into small balls, using about 1 teaspoon sausage mixture and fry slowly until done, but not too crusty. Cool balls. Use cheese pastry that is given for Olives in Cheese Pastry and pinch off enough dough to cover each sausage ball with a thin coating of pastry. Freeze. When ready to bake, put unthawed balls on cookie sheet and bake at 400° until lightly brown, 15 or 20 minutes. The balls hold their shape better if they are not thawed. Serve hot. Makes about 40 balls.

SAUSAGE ROLL UPS

Make "Baking Powder Biscuit," using 4 tablespoons of shortening instead of three. Cook sausage slightly, spread in a flat sheet. Roll dough thin and cover with sausage, patting it down on the dough. Roll up in a small cylinder as you would roll a jelly roll. Put in refrigerator for a short while to harden and then slice in ¾ inch slices. Put in biscuit pan, cut side down and bake until brown. Serve hot.

SHRIMP TURNOVERS

1 cup cleaned and cooked shrimp
1 tablespoon lemon juice
2 tablespoons mayonnaise
1 package pie crust mix

¼ teaspoon tobasco sauce
1 teaspoon Worchestershire Sauce
Dash of onion salt

Roll pie crust thin and cut in 3 inch circles; mash shrimp and add other ingredients, making a paste. Put a spoonful on each pastry circle. Fold over and press together with tines of fork. Bake until turnovers are brown. Serve hot.

BEVERAGES

CHRISTMAS PUNCH

2 quarts cranberry juice cocktail
2 6-ounce cans lemonade concentrate
2 6-ounce cans orange juice concentrate

1 quart canned sweetened pineapple juice
1 quart ginger ale

Combine thawed lemonade and orange juice concentrates with the rest of ingredients. Taste, add sugar if necessary. Serve with ice ring in punch bowl (see Fruit-Filled Ice Ring) but freeze cherries and green leaves (arranged to resemble bunches of holly) instead of fruit. This will serve about 25 punch cups. If cups are small it will serve 30.

PARTY PUNCH

4 6-ounce cans frozen orange juice
6 6-ounce cans frozen lemonade
1 46-ounce can pineapple juice

6 quarts ginger ale
1 bottle maraschino cherries
6 thinly sliced oranges

Have all ingredients thoroughly chilled. Combine fruit juices. Sweeten if necessary. Pour fruit juices over ice in punch bowl and add cherries and juice, and sliced oranges. A fruit-filled ring of ice (easy to make in a deep freeze) can be floated in the punch bowl instead of ice block if preferred. Add ginger ale just before punch is served.

BREADS

APRICOT BREAD

½ pound natural-colored dried apricots
2½ cups flour
¾ cup sugar
4 teaspoons baking powder
½ teaspoon soda

½ teaspoon salt
1 cup buttermilk
1 egg, beaten
3 tablespoons vegetable oil
½ cup chopped pecans

Cover apricots with boiling water and let stand for 10 minutes. Drain and dry between paper towels. Cut in thin slivers. Sift dry ingredients. Combine buttermilk, beaten egg and vegetable oil. Stir into dry ingredients until well mixed. Add apricots and nuts which have been dredged in ¼ cup extra flour. Put in well greased loaf pan and bake in preheated 350° oven for about 1 hour or until done. Turn out on rack until cold. Wrap in waxed paper and store in refrigerator until ready for use.

BISHOP BREAD

2½ cups flour
2 cups brown sugar
½ teaspoon salt
½ cup Crisco
¾ cup sour milk

½ teaspoon soda
1 teaspoon baking powder
2 teaspoons powdered cinnamon
2 eggs beaten together
½ cup chopped pecans (optional)

Mix flour, sugar, salt and Crisco. Reserve ¾ cup of this mixture for topping. To the remainder add sour milk with soda in it, baking powder, cinnamon and eggs. Beat to a smooth batter. Pour into two greased bread pans and scatter crumbs of the reserved mixture on top of batter. Bake in preheated 350° oven for about 35 or 40 minutes. Nuts can be added to the batter if desired.

ORANGE-DATE BREAD

2 oranges
2 well beaten eggs
1¼ cups brown sugar
¼ cup melted margarine
¼ cup fresh orange juice

2½ cups sifted flour
3 teaspoons baking powder
½ tsp. salt
½ cup chopped pecans
½ cup chopped dates

Grind oranges, drain and reserve juice. Use ¼ cup of this juice for the above recipe. Sift dry ingredients; add sugar and margarine to beaten eggs; combine with dry ingredients and orange juice, add ground oranges, pecans and nuts. Pour in greased and floured pan and bake 350° about an hour. When cool store in the refrigerator until ready to cut in thin slices. Put two slices together with butter between.

CRANBERRY BREAD

1 cup raw cranberries
1 cup chopped nuts
1 orange juice and rind
1 beaten egg
2 tablespoons Wesson Oil

1 cup sugar
2 cups flour
½ teaspoon salt
1½ teaspoons baking powder
½ teaspoon soda

Sift dry ingredients together. Slice cranberries in 3 or 4 slices, using a sharp knife. Grate rind of orange to use in bread and squeeze out juice. Put juice in a cup with the Wesson Oil and add enough boiling water to make ¾ cup of liquid. Combine liquid with dry ingredients and beaten egg; add sliced cranberries and nuts; put in greased and floured bread pan and bake for about an hour in 325°. When cool put in refrigerator, wrapped in foil, until ready to slice. Pretty and delicious. Serve buttered.

TOASTED FRENCH BREAD

1 loaf French bread
1 stick butter or margarine, melted
1 teaspoon parsley flakes (optional)

½ teaspoon garlic powder
Parmesan cheese

Slice bread diagonally into ¾-inch slices. Combine melted butter, parsley flakes and garlic powder. Brush each slice with butter mixture. Cut a length of aluminum foil 8 inches longer than loaf of bread. Put slices back together again in the middle of the foil. Twist each end of the foil and roll back the sides so that the bread is not covered. Brush from the top of the loaf with the seasoned butter. Sprinkle with Parmesan cheese and put in 400° oven until toasted, about 10 or 15 minutes. The bread can be served right in the foil if desired or taken out of it and put on a tray. This method eliminates the scattered crumbs which we get when cutting the bread part of the way through before serving.

FRUIT BREAD

½ cup crystallized cherries
¼ cup crystallized pineapple
¼ cup citron
½ cup pecans
2 cups flour
4 teaspoons baking powder

¾ cup sugar
¼ teaspoon salt
2 eggs beaten together
3 teaspoons vegetable oil
1 cup milk

Cut fruit and pecans in small pieces. Sift dry ingredients together and combine with fruit and nuts. Add beaten eggs and vegetable oil to milk. Stir into flour mixture just enough to moisten flour well. Pour into greased bread pan 9 x 5 x 3 and cook about 1 hour in oven that has been preheated to 350°. Turn out on wire rack when done. When cold, wrap in waxed paper and store in refrigerator until ready to use.

GARLIC BREAD STICKS

1 package long frankfurter buns
2 sticks butter, melted

¼ teaspoon garlic powder
Sesame or caraway seed

Split rolls in half lengthwise, then cut each half into two lengthwise strips. Trim edges. To melted butter add ¼ teaspoon garlic powder (or to taste). Brush bread sticks on all sides with melted butter or dip sticks lightly in the butter. Sprinkle with sesame or caraway seed. Put on baking sheet and toast in oven preheated to 450° until brown. This will take about 5 minutes. Watch while cooking.

SESAME BUN BITES

1½ sticks butter
½ teaspoon garlic powder

1 8-ounce package hamburger buns
Sesame seed

Combine butter and garlic powder and spread on both sides of buns. Put backs of halves together. Brush tops with butter and sprinkle with sesame seed. Place on a cookie sheet. Cut each bun in quarters and spear together with cocktail pick after toasting. Nice to serve with meatballs at cocktail parties.

CAKES AND COOKIES.

CHRISTMAS COOKIES

2/3 stick butter or margarine
½ cup brown sugar
2 eggs beaten together
1½ cups flour
½ teaspoon soda
1 teaspoon cinnamon
1 teaspoon ginger

½ cup whiskey
2 cups crystallized cherries
cut in half
1 cup chopped dates
1 cup crystallized pineapple
1 cup citron, chopped
1½ cups chopped pecans

Cream butter. Add sugar and beaten eggs. Sift flour with soda and spices. Add flour mixture and whiskey alternately to butter and sugar mixture. Chop fruit and nuts coarsely and add to batter. If batter seems too stiff add a tablespoon of milk. It should be stiff enough not to spread. Put out by teaspoonfuls on greased cookie sheet. Cook at 325° about 15 minutes.

YELLOW CORNFLAKE COOKIES

4 egg whites
2 cups sifted yellow sugar
½ teaspoon cream of tartar

4 cups cornflakes
1 cup broken pecans

Beat egg whites with cream of tartar until very stiff; add sifted yellow sugar, a small amount at a time; fold in cornflakes and nuts and bake slowly on a greased cookie sheet, using a tablespoon of the mixture for each cookie. Bake in slow oven until firm to the touch; cool slightly and remove before cookies get cold.

DROP COOKIES

½ cup Crisco
½ cup margarine
1 cup sugar

1½ cups sifted flour
2 eggs
1 teaspoon vanilla

Cream shortening with sugar; add beaten eggs and vanilla and fold in flour. Drop by teaspoon on greased cookie sheet and remove from sheet as soon as they are done.

BROWN-EDGED WAFERS

1 cup butter or margarine
1 cup sugar
2 eggs beaten together

1½ cups flour
½ teaspoon salt
1 teaspoon vanilla

Cream butter and sugar together. Add beaten eggs and flour that has been sifted with salt. Add vanilla. Drop by small spoonfuls (they will spread) on greased baking sheet. Bake at 350° about 10 minutes.

CINNAMON CRISPS

1 box (about 8 ounces) cinnamon graham crackers
2 sticks margarine

1 cup brown sugar
1 cup finely chopped pecans

Line a greased 13 x 11 inch pan with whole cinnamon graham crackers. Melt 2 sticks margarine. Add brown sugar and bring to a boil. Stir in chopped pecans. Remove from heat. Cover the crackers with this syrup, pouring it on with spoon. Bake for 10 minutes at 350°. Cut between crackers and take from the pan as soon as they come out of the oven. Otherwise they will stick to the pan.

ROCKY ROAD FUDGIES

2 sticks butter
3 envelopes Redi-Blend chocolate or 3
squares bitter chocolate (3 ounces)
4 eggs beaten together
2 cups sugar

1½ cups flour
1 teaspoon baking powder
2 teaspoons vanilla
1 cup chopped pecans
1 bag miniature marshmallows

Melt butter in top of double boiler and blend with chocolate. Beat eggs together, add sugar and chocolate mixture. Sift flour and baking powder together and add to above. Flavor with vanilla, add chopped nuts and put in greased and floured pan about 9 x 13. Cook at 325° about 35 minutes. Take from oven and while still hot cover the top completely with marshmallows and carefully spoon the following chocolate icing over them while cake is still in the pan.

ICING: Melt 1 stick of margarine in double boiler. Add 3 envelopes of Redi-Blend chocolate. Or if you prefer, 3 squares of bitter chocolate (3 ounces) and 1 cup of sugar. Combine with ½ cup strong coffee and flavor with 1 teaspoon vanilla.

Cook until well blended. Remove from heat and stir in 1 pound confectioners' sugar that has been sifted to remove any lumps. Put over marshmallows at once. The icing may seem a little thin. Pour carefully over the marshmallows with a spoon to completely cover them.

Cool and cut cake in the pan. This cake is best made and iced a day ahead. A packaged brownie mix can be used instead of the cake recipe.

FILLED CUP CAKES

½ cup margarine
1 cup sugar
1½ cups flour
2 eggs, beaten separately

½ cup milk
1 teaspoon baking power
½ teaspoon vanilla
Custard filling

Cream butter and sugar; add beaten yolks. Sift dry ingredients; add alternately to butter and sugar with the milk; and beaten whites; flavor. Put in small greased tins and bake at 375° about 20 minutes. Remove from tins; cool; cut off tops and remove small amount of cake to make a place for the filling—fill these cakes and sprinkle chocolate candy sprinkles or grated chocolate over the tops.

FILLING

⅛ cup sugar
¼ teaspoon salt
1¼ tablespoons cornstarch
½ tablespoon flour

2 egg yolks
1½ cups milk
2 teaspoons butter
1 teaspoon vanilla

Sift dry ingredients; heat milk; beat yolks slightly—make a thick custard by adding dry ingredients to yolks and pouring heated milk over them. Return mixture to double boiler and cook until very thick; add butter and vanilla; chill thoroughly before filling cakes. This is the basic recipe but it has many variations. For almond filling add 1 teaspoon almond flavoring and a half cup of chopped toasted almonds. For banana filling add a small amount of chopped bananas and top with half a slice of banana. Chopped moist canned coconut can be added for a coconut nut filling. This recipe will make 24 very small filled cup cakes.

TOASTED ANGEL FOOD CAKE

Break off small pieces of angel food cake with 2 forks. Dip lightly in melted butter and then in sifted brown sugar. Place on greased cookie sheet and toast at 400°. Watch closely as they brown easily.

BUTTERSCOTCH FUDGE CAKE

2 sticks margarine
1 box light brown sugar
4 egg yolks, beaten
2 teaspoons vanilla

2 cups flour
1 teaspoon baking powder
1 cup chopped pecans
4 egg whites, beaten

Melt margarine in a large saucepan and stir in the brown sugar. *Mix well.* Add beaten yolks to this and flavor with vanilla. Sift flour and baking powder together and add to the mixture with the chopped nuts. Add beaten whites last. Pour in greased rectangular pan and bake at 275° for 45 minutes. Cool in pan and cut in squares. Sift confectioners' sugar on cake squares. Do not overcook this (cake should be chewy).

CARAMEL CAKE BARS

1 box yellow cake mix
1 stick margarine
1 pound light brown sugar
2 tablespoons flour

2 eggs, beaten
1½ cups broken pecans
1 teaspoon vanilla

Make cake by directions on box, only put it in two oblong pans 13 x 10 x 2 inches. This will make thin layers of batter. Bake in 350° oven about 25 minutes. Remove from heat to cool. While cooling make the caramel topping as follows: Melt margarine in iron skillet. Mix sugar with beaten eggs and flour and add to the margarine. Cook over low heat about 3 minutes. Remove from heat and add vanilla and nuts. Spread this evenly over cakes while still in pan. Return to the oven and bake at 400° for 8 minutes. Cool and cut in bars 1½ inches long. This will make 50 to 60 bars. If you need a smaller quantity, use half the cake batter for the bars and the other half for cup cakes. These make nice cakes for parties. They have an icing about as thick as the cake part.

RAISIN CAKE

1 cup sugar
1¼ cups brown sugar
1 cup margarine
4 eggs, beaten separately
2 cups butter-milk
Peeling, only, of 1 orange

4 cups flour
2 tsp. soda
1 tsp. salt
2 cups seeded raisins
1 cup chopped pecans

Cream margarine and both kinds of sugar together; add beaten yolks;

grind raisins and orange peel and sift a small amount of the flour over them. Sift dry ingredients together and add to butter and sugar mixture, alternating with milk and beaten egg whites. Fold in nuts and fruit mixture and put in a greased biscuit pan or in two 8 inch cake pans. Bake at 350° for about one hour. When cool, ice with "Uncooked Orange Icing." Serve while fresh.

CANDY

APRICOT BALLS

1 box dried apricots
Juice ½ lemon

2 cups Bakers Cocoanut Southern style
Condensed milk, about ½ cup or less

Grind apricots; add cocoanut and bind together with Eagle Brand condensed milk—sprinkle lemon juice over the combination and knead it all together. Form into small balls and roll in powdered sugar. Chill. Makes about 20 balls.

NEW ORLEANS PRALINES

1½ cups sugar
⅛ cup white Karo
⅔ cup water

1 tablespoon butter
⅛ teaspoon salt
2 cups pecans

Combine sugar, Karo, water and salt; cook over low heat to 238° or soft ball stage; add butter and pecans and beat until it thickens; drop on buttered sheet. This is the sugary kind rather than the creamy variety of praline.

DATE ROLL

1 package dates
1 cup pecans
1 teaspoon vanilla
1 pinch salt

2 cups sugar
1 cup milk
1 tablespoon Karo
1 tablespoon butter

Cut dates in 4 pieces; chop nuts; cook sugar, milk, Karo and salt, slowly to soft ball stage 238°, add dates and simmer until it again reaches 238°, add butter and vanilla and beat until very thick and stiff. Spoon onto a damp cloth and roll into a cylinder about one and a half inches in diameter. Chill; unroll and roll over and over in additional finely chopped pecans. Roll in waxed paper and slice when ready to use.

DESSERTS

ANGEL PIE (With Variations)

4 egg whites
1 cup sugar
¼ teaspoon cream of tartar
1 pinch salt
1 pint whipping cream

4 egg yolks
½ cup sugar
3 tablespoons lemon juice
1 tablespoon grated lemon rind

Add salt to egg whites; beat until foamy; add cream of tartar; beat until stiff and add sugar slowly to make a meringue. Lightly grease a glass pie pan and line bottom and sides with meringue. Do not let it come over the edge of pan. Press down in center with a spoon and bake at 250° until firm, about one hour. Cool and fill the meringue with the following mixture:

Filling

Beat egg yolks slightly; add the half cup sugar, lemon juice and grated rind. Cook in double boiler about ten minutes or until very thick; chill and add half of the cream which has been whipped. Fill meringue shell and cover with remaining whipped cream. Refrigerate 4 to 6 hours.

Another version has a chocolate filling made in the same way, adding 8 tablespoons cocoa to the cooked egg mixture and flavoring it with 1 teaspoon vanilla instead of lemon. Taste and add more sugar as desired. Then add half the whipped cream and put in meringue shell. Cover with remaining whipped cream and sprinkle with grated chocolate or with chocolate candy sprinkles. Refrigerate for 6 hours before using.

Angel Pie—Peach Filling

Make angel pie shell; when ready to serve fill with alternate slices of fresh peaches and sweetened whipped cream that has been flavored with almond extract. Decorate top with overlapping slices of peaches around the outer edge. This will take a pint of whipping cream and 10 to 12 peaches.

COFFEE ALASKA

One "Fudge Cake" recipe	6 egg whites
3 pints Coffee Ice Cream	1½ cups sugar
1 tablespoon powdered coffee	½ teaspoon cream of tartar

Turn fudge cake out on a greased cookie sheet with open end; cool; spread with spoons of coffee ice cream and cover completely with meringue made of the last four ingredients. The powdered coffee should be added last. Run in preheated, very hot oven—about 500°. Watch carefully as it will brown in less than five minutes. Slide off onto platter and serve at once. This serves at least twelve people. The recipe can be cut in half and one layer of packaged fudge cake can be substituted if desired. Be very careful that the meringue seals in all the ice cream.

CHRISTMAS SHERBET

Little tree-shaped salad molds are available in most stores and they can be used to make a very attractive Christmas dessert. Pack them as firmly as possible with bought green lime sherbet and put them in the deep freeze. You can unmold them and decorate them and return them to the freezer until ready to use. Decorate with chopped crystallized cherries, both red and green; crystallized pineapple or bits of green citron —all in very small pieces. Put on each tree by hand in a decorative manner. It is best to take one or two trees from the freezer at a time to prevent melting. Ring-shaped salad molds can be treated in the same manner and decorated in red and green fruits to resemble holly. Put a fluffy red bow of narrow ribbon at the top of the wreath. Serve Snow Ball Cakes with each of these desserts and decorate the top of cakes with a sprig of holly made of the cherries with citron leaves. When turning the sherbet out of the mold to decorate, run a knife around edges and they will usually come right out. If they do not, put the mold on top of a cloth that has been rung out in hot water for a second. After they have been decorated do not return to the molds, but put on a tray covered with wax paper and return to freezer until ready to use.

CRANBERRY SHERBET

2 cans cranberry sauce	2 tablespoons gelatin
2 oranges	½ cup water
2 lemons	1 quart gingerale
½ cup sugar	2 beaten egg whites

Melt cranberries in double boiler; add gelatin that has softened in ½ cup water; dissolve thoroughly; cool. Grind oranges and lemons; add to mixture and then add sugar and gingerale. Freeze until mushy and add beaten whites. Freeze again. This is good served as a first course in the center of a grapefruit half. Serves 8.

DUTCH APPLE CAKE

1 package yellow cake mix	⅛ cup butter
1 can apple pie slices	2 cups brown sugar
Powdered cinnamon	

Put cake batter in pan and lay slices of apple over the uncooked batter. Cream butter; add sugar and powdered cinnamon to taste. Crumble this over the apples. Sprinkle with more cinnamon and bake. Serve warm with whipped cream. A favorite with men.

FRUIT-FILLED ICE RING

This should be done the day before it is to be used. Get the largest ring mold available that will fit into your punch bowl. A 12-cup salad ring usually is about the right size. Half fill and put in a level place in the coldest section of the deep freeze. The clearness of the ice depends on quick freezing. When it is frozen hard remove from deep freeze and arrange small colorful fruits in season (or canned fruits if necessary) in attractive designs around the ring. Combine small green leaves of some kind with the fruit. I use cherry laurel leaves or mint leaves when possible. After they are arranged pour a small amount of water carefully around fruit and put back in deep freeze. (Use only enough water to anchor the fruit securely.) In an hour take out. Either add a little more water or completely cover the fruit with water and refreeze. When ready to use, put hot towel on bottom and sides until the ring is loosened. Carefully slide it in punch bowl, fruit side up. If preferred the ice can be replaced by sherbet, using about 2 quarts. In this case the fruit juices should be icy cold before pouring over sherbet. It would be wise to chill the punch bowl with a block of ice, removing it before putting in the punch. Serves 40 to 50 punch cups.

GINGER ICE CREAM

3 egg yolks	1 pint whipping cream
½ cup sugar	1 cup preserved ginger
2 level teaspoons cornstarch	¾ cup sherry wine
1 quart milk	

Beat yolks. Add sugar and cornstarch. Put in double boiler over hot water. Add milk gradually and cook until thick. Cool and chill. Whip cream and combine with custard. Freeze until about half frozen. Add preserved ginger and the wine. Freeze until quite firm. Serve with Toasted Angel Food Cake.

GINGER SHERBET

1 cup sugar	Juice of 6 lemons
1½ cups water	Juice of 6 oranges
Rinds of 2 lemons	1 quart ginger ale
1 tablespoon gelatin	2 egg whites, whipped
¼ cup cold water	¼ pound crystallized ginger

Boil sugar, water, and lemon rinds for 5 minutes. Soak gelatin in cold water and dissolve in boiling syrup. Remove lemon peel. Cool. Add lemon and orange juice to ginger ale and combine with cold syrup. Taste and add more sugar or lemon if needed. Put in dessert tray and partially freeze. Take out of refrigerator and beat in stiffly beaten whites and ginger. Refreeze. Serve with Brown-Edged Wafers; a most refreshing summer dessert.

MACEDOINE OF FRESH FRUITS

Select fruits in season. Pineapple—cut in slices and then in small pieces, discarding hard centers; apricots—cut in half; blue plums—cut in half; watermelon, cantaloupe and honeydew balls (cut with large baller) ; pears and peaches—cut in quarters; whole strawberries; seeded grapes; blueberries and any other desired fruit. I do not use bananas as they discolor and get soft so quickly.

Use enough confectioners' sugar to sweeten the amount of fruit you have. Mix sugar and kirsch or rum if you prefer, until well dissolved, before combining with fruit. Allow about 1 tablespoon kirsch for each serving of fruit. Combine with fruit and let stand a while before putting it in a large crystal bowl or a scooped out watermelon shell with top cut in scallops. It is also pretty served in huge brandy snifters if they are available. Put on buffet table surrounded with small punch cups. Garnish with sprays of fresh mint. Another delightful way to sweeten the fresh fruit is to put a quart of pineapple sherbet in the containers and add 4 to 6 ounces of crème de menthe before putting the well-chilled fruit in the bowl. A winter fruit bowl can be made of grapefruit and orange sections, pears and grapes with any other fresh fruits available. Combine with canned pineapple and peaches.

MINT SHERBET RING WITH FRESH FRUIT

1/2 gallon lemon sherbet	Green coloring
2/3 cup green crème de menthe	Strawberries or red raspberries

Turn sherbet into electric beater bowl. Let soften slightly and stir in crème de menthe. If it is not a pretty green color add a few drops of green coloring. Put in 9½-inch ring mold; place mold in deep freeze for at least 24 hours. To unmold invert on serving platter after running around edges of mold with a cake knife. (It will probably come right out, but if not wring a cloth out in hot water and wipe around bottom of mold with it. Shake mold slightly.) Put platter back in deep freeze until ready to use. Fill center with red raspberries or strawberries, and tuck green leaves, such as ivy leaves, around base of ring. Lime sherbet can be used the same way without the crème de menthe. It can also be molded in individual ring molds and any kind of fresh fruit used in the center of the rings.

MOCK CHOCOLATE SOUFFLE

1 box devil's food cake mix	1/2 cup cocoa
1 cup brown sugar	2 cups boiling water
	1 large bag miniature marshmallows

Make cake according to directions on box. Combine sugar, cocoa and boiling water in the bottom of an ungreased oblong pyrex dish 13x10x2. Float the marshmallows on top of the liquid. This will make a raft to pour the cake batter over. Spoon batter carefully on top of marshmallows. Bake in 350° pre-heated oven for about 30 minutes. The marshmallows make the cake puff up very much like a soufflé. Do not overcook as the syrup at the bottom of the cake will cook away. When serving, spoon some of the syrup over each portion. Pass ice cream balls to top soufflé—vanilla, coffee or peppermint ice cream can be used. Serves about 10.

ORANGE CHARLOTTE

2 cups unstrained orange juice	3/4 cup boiling water
1/8 cup lemon juice	2 cups sugar
3 tablespoons gelatin	6 egg whites
3/4 cup cold water	1 cup whipping cream

Soak gelatin in cold water; dissolve in boiling water; add sugar and fruit juice. Chill when very thick, beat or whip until smooth and frothy. Add beaten egg whites and whipped cream and pour in ring mold. When ready to serve unmold. Fill center with extra whipped cream with sections of 2 large oranges folded into cream. Press split lady fingers around sides if desired.

ORANGE ICE CREAM RING

½ gallon vanilla ice cream
2 large cans frozen orange juice
concentrate

2 tablespoons grated orange rind
12 ladyfingers

Soften commercial ice cream and beat in orange juice concentrate and orange rind. Put in a large 9½-inch ring mold and refreeze in freezing compartment of refrigerator. When ready to use take out and dip mold quickly in hot water. Run knife around sides and turn out on serving platter. Press ladyfinger halves around the outside of ring and fill the center with whipped cream. Garnish around the ring with ivy leaves and assemble small flowers on some of the leaves with three overlapping sections of canned mandarin orange sections. This should be taken from the freezer about 15 minutes before serving to soften slightly. If it seems to be getting too soft put the platter in refrigerator until serving time. Serves 8 to 10.

PEACHES WITH ICE CREAM

Peel and cut large fresh peaches in 6 or 8 sections, according to size of peach. Arrange sections in a 4-inch circle overlapping each section. Fill the circle with vanilla ice cream. Peach circles can be arranged ahead of time if sprinkled with lemon juice.

PEACHES, ICE CREAM AND PORT WINE

Put a large peach half in each compote. Cover with 2 tablespoons of port wine. Fill compote with vanilla ice cream. Delicious and easy to fix. Serves 1.

SABAYON WITH FRESH PEACHES

6 egg yolks
1 cup sherry wine

1 cup sugar

Cook in double boiler over hot (not boiling) water until thick. Chill. Serve in a bowl covered with whipped cream, or cream can be folded in sauce. Set bowl in center of a platter and surround bowl with halves of large fresh peaches. Serves 6.

MOLDED SABAYON FOR 25

16 egg yolks
1 cup sugar
1 bottle cream sherry wine
1 box (4 envelopes) gelatin
¾ cup cold water
16 egg whites
¼ teaspoon salt

½ teaspoon cream of tartar
1 additional cup of sugar
1 pound almond macaroons
2 cups crystallized cherries
½ cup crystallized orange peel
½ cup citron
1 cup slivered almonds

Beat yolks until light and fluffy. Add sugar and beat until thoroughly blended. Pour wine into egg mixture slowly. Put over hot water and cook until it coats a spoon. Add gelatin that has been softened in ¾ cup cold water. Stir until dissolved. Remove from heat and chill until slightly thick. Beat whites with salt and cream of tartar until stiff. Add the other cup of sugar slowly, beating constantly. Combine with yolk mixture. Break macaroons in small pieces and chop fruit. Add to the above with slivered almonds. This can be molded in two large ring molds or can be poured directly into crystal compotes if you have room to refrigerate so many. If you put the rings on platters to serve, fill centers with unsweetened whipped cream. The compotes can be put on the buffet table if desired with a spoon of whipped cream on each, topped with chopped toasted almonds or with chocolate sprinkles.

STRAWBERRY FLUFF DESSERT

1 large angel food cake	1 box frozen strawberries
1 quart vanilla ice cream	1 egg white
1 quart fresh strawberries	½ cup sugar

Break up frozen berries with a fork; put in the large bowl of an electric beater with the unbeaten egg and sugar. Turn it on low speed until it is well mixed, then increase speed and beat for 15 or 20 minutes. At this point you will have a bowl completely full of a fluffy pink icing. Turn it back on low speed if you are not ready to use it. We find that if it is started when the luncheon guests are seated that it will be just right at dessert time. Slice angel food cake crosswise; fill sandwich fashion with the vanilla ice cream; ice with the Strawbery Fluff, swirling it around the cake. Fill center with fresh strawberries and you will have a beautiful dessert. This will serve 12 generously. Any portion that is left can be frozen in a refrigerator dessert tray for future use. When fresh strawberries are not available fill center of cake with whipped cream.

STRAWBERRIES ROMANOFF

2 quarts large strawberries	1 pint vanilla ice cream
1 cup sugar or as needed	½ pint whipping cream
Wine glass of rum	1 tablespoon grated orange peel

Combine berries, orange peel, sugar and rum and let stand for an hour. Soften vanilla ice cream and stir in whipped cream. Add berries to this and serve at once over slices of angel food cake or in compotes.

SIMPLE PARTY DESSERT

Individual meringue shells can be filled with ice cream and topped with contrasting color sherbert to make attractive desserts. Pistachio ice cream topped with raspberry sherbert or vanilla ice cream topped with lime or orange sherbet are nice combinations and can be quickly assembled.

EGGS

CURRIED EGGS II

6 hardboiled eggs
1 4 oz. can mushrooms
1 5 oz. can water chestnuts
2 pimentoes
2 cups milk
3 heaping tablespoons butter
3 heaping tablespoons flour

1 teaspoon salt
¼ teaspoon cayenne pepper
1 teaspoon onion juice
2 teaspoons Worcestershire Sauce
1 teaspoon curry powder
1 tablespoon water

Slice eggs and water chestnuts; chop mushrooms and pimentoes. Make cream sauce and season with remaining ingredients, smoothing curry powder in the water before adding it to cream sauce. Combine. Put in small casserole or in 4 baking shells and cover with fine bread crumbs which have been mixed with grated Italian cheese. Heat until brown. Serves 4.

EGGS AND MUSHROOMS

6 hard-boiled eggs sliced
½ pound fresh mushrooms
1 bell pepper
1 small package Old English Cheese
1 small can pimentoes
1 small onion

2 cups milk
3 heaping tablespoons butter
3 heaping tablespoons flour
1 tsp. salt
¼ teaspoons cayenne pepper
1 tablespoon Worcestershire Sauce

Chop bell pepper and onion and cook in several tablespoons of butter until tender but not brown; add chopped mushrooms and cook for five minutes. Make cream sauce of remaining ingredients and add grated cheese. Stir until melted. Combine all with eggs. Serve over canned Chinese noodles. Serves 6.

EGGS, SWEETBREADS AND PEAS

1½ lbs. sweetbreads
6 hard boiled eggs

1 small can peas
3 cups medium cream sauce

Make cream sauce (see Index) season highly. Add 1 tablespoon Worcestershire sauce. Drain peas, chop eggs and combine ingredients. 2 tablespoons sherry can be added if desired. Serves 8.

FISH AND SEAFOOD

SALMON IN SEA SHELLS

1 pound can red salmon
1 cup "medium white sauce"

1 small can green peas
1½ cups moist creamed Irish potatoes

Remove liquid and bones from salmon; combine with the cup of white sauce and the peas. Season to taste: and fill shells or a small casserole.

Pipe potato flowers around edges through a pastry tube using instant creamed Irish potatoes or making the regular creamed potatoes. Bake in oven about 15 minutes until potatoes are browned. If preferred the potatoes can be spooned roughly over the salmon in a casserole. Serves 4 to 6.

SALMON CASSEROLE

1 pound can red salmon	1 cup milk
3 cups cooked rice	1 cup grated yellow cheese
10½ oz. can condensed celery soup	1 tablespoon lemon juice

Drain and pick salmon from bones. Combine with other ingredients reserving cheese to put on top. Bake at 350°. Serves 6.

STUFFED RED SNAPPER

3 or 4 pound tail end of red snapper	1 tablespoon minced parsley
½ cup water	1 beaten egg
Juice of 1 lemon	2 tablespoons melted butter
2 tablespoons melted butter	½ teaspoon salt
2 cups bread crumbs	½ cup minced celery
1 onion, grated	Dash cayenne pepper

Rub fish with salt and butter, and dredge with flour. Mix water, lemon juice and melted butter together to use for basting fish as it cooks. Combine the remaining ingredients to make the stuffing. After it is put inside the fish the sides should be sewed together with a large needle and coarse thread, or it can be tied together with wrapping cord which is cut and removed before sending fish to the table. As the fish is somewhat difficult to remove from the baking pan to the serving dish, it is wise to butter a shallow pan well and put a piece of cheese cloth over the butter with edges extending beyond the fish. Place the stuffed fish on this and bake at 350° about 45 minutes or until fish flakes. Baste at intervals with the water, lemon juice and butter while it is cooking. Take fish up by lifting edges of cheese cloth. Put fish on serving dish and slide from under the fish. Serve with Egg Sauce to which 1 tablespoon of capers may be added.

BAKED FISH FILLETS

2 pounds frozen cod or haddock fillets	¾ teaspoon dry mustard
3 tablespoons butter	¾ cup grated cheese
3 tablespoons flour	1 tablespoon lemon juice
1½ cups milk	¾ teaspoon salt, dash cayenne

Thaw and arrange fish fillets in oblong casserole. Melt butter in top of double boiler. Smooth in flour, add milk, reserving one tablespoon to smooth dry mustard to a paste. Add this to sauce. Stir in cheese, lemon juice and seasonings. Spread this sauce over the fish. Sprinkle additional grated cheese over same and bake at 375° for 45 minutes. If desired 2 cans of frozen shrimp soup thawed can be substituted for the cream sauce and the cheese sprinkled on top of the dish. Serves 7 or 8.

CRAB AND ARTICHOKE HEARTS CASSEROLE

1 stick butter	1 cup grated cheese
4 tablespoons flour	3 6-ounce cans crab meat
1 pint milk	6 hard-boiled eggs, sliced
1 teaspoon Worcestershire sauce	1 large can artichoke hearts
Salt and cayenne pepper	½ cup fine bread crumbs
1 teaspoon grated onion	

Melt butter in top double boiler. Stir in flour. When a smooth paste add milk slowly. Stir until sauce is thick, add seasonings, onion and ¾ cup of the grated cheese. Flake crab meat. Slice hard-boiled eggs. Slice drained artichoke hearts in half lengthwise. Put in oblong casserole and cover with sauce. Add the remaining ¼ cup grated cheese to ½ cup fine bread crumbs and sprinkle this over top of cream sauce. Bake at 325° about half an hour. Chopped chicken breast can be substituted for crab meat if desired. Serves 8 or 10.

CRAB IMPERIAL

3 cans crab meat 6 oz. size	½ chopped green peppers
1 cup mayonnaise	1 chopped pimento
2 beaten egg yolks	2 teaspoons prepared mustard
1 tablespoon lemon juice	1 teaspoon grated onion
Salt and red pepper to taste	3 tablespoons sherry

Pick bones from crab meat and pull off in pieces. Smooth mustard in sherry and add to mayonnaise with seasoning and beaten yolks. Add chopped peppers, onion and lemon juice and fold crab meat into the combination. Pile in shells with a coating of more mayonnaise. Sprinkle with crumbs and paprika and bake. Serves about 8.

CRAB OR LOBSTER FONDUE

2 6½ ounce cans crab or lobster	Butter
⅓ cup mayonnaise	½ pound sharp cheese
2 tablespoons prepared mustard	3 cups milk
½ teaspoon salt	4 eggs slightly beaten
½ teaspoon paprika	1 teaspoon Worcestershire sauce
12 slices bread	

Pick over and flake crab or lobster and add to next four ingredients. Trim crusts from bread and spread each slice with softened butter. Make 6 sandwiches by spreading one buttered slice with fish mixture and covering it with another slice buttered side up. Cut these sandwiches in quarters. Put a layer of these squares in buttered oblong casserole and cover the layer with cheese sliced thin. Pour over this the milk to which the slightly-beaten eggs and Worcestershire sauce have been added. Put in refrigerator for several hours. Take out and put casserole in pan with a little hot water in it. Bake at 325° for an hour. This can be made hours ahead of time and left in refrigerator until time to bake. Serves 8.

CURRIED OYSTERS AND EGGS

1 onion, grated	1 teaspoon salt
1 stick butter or margarine	⅛ teaspoon cayenne pepper
6 tablespoons flour	1 quart oysters
3 cups milk	5 hard-boiled eggs, sliced
1 teaspoon curry powder or to taste	6 cups fluffy cooked rice

Sauté onion in butter until tender but not brown. Remove to top of double boiler and add flour. When smooth add most of the milk and make a cream sauce. Smooth curry powder in the rest of the milk and add to sauce with salt and pepper. Taste and add more salt or curry to suit you. Simmer oysters for 5 minutes in a separate vessel and add to the sauce. Then add the sliced hard-boiled eggs. These should have been simmered for 20 minutes and peeled while still warm. Serve over hot rice. Serves 8.

NEW ORLEANS SEAFOOD GUMBO

3 large onions, chopped	⅛ teaspoon cayenne pepper
3 tablespoons bacon drippings or butter	1 teaspoon nutmeg
3 tablespoons flour	2 pounds sliced okra (can use frozen)
3 No. 2 cans tomatoes	2 medium-size bell peppers, diced
3 cups water	2 cups crab meat, fresh or frozen
2 sprigs parsley	2 cups deveined shrimp
1 bay leaf	1 pint oysters with liquor
2 cloves garlic	2 teaspoons gumbo filé powder
1 teaspoon salt (more if needed)	4 to 6 cups hot fluffy rice

Cook onions in bacon drippings or butter until tender but not brown. Add flour and stir until smooth. Combine with tomatoes and water. Cook for half an hour. Tie parsley, bay leaf and garlic in cheese cloth and add to above mixture with seasonings, okra and bell peppers. Cook at medium heat for one hour, stirring frequently. Now add crab and shrimp and cook 30 minutes more. A short while before serving add oysters and filé powder (this powder can be found on the spice shelf at better groceries, especially in the South). Cook about 20 minutes more and serve over hot fluffy rice in soup bowls. I use a heavy vessel for this to prevent burning. Do not use high heat at any time. Remove cheese cloth bag before serving. This can be served as a main course with a green salad to make a complete meal. Serves 10 or more.

FRUITS

GLAZED RED APPLES

Peel and core winesap apples. Fill centers with whole cranberry sauce using one can to every six apples. Fill centers with the sauce and put remaining sauce around apples. Sprinkle apples with sugar. Add a little water to the sauce around apples and bake slowly, basting with the red syrup until the apples are glazed and tender. Nice with turkey or chicken.

BAKED APRICOTS

2 2½-sized cans apricots
1 cup chopped pecans
4 ounces Cheddar cheese, grated
  Juice from apricots
2 tablespoons lemon juice

2 tablespoons sugar
1 egg, beaten
2 tablespoons flour
  Cheese crackers, crumbled

Drain apricots and arrange cut-side down in a small buttered oblong casserole in layers with pecans and grated cheese. Make a syrup by boiling together apricot juice, lemon juice and sugar until it thickens. Beat egg and add flour. Pour hot juice over egg mixture and cook until thickened. Pour over apricots and cover with cheese crackers which have been rolled into crumbs. Bake until cheese melts and it is well heated. This is nice with chicken dishes.

CURRIED FRUIT

1 large can peaches
1 large can pears
2 small cans pineapple tidbits
1 large can apricots

1 can seeded black cherries
1 stick butter or margarine
¾ cup brown sugar
1 teaspoon curry powder

This can be made ahead and reheated. Drain fruit. Melt butter and add sugar and curry powder. Arrange fruit in two layers in a buttered casserole, pouring syrup over each layer. Bake at 300° for an hour. A nice addition is a little chopped crystallized ginger over the top or a small bottle of maraschino cherries arranged to decorate top of the casserole. More curry can be used if desired; I like the faint taste of it best. Serves 10. This can be made in smaller quantity by using the small cans of fruit and cutting down, proportionately, on the sugar.

FRUIT PLATTER

To Be Passed at Morning Coffees

Cut balls from honey dew, watermelon and cantaloupes using the largest sized melon ball scoop. Sprinkle lightly with salt and put on platters surrounded by fresh mint sprays. Put a colored cocktail pick in each melon ball. These platters should be re-arranged and passed several times. When melons are out of season "pineapple points" or "frosted grapes" can be substituted.

FRUIT IN TINY MERINGUE SHELLS

Make small meringue shells tinted a pastel shade, cook in slow oven, put 2 specimen strawberries in each. Or fill the meringue with a tablespoon of fruit ice cream and pass as a sweet at morning coffees. In making meringues be sure to make a bottom circle and build a rim around it. They should be about 2 inches in diamenter.

STUFFED ORANGES

6 oranges	1 tablespoon lemon juice
12 chopped dates	2 tablespoons cocoanut
½ cup pecans chopped	2 egg whites
¼ cup raisins chopped	4 tablespoons sugar

Cut tops from oranges; cut out pulp and clean shell; mix the pulp, which has been separated from the inside of orange with raisins, dates, pecans and half of the cocoanut; add lemon juice. Fill shells and put them in a large skillet. Surround with ¼ cup water to which ¼ cup light corn syrup has been added; cook in oven at 375° for 20 minutes basting once or twice with the liquid; remove from oven and cover tops with meringue made of egg whites and sugar. Sprinkle remaining cocoanut over meringue; return to oven and cook until meringue has browned. Serve hot or cold. If preferred the oranges can be filled with mincemeat to which has been added a little sherry wine. After they have been cooked put a cherry on top instead of the meringue.

MEATS AND POULTRY

CORNISH HEN OR CHICKEN
BING CHERRY SAUCE

If Cornish hens are used, get the large 22 oz. size and have them split half in two like spring chickens. Rub with salt and pepper. Broil in butter until brown. For six servings add 6 sliced shallots; lower heat; cover skillet and cook slowly for half an hour. Cover with cherry sauce and bake in covered skillet inside slow oven for half an hour, basting at intervals with the cherry sauce. When ready to serve remove hen or chicken to platter and cover each piece with some of the cherries.

BING CHERRY SAUCE

Cook 2 tbsp. sugar and 2 tbsp. vinegar over low heat until dark brown in color; set aside. In separate skillet melt 1 tablespoon butter, smooth in two tablespoons flour; add one can beef bouillon and stir until smooth; add ½ cup orange juice, 2 tablespoons lemon juice, 2 tablespoons sherry and 3 tablespoons grated orange rind. Add to vinegar and sugar with one cup of the juice from a large can—size 2½—of Bing cherries, cook over low heat for 15 minutes; add the drained cherries.

BROILED CHICKENS WITH STUFFED MUSHROOMS

Have two broilers split in half. Rub the chickens inside and out with a little salt and pepper. Panbroil them in butter on both sides. When nicely browned, reduce heat. Add a very little water or chicken broth, if you have it, cover and let cook until tender. When ready to serve put several stuffed mushrooms on each chicken half. Additional butter can be put in skillet and cooked in the drippings a few minutes. Scrape the brown particles up from the skillet to mix with the butter, and put a spoonful over each chicken half. Half a pound of large mushrooms should be sufficient to garnish the four chicken halves. Wash, but do not peel them. Cut off stems and chop them. Dip mushroom caps in butter and then panbroil them with the stems in additional butter for 5 minutes. Remove mushroom caps but leave stems. Add to them ¼ cup ground onion, ¼ cup ground celery (cut in small pieces before grinding to avoid strings), ¼ cup ground bell pepper and 1 tablespoon minced parsley. Cook a few minutes until tender. Stir in a little salt and pepper and enough bread crumbs to hold mixture together. Stuff mushroom caps with this mixture. Sprinkle more fine crumbs on top and bake until brown. This only takes a few minutes. Serves 4.

CHICKEN LIVERS AND MUSHROOMS

1 lb. chicken livers	3 tablespoons flour
½ lb. fresh mushrooms	1 teaspoon salt
1½ cups of cream	Large pinch black pepper
3 tablespoons butter	½ teaspoon paprika

Slice mushrooms; cut livers in half, dredge them in the combined flour and salt and sauté them in the butter until browned. Add mushrooms and cook about five minutes; add cream and paprika and stir until thickened. Put on toast points. Serves 4 to 6. These are delicious when served in the center of a cheese souffle ring. (See index.)

OVEN-FRIED CHICKEN BREASTS

8 small whole chicken breasts	2 cups crushed cornflakes
½ pound butter	¾ cup grated Parmesan cheese
Small amount garlic salt	½ cup sesame seed

Remove ribs from breasts if they have been left on them. Season with salt and pepper rubbed on each breast. Melt butter and add a small amount of garlic salt. Crush cornflakes slightly and add Parmesan cheese. Dip breasts in butter and roll in crushed cornflakes, being sure to cover each piece evenly. Put in a shallow oblong Pyrex dish, not touching, and add any leftover crumbs or butter. Bake for about an hour in oven heated to 325°, or until tender and brown. If preferred, substitute half a cup of toasted sesame seed for the Parmesan cheese. To toast the seed put in a shallow ungreased pan and cook in 350° oven for about 10 minutes, stirring once or twice. Add these to finely crushed cornflakes. Serves 8. Can serve with Mushroom Sauce (see Index) if desired.

CHICKEN BREASTS—ORANGE SAUCE

6 small chicken breasts	2 cups fresh orange juice
⅓ cup sugar	Grated rind one orange
2 tablespoons flour	2 tablespoons lemon juice
Salt and pepper to taste	

Allow a whole breast for each serving or substitute a half broiler for each person. If breasts are used bone them with a small sharp knife— broil in butter until brown, then cover skillet and put in oven and bake at 350° about 40 minutes or until tender. Combine sugar and flour and smooth in a small amount of the orange juice. Put the rest of juice in a double boiler; heat and add to the first mixture, cook until thick. Pour over chicken breasts and cook a short while, basting chickens with sauce. Garnish with orange slices topped with orange marmalade. Serves 6.

CHICKEN PAPRIKA

2 pounds frying chicken	1 tablespoon paprika
1 onion chopped	1 bay leaf, small
1 small can mushrooms	½ teaspoon salt
1 can tomato puree	¼ teaspoon black pepper
1 cup sour cream	1 pinch sugar

Cut chicken in serving portions; dredge in flour and brown in 2 large tablespoons fat. Pour off a little of the fat and add the remaining ingredients—cover and cook over low heat for 45 minutes or until tender. Stir occasionally.

CHICKEN SUPREME II

3 large chicken breasts	1 cup ½ and ½ milk and cream
½ pound fresh mushrooms	½ cup Sauterne
6 slices baked ham	1 tablespoon flour
1 small bunch spring onions	Salt and pepper

Have butcher split breasts in half; remove as many bones as possible with a small sharp knife. Rub salt and pepper into breasts and broil until brown on both sides; add onions and cook slowly for 5 minutes, then add mushrooms and cook 5 minutes more. Cover skillet and cook slowly until tender. Remove chicken; pour off excess fat, and make a sauce by smoothing the flour in remaining fat. Add milk, wine and seasoning and cook until thick. Broil ham slices slightly, put a half chicken breast on each slice and pour mushroom sauce over each serving. Serves 6.

INDIVIDUAL TURKEY DIVAN ROLLS

6 large thin slices baked turkey breast	Dash of cayenne pepper
2 10-ounce packages frozen broccoli or	4 egg yolks
asparagus	½ cup sherry wine
½ cup flour	½ cup grated Parmesan cheese
½ cup butter	1 tablespoon Worcestershire sauce
3 cups milk	1 cup whipped cream
1 teaspoon salt	

Cook broccoli or asparagus according to directions on box. Drain. Divide the spears into six portions. Mix a little melted butter and lemon juice, and drizzle over the broccoli or asparagus. Roll a slice of turkey breast around each portion of the vegetable. These can be made ahead of time and kept warm over hot water. When ready to serve, put rolls of turkey and vegetable on each plate. Cover generously with hot sauce and garnish with parsley. To make the sauce, melt butter in top of double boiler. Smooth in flour and gradually stir in milk. Stir constantly until smooth and thick. Add cheese, seasoning and wine. Reduce heat and add beaten egg yolks. (Do *not* let water boil in bottom of double boiler after eggs are added.) Cook until thick. Remove from heat and add whipped cream.

HAM AND SWEETBREADS

1 pound cooked ham, diced	1 cup sliced ripe olives
1½ pounds sweetbreads	4 cups medium cream sauce
2 tablespoons Worchestershire Sauce	

Cook and dice sweetbreads; make cream sauce (see Index). Season highly and add Worchestershire sauce, and a teaspoon of grated onions if desired. Combine ingredients. Serve in pastry shells or on toast.

SWEETBREADS WITH OLIVES

1 pound sweetbreads	Salt and cayenne pepper to taste
4 tablespoons margarine	1 teaspoon Worcestershire sauce
4 tablespoons flour	1 cup shell noodles
2 cups milk	½ cup sliced stuffed olives

Soak sweetbreads in cold water with juice of half a lemon for 20 minutes. Boil with ½ teaspoon salt and a sliced union for 20 minutes. Blanch in cold water before removing membrane and pipes. Break in pieces. Melt margarine in top of double boiler. Smooth in flour and add milk gradually, stirring until thick. Season with salt, cayenne pepper and Worcestershire sauce. Cook shell noodles according to directions on package. Drain. Add noodles and sweetbreads to cream sauce. Just before serving add sliced olives. Serve on pastry or toast rounds garnished with parsley. Serves 6.

PASTRY

RUM TARTS

1 envelope gelatin	1 cup milk
¼ cup cold milk	½ cup sugar
3 egg yolks, beaten	pinch nutmeg
1 beaten egg white	¼ cup rum
½ pint whipping cream	

Soak gelatin in the ¼ cup of cold milk; make custard of egg yolks, sugar and milk and dissolve gelatin in this. When very cold and thick add 1 beaten egg white and season with rum and nutmeg. Then add the whipped cream and pour in ready baked tart shells. The very small tart shells filled with this filling are especially nice to serve for morning coffees. Refrigerate for several hours before serving and cover tops with chocolate candy sprinkles or with grated chocolate.

MINCEMEAT CHESS TARTS

Line very small tart shells with pastry and put mincemeat chess filling in them. Bake about 15 minutes at 400° or until brown.

Filling

2 eggs beaten together
4 tablespoons sugar
⅔ stick of margarine

½ cup mince meat
2 tablespoons sherry wine

Soak mincemeat in wine; cream margarine and sugar and add beaten eggs slowly. Beat well; fold in mincemeat and spoon into shells and bake slowly until firm.

LEMON CHIFFON PIE

1 tablespoon gelatin
¼ cup cold water
4 egg yolks, beaten
½ cup sugar
½ teaspoon salt
3 tablespoons lemon juice

2 tablespoons frozen orange juice concentrate
½ teaspoon grated lemon rind
4 egg whites, stiffly beaten
4 tablespoons additional sugar
9-inch baked pie shell (either pastry or crumb)

Soak gelatin in cold water. Add sugar and salt to beaten yolks. Then add fruit juice and rind. Cook in double boiler until thick. Add soaked gelatin to hot mixture and chill until partially set. Add sugar gradually to beaten whites and fold into the gelatin mixture. Pour into shell and chill until firm. Top with whipped cream. Serves 6.

GRASSHOPPER PIE

1½ cups chocolate wafer crumbs
¼ cup sugar

¼ cup melted butter

This is for crumb pie crust. Combine crumbs, sugar and melted butter and put into a well-greased pie pan. Cook 4 minutes in 425° oven. Watch carefully to prevent burning.

Pie Filling

1 envelope gelatin
¼ cup cold water
4 egg yolks
¼ cup sugar

⅜ cup green crème de menthe
½ pint cream, whipped
Chocolate sprinkles

Soak gelatin in cold water and stir over hot water until dissolved.

Beat egg yolks until light. Add sugar and beat again until fluffy. Add crème de menthe and the dissolved gelatin. Chill until very thick and fold in whipped cream. Pour over chocolate pie crust and chill until firm. When ready to serve cut in wedges and top with chocolate sprinkles. If the filling is not a pretty green color add a few drops of green coloring before pouring it into the pie crust.

SALADS AND SALAD DRESSINGS

ANCHOVY DRESSING

1 small can anchovy fillets	1 teaspoon prepared mustard
1 bunch green onions	1 lemon (juice of)
1 cup salad oil or half olive oil	6 tablespoons vinegar
½ teaspoon salt (or less)	2 tablespoons minced parsley

Mash anchovies thoroughly with silver fork. Chop onions very fine, using some of the green tops. Gradually add oil and seasonings to anchovies, alternating with lemon juice and vinegar. Stir in parsley and onions last. Blend well and refrigerate. Serves 6.

ASPARAGUS AND ARTICHOKE SALAD

2 cans green or white asparagus tips, chilled	2 cans artichoke hearts, chilled
	Iceberg or Bibb lettuce

To serve, make individual lettuce cups; put in evenly-divided contents of cans of asparagus and artichokes. Loosen the petals of the artichoke hearts with a silver fork, working carefully from the tops and press open slightly to resemble a flower. Pour over Anchovy Dressing. Serves about 8.

AVOCADO AND CUCUMBER MOLD

2 large avocados	2 tablespoons boiling water
1 lemon (juice of)	½ cup mayonnaise
1 cup grated cucumber	½ cup cream, whipped
1 cup minced celery	4 tablespoons French dressing
3 tablespoons gelatin	Salt and cayenne pepper
¾ cup cold water	

Peel and sieve avocados. Sprinkle lemon juice over them to help retain the green color. Grate cucumber and chop celery. Soak gelatin in cold water. Pour boiling water on gelatin and stir over more boiling water until dissolved. Cool. Add to mayonnaise. Fold in whipped cream. Add avocado and cucumber that has been marinated in French dressing and drained. Salt and cayenne pepper to taste. Makes 6 small molds. Serve in lettuce cups surrounded by a circle of grapefruit sections.

AVOCADO, PINEAPPLE AND CHEESE SALAD

1 package lemon jello	1 large avocado
1 small can sliced pineapple	1 3 oz. package Philadelphia Cheese
1 lemon (juice)	

Drain pineapple and cut in pieces; add lemon juice to pineapple juice and then add enough water to make one pint of liquid. Heat this and dissolve jello in hot juice—chill until almost congealed. Cut small balls from avocado with melon scoop and form small balls of cheese which has been mashed and seasoned with Worcestershire sauce and onion juice. Add these balls and the pineapple to the gelatin mixture. Pour into small molds and serve with mayonnaise. Serves 6.

MOLDED BEET SALAD

1 tablespoon gelatin	2 tablespoons sugar
¼ cup cold water	½ teaspoon salt
¾ cup boiling water	1 tablespoon grated onion
1 cup beet juice	½ cup finely-diced celery
1 tablespoon lemon juice	1½ cups finely-diced beets
1 tablespoon horse-radish	½ cup sliced radishes
(optional)	

Soak gelatin in cold water. Add boiling water and stir until completely dissolved. Add beet juice, lemon juice and seasonings. Chill. Refrigerate until partially congealed. Add onion, celery, beets and radishes. This should be a pretty red color suitable for Christmas or Valentine's Day parties. If it is not red enough add a very little red coloring to make the desired shade. Serves 6.

CAPER DRESSING

½ onion, grated	1 teaspoon paprika
⅛ teaspoon cayenne pepper	½ cup vinegar
1 teaspoon dry mustard	½ cup salad oil
1 teaspoon salt	½ cup olive oil
2 teaspoons sugar	2 tablespoons capers

Mix dry ingredients and smooth to a paste with part of the vinegar. Add this slowly to oil, alternating with remaining vinegar. Put capers in last. Refrigerate and stir well before using.

CAESAR SALAD

2 cloves garlic	1 can anchovy fillets, drained and
¾ cup olive oil	chopped
6 cups mixed salad greens	2 teaspoons Worcestershire sauce
4 tablespoons grated Parmesan cheese	½ cup crumbled Roquefort or blue cheese
1 egg	2 cups croutons
Paprika	¼ cup wine vinegar
2 teaspoons lemon juice	

Soak garlic in the olive oil for several hours and then discard garlic. Wash and dry salad greens and break into bite-size pieces. Romaine, endive and iceberg are a good choice of greens. Sprinkle cheese over greens, then paprika and part of the olive oil. Now drop a raw egg over all and add lemon juice and vinegar, and toss lightly. Add remaining ingredients, except croutons, and toss again. The croutons should be added the very last moment so they will be very crisp. These can be made ahead of time. They are tiny squares of bread that have been drizzled with melted butter which has had a small amount of garlic salt added to it; then they are toasted in a 325° oven until golden brown; you will have to shake the pan occasionally. Serves 8.

CHERRY SALAD

1 can No 2 pie cherries and juice
1 orange, juice and grated rind
1 lemon, juice and grated rind
1 cup sugar
1 cup chopped pecans

1 small can grated pineapple with juice
1 package lemon flavored gelatin
1 envelope Knox gelatin
¼ cup cold water

Heat first five ingredients and pour over the package of lemon flavored gelatin. Soak Knox gelatin in ¼ cup cold water and dissolve in first mixture. When cool and partially congealed add nuts and pour in 8 molds. This is delicious.

FROZEN CHEESE AND CRANBERRY SALAD

2 3 ounce packages Philadelphia Cheese
1 cup cream, whipped
½ cup mayonnaise

½ cup blanched almonds
1 small can grated pineapple with juice
1 can whole cranberry sauce

Break up cranberry sauce with a fork; soften cheese with whipped cream and mayonnaise; combine ingredients and freeze in refrigerator tray. Cut in squares to serve overlapping grapefruit sections around the cheese squares. This salad does not need extra mayonnaise. Serves 6 or 8.

HAWAIIAN CHICKEN SALAD

1½ cups chicken breast, chopped
1 cup chopped celery
1 cup chopped pineapple
½ cup chopped blanched almonds
    Salt and red pepper to season highly
1 cup mayonnaise

1 tablespoon lemon juice
1 cup cream, whipped
1½ envelopes gelatin
¼ cup cold water
1 cup white grapes

Soak gelatin in cold water and dissolve over hot water. When cold add to combined mayonnaise, lemon juice and whipped cream. Chill and when nearly congealed fold in the rest of· the ingredients. Be sure to season highly. Fills 8 small molds or a ring mold.

FROZEN CUCUMBER SALAD I IN AVOCADOS

1 large cucumber grated or chopped fine
2 cups tomato juice
½ onion grated
2 teaspoons gelatin
4 tablespoons cold water

1 teaspoon salt
1 tablespoon sugar
    Juice & grated rind 1 lemon
2 stiffly beaten egg whites
1 teaspoon horse radish

Soak gelatin in cold water; heat tomato juice with seasoning and dissolve gelatin in hot juice. Chill; add cucumber and freeze to a mush. Beat egg whites into this, add lemon juice and rind and freeze again. This is good served in half avocado pears that have been marinated in French dressing. Serves 6.

FROZEN CUCUMBER II

3 large cucumbers
1 small onion
Salt and cayenne pepper
¼ cup vinegar

2 teaspoons gelatin
¼ cup cold water
green coloring

Grate cucumber, remove seeds; grate onion; combine and add seasoning and a few drops of green coloring—soak gelatin in cold water; heat vinegar and dissolve gelatin. When cold add to cucumbers. Freeze until mushy; add 1 beaten egg white and beat well. Refreeze. Serve in tomatoes for a refreshing summer salad. Garnish with "Cheese Balls" rolled in parsley.

CRAB MEAT LUNCHEON SALAD

3 6-ounce cans crab meat
8 Holland rusks
1 tube anchovy paste
3 tomatoes
Shredded lettuce

1 cup minced celery
1 bunch spring onions, sliced
Mayonnaise
12 hard-boiled eggs
24 large stuffed olives

Pick over crab meat and flake in large pieces. Spread Holland rusks with anchovy paste. Peel and slice tomatoes. Put shredded lettuce on each salad plate. Top with a rusk and put a slice of tomato on rusk. Mix crab meat with celery and onions, and just enough mayonnaise to moisten. Divide crab meat mixture into portions and put on tomato slices. Rice hard-boiled eggs in a bowl and use to completely cover the salads. Slice large stuffed olives lengthwise and surround the base of each salad with 6 olive halves, standing slices up lengthwise against the base of the salad. Serve this with Roquefort Cheese Dressing (2) or with Thousand Island Dressing. I sometimes pass around bowls of each and let the guests take their choice. This makes a nice lunch salad and is a satisfying meal. Serves 8.

GREEN GODDESS DRESSING OR DIP

1½ cups mayonnaise
¾ cup sour cream
1 teaspoon dry mustard
¼ cup wine vinegar
1 teaspoon grated onion

Salt and cayenne pepper to taste
1 teaspoon Worcestershire sauce
3 tablespoons anchovy paste
2/3 cup finely-chopped parsley
¼ cup snipped chives

Combine mayonnaise and sour cream. Smooth mustard with the vinegar and add. Add onion, seasonings, and parsley and chives last. Freeze-dried chives that come in small cans on the grocery spice shelf are wonderful to keep on hand. Refrigerate dressing, closely covered, until ready to use. It is better after it sets a while. This can also be used as a cocktail dip when two hard-boiled eggs are sieved into it and a small can of shrimp chopped fine is also added.

FRUIT AND GINGER SALAD

1 No. 2 can pears	1 pint ginger ale
1 No. 2 can pineapple	1 pound seedless white grapes
1 lemon	6 tablespoons crystallized ginger
2 packages lemon jello	8 ounces cream cheese

Drain fruit, reserve pineapple juice. Add to it juice of lemon and water to make one pint liquid. Heat and pour over jello. Stir until dissolved. Cool. When cold add ginger ale and put in the refrigerator to partially congeal. Cut pears and pineapple in small pieces. Wash and pick over grapes. When gelatin is thick, add fruit and 3 tablespoons chopped ginger, and pour in molds to congeal. This makes a large ring mold or 12 small ones. The recipe can be cut in half for a small group, using the 8-ounce cans of fruit. Instead of mayonnaise use a fluff of cheese topping on each mold. To make this, mash cream cheese and thin slightly with orange juice concentrate and grated orange rind. Care should be taken not to get it too thin as it must stand up in peaks. Add to this the other 3 tablespoons of chopped ginger. Makes 12 small molds.

SPICED PEACH SALAD

1 can spiced peaches 2½ size	1 lemon (juice)
1 package lemon flavored gelatin powder	¼ cup chopped pecans
1 3 oz. package Philadelphia Cream cheese	

Combine juice from peaches, lemon juice and enough water to make one pint of liquid; heat and pour over lemon flavored gelatin. Remove seed from peaches from the stem end, using a small sharp knife. Stuff peaches with combined cheese and nuts. Place each peach in a tea cup and pour partially congealed gelatin around it. Serves 6.

D'ANJOU PEAR SALAD

Peel and core pears, sprinkle with lemon juice, and serve in lettuce cups covered with the following dressing: to 2 cups of mayonnaise add 2 tablespoons tomato catsup, 1 teaspoon grated onion, 1 teaspoon Worcestershire sauce, and ½ pound cottage cheese that has been drained in a colander until dry. This is especially good with the firm winter pears.

BLUE PLUM SALAD

6 dark blue plums	1 package lemon flavored gelatin
2 bananas	1 lemon (juice)
1 small can pineapple	Cold water as needed

Seed plums and cut each half in 4 or 5 sections. Slice bananas and cut up pineapple. Combine pineapple juice and lemon juice with enough water to make one pint of liquid. Heat and pour over lemon flavored gelatin. Chill; partially congeal; add fruit and pour in 6 molds that have been rinsed with cold water.

TOMATO-CHEESE SALAD

1 8 oz. can tomato sauce	1 cup hot water
8 tablespoons mayonnaise	½ cup celery
4 tablespoons lemon juice	¼ cup chopped green peppers
2 tablespoons gelatin	½ cup sieved cottage cheese
¼ cup cold water	Salt and cayenne pepper to taste

Soak gelatin in cold water; dissolve in hot water; add tomato sauce and lemon juice. When cool add mayonnaise and other ingredients. Season to taste and pour into six molds.

POND LILY SALAD

5 cantaloupes	5 fresh pears
1 honeydew melon	5 large fresh red plums
½ watermelon	1 small can concentrated orange juice
1 fresh pineapple	2 tablespoons grated orange rind
10 fresh apricots	3 3-ounce packages cream cheese
5 bananas	1 pint blueberries

Cut each cantalope in five deep points and pull apart. (See directions for Cantaloupe Pond Lily. Cut balls with a large melon-ball cutter from honeydew and watermelon. Peel pineapple and cut in ¾-inch blocks (do not use hard core at center of pineapple). Peel pears and sprinkle with lemon juice to prevent discoloration. Cut each plum in 6 sections away from the seed. Do not peel either plums or apricots. Cut apricots in quarters. Slice bananas just before serving salad. The rest of the fruit can be prepared ahead. Mash cream cheese and add enough concentrated orange juice to thin cheese to the consistency of thick mayonnaise that will stand up in swirls. Add grated orange rind to cheese. To assemble each salad, put half a cantaloupe on each dinner plate, and pull back the rind of each "petal" as described. Tuck small pieces of lettuce hearts or Bibb lettuce between each petal. Fill each pond lily cup with the assembled fruit. I usually put the pear sections and pineapple in first and cover with the rest of the fruit letting it spill out around the petals. On top of each salad put a large spoon of the orange-flavored cheese which serves as a salad dressing instead of mayonnaise. Sprinkle a few blueberries over the top of each serving. I serve these with the hot Cheese Dreams and tiny hot biscuits filled with baked ham. A dessert is not really necessary with this salad. It makes a beautiful luncheon plate and is a completely satisfying meal. While the pond lily is more of a conversation piece, rings of cantaloupe can be substituted if preferred for the base of the salad. Poppy Seed Dressing can also be substituted for the cheese if desired. This can be assembled ahead of time, adding the banana slices just before serving. Serves 10.

SANDWICHES

SUPPER OR LUNCHEON SANDWICH

For each sandwich allow one king-size slice of rye bread. Cut off crust. Spread with butter. Cover with lettuce leaf, two slices of Swiss cheese, another lettuce leaf, then two slices of cooked chicken breast or one of turkey breast. Cover this generously with several spoonfuls of Thousand Island Dressing. Top with a slice of tomato and a Stuffed Egg. Garnish with crisp bacon and black olives. Pass extra Thousand Island Dressing.

ASPARAGUS SUPPER OR LUNCHEON SANDWICH

Trim crusts from largest size sandwich bread slices and toast on one side. Put a slice of processed American cheese on untoasted side and run under the broiler until it begins to melt. Remove from heat and place four spears of large, heated asparagus over the melted cheese. Cover with Shrimp Sauce and garnish each plate with parsley. Serve at once. This makes a satisfying meal when served with a grapefruit salad. One recipe for Shrimp Sauce should cover 6 servings.

SAUCES

EGG SAUCE: Make cream sauce by melting 4 tablespoons butter in top of double boiler, then smooth in 4 tablespoons flour and add 2 cups milk slowly. Stir until sauce thickens. Add 1 teaspoon Worcestershire sauce, 1/2 teaspoon salt, 1/8 teaspoon cayenne pepper, 1 tablespoon lemon juice and 2 chopped hard-boiled eggs.

SHRIMP SAUCE

3 tablespoons butter	1 teaspoon Worcestershire sauce
3 tablespoons flour	1 tablespoon lemon juice
2 cups milk	1/2 pound chopped cooked shrimp
Salt and cayenne pepper	2 egg yolks

Melt butter in top of double boiler. Add flour. When smooth gradually stir in milk and seasonings. Add chopped shrimp. Beat yolks until light and add to sauce. (Do not let water boil in bottom of double boiler for the sauce might curdle.)

SHE-CRAB SOUP

Charleston, South Carolina is famous for "She-Crab Soup" and I found that by adding crab roe to my Tennessee recipe it made a delicious change. The canned roe is available in the South in Charleston as well as Savannah, Georgia, but I found it difficult to get farther North. This is my version of the famous recipe.

1 medium onion, grated
1 stick butter or margarine
1 pound crab meat or 2 (6-ounce) cans crab meat
3 level tablespoons flour

1 quart milk
1 pint half milk and half cream
Salt and cayenne pepper to taste
½ cup sherry wine
¼ pound (4 ounces) crab roe, chopped fine

Sauté onion in part of the butter in top of double boiler placed over direct heat until tender but not brown. Put the top over hot water and melt the rest of the butter. Stir in flour and gradually add the milk and half-and-half cream, stirring until smooth after each addition. Season with salt and cayenne pepper. If desired a teaspoon of Worcestershire sauce can also be added. Cook until slightly thickened. Add crab meat, wine and roe. Serve in soup cups with a sprinkle of paprika.

SENEGALESE

1 small onion, chopped
¼ stick butter
1 heaping tablespoon flour
2 teaspoons curry powder (or less)
4 cups chicken broth

4 egg yolks
1 pint cream
Salt and cayenne pepper
2 chicken breasts, boiled and diced

Sauté onion in butter until tender. Add flour and curry powder. Gradually add stock and bring to boiling point. Put in top of double boiler. Beat the yolks and the cream together and combine with chicken stock. Cook several minutes until it begins to thicken. (Do not let water boil under the soup after egg is added.) Season with salt and cayenne pepper. Strain through a fine sieve and refrigerate until very cold. When ready to serve add diced chicken breasts. Serve in cups with a sprinkle of paprika on each. Serves 6 or 8.

GAZPACHO

6 large red ripe tomatoes, peeled and chopped
2 cucumbers, peeled and chopped
3 sticks celery, diced fine
1 bell pepper, diced
1 small onion, minced
Dash of Tabasco sauce

½ teaspoon salt or more to taste
Cayenne pepper to taste
1 teaspoon Worcestershire sauce
1 tablespoon vinegar
2 tablespoons olive oil
1 small can tomato juice

You can put vegetables through food chopper or a blender. Add seasonings to olive oil and combine with vegetables and tomato juice. Put in bowl that has been rubbed with a clove of garlic. Refrigerate for several hours. Serve in chilled mugs. Serves 6.

EASY VICHYSSOISE

1 box instant mashed potatoes
1 onion
1 stalk celery
2 cups chicken broth or stock

Salt and cayenne pepper to taste
1 pint half milk and half cream
Freeze-dried chives

Simmer onion and celery in a strong chicken stock. Season with salt and pepper and strain. You should have two cups of this to replace the milk and water suggested on the box for mashed potatoes. Follow directions on box, and when potatoes are smooth, thin the mixture to a thick soup consistency with the half milk and half cream. Add 1 tablespoon freeze-dried chives. These come in small cans and can be found on the spice shelves at better groceries. Refrigerate and serve very cold in chilled cups with additional chives sprinkled on top. (Fresh or frozen chives can be used, but the dried chives are a great boon as they are always on hand when needed; they look exactly like fresh chives when the air hits them. Also, canned chicken stock or consommé can be used if you do not have chicken stock on hand.) Serves 5 or 6 cups.

VEGETABLES

HARVARD BEETS

½ cup sugar
½ teaspoon salt
1 tablespoon cornstarch
½ cup vinegar

1 can tiny whole beets
2 tablespoons butter
1 tablespoon orange marmalade or
1 orange ground in food chopper

Cook sugar, salt, cornstarch and vinegar in double boiler until clear. Add drained beets and heat thoroughly but do not boil. When hot add 2 tablespoons butter and orange marmalade. Do not let stand too long as beets will turn dark. (If marmalade is not on hand, grind one orange and add pulp and rind to the sauce.) These can be served alone or used to replace Hollandaise Sauce to fill center of Broccoli Ring.

CAULIFLOWER WITH SOUFFLE TOPPING

1 large cauliflower
1 scant teaspoon salt in water
4 tablespoons melted butter
½ cup mayonnaise

2 teaspoons lemon juice
2 egg whites, stiffly beaten
Salt and cayenne pepper
Grated Parmesan or Cheddar cheese

Soak cauliflower in cold water for 30 minutes. Cook, head up, in salted water until barely tender. Drain in colander. Pour 4 tablespoons butter over cauliflower just before putting on the following topping: fold the mayonnaise and lemon juice into the stiffly-beaten egg whites. Add a little salt and cayenne pepper and spread over cauliflower. Sprinkle with grated cheese and put in hot oven until puffy and lightly browned. Put on platter and surround with sprigs of parsley with stems removed. Serves 6.

ONIONS STUFFED WITH CHICKEN LIVERS

6 large Bermuda onions
1 small can mushrooms
1 cup chicken livers

1 can mushroom soup
½ cup dried bread crumbs
Salt and pepper to taste

Boil onions until tender; drain; scoop centers out; turn upside down to drain. Broil chicken livers in butter about 5 minutes; remove from heat and chop. Add mushrooms, seasoning bread crumbs and centers of onion that have been chopped. Bind together with some of the mushroom soup undiluted; stuff onions and cover tops with crumbs and bits of butter. Place in flat casserole and surround with the rest of the mushroom soup that has been slightly diluted with hot water. Bake at 375° until crumbs have browned.

POTATO PUFFS

1 envelope dehydrated Irish potatoes
1½ cups boiling water
½ cup milk
¼ tsp. salt

1½ cups grated yellow cheese
2 well beaten eggs
2 tablespoons melted butter

Make creamed Irish potatoes of first four ingredients; add melted butter, grated cheese and eggs that have been beaten together. Put in ramekins or shells. Bake until brown and puffed. Fills 8 small shells.

SCALLOPED POTATOES AND EGGS

4 large baking potatoes
2 cups milk
4 tablespoons flour
4 tablespoons butter
1 teaspoon salt

⅛ teaspoon cayenne pepper
8 hard-boiled eggs
2 tablespoons minced parsley
1 large onion sliced very thin, parboiled
  and drained
1½ cups grated cheese

Parboil potatoes with skins on until barely tender. Cool slightly and peel. Slice in. thin slices. Make cream sauce of milk, flour and butter. Season with salt and cayenne pepper. Slice hard-boiled eggs. Arrange slices of potatoes, parsley, eggs and onions in alternate layers in buttered casserole. Sprinkle a little extra salt over each layer, and then sprinkle a little cheese over the salt. Cover with cream sauce. This should make three or four layers. Save enough cheese for the top layer. Bake in a 350° oven for about 45 minutes. Serves 8. This is especially good served with baked ham.

BROWNED RICE

1 cup raw rice
1 can onion soup

1 can beef broth bouillon
3 tablespoons butter

Fry the raw rice in the butter in a skillet stirring constantly until golden brown. Add the two cans of undiluted soup and pour in a small greased casserole. Bake for 45 minutes or longer if necessary to absorb liquid at 350°. Delicious with broiled chickens or Cornish hens. Serves 4 to 6.

MIXED VEGETABLES WITH EGG SAUCE

2 12-ounce boxes frozen mixed vegetables	1 teaspoon prepared mustard
3 hard-boiled eggs, riced	1 teaspoon Worcestershire sauce
1 grated onion	4 drops Tabasco sauce
½ cup vegetable oil	1½ cups lemon mayonnaise

Cook vegetables according to directions on box and drain. Keep very hot. Stir riced eggs, onion, vegetable oil and seasonings into mayonnaise. When ready to serve, put mixed vegetables on a flat platter. Cover with a thin layer of the egg sauce and dust with paprika. This sauce is also good on cauliflower, asparagus, and broccoli. It keeps well in the icebox and can be made ahead of time. It can be substituted for Hollandaise Sauce. A small meat dish would be just right with this.

MIXED RICE RING—RIPE OLIVE SAUCE

Cook wild rice and white rice separately. Use a cup of white rice and half a cup to one cup of wild rice. Cook as directed in "Plain Rice Ring"; mix the two varieties together with 2 silver forks. Pack in well greased ring mold and put in pan of hot water at 350° for a half hour. Cover top of ring with waxed paper while cooking. Invert rice ring on a platter; decorate with strips of pimento put about 3 inches apart crosswise around the top of the ring; surround by parsley and put a bowl of "Ripe Olive Sauce" in center of ring—mixed rice is also pretty served as a side dish. It is more reasonable than all wild rice and the combination makes an attractive dish that is good with meats.

SQUASH CASSEROLE

8 medium sized squash	1 can condensed mushroom soup
1 onion	½ cup sliced almonds

Boil squash and onion in salted water until tender. Run through a sieve and mash out as much liquid as possible. Combine with condensed mushroom soup and almonds and put in a small casserole. Cover with crumbs and bits of butter and heat until brown. Serves 5 or 6.

TOMATOES STUFFED WITH CORN

6 tomatoes	4 tablespoons soft bread crumbs
3 tablespoons bell pepper	⅛ tsp. salt
½ cup chopped onions	4 large ears corn
¼ stick butter	Cayenne pepper to taste

Scoop out and drain tomatoes. Reserve pulp, sauté onions and peppers in butter until tender; add tomato pulp, bread crumbs and seasoning and cook until very thick. Add corn that has been cooked and cut from the cob. Sprinkle inside of each tomato with a pinch of salt, and stuff with corn mixture. Cover tops with bread crumbs and dot with bits of butter. Bake for 15 or 20 minutes or until brown. Serves 6.

☆ SETTING THE TABLE— ☆
SERVING THE PARTY

Formal luncheons and dinners should be carefully planned so that the linens, decorations and china harmonize.

Flower arrangements are a matter of taste but the central decoration should be low enough for the guests to see each other. Sometimes it is necessary to have a long table where candelabra are used as part of the decoration and since they are tall, the centerpiece should be tall enough to be in balance with them.

Candlesticks and candelabra are never used for breakfasts or luncheons but they add a great deal of charm to a tea, dinner or buffet supper. They should always be lighted when used. Silver compotes of candies or nuts can be added as a part of the decoration for a very long table.

Tablecloths of embroidered linen, lace or damask are usually preferred for dinners, while dainty place mats and runners can be substituted for luncheons.

A space of twenty-four inches should be allowed for each guest at the table and a service plate should be put in the center of each space. Plates should be spaced evenly so that they will be directly opposite the ones on the other side of the table.

Glasses should be placed to the right and slightly above the service plate and bread-butter plates placed to the left in the same manner. The latter are rarely used for formal dinners, although they can be used for luncheons. When they are used, the butter knife is placed across the top of the plate at right angles to the other silver.

In placing the silver there is one rule to be followed: All knives and spoons should be placed to the right of the service plates with the cutting edge of the knife turned toward the plate. The forks should be placed to the left of the service plate with the exception of the cocktail or oyster fork which should be put on the right side with the knives and spoons. All of the silver should be placed so that the lower edges are on a straight line about an inch from the edge of the table. Since it does not look well to have too much silver on the table, the dessert fork and spoon are usually brought in on the dessert plate and the after dinner coffee spoon is sent in with the coffee. The table silver is placed in the order in which it is to be used, working from the outside toward the plate.

The napkins are put on the service plates if the first course is soup, which is brought in after the guests are seated; but if the first course is already in place when dinner is announced, the napkins are folded in a rectangular shape and placed to the left of the dinner fork on an even line with the lower edge of the silver.

Place cards are usually used for a formal dinner. The woman guest of honor should be seated to the right of the host and the man guest of honor should be to the right of the hostess. At a luncheon where only women are served, the guest of honor should be seated to the right of the hostess.

Good service is one of the most important parts of a formal dinner or luncheon. One maid can serve at least eight guests if she does nothing but serve. In the event the maid is to cook and serve the dinner also, it should be planned on simple lines and the guests should never number more than six.

Black uniforms with white aprons, collars and cuffs are always in good taste for the maids. They can be replaced by the same uniform in white during the summer months if desired.

The present-day rule is that the guest of honor should always be served first. When the dinner is large and more than one maid is to serve, they should start serving at opposite ends of the table. If the first course is an appetizer, it can be placed on the service plate before dinner is announced; but if it is a soup, the guests should be seated before the maids start serving. The soup plate is brought in and put on top of the service plate. The object of the service plate is to always have a plate in front of each guest during the meal with the exception of a short time before the dessert is served. The service plate is left in place and each course is put on it until the main course is served. The maid brings each plate in on a serviette, which is a square, lace-edged linen envelope with a quilted pad slipped inside of it. When she brings in the main course, she removes both the service plate and the soup bowl on it with her left hand and immediately replaces it with the hot plate which is in her right hand. When the guests have finished the main course, she removes that plate and does not bring in the dessert plate until the table has been cleared and the crumbs removed with a folded napkin.

The dessert plate is then brought in and placed before the guest. This plate should have a small lace doily on it, on which a finger bowl partially filled with water is placed. When possible, a small flower matching the table decorations should be floated in the finger bowl. The dessert fork is put on the plate to the left of the finger bowl and the dessert spoon is placed to the right. The guest removes the silver from the plate and places it on the table, the fork to the left and the spoon to the right, and also removes the finger bowl and doily, placing them to the upper left of the dessert plate. Now all is in readiness for the maid to serve the dessert. If the dessert is to be passed, each guest takes a portion from the platter and places it on the dessert plate, using both the fork and serving spoon that are sent in on the platter. If the dessert is to be served from the pantry, the maid brings in the filled dessert plate, removes the original dessert plate with her left hand and replaces it with the filled dessert plate which is in her right hand. All

319

dishes are passed to the left of the guest and removed in the same manner with the exception of the cup and saucer and glasses. Water is poured to the guest's right, the glasses being left on the table when this is done.

Coffee can be served in several ways. It can be sent to the table from the pantry with the coffee spoon on each saucer or the hostess can serve it either from the table or in the living room. The latter method is often a helpful idea as the guests leave the table and there is no delay in clearing it. The coffee service, cups and spoons are put on a large silver tray and placed before the hostess who either hands each filled cup to the guests as she pours or has a maid standing by to pass it.

SILVER ARRANGEMENT

The flat silver arrangement for a formal dinner, consisting of appetizer, soup, fish, main course, salad, dessert and coffee, is placed as follows: Start at the outside and work toward the plate. On the right side put a cocktail fork for the appetizer, next put a soup spoon, then a fish knife. (The breakfast knife can be used for this if you do not have fish knives.) Next to the plate put the dinner knife with the cutting edge toward the plate. "On the left of the plate, working from the outside toward the plate, first put the fish (or breakfast fork) then the dinner fork, and next to the plate put the salad fork. The guests always start using the silver farthest from the plate when it is placed in this manner. The dessert spoon and fork and the after-dinner coffee spoon are sent in from the pantry when they are needed.

For a less formal dinner, consisting of a fruit course, main course, dessert and coffee, place the silver as follows: On the right side, working from the outside toward the plate, put a fruit spoon, then a dinner knife next to the plate. On the left side put the dinner fork. The dessert silver and after-dinner coffee spoon are sent in from the pantry. When a breakfast menu is served, substitute a breakfast knife and fork for the larger ones used for dinner.

INDEX ☆

321

INDEX